W9-AQH-342

Methods for Teaching

Promoting Student Learning in K–12 Classrooms

Eighth Edition

David A. Jacobsen

Paul Eggen
University of North Florida

Donald Kauchak
University of Utah

Allyn & Bacon
is an imprint of

Boston   New York   San Francisco
Mexico City   Montreal   Toronto   London   Madrid   Munich   Paris
Hong Kong   Singapore   Tokyo   Cape Town   Sydney

Vice President and Executive Publisher: Jeffery W. Johnston
Executive Editor: Darcy Betts Prybella
Editorial Assistant: Nancy J. Holstein
Senior Managing Editor: Pamela D. Bennett
Project Manager: Sarah N. Kenoyer
Production Coordinator: Roxanne Klaas
Design Coordinator: Diane C. Lorenzo
Photo Coordinator: Valerie Schultz
Cover Design: Kristina Holmes
Cover Image: SuperStock
Operations Specialist: Susan W. Hannahs
Director of Marketing: Quinn Perkson
Marketing Coordinator: Brian Mounts

For related titles and support materials, visit our online catalog at www.pearsonhighered.com.

Copyright © 2009 by Pearson Education, Inc.

All rights reserved. No part of the material protected by this copyright notice may be reproduced or utilized in any form or by any means, electronic or mechanical, including photocopying, recording, or by any information storage and retrieval system, without written permission from the copyright owner.

To obtain permission(s) to use material from this work, please submit a written request to Pearson/Allyn & Bacon, 501 Boylston Street, Suite 900, Boston, MA 02116 or fax your request to 617-671-2290.

Between the time website information is gathered and then published, it is not unusual for some sites to have closed. Also, the transcription of URLs can result in typographical errors. The publisher would appreciate notification where these errors occur so that they may be corrected in subsequent editions.

Library of Congress Cataloging-in-Publication Data

Jacobsen, David (David A.)
  Methods for teaching: promoting student learning in K–12 classrooms/David A.
Jacobsen, Paul Eggen and Don Kauchak.—8th ed.
    p. cm.
  ISBN-13: 978-0-13-514572-2
  ISBN-10: 0-13-514572-4
  1. Teaching. 2. Classroom management. 3. Lesson planning. 4. Learning. I. Eggen, Paul D., 1940- II.
Kauchak, Donald P., 1946- III. Title.
  LB1025.3.J336 2009
  371.102—dc22

                                                                      2007052558

Photo Credits: ©Royalty–Free/CORBIS, Page 2; Scott Cunningham/Merrill, Page 39; Masterfile Royalty Free Division, Page 40; Karen Mancinelli/Pearson Learning Photo Studio, Page 68; Anthony Magnacca/Merrill, Page 93; Anthony Magnacca/Merrill, Page 94; Anthony Magnacca/Merrill, Page 130; Anthony Magnacca/Merrill, Page 156; Superstock Royalty Free, Page 191; Patrick White/Merrill, Page 194; Patrick White, Page 222; Anthony Magnacca/Merrill, Page 258; Laura Bolesta, Page 294, Bob Daemmrich/Bob Daemmrich Photography, Inc., Page 325; Corbis Royalty Free, Page 326.

Allyn & Bacon
is an imprint of

Printed in the United States of America
10 9 8 7 6 5 4 3 2   **CMA** 12 11 10

To Lorrie, Judy, and Kathy

Tell me, I forget.
Show me, I remember.
Involve me, I understand . . . Eureka!
  —An ancient Chinese proverb

Preface

- Planning
- Implementing
- Assessing

Effective classroom teaching requires professional commitment. Although exciting experiences may occur spontaneously, such happenings are the exception, not the rule. If teachers are to sustain a success-oriented environment by promoting student learning throughout the academic year, they must continually and thoroughly address the teaching act, which is founded on the planning and implementing of instructional activities and the assessing of student performance.

These planning, implementing, and assessing components represent a continual or cyclical process in which professional teachers strive to increase the quality of their instruction—that is, to promote learning in increased numbers of students. The purpose of this textbook is to provide the tools that will enable in-service and preservice teachers to plan, implement, and assess effectively. In doing so, teachers will constantly make decisions about goals and resources needed to facilitate standards and reflect on whether those goals were met.

It is impossible for one textbook to cover the entire discipline of teaching methods. However, we believe that we are offering a foundation that will promote student learning by fostering effective classroom teaching and providing a solid framework for in-depth study in the areas presented.

CONCEPTUAL FRAMEWORK

Two major goals structure this text. The first is to develop in readers the conceptual tools needed to serve as a foundation for continued professional growth. The second is to provide teachers with the latest research on teaching and describe implications of this research for classroom practice.

For the first time, a substantial body of research literature is exerting a prominent influence on educational decisions. This literature falls under a somewhat general category of teacher effectiveness. Simply stated, the research identifies what "good," or effective, teachers do compared to what is done by those who are less effective. The research is wide and varied and addresses a multitude of practical questions. For example, what effect would reducing class size have on both teachers and students? Research shows that reductions in class size can have both short- and long-term positive effects (Nye, Hedges, & Konstantopoulous, 2001; Viadero, 1999). In Tennessee, where class sizes were reduced from 25 to 15 students, researchers found immediate gains in reading and math scores. Follow-up studies revealed that the positive effects lasted through 12th grade. Fewer students in the smaller class dropped out of school, they took more challenging courses, and they were more likely to attend college than their counterparts in larger classes. These positive effects were especially strong for African American students. Smaller class sizes also positively affect teachers' lives (Muñoz & Portes, 2002). When class sizes are reduced, teachers' morale and job satisfaction increase. In smaller classes, teachers spend less time on discipline and more time on small-group work and diagnostic assessment. Overcrowded classrooms are among the most talked about topics in American education today, but critics question whether this educational change is worth the price tag. Research provides answers to questions such as these.

Historically, education has been vulnerable to opinion and influenced by prominent thinkers or, at the worst, unexamined beliefs or whim. That is no longer the case. Because of this second theme, appropriate research studies that document teaching effectiveness are used extensively throughout the text.

Learning to Teach

Learning to teach is complex and multifaceted in that it requires many different kinds of knowledge. Among these are the following:

- Content knowledge
- Pedagogical knowledge
- Teaching skills

Let's examine each of these.

It has long been held that "you can't teach what you don't know." Your *content knowledge* is based on the hours you have spent in liberal arts courses and in courses in your major and minor. However, according to Rudolph Dreikurs (1968b), "Knowledge of subject matter alone is not sufficient for being proficient in the classroom . . . or even the ability to convey that knowledge". Teachers must also know how to translate complex and difficult ideas into learnable topics.

Pedagogical knowledge, which involves knowing about classrooms, how they work, and how they promote learning, is a second kind of critical teacher knowledge. Some examples of concepts embedded in the domain of pedagogical knowledge include the following:

- Levels of learning in the cognitive domain
- Instructional goals and objectives
- Lesson planning
- Wait time
- Inquiry
- Rules and procedures
- Criterion-referenced tests

One of our goals in writing this text is to provide you with a knowledge of these concepts that will allow you to think about and analyze your role as a teacher and to dialogue with other professionals about important educational issues.

A third kind of teacher knowledge includes *teaching skills,* or the ability to use knowledge in strategic ways to bring about student learning. The teaching skills examined in this book are organized around the three interrelated tasks of planning, implementation, and assessment. We hope this book will provide you with the necessary skills to become competent during your first years of teaching.

ORGANIZATION OF THE TEXT

This text is organized into four units:

Unit One: Managing Classrooms for Effective Instruction (Chapters 2–3)

Unit Two: Standards and Planning for Instruction (Chapters 4–6)

Unit Three: Standards and Implementing Instruction (Chapters 7–10)

Unit Four: Standards and Assessing Instruction (Chapter 11)

In an attempt to streamline the readability of the text, we have implemented a standard format for each chapter that includes the following:

1. *Introduction.* An orientation to the material and a rationale for its inclusion in the book, including a scenario to focus the material to be studied.
2. *Learner Objectives.* A listing of the general knowledge you will possess after reading the chapter.
3. *Applying . . . in the Classroom.* A case study and a series of questions designed to serve as an advance organizer for the content of the chapter.
4. *Content.* Ideas and concepts that facilitate your attainment of the objectives by providing explanations, descriptions, and examples. Subheadings include sections on how diversity influences teaching and learning, how you can use diversity to make your classrooms richer learning environments, and how technology can enhance teachers' effectiveness and make their instructional tasks more efficient.
5. *Reflecting On . . .* This feature, which keys the content of the chapter to INTASC standards, provides opportunities for you to reflect on the material presented through specific questions.
6. *Summary.* Brief concluding statements relating the work to the overall conceptualization of the book.
7. *Key Concepts for Review.* Important terms and concepts that are listed in this section and marked in bold in the chapter.
8. *Preparing for Your Licensure Examination.* This feature presents a teaching scenario followed by a number of questions designed to help you focus on key chapter topics and provide opportunities and experience for the types of questions you will likely encounter on PRAXIS II.
9. *Video Exercise.* This feature presents a specific video that can be viewed online. After viewing the video, students respond to a series of questions.

10. *Developing Your Portfolio.* Suggestions regarding topics covered in the chapter that can be addressed in your academic portfolio.
11. *Questions for Discussion.* Questions designed to stimulate thinking about chapter content.
12. *Suggestions for Field Experience.* A list of activities that can be undertaken in schools and classrooms.
13. *Tools for Teaching.* This section presents suggested printed annotated references and suggested annotated Web sites.

This text is designed to be interactive—to help you actively use the information in it to construct a comprehensive view of effective teaching. We encourage you to use the different components of each chapter as you define yourself as a teacher.

NEW TO THIS EDITION

In addition to the contemporary references and updated research on teacher effectiveness throughout the text, the eighth edition includes significant additions:

- New and expanded discussions on national and state standards and their impact of the three-phase model of teaching
- An increased focus throughout the text on teaching strategies in the classroom
- A new chapter that establishes the relationship between sources of goals, the taxonomy of education, and content in the cognitive domain
- An "*Applying . . . in the Classroom*" section that presents a case study and follow-up questions that serve as advance organizers for the content of the chapter
- A glossary that presents the key concepts found in the text
- A "*Video Exercise*" section integrates Pearson's myeducationlab.com online video with follow-up questions and feedback. See further information about MyEducationLab below.
- A "Tools for Teaching" section that presents selected, annotated print references and selected annotated Web sites.

Finally, as with the previous seven editions, we have attempted to produce a methods book that is even more practical and applicable to classroom teaching. To this end, additional revised and expanded scenarios, examples, and exercises are offered throughout the text.

Where the Classroom Comes to Life

"Teacher educators who are developing pedagogies for the analysis of teaching and learning contend that analyzing teaching artifacts has three advantages: it enables new teachers time for reflection while still using the real materials of practice; it provides new teachers with experience thinking about and approaching the complexity of the classroom; and in some cases, it can help new teachers and teacher educators develop a shared understanding and common language about teaching. . . ."[1]

[1] Darling-Hammond, I., & Bransford, J.,Eds. (2005). *Preparing Teachers for a Changing World.* San Francisco: John Wiley & Sons.

As Linda Darling-Hammond and her colleagues point out, grounding teacher education in real classrooms—among real teachers and students and among actual examples of students' and teachers' work—is an important, and perhaps even an essential, part of training teachers for the complexities of teaching today's students in today's classrooms. For a number of years, we have heard the same message from many of you as we sat in your offices learning about the goals of your courses and the challenges you face in teaching the next generation of educators. Working with a number of our authors and with many of you, we have created a Web site that provides you and your students with the context of real classrooms and artifacts that research on teacher education tells us is so important. Through authentic in-class video footage, interactive simulations, rich case studies, examples of authentic teacher and student work, and more, **MyEducationLab** offers you and your students a uniquely valuable teacher education tool.

MyEducationLab

It is easy to use! Wherever the MyEducationLab logo appears in the margins or elsewhere in the text, you and your students can follow the simple link instructions to access the MyEducationLab resource that corresponds with the chapter content. These include:

Video

Authentic classroom videos show how real teachers handle actual classroom situations.

Homework & Exercises

These assignable activities give students opportunities to understand content more deeply and to practice applying content.

Case Studies

A diverse set of robust cases drawn from some of our best-selling books further expose students to the realities of teaching and offer valuable perspectives on common issues and challenges in education.

Simulations

Created by the IRIS Center at Vanderbilt University, these interactive simulations give hands-on practice at adapting instruction for a full spectrum of learners.

Student & Teacher Artifacts

Authentic student and teacher classroom artifacts are tied to course topics and offer practice in working with the actual types of materials encountered every day by teachers.

Readings

Specially selected, topically relevant articles from ASCD's renowned *Educational Leadership* journal expand and enrich students' perspectives on key issues and topics.

OTHER RESOURCES

Lesson & Portfolio Builders

With this effective and easy-to-use tool, you can create, update, and share standards-based lesson plans and portfolios.

News Articles

Looking for current issues in education? Our collection offers quick access to hundreds of relevant articles from the ABC News Feed.

MyEducationLab is easy to assign, which is essential to providing the greatest benefit to your student.

Visit www.myeducationlab.com for a demonstration of this exciting new online teaching resource.

ACKNOWLEDGMENTS

We express our gratitude to the hundreds of students and teachers who provided critical feedback and served as invaluable sources in the preparation of the eighth edition. We also thank our reviewers: Phyllis J. Anthony, Holy Family University; Julie Ashworth, Augustana College; Edward Case, Western Carolina University; Gail P. Gregg, Florida International University; Cordelia M. Nava, Texas A&M International University; and David Pugalee, University of North Carolina, Charlotte.

Finally, our thanks to Roxanne Klaas who provided invaluable input throughout the copy editing process; our project manager, Sarah Kenoyer, who dotted all the i's and crossed all the t's; our associate editor, Christina Robb, who was instrumental in the conceptualization of the eighth edition; and our executive editor, Darcy Betts Prybella, who guided the entire process and enabled the completion of this work.

D. A. J.   P. D. E.   D. P. K.

Brief Contents

Contents

UNIT ONE:
MANAGING CLASSROOMS FOR EFFECTIVE
INSTRUCTION   39

Chapter 2

CLASSROOM MANAGEMENT: PREVENTION   40

Chapter **3**

CLASSROOM MANAGEMENT: INTERVENTIONS 68

UNIT TWO:
STANDARDS AND PLANNING
FOR INSTRUCTION 93

Chapter **4**

STANDARDS AND THE GOALS OF INSTRUCTION 94

Chapter 5

FORMULATING GOALS AND OBJECTIVES USING STANDARDS   130

Chapter 6
PLANNING FOR ASSESSMENT WITH STANDARDS   156

UNIT THREE:
STANDARDS AND IMPLEMENTING INSTRUCTION   191

Chapter 9

MEETING STANDARDS THROUGH LEARNER-CENTERED INSTRUCTIONAL STRATEGIES   258

CHAPTER 1

Teaching in an Era of Standards and Accountability

INTRODUCTION

You are probably reading this book because you are either enrolled in an undergraduate general methods course or a teacher interested in improving your instructional effectiveness. As we write this book, we are assuming that while you have had experience with schools and classrooms—as we all have had as students, parents, aides, or tutors—you may not have done any formal teaching yourself. Based on this assumption, we will provide you with the background and basic tools needed to make intelligent decisions about planning learning activities, implementing those activities with children, and assessing their success in an era of standards and accountability. We hope that when you finish your study, you will have the conceptual and intellectual tools to continue to grow as a professional throughout your career.

For those of you who have had formal experience with teaching, we hope this material will help make your work more systematic and effective and will further assist you in making even better decisions about teaching.

We begin by familiarizing you with the influence that standards have had on classroom teaching and how federal and state standards as well as professional organizations have impacted the planning, implementing, and assessing of instruction.

LEARNER OBJECTIVES

After completing your study of Chapter 1, you should be able to do the following:

- Identify ways in which standards influence the act and process of teaching
- Discuss the primary role of the teacher
- Describe a variety of strategies teachers use to promote student growth and achievement
- Discuss ways in which teachers serve as decision makers
- Describe the importance of reflection in classroom teaching
- Identify the components of the three-phase model of teaching

APPLYING TEACHING AND STANDARDS IN THE CLASSROOM

Following is a case study in which a kindergarten teacher presents a lesson on dental health. As you read the case study, consider the following questions:

- Is the teacher promoting social and emotional growth in the children? If so, how?
- Are the students actively involved in the lesson?
- What are some of the different activities that Mrs. Warner employs?
- Is the learning environment primarily teacher centered (the teacher is the *sage on the stage*) or student centered (the teacher is the *guide on the side*)?

Mrs. Joy Warner wanted her kindergartners to learn about dental health. She organized her room into several learning centers, including a dentist's office where the children counted each other's teeth, cavities, and fillings and put information on a chart; a play-dough center where the children made models of teeth; an art center where the children painted the different parts of a tooth; a center by the sink where students practiced correct toothbrushing strokes; and a nutrition center where she interacted with a few children at a time. Three children sat with Mrs. Warner while an aide and a parent volunteer worked with children in the other learning centers.

To begin, she showed them a picture of some food.

"What kind of food is this?" Mrs. Warner asked.

"It looks like meatloaf," JuRelle said.

"Look a little closer."

"Cake."

"Yes, it does look like cake. And what is the stuff on top?"

"Icing," Melina said.

"And maybe nuts," Nirav added.

"Great, Mrs. Warner said. "Now what do we have here?"

"Strawberries."

"Good, Jessica. What about this one?"

"A tomato," Preston said.

"Good," Mrs. Warner said as she continued to hold up the pictures and ask the children to iden-tify the food in each. She then turned toward the felt board, on which she had a cutout happy face.

"What we are going to do now is sort these pictures. Some of these are pictures of food that can make your teeth happy, while others make your teeth not so happy. I'm going to put all the pictures in the middle and choose one, and then you can tell us where the pictures go.

"OK, now let me model it first to show you. This is cake, and I am going to put cake right up here under the sad tooth. Why do you think the cake would make the tooth unhappy . . . Melina?"

"Cavities," Melina replied.

"What might cause a cavity?" Mrs. Warner asked.

"Sweet things," Melina said.

"Yes. Cavities are caused by eating too many sweet things, but what makes them sweet?"

"I know. It's sugar!" Melina exclaimed.

"Very good," Mrs. Warner said. "You put sugar in things to make them sweet. Now let's go back to our pictures to see if they should go under the happy face or the sad face. . . . JuRelle, you do one for us."

JuRelle reached out, picked up a picture, and said, "Tomatoes."

"Can you say that in a complete sentence, please?"

"Tomatoes are healthy for your teeth."

"Nice job, JuRelle. I like that word healthy. OK . . . Preston?"

"Strawberries are good for your teeth."

"Right. A strawberry is a fruit, and it does have some sugar in it. But if you are going to eat the natural sugar in it, we know that is better than when you put sugar into foods to make them sweet like candy and cake."

Mrs. Warner continued to have the students classify the pictures and place them on the felt board. "Now," she asked, "how many things do we have that are not good for your teeth?" The children counted aloud, one through seven.

"And how many things do we have that are good for your teeth?" The children counted again, one through eight.

"So which foods do we have the most of?"

"Healthy food," the children replied.

"Good. Now I want everyone to listen. When we go over to our mural on the floor, you are going to draw either one healthy food or one unhealthy food."

"I'm going to draw a strawberry," Preston said.

"And where are you going to draw it? Under healthy things or unhealthy things?"

"Healthy."

"Good, Preston," Mrs. Warner said. "You are going to draw your strawberry under healthy, and after you draw it, write the word for the food right under your drawing."

Mrs. Warner then sat on the floor next to the children and monitored their progress with a focus on an inventive spelling exercise that allowed her to diagnose the children's progress on writing and their use of phonetics. These observations gave her information for future, individualized instruction.

She was also able to review with them their work in this integrated learning experience, including numbers, sets, language development, health, communication skills, writing, and art.

Before we see how responses to this relate to teaching and the role of the teacher, let's begin by examining how standards and professional organizations impact what is taught in the classroom.

STANDARDS AND PROFESSIONAL DEVELOPMENT

Several organizations aim to improve education through the publication of guidelines or standards to guide the profession. These guidelines and standards influence teachers' roles both directly and indirectly. In this section, we describe national and state efforts to improve education and their effects on teachers.

Interstate New Teacher Assessment and Support Consortium

The Interstate New Teacher Assessment and Support Consortium (INTASC) was created in 1987 to help states develop better teachers through coordinated efforts of support and assessment. INTASC developed 10 teacher performance standards or principles. These principles, found in Figure 1.1, present a wide range of content knowledge, pedagogical methodologies and strategies, and personal behaviors that promote student learning. For example, in the scenario that opens this chapter, Mrs. Warner is clearly addressing principle 5, in which the teacher uses an understanding of individual and group motivation and behavior to create a learning environment that encourages positive social interaction, active engagement in learning, and self-motivation.

National Board for Professional Teaching Standards

The INTASC standards were developed to guide the professional development of all teachers but have been especially helpful for beginning teachers. A comparable movement focusing on the professional development of experienced teachers is the National Board for Professional Teaching Standards (NBPTS). Created in 1987 as an outgrowth of a Carnegie

Figure 1.1   Principles of the Interstate New Teacher Assessment and Support Consortium (INTASC)

1. The teacher understands the central concepts, tools of inquiry, and structures of the discipline he or she teaches.
2. The teacher understands how children learn and develop.
3. The teacher understands how students differ in their approaches to learning.
4. The teacher understands and uses a variety of instructional strategies.
5. The teacher uses an understanding of individual and group motivation.
6. The teacher uses knowledge of effective verbal, nonverbal, and media techniques.
7. The teacher plans instruction based on knowledge of subject matter.
8. The teacher understands and uses formal and informal assessment strategies.
9. The teacher is a reflective practitioner.
10. The teacher fosters relationships with colleagues, parents, and agencies.

Forum Report, *A Nation Prepared: Teachers for the 21st Century*, the board is composed mostly of K–12 teachers but also includes union and business leaders and university faculty. NBPTS seeks to strengthen teaching as a profession and raise the quality of education by recognizing the contributions of exemplary teachers, compensating them financially, giving them increased responsibility, and increasing their role in decision making (Serafini, 2002).

National Board certification is based on standards that grew out of the report *What Teachers Should Know and Be Able to Do*. Certification is directed by five core propositions about professional educators. These propositions and descriptions of how they play out in practice are outlined in Table 1.1.

Clearly, the NBPTS standards, when properly implemented, are critical to the promotion of student learning and serve as focal points for much of the material presented in the text.

Table 1.1   Propositions of the National Board for Professional Teaching Standards

Proposition	Description
1. Teachers are committed to students and their learning.	■ Accomplished teachers believe that all students can learn, and they treat students equitably.
	■ Accomplished teachers understand how students develop, and they use accepted learning theory as the basis for their teaching.
	■ Accomplished teachers are aware of the influence of context and culture on behavior, and they foster students' self-esteem, motivation, and character.
2. Teachers know the subjects they teach and how to teach those subjects to students.	■ Accomplished teachers have a rich understanding of the subject(s) they teach, and they appreciate how knowledge in their subject is linked to other disciplines and applied to real-world settings.
	■ Accomplished teachers know how to make subject matter understandable to students, and they are able to modify their instruction when difficulties arise.
	■ Accomplished teachers demonstrate critical and analytic capacities in their teaching, and they develop those capacities in their students.
3. Teachers are responsible for managing and monitoring student learning.	■ Accomplished teachers capture and sustain the interest of their students and use their time effectively.
	■ Accomplished teachers are able to use a variety of effective instructional techniques, and they use the techniques appropriately.

4. Teachers think systematically about their practice and learn from experience.

- Accomplished teachers can use multiple methods to assess the progress of students, and they effectively communicate this progress to parents.
- Accomplished teachers are models for intellectual curiosity, and they display virtues—honesty, fairness, and respect for diversity—that they seek to inspire in their students.
- Accomplished teachers use their understanding of students, learning, and instruction to make principled judgments about sound practice, and they are lifelong learners.
- Accomplished teachers critically examine their practice, and they seek continual professional growth.

5. Teachers are members of learning communities.

- Accomplished teachers contribute to the effectiveness of the school, and they work collaboratively with their colleagues.
- Accomplished teachers evaluate school progress, and they utilize community resources.
- Accomplished teachers work collaboratively with parents, and they involve parents in school activities.

Source: Reprinted with permission from the National Board for Professional Teaching Standards, *What Teachers Should Know and Be Able to Do,* www.nbpts.org. All rights reserved.

National Council for Accreditation of Teacher Education and Teacher Education Accreditation Council

Additional attempts to improve the quality of education in the United States have focused on teacher education. Both the National Council for Accreditation of Teacher Education (NCATE) and the Teacher Education Accreditation Council (TEAC) have created standards for teacher education. The standards of these councils are designed to ensure that their accredited institutions produce competent, caring, and qualified teachers and other professional school personnel. Through this process, NCATE provides assurance to the public that graduates of those institutions have acquired the knowledge and skills necessary to help all students learn (NCATE, 2000). NCATE also addresses the need for teacher education institutions to identify teacher dispositions, examples of which could include the following (Adams State College, 2002):

- A belief that all students can learn
- A vision of high and challenging standards
- A commitment to personal professional development and to a safe and supportive learning environment

- An ability to accept responsibility
- An understanding of school operations as an integral part of the larger community
- An acceptance of families as partners in the education of their children
- A dedication to bringing ethical principles into the decision-making process

For TEAC, three quality principles are the means by which a teacher education faculty makes the case that its professional education program has succeeded in preparing competent, caring, and qualified professional educators. Those principles are the following (TEAC, 2004):

- Evidence of student learning, including subject matter knowledge, pedagogical knowledge, and caring teaching skill
- Valid assessment of student learning
- Institutional learning, including program decisions and planning based on evidence and influential quality control system

Federal Efforts to Improve Teaching

Goals 2000.   In addition to accreditation agencies, national goals and federal mandates are fueling the reform movement to reorganize schools around standards. Because education of children is constitutionally a state's right, standards were put forth in the 1980s in the form of reports, not mandates, such as *A Nation at Risk*. When that now-famous exposé on public education, along with other white papers, produced disappointing results, educational leaders turned to national goals and the notion of voluntary compliance (Marzano & Kendall, 2003). In 1989, the first President Bush convened an educational summit of governors, led by Governor Bill Clinton of Arkansas, that focused on educational reforms and included the following six national educational goals, which were part of Goals 2000. By 2000, the following goals were to have been met:

1. All children in America will start school ready to learn.
2. The high school graduation rate will increase to at least 90%.
3. All students will leave grades 4, 8, and 12 having demonstrated competency over challenging subject matter, including English, mathematics, science, history, and geography, and every school in America will ensure that all students learn to use their minds well, so that they may be prepared for responsible citizenship, further learning, and productive employment in our nation's modern economy.
4. American students will be first in the world in science and mathematic achievement.
5. Every adult American will be literate and will possess the knowledge and skills necessary to compete in a global economy and exercise the rights and responsibilities of citizenship.
6. Every school in the United States will be free of drugs, violence, and the unauthorized presence of firearms and alcohol and will offer a disciplined environment conducive to learning.

It is important to note that goals 3 and 4 specifically addressed academic achievement and that, during the Clinton administration, goal 4 was expanded to include foreign languages, the arts, economics, civics, and government. Two additional goals were also added:

7. By 2000, the nation's teaching force will have access to programs for the continued improvement of their professional skills and the opportunity to acquire the knowledge and skills needed to instruct and prepare all American students for the next century.
8. By 2000, every school will promote partnerships that will increase parental involvement and participation in promoting the social, emotional, and academic growth of children.

The establishment of these goals provided the impetus for a wide variety of national councils and associations to publish standards in their given disciplines and field of study.

No Child Left Behind.   Although many critics found the standards reform effort problematic because of the overwhelming number of standards and their minimal and ambiguous nature, the focus led to more specific federal proposals, such as No Child Left Behind (NCLB). This legislation, signed by President George W. Bush in 2002, is a reauthorization of the Elementary and Secondary School Act of 1965 and provides, among other things, guidelines for teacher and school accountability and low-performing schools that include the following:

- By 2005–2006, schools will test all children in reading and math in grades 3 to 8. Schools failing to meet standards run the risk of losing federal funds in addition to funding transfers to high-performing schools, while schools meeting standards could be eligible for additional funding.
- Scientifically based methods, such as phonics, will be employed.
- By 2005, school systems will be required to ensure high-quality teachers.

Although professional education associations and school systems support much of this legislation, concerns include the expanded role of the federal government in education and the perceived lack of financial support to enact these mandates (Hardy, 2002; Jennings, 2002). While state education officials and school boards grapple with NCLB compliance, principals are the frontline interpreters for parents and teachers. That means they must explain accountability (e.g., testing students, offering extra services for low achievers, and improving educator quality), give parents more information (e.g., written parent involvement policy and state report cards), and provide choice (e.g., transfers to higher-performing public schools) (National Association of Elementary School Principals, 2004).

State Standards

The U.S. Constitution makes it clear that states have the responsibility for educating citizens. To that end, the standards movement at the state level encompasses not only content knowledge and skills but also how courses and subjects are defined, how student performance is described, and how student performance is graded and reported (Marzano & Kendall, 2003). For example, Mrs. Warner's dental health lesson addresses Colorado's standard 1: Students understand the process of scientific investigation and design, conduct, communicate about and evaluate such investigations. More specifically, at the kindergarten level, the students "use data based on observations to construct a reasonable explanation." Colorado has been identified as one of four states with the clearest model content standards for grades K–12, along with suggested grade-level expectations. Let's take a look at some examples of standards at different grade levels in mathematics:

Standard 1: Students develop number sense and use numbers and number relationships in problem-solving situations and communicate the reasoning involved in solving these problems.

- Kindergarten students will, using objects and pictures, represent whole numbers from 0 to 50 in a variety of ways.
- Fourth-grade students will, using objects and pictures, represent whole numbers, including odds and evens, from 0 to 1,000,000.
- Seventh-grade students will locate integers and positive rational numbers on the number line.
- High school students will demonstrate relationships among subsets of the real-number system, including counting, whole, integer, rational, and irrational numbers, one to the other.

In addition to academic standards, Colorado also established performance-based standards for its teachers that serve as required knowledge and skills for the licensing of all teacher education candidates in that state. The six standards, which include 45 elements, are the following:

- Knowledge of literacy
- Knowledge of mathematics
- Knowledge of standards and assessments
- Knowledge of content
- Knowledge of classroom and instructional management
- Democracy, educational governance, and careers in teaching

For a complete review of both K–12 Academic Standards and the Performance-Based Standards for Colorado Teachers, see the Web site listing in the "Technology in the Classroom" section on pp. 30–32.

The reform efforts you have read about in this section attempt to improve education by clearly stating educational goals and purposes. Another way to improve education is through an analysis of teaching and the role of the teacher.

THE TEACHER'S ROLE

An often-held and stereotypical view of a teacher is that of an informed person disseminating information to a group of people hungry for knowledge. The group is often viewed as passive, and the main activity in such a learning environment involves the teacher *telling* the students what they need to know. However, most educators agree that this view is extremely narrow and that telling is only one of many strategies a teacher may employ. To begin our study of the different roles teachers play, refer to the case study at the beginning of this chapter, which follows a teacher implementing a primary science unit.

Promoting Growth and Achievement

Several teacher roles are undertaken in this teaching scenario, and they are often found in the form of contrasting dualisms. For instance, by providing several interactive learning centers, Mrs. Warner hoped to promote social and emotional growth in the children, while the teaching strategy she employed to facilitate students' understandings of healthy and unhealthy foods promoted both the acquisition and the internalization of knowledge. Thus, in this particular activity, Mrs. Warner had dual goals—the development of social and emotional growth and knowledge acquisition.

It is important to note that when asked to classify healthy and unhealthy foods, the student JuRelle said, "Tomatoes are healthy for your teeth." Mrs. Warner, up to that point, had the children thinking about pictures of food items by placing them under either a sad tooth or a happy tooth. It was JuRelle, not Mrs. Warner, who verbalized the concept and made the connection between food items and healthy teeth. Her emphasis on engaging the student as an active learner is one aspect of constructivism, a developing view of learning that we will discuss later in the chapter.

In addition to the acquisition of desired knowledge, both the social and the intellectual enhancement of children are primary aims that teachers address as a significant part of their role as professional educators. Socially, Mrs. Warner had the children interacting with one another in many of her learning centers, particularly the "dentist's office," where the children worked with one another to complete their chart. The center in which she participated with the children was focused on intellectual or cognitive activities. The dualism here and in many other aspects of teaching is not an either/or situation but one of priority.

A major question facing teachers is, What component of a student's growth is most important for public school institutions to address? Is it intellectual-academic or emotional-social growth? Stated in terms of what should be taught, should the curriculum be based on a storehouse of knowledge that has enabled humankind to advance civilization, or should our instruction focus on helping students interact better with their peers to improve self-esteem and academic achievement and provide opportunities to develop friendships (Campbell, Campbell, & Dickinson, 2004).

We contend that the central role of a teacher is to facilitate student learning, broadly defined, in a variety of ways. This brings up a fundamental question: How do we learn? We learn in many different ways, ranging from pure experiential learning to learning from others. We see these types of learning illustrated in Mrs. Warner's classroom in the different activities she organized to promote learning. On closer inspection, however, we also see that her learning environment is primarily student centered, practical, and action oriented, all of which reflect a constructivist approach to learning.

Constructivism in the Classroom

Although **constructivism** is multifaceted, a common view argues that knowledge resides only within learners and that we cannot teach precise representations of "truth." We can only negotiate shared meanings with students and provide them with opportunities to construct useful understanding as students engage in purposeful activity (Jacobsen, 2003a).

Although this *radical* view of constructivism is highly valued by many academicians, it often fails to translate or apply to the practical realities teachers face in today's classrooms. While evidence overwhelmingly indicates that learners do indeed construct understanding, not all forms of understanding are equally valid, and a reality independent of individual understanding exists (Eggen & Kauchak, 2007). If this were not true, teachers would have little role in education, and an "anything goes" constructivism could result. That would fly in the face of the fact that teachers are being increasingly held accountable for facilitating the acquisition of a concrete cognitive body of knowledge measured by standardized, high-stakes assessments.

A constructivist learning environment prioritizes and facilitates the student's active role. A constructivist learning environment shifts the focus from teacher dissemination, which promotes a passive role for students, to student autonomy and reflection, which promotes an active role. **Active learning** suggests learning activities in which students are given considerable autonomy and control of the direction of learning activities. Active learning activities include problem solving, small-group work, collaborative learning, investigational work, and experiential learning. In contrast, **passive learning** activities, in which the students are basically receivers of information, include listening to what the teacher says and commonly being asked low-level questions. This constructivist shift is based on the idea that learners are naturally active and curious, both of which suggest a deemphasis on lecture and textbooks. This deemphasis does not imply that teachers should not explain content to students; it does suggest that we should be skeptical about how much understanding learners develop on the basis of our explanations and their recording of that knowledge. Believing that learners *construct* rather than *record* understanding has important implications for the way we teach. In addition to the note of caution listed previously, as teachers we should do the following (Eggen & Kauchak, 2007):

- Provide learners with a variety of examples and representations of content
- Promote high levels of interaction in our teaching
- Connect content to the real world

Even though there is no single constructivist theory, many constructivist approaches recommend the following (Ormrod, 2000):

- Complex challenging learning environments and authentic tasks
- Social negotiation and shared responsibility as a part of learning
- Multiple representations of content
- Understanding that knowledge is constructed
- Student-centered instruction

The focus on **student-centered instruction** is multifaceted. As students construct their own understanding of content, they develop a personal feeling that the knowledge is their own. Second, student centeredness implies a heavy emphasis on inquiry and problem-based learning and group work. Much of the focus on problem-solving activities in the classroom, along with other student-centered components of constructivist theory, is founded on the philosophy of John Dewey (1906, 1938), probably the most influential American educational philosopher. Prior to Dewey, the aim of education in the United States was facilitating a student's acquisition of knowledge. With the appearance of Dewey's theories and reflective method, educators became increasingly interested in students' ability to think about information and engage in realistic problem solving. Teachers applying his theories to their classroom teaching emphasize a student-centered, activity-oriented curriculum (Jacobsen, 2002b). Dewey further believed that these activities should be meaningful and of practical value, that the most effective learning activities for students involved *learning by doing*, and that learning should be a continuous lifelong experience in which "an active mind interacts with a wide-open world to solve genuine problems that are continuous with, yet different from, previous experiences" (Reed & Johnson, 2000, p. 91).

Constructivist theories of learning were also influenced by the developmental theories of Piaget (1952, 1959) and the social learning theories of Vygotsky. Piaget's work focuses on direct, individual experiences that move the learner, sequentially over a period of time, to construct perceptual, concrete, and finally abstract knowledge. Vygotsky's work emphasizes the importance of social interaction as students participate in meaningful learning tasks. Learners advance their own thinking through exposure to the views and insights of others. One of the most commonly implemented group-work learning strategies is **cooperative learning,** in which the teacher's role is to promote learning by emphasizing a team, as opposed to a competitive approach to learning. In this role, teaching can, once again, facilitate students' construction of knowledge.

However, a word of caution is necessary: the operable word in the previous sentence is *can*. Specifically, the view that social interaction facilitates the construction of understanding is an underlying principle of constructivist learning theory. This is sometimes intended to mean that a teacher who uses cooperative learning is "constructivist," whereas one who relies on large-group learning activities is not. In fact, both teachers may be basing their instruction on constructivist views of learning, or neither may be. Large-group instruction, effectively undertaken, can promote the construction of understanding, while cooperative learning, improperly undertaken, may not (Eggen & Jacobsen, 2001). Therefore, the bottom line is not how teachers teach but rather what and how students learn. The effectiveness of a strategy is found not in how it was implemented but in whether it promoted students' personal acquisition and understanding of knowledge. This suggests that during the planning process, teachers consider all the traditional questions of teaching—how to organize and implement learning activities, how to motivate students, and how to assess learning—but ultimately analyze these in terms of student learning (Eggen & Kauchak, 2007). In later chapters, we discuss constructivist considerations regarding planning, implementing, and assessing, but now let's consider how motivation influences learning.

Motivating Students

A critical teacher role in promoting student learning is increasing students' desire or **motivation** to learn. To accomplish this task, you need to know your students well enough to be able to provide learning experiences that they will find interesting, valuable, intrinsically motivating, challenging, and rewarding (Kellough, 2000). The better you know your students, understand their interests, and assess their skill levels, the more effective you can be in reaching and teaching them. Some of the questions you might want to get your students to answer are the following: (McCarty & Siccone, 2001):

- What are some of the things you think an "educated adult" needs to know?
- What are your interests, hobbies, and favorite ways to spend time?

motivational factor. Personal teaching strategies to enhance motivation include being sincere, positive, enthusiastic, and supportive. In addition, one of the most powerful ways of communicating our interest is simply by listening to what students are saying and letting them know we value their thoughts and contributions to the class. Finally, humor can be an indispensable tool in promoting a positive relationship with your students.

A negative factor regarding motivation involves mistakes. Overemphasis on mistakes can damage a child's positive self-concept and eventually inhibit the child's desire even to attempt the task at hand. This can also happen when "winning" becomes an end goal. Teachers can deemphasize competition and student comparisons by focusing on a cooperative learning environment with an emphasis on the mastery of learning outcomes.

In motivating students, teachers cannot internalize concepts or behaviors for students because internalization is a personal, unique process that all of us must undertake for ourselves. However, teachers can do many things to facilitate the process. For example, in teaching a child to ride a bicycle, we can demonstrate bicycle functions, such as the use of brakes and pedaling. We can have the child sit on the bike with us, roll it slowly, and lean from side to side, thereby demonstrating balance. We can put the child on a stationary bicycle and allow him or her to experience pedaling and using the brakes. We can run alongside the child, aid in corrections, and constantly encourage and reinforce appropriate behaviors. In short, we can provide instructional support by demonstrating or modeling riding a bicycle; providing a knowledge base regarding operation, and providing appropriate, sufficient, and supportive practical experiences. These instructional scaffolds enable the child to ultimately learn to ride and develop pride in his or her developing ability to cope with the world.

Mistakes are a natural part of learning and are part of the process of challenge. Rudolph Dreikurs (1968a) provided us with a classic example of this. When children learn to ride a bicycle, they frequently go down a street. If there is a rock in the middle of the road, they attempt to hit it because they want to experiment, to experience what it is like to hit a rock when learning to ride. Challenge and the mistakes that go with it are essential to learning.

Likewise, many students are prone, metaphorically, to hit rocks. We cannot teach them to do otherwise. What we can do is provide educational experiences that promote positive learning environments laden with a variety of extrinsic motivational factors that, we hope, students will transfer to the intrinsic plane. In this way, teachers enhance and, to some degree, direct the internalization process, the final product of which is determined by the child.

Throughout history, great teachers have facilitated that which students think or do, and an educator's value is found in paving the way for students' transfer from what they do to what they know or become.

EXERCISE 1.1

Review the discussion on motivation and list three ways you would facilitate student motivation.

TEACHING: AN ANALYSIS

How do effective teachers promote student learning and motivation? To answer this question, let's look at three examples of teachers working in classrooms.

Scenario 1. Mrs. Shafer is a sixth-grade teacher at Plainview Elementary School. Plainview is an older school in a lower-middle-class neighborhood of Laqua, Florida. While the school is not new, the administration has kept the grounds and building attractive. Everyone cooperates in keeping the small areas of grass from being trampled on and killed, and the paved and cemented areas are kept free of debris. There are no broken windows, and the water fountains and lavatories work well and smell fresh.

Mrs. Shafer's room has a high ceiling that makes it seem big, but she has grouped large boxes to make cubbyholes and privacy corners for her children. She asked for and received permission to paint designs and graphics (sayings or pictures such as rainbows) on her walls in addition to her use of several large bulletin boards for decoration.

Mrs. Shafer is beginning a unit in geography, and students have studied various geographic regions and their physical features. The children are now familiar with regions such as the American central plains, the Russian steppes, the Argentine pampas, the American Rocky Mountains, the Swiss Alps, and the South American Andes. They know how the regions are similar and how they differ. Mrs. Shafer now wants her children to understand the influence of geography on people's lifestyles and culture. She decides to use pictures of people in different regions to get students to link the regions with the people's appearances and activities. She gathers her pictures and begins the lesson. She starts by showing a picture of children playing in front of some grass huts.

"Look at the picture, everyone," Mrs. Shafer says, smiling. "Tell me anything at all you see about the pictures."

"They're in Africa," Carol says immediately.

"Excellent, Carol, but how do you know that?"

"My dad is in the navy, and we lived in Greece, and we took a trip to Africa, and we saw houses like those."

Jimmy's eyes open wide. "You went to Africa? I've never been out of Laqua in my life."

Mike adds, "I've never been there, but I've read about it, and those children could live in India maybe'cuz they don't wear many clothes in India either."

David is whispering and grinning at Billy as Mike is talking, and Mrs. Shafer gives him a stern look.

"What did we agree was one of our important rules, David?" Mrs. Shafer asks.

"We always respect others," David says quietly.

"And what is one way we do that?"

"We listen to what they have to say whether we agree or not and then express our opinion when it's our turn."

"Very good, David," Mrs. Shafer says with a smile. "That's a good reminder for all of us. Now let's go on. What else do you see in the picture?"

The children continue describing what they see, and then Mrs. Shafer shows two Russian children playing with a sled in front of a log structure. Again she asks for a description of what the children see. She continues this process, showing pictures of Indian shepherds in Ecuador and Bedouin tribesmen in the Middle East. She asks the students to compare all the pictures by showing similarities and differences. Finally, she asks the children to summarize what they saw.

"Well, people live in different places and their houses are different," Joan suggests.

"Fine, Joan. Now, anything else?"

"They dress different," Kim adds.

"OK."

"They're playing different games and stuff," Susan says.

"Very good. What more can you say about what we've seen—people's houses, clothes, games they play, and so on?"

"Well," Jimmy says somewhat hesitantly, "they're things about people."

"Fine, and what things about people?"

"Oh, how they live and everything."

"Very good. So we're saying geography and climate affect people's lifestyles."

Mrs. Shafer next discusses Florida's climate, geography, and lifestyle and asks the children to compare that to how they would expect to live in northern Michigan or Minnesota.

After a number of comparisons are made, Mrs. Shafer announces, "Now, everyone, I have two short paragraphs that I want you to read. Then I want you to write four examples from the paragraph that show how geography and climate affect lifestyle."

The paragraphs she gives the children are as follows:

José and Kirsten are two children about your age who live in faraway lands. Kirsten lives in the mountains of Norway, which is quite far north. José lives on the flat plains of western Mexico, where it is very hot and dry. Kirsten loves to ski and does so nearly every day in the winter. In the summer she and her brother put on light wool sweaters and go hiking in the mountains. They love to sit atop the peaks and look down over the valleys. In the evenings, Kirsten's mother builds a fire, and everyone in the family reads quietly.

José loves to play, just as Kirsten does. He swims every afternoon in a pond formed by a spring near his village. He becomes impatient because he has to wait until after the nap his mother takes every day at noon. The children go outside and play in the evening, enjoying the breeze that cools the village. They usually play until it is so dark they can't see.

Mrs. Shafer collects the students' papers and ends the class by saying she will introduce the idea of culture the following day and relate culture to geography and climate. She reviews the papers during her planning period and finds the following responses:

1. *Kirsten skiing in the winter*
2. *Kirsten's family sitting and reading by the fire in the evening*
3. *Kirsten and her brother hiking in the mountains*
4. *José's mother napping every noon*
5. *José playing in the evening*
6. *José swimming in the afternoon*

Scenario 2. *Mr. Adams works in a kindergarten classroom. He has his room arranged in sections. Today is Monday, so Mr. Adams arrives at school early to set up his room for the week. He changes his activities on a weekly basis and spends his Friday afternoons and Monday mornings getting them ready. This week he wants to put particular emphasis on manipulative skills and wants to be sure all the children can perform tasks such as buttoning coats and tying shoes. In one corner he puts some flashlight bulbs in little holders, some dry-cell batteries, and some wire. In another corner he places a large flannel board with different numbers of beans glued on it so children can match numerals such as 2 or 3 with the appropriate number of beans. He arranges similar activities in the other corners of the room.*

As the children come in, Mr. Adams asks them what activities they would like to choose and sends them each to a corner to begin. He then sits down on the floor with three boys to help them learn to tie the shoelaces on a large doll they've named Fred. Each day the children button Fred's shirt, tie his shoes, and comb his hair. Jimmy is struggling to get Fred's shoe tied and appears slightly uninterested to

Mr. Adams. He feels his forehead, which appears to be warm, and immediately takes him by the hand down to the nurse's office. Jimmy is often ill, so Mr. Adams is sensitive when he appears listless.

As he returns, he sees Scott throw a beanbag at Lisa. Mr. Adams admonishes him, gently saying, "Scott, you're not supposed to throw the beanbag at Lisa; you're supposed to throw it so she can catch it."

"She threw it at me first."

"Did you, Lisa?"

Smiling shyly, Lisa nods.

"Throw it to each other and count to see if you can do it 10 times each without missing."

Mr. Adams continues working with groups of children until 11:30 a.m., when it is time for dismissal. He helps the children get safely on the bus and then goes back to his room.

Taking stock of his morning, he grins to himself as he recalls that David had improved significantly in tying Fred's shoes. He takes out a sheet that has the children's names on it and puts a check by David's name. He notices as he glances at the sheet that Bobby had trouble walking the balance beam and prepares a note for his mother suggesting some exercises he could do at home. With this done, he prepares for his afternoon class.

Scenario 3. *Mrs. Tyler is a history teacher in a large high school. She is working on a unit in group processes, and while her ultimate goal is for the students to understand the effects of group processes on democratic decision making, her particular goal in this lesson is to have her students learn to understand their own views more clearly and to learn to cooperate by making decisions in groups. To accomplish this, she splits the class into two groups and presents each group with a perplexing dilemma. The situation describes a shipwreck with some sick and injured people. The party is marooned on a deserted island, short of food and water fit for drinking. Fortunately, they're rescued, but the ship can handle only part of the people in one trip. In all likelihood, many of the sick and injured won't survive the trip back to civilization, but they'll surely die if left on the island. If the healthy are left until the second trip, many will die of starvation or thirst before the ship returns. She asks the students to discuss the issue during the class period, recording notes and decisions. Each group is to report the following day.*

As the groups discuss the problem, Mrs. Tyler listens and periodically raises questions if students appear to drift away from the task at hand or suggests issues that aren't considered by the group.

The next day Mrs. Tyler has the students discuss the process they went through, their feelings as they were involved in the discussion, and the bases for the decisions they made. As the year progresses, Mrs. Tyler makes short notes about each student, describing the student's progress in working in group situations.

Now let's analyze these three teachers involved in activities with students at three different levels and in three different content areas and see how they illustrate a framework for subsequent chapters in this book.

Areas of Emphasis: Differing Goals Influence Learning

First, let's look at what the three teachers hoped to accomplish. Mrs. Shafer wanted her students to understand the influence of geography and climate on lifestyle. Mr. Adams had his children doing a variety of things; some worked with trying to light the bulb, some counted beans, and others worked on skills like tying shoes and buttoning coats. Mrs. Tyler wanted her students to learn to cooperate in groups and did this by involving them in a problem-solving, decision-making activity. While each teacher had a primary instructional focus, their classrooms also focused on other goals. For example, while Mrs. Shafer wanted her students to learn about the relationship among geography, climate, and lifestyle, she also viewed respect for others as important. She demonstrated this view when she reminded David and Billy to listen when Mike was talking. Also, to perform psychomotor skills, such as carpentry and hitting a tennis ball properly, knowledge of technique is required. All this illustrates that three areas—**knowledge, skills,** and **attitudes**—are closely interrelated and cannot be completely separated in any reasonable way.

Based on the three scenarios, we see that students' learning is more varied and complex than we might expect at first glance. Mrs. Shafer's students were learning information, or knowledge, and how it can be used to explain objects and events that occur in the world. By comparison, many of Mr. Adams's activities were related to manipulative or psychomotor skills such as buttoning Fred's coat and tying his shoes. Many other psychomotor skills are taught in schools—typing, carpentry, leatherwork, mechanics, and physical education skills. Mrs. Tyler's activity was different from both Mrs. Shafer's and Mr. Adams's. She wanted her students to develop interpersonal communication skills and acquire certain attitudes and values, such as cooperation, willingness to listen to a contrasting view, and respect for others.

We see now that students learn much more than information in schools. Student learning can be described as existing in three forms: (a) information and knowledge, (b) psychomotor skills, and (c) attitudes and values.

All three areas are extremely important and need to be addressed in schools. However, a complete discussion of the learning of all three—knowledge, skills, and attitudes—is beyond the scope of a single text. Although we will discuss the other two areas, we have chosen to emphasize the area of knowledge and information. The reason is simple. While attitudes and psychomotor skills are important and valued by both the public and educators, relatively greater emphasis is placed on the acquisition of knowledge and the ability to think. We will take a closer look at knowledge, skills, and attitudes in Chapter 4.

Learning Environments Influence Learning

In addition to goals, learning is also influenced by the kinds of learning environments teachers create. Let's look again at the three scenarios and see how the learning environments differed. Mrs. Shafer worked with her whole class, while Mr. Adams worked with small groups and had learning centers set up. Mrs. Tyler worked with two large groups. Adding one-on-one encounters to our list, the different grouping arrangements appear in Figure 1.2. Different group arrangements provide different opportunities for students to learn different things. We discuss these different arrangements in more detail in later chapters.

Figure 1.2 Group Arrangements for Learning Activities

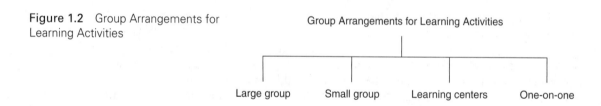

Group Arrangements for Learning Activities

Large group   Small group   Learning centers   One-on-one

Other Influences on Learning

While group arrangements affect the way children learn, many other factors influence what children take away from school. For instance, in Mr. Adams's activity, Jimmy appeared listless, and it turned out that he did not feel well. Health is certainly a factor that affects learning, and the younger the child, the more important it is to support good nutrition (Berk, 2003). Nutrition is another factor; its importance, in addition to promoting general health, is evidenced by schools implementing free breakfast and lunch programs for needy children. In doing so, schools address two issues: hunger and nutrition. Children can not concentrate, enjoy school, or truly learn if they are hungry and it is well documented that children need adequate nutrients for their cognitive development.

Background experiences also influence learning. Again, think about Mrs. Shafer's lesson. In discussing the picture of children playing in front of the grass huts, Carol reacted quite differently from Jimmy because she had been to Africa and had seen huts and children similar to those in Mrs. Shafer's picture, while Jimmy had no frame of reference whatsoever. Mike's reaction was somewhere in between. He had no firsthand experience but was familiar with the ideas from pictures and stories. All this illustrates how experience can affect what children learn. In the situation just described, Carol was certainly in the best position to derive the most benefit from the lesson because of her experience, while Jimmy was in the least advantageous position. Obviously, we as teachers cannot control students' backgrounds, but we can provide the most realistic examples possible, promote as much student involvement as possible, and design learning activities that allow students to share their background experiences. These examples illustrate the teacher's crucial role in influencing student learning, which brings us to the central theme of this text.

As you reflect on your role as a teacher, you see that as an individual teacher, you can do little about children's ability, health, outside experiences, or emotional makeup. You can, however, significantly influence their learning by providing school experiences that promote thinking and by making learning as positive an experience as possible. That is what this book is all about. In succeeding chapters, we will help you learn to plan, implement, and assess activities to promote as much student learning as possible.

DIVERSITY IN THE CLASSROOM

Accommodating Through Standards

As we saw in the previous section, what students bring to our classrooms strongly influences learning. **Learner diversity** presents both challenges and opportunities for the classroom teacher. The children we teach differ in significant ways, including physical characteristics, interests, home life, intellectual abilities, learning capacities, motor abilities, social skills, aptitudes and talents, language skills, background experiences, ideals, attitudes, hopes, and dreams (Jarolimek, Foster, & Kellough, 2005). Today's classrooms are more diverse than at any time in the history of American education because of significant changes in the ethnic/racial makeup of student populations and the rise in the number of children with exceptionalities in our classrooms. In terms of the former, immigration has increased to the extent that by the

Table 1.2   Examples of Three-Phase Approach

	Planning	Implementing	Assessing
Mrs. Shafer	Wanted students to know how lifestyle and geography relate. Selected pictures and planned discovery.	Had children observe pictures and discover relationship.	Gave children a paragraph and had them identify illustrations in it.
Mr. Adams	Wanted students to develop manipulative skills. Decided on practice. Decided to use the doll.	Had students practice on the doll.	Observed students and checked their names on a checklist.
Mrs. Tyler	Wanted students to learn to work in groups. Chose a dilemma for groups to discuss.	Had students discuss the dilemma and arrive at group decision.	Observed students work in groups during the year.

Although described as three separate phases, the continuity and interrelationships of the phases should be emphasized. To see this interrelationship between the different phases, let's begin with planning. The goal that a teacher has for a particular group of students should determine both what is taught and how it is taught and should also influence the manner in which the learning is assessed. These relationships are shown in Figure 1.3.

Some of the relationships shown in Figure 1.3 are readily apparent, while others require some discussion. The effect of goals on implementation strategies and assessment procedures is apparent in that the goal being taught influences how the lesson is taught and how the effectiveness of the lesson is measured. Assessment procedures also influence the goals chosen and the implementation procedures used. For example, if assessment procedures show that the desired learning has not taken place, the teacher may wish to reconsider both the goals and the instructional strategies used. Perhaps the goals were overly ambitious or inappropriate for students. In a similar way, the teaching strategy may have been unsuitable for attaining the chosen goal. With feedback from one phase of the teaching act, the teacher can critically examine and reflect on the effectiveness of the other components as well as the total learning experience.

THE TEACHER AS DECISION MAKER

Teachers make a wide range of decisions that clearly affect the effectiveness of their classroom teaching. Decision making implies making choices; some of the most common examples involve deciding what to teach, how to teach it, and how to assess student

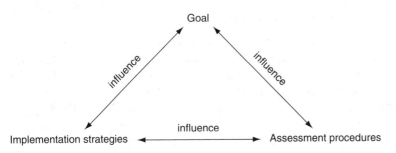

Figure 1.3 The Three-Phase Approach to Teaching

achievement. Using how to teach as an example, a number of sources influence decision making and run the gamut from believing a specific strategy to be the most effective way of teaching something to having case studies and hard research information establishing its effectiveness.

One way to bypass these important decisions is to implement the content, strategies, and assessments found in teachers' guides and instructional materials that often accompany textbooks. Such resources may provide the most effective instruction for a given lesson, but we take the position here that anything we undertake in our classrooms should be weighed against other alternatives in a conscious and deliberate effort. Effective teachers draw from several areas of knowledge as they face a great variety of decisions in the classroom arena, and the ability to make professional decisions is vital to teaching (Doebler, 1998).

Factors Influencing Decision Making

Three major ways of evaluating the professional decisions we make as teachers are research, experience, and context. A growing body of research provides useful information about the relationship of teacher actions to student learning (Bruning, Schraw, Norby, & Ronning, 2004; Eggen & Kauchak, 2007); we introduce you to this research as we consider different aspects of decision making in later chapters.

A second factor influencing professional decision making is experience. Research is clear that veteran teachers draw heavily on their experiences to guide their decisions (Berliner, 1994). This has several implications for beginning teachers. First, research on the effective practices of experienced teachers needs to be considered. Second, beginning teachers need to observe and talk with experienced teachers as they learn to teach. Finally, beginning teachers need to reflect on their own growth as they progress and, by doing so, grow through experience and learn from their successes and failures.

Context is a third factor that influences teachers' decision making. No two students and no two learning environments are alike. In addition, instructional decision making is also influenced by the kind of content being taught, the resources available, and even the time of day or point in the school year. As we learn about alternative teaching methods and instructional strategies, we need to continuously ask ourselves, Will these work for me, and will they effectively promote student learning in my classroom?

The Importance of Goals in Decision Making

Weighing alternatives requires making choices that influence learning. This can be done only when teachers have clear goals. Teachers should always have goals in mind when they teach because goals provide direction for teaching and guide decision making. Decision making is strategic in the sense that decisions are based on purposeful and explicit goals. Here is an effective sequence to follow in goal-based decision making (Beyer, 1988):

- Identify the desired goal
- Identify obstacles to reaching that goal
- Identify options for overcoming each obstacle
- Examine the options in terms of time, resources, costs, and constraints on their use
- Choose the best option or combination of options

The consideration of goals is undertaken in the planning phase, which we identified as the first of three phases in which teachers make decisions. In the planning phase, teachers not only consider goals but also design learning activities that will help students reach those goals. Decision-making questions for consideration include the following:

- How should I explain a given idea or concept?
- How should I relate that topic to material we have already studied?
- How can I use concrete examples to illustrate the topic?
- What kinds of learning tasks can I design to encourage meaningful learning?

In the second phase, implementing, teachers do not engage in advanced decision making, such as the examples provided previously, but are required to make a number of split-second decisions as they interact with students in classrooms. Many of these interactions are in the form of questions. The effective teacher needs to know the art of asking questions and how to use different question formats—fact questions, process questions, convergent questions, and divergent questions—to promote learning (Good & Brophy, 2008). Decision-making considerations during this phase include the following:

- What kinds of questions will encourage student thinking and also allow me to gauge student understanding?
- Should questions be addressed to the whole group or individual students?
- How long should the teacher wait for a student response?
- What should the teacher do if a student response is incorrect? Should I prompt (a questioning technique discussed in Chapter 7), provide the answer, or call on another student?

The third phase, assessment, also requires teachers to make decisions. Teachers continually ask themselves whether students understand new ideas and what modifications need to be made to promote student learning. Questions that address assessment decisions include the following:

- What kinds of assessments can be used to determine whether students understand the topic being taught?
- Which aspects of the content do students clearly understand, and which require additional instruction?

- Which students need extra help, and which do not?
- In what ways can the assessment results be communicated to students, parents, and other professionals in need of this information?

At this point, it should be increasingly clear that teaching is extremely complex and requires continual decision making. Several factors complicate the process. There are no easy, clear-cut answers in teaching, but there are decisions only teachers can make. In the presence of confusing and ambiguous issues, teachers must search for appropriate courses of action rather than resolution. Even in the best of times, teachers may have to choose between several less-than-good alternatives, and many instructional problems cannot be solved completely (Wassermann, 1999). Nevertheless, the quality of the professional decisions you make will directly influence the kinds of learning experiences you provide and ultimately affect the degree to which you promote student learning.

THE IMPORTANCE OF REFLECTION IN TEACHING

A major way that teachers improve their decision making is through **reflection**. Reflective teachers are thoughtful, analytical, and even self-critical about their teaching. After you have taught a lesson, you will want to reconsider your planning and the decisions you have made. Reflection, whether written or mental, is an effective tool for refining professional thoughts, ideas, and beliefs. Reflection enables us to evaluate our experiences, learn from mistakes, repeat successes, and revise and plan for the future.

Reflective teaching is complex and multifaceted. It is a review of one's practices in an attempt to determine whether you accomplished what you set out to do and to gain insight on more effective ways of doing what you did. A reflective teacher willingly takes responsibility for considering personal actions; is committed to thinking through difficult issues in depth, persistently seeking more knowledge and better ways to teach and to manage classrooms; maintains a healthy skepticism about educational theories and practices; and gathers as much information as possible about any given problem, weighs the value of the evidence against suitable criteria, and then draws a conclusion and makes a judgment (Ely, 1994).

Basically, reflection asks, How effective were the decisions I made? Specifically, reflection tries to answer questions such as the following:

- How appropriate were the topics—that is, should they be taught again?
- Was the sequence of topics appropriate? If not, how should they be resequenced?
- Was my goal(s) appropriate for my students?
- Was my instruction aligned? Did my lesson plans facilitate my unit plan? Were the procedures and assessments I specified consistent with my goals?
- Were the procedures I used as effective as they might have been? If not, what procedures might have been better?
- Did the materials I used adequately represent the topic?
- What representations or resources would have made the topic more understandable?
- Is there a way I could have made the overall environment more conducive to learning?

Finally, much of what has been said to this point refers to reflection as a process of questioning our practice in a variety of rational ways, but reflection can also be viewed as creative

and "examples." For additional practice, find the Web site for the department of education for your state and complete the same exercise.

5. On page 35, we provide introductory information on academic portfolios, and, using whatever resources of your choice, we urge you to research the pros and cons of electronic portfolios. To begin this undertaking, we suggest that you employ a search engine with the key word "portfolios" and then click on "electronic portfolios."

EXERCISE 1.4

Using the INTASC, NCATE, and TEAC standards listed previously in this chapter, reread the opening scenario involving Mrs. Warner and identify all those she is addressing in her dental lesson.

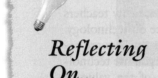

INTRODUCTION: A MODEL FOR TEACHING

INTASC Principles 1, 2, 3, 4, 5, 7, 8, and 9

Think about the different teacher roles and influences on learning. Think about ways in which you will promote student learning in your classroom.

Reflecting On...

SUMMARY

A number of national standards have been formulated to guide teachers' professional development. The Interstate New Teacher Assessment and Support Consortium (INTASC) provides guidelines for new teachers. The National Board for Professional Teaching Standards (NBPTS) provides comparable standards for experienced teachers. The National Council for Accreditation of Teacher Education (NCATE) and the Teacher Education Accreditation Council (TEAC) create guidelines for teacher preparation programs. Federal efforts to improve teaching include the Goals 2000 initiative and No Child Left Behind (NCLB). States have also created content-related standards, and these will have a direct effect on both teachers and students.

Teachers perform multiple roles in the classroom, ranging from promoting academic and cognitive growth to moral and psychomotor development. Constructivism, a developing theory of learning, emphasizes the teacher's role in guiding and facilitating learning. In addition, teachers play a critical role in developing student motivation for learning.

In their instruction, teachers have multiple goals, ranging from cognitive to affective and psychomotor. Because of the heavy emphasis on cognitive outcomes in the schools, this text will focus primarily on cognitive growth and development. In attempting to promote growth in students, teachers create productive learning environments that attempt to build on other contextual factors in learning.

The conceptual foundation for the text is a three-phase approach to instruction that begins with planning. A central focus of planning is the creation of clear learning goals and the selection of teaching strategies. During the implementation phase, teachers use instructional strategies to help students reach learning goals. In the final phase of the conceptual model, teachers assess learning, attempting to ascertain what students have learned.

This text emphasizes the central role of decision making in effective teaching. Research, experience, and context all influence the complex decisions teachers make in the classroom. Goals, when clearly conceptualized, can provide both focus and clarity in teachers' instructional decisions.

Reflection provides opportunities for teachers to think about the effectiveness of their actions. Linked to decision making, reflection encourages teachers to ask, How effective were the decisions I made?

This text is divided into three main sections that correspond to the conceptual model for the text: planning, implementation, and assessment. These three sections are designed to provide teachers with the knowledge and skills necessary for effective instructional decision making and insightful professional reflection.

KEY CONCEPTS

Active learning 12	Knowledge 20
Assessing 25	Learner diversity 21
Attitudes 20	Motivation 13
Constructivism 11	Passive learning 12
Cooperative learning 13	Planning 23
Extrinsic 14	Reflection 29
Implementing 24	Skills 20
Intrinsic 14	Student-centered instruction 12

PREPARING FOR YOUR LICENSURE EXAMINATION

Let's look now at another teacher who is working with a group of second-grade students. Read the following case study and, using specific information from this chapter, answer the questions that follow.

Mrs. Lori Guthrie, a Title VI teacher, began her class by letting her children know they were going to have another one of their "adventures," which, as usual, made them eager to find out the subject of today's lesson.

"OK, guys," she said, "let's take a walk outside and grab one of the bags on the way." The children scampered to the door, and out they went. "Boy," Mrs. Guthrie continued, "what kind of a day do we have today?"

"Sunny, Mrs. G.," José said.

"It's beautiful out," Maria added.

"What are we going to do?" Katy inquired.

"Well," Mrs. Guthrie responded, "with it being such a nice day, let's look for some different kinds of things that we can use in making up fun addition and subtraction problems. Start looking around, and let me know when you find something."

"Oh, Mrs. G., I found some leaves . . . and lots of them. Does anyone want some too?" Nate asked.

"I want some," Maria said.

"Me, too," Marley said as both children joined Nate and scooped up handfuls of leaves.

"Mrs. G., I found some stones," Alex said, "and this big rock. Can I keep it, too?"

"Hey," Mrs. Guthrie replied, "whatever works for you."

"I found some big twigs, and look at this pop can. This is fun. I want to use the pop can, too," José said.

"Great idea," Mrs. Guthrie said. The children continued to scavenge about for a few minutes before she led them back to the classroom. "OK, guys," she began, "you've got real neat stuff, so what are you going to need now?"

"Some paper and some glue," Katy responded.

"Anything else?"

"Yeah, something to write our addition and subtraction problems with," Maria added.

"Fine, come and get the things you'll need." The children came to Mrs. Guthrie, and each took a piece of construction paper, a bottle of glue, and a magic marker.

After the children had been working for a few minutes, Mrs. Guthrie said, "Look at the way Marley has arranged his sticks. He put them in one group of six and one group of two, and then he wrote the problem beside them and showed us that six sticks plus two sticks equals eight sticks. Terrific!"

"And look at Alex's subtraction problem," Mrs. Guthrie continued enthusiastically. "Two leaves take away two leaves equals no leaves. Now I saw her leaves glued down, and then she had to take them off, and there was just glue left. Good thinking!"

After commenting on all the students' work and encouraging them to offer their own observations, Mrs. Guthrie then said, "OK, class, it's time to take everything upstairs."

1. After reading the comment from Campbell found on page 11, which of the primary aims of education does this lesson primarily reflect? Why?

2. What motivational techniques did Mrs. Guthrie employ in her lesson, and why is intrinsic motivation considered to be more desirable or powerful than extrinsic motivation?

3. How did Mrs. Guthrie incorporate the three forms of student learning—information and knowledge, psychomotor skills, and attitudes and values—into her lesson, and which do you believe should have received the primary focus? Why?

4. What three characteristics of a constructivist learning environment did Mrs. Guthrie incorporate into her lesson? Discuss each one briefly.

5. What were a few of the most common classroom decisions Mrs. Guthrie had to make regarding this lesson?

6. The three-phase approach to teaching is a cyclical or closed loop. Regarding this particular lesson, having completed one complete cycle, what would Mrs. Guthrie do now?

VIDEO EXERCISE

Go to MyEducationLab™ and select the topic "Effective Teaching and the Effective Teacher" and watch the video "Using Student Ideas and Contributions." After viewing the video, respond to the following questions:

1. Is Ms. Rebecca Adkins's primary role that of "sage on the stage" or "guide on the side"? Provide a brief explanation.

2. Regarding the planning stage of the three-phase model of teaching, what do you think Ms. Adkins wants the children to learn?

3. Regarding the implementation stage of the three-phase model of teaching, what are a few of the strategies Ms. Adkins employed to promote student growth and achievement?

4. Regarding the assessment stage of the three-phase model of teaching, what could Ms. Adkins do to determine whether the students had "learned" the lesson?

5. In terms of reflection, what do you think Ms. Adkins could do to improve the lesson?

DEVELOPING YOUR PORTFOLIO

Portfolios are increasingly becoming one means of demonstrating the skills, experiences, and accomplishments of the beginning teacher (Goethals, Howard, & Sanders, 2004). Unlike a professional portfolio that is designed to provide administrators or a school system with your qualifications for employment, an academic portfolio provides opportunities to organize and reflect on resources that include both theoretical and practical experiences in your teacher preparation program of study. Components of an academic portfolio commonly include the following:

- Table of contents
- Student information/résumé
- Philosophy statement
- Reflections on teaching
- Additional documentation, such as letters of recommendation and awards
- Artifacts such as sample lesson plans, assessments, examples of student work, and photos of creative activities (e.g., learning centers or videotapes of dynamic lessons)

As evidence that you are attaining the stated goals and objectives of courses in your professional program of study, we offer an academic portfolio task at the end of each chapter. For example, in Chapter 5, we suggest that you write three goals objectives in your area of emphasis and key them to selected state standards.

A philosophy statement is often found in an academic portfolio and a professional portfolio. Therefore, your academic portfolio task for this chapter is the following:

Philosophy statements are designed to express views on the nature and needs of students and society, the knowledge base to be taught, and the methods and strategies (pedagogy) to be employed in classroom teaching. Using the discussions in this chapter on constructivism, motivation, and national and state standards, write your own philosophy statement in terms of how teachers promote student learning. Be sure to address the following three questions:

- How can teachers facilitate learning for all students?
- What kinds of decisions do teachers make?
- What kinds of abilities and competencies should a teacher bring to the classroom?

QUESTIONS FOR DISCUSSION

1. Why is intrinsic motivation considered to be more desirable or powerful than extrinsic motivation?

2. Of the three forms of students learning—information and knowledge, psychomotor skills, and attitudes and values—which do you believe should receive the primary focus? Why?

3. What are three characteristics of a constructivist learning environment?

4. What are some of the most common decisions classroom teachers make on a daily basis?

5. What is the relationship between decision making and teacher reflection?

6. Most classroom teachers consider the three-phase approach to teaching to be cyclical or that of a closed loop. What does this mean, and how does it work?

SUGGESTIONS FOR FIELD EXPERIENCE

1. Interview a teacher and ask him or her to share strategies used in the classroom to motivate children. Also ask for suggestions on how you can increase your knowledge of a student, which in turn can affect the success of your motivational techniques.

2. Having identified characteristics of a constructivist learning environment in item 3 under "Questions for Discussion," look for examples of these characteristics in your field classroom.

3. If available, examine a series or number of objectives in a lesson plan, curriculum guide, or teacher's edition and determine whether they primarily address the areas of knowledge, skill, or attitude. You might also discuss with a classroom teacher how or if she or he sets priorities for these three areas.

4. Review either district or state curriculum guides to see if you can identify areas in which teachers must engage in decision making. Specifically, look for opportunities for choice in the areas of content, strategies, and assessments.

5. If sharing information with other preservice teachers is possible at your school site, discuss the role of reflection as a critical part of the three-phase approach to teaching.

6. Given the opportunity, select a goal that appears in a curriculum guide, unit plan, or text and decide what available materials would provide the most effective instruction.

TOOLS FOR TEACHING

Print References

Gagnon, G., & Collay, M. (2006). *Constructivist learning design: Key questions for teaching to standards*. Thousand Oaks, CA: Corwin Press. Reviews the process of learning, assumptions about the processes, and descriptions of how to organize for learning.

Redman, P. (2006). *Don't smile until December and other myths about classroom teaching*. Thousand Oaks, CA: Corwin Press. A thorough review of key qualities necessary to become a good teacher with a focus on the quality of humanness and the ability to touch the lives of students.

Snider, V. (2006). *Myth and misconception about teaching*. Lanham, MD: Rowman & Littlefield Education. Present a different way of thinking about teaching and learning with an emphasis on how myth stands in the way of developing a science of teaching that focuses on results as opposed to unsubstantiated beliefs.

Weinstein, R. (2002). *Reaching higher: The power of expectations in schooling*. Cambridge, MA: Harvard University Press. An in-depth presentation of the academic expectations of students and educators and how they shape children's lives in school.

Web Sites

http://home.capecod.net~tpanitz/tedsarticles/coopbenefits.html Here you will find the academic, social, and psychological benefits of student-centered instruction via collaborative learning paradigms.

www.secondaryenglish.com/approaches.html Here you will find an experiment using teacher-centered instruction versus student-centered instruction as a means of teaching American government to high school seniors for the purpose of identifying the effectiveness of nontraditional instruction.

www.weer.wisc.edu/step/ep301/Fall2000/Techonites/stu_cen.html Here you will find answers to the following questions: What is student-centered teaching? Why do we want to promote student-centered teaching? What are the benefits of student-centered teaching? How do authentic learning, active learning, cooperative learning, and cognitive apprenticeship promote a student-centered environment? How is thematic instruction student centered?

http://agpa.uakron.edu/k12/best_practices/student_instruction.html Here you will find information to suggest that teachers who permit students to play an active role in selecting topics and answer their own questions stimulate motivation and reasoning.

www.funderstanding.com/constructivism.cfm Here you will find a definition of constructivism and a brief discussion on several guiding principles of constructivism.

http://carbon.cudenver.edu/~mryder/itc_data/constructivism.html Here you will find an excellent resource for a wide range of definitions of constructivism as well as a number of printed references.

http://chiron.valdosta.edu/whuitt/col/motivation/motivate.html Here you will find definitions of motivation as well as the importance of motivation, the relationship of motivation and emotion, and explanation of motivational influences, and selected motivational theories.

Managing Classrooms for Effective Instruction

CHAPTER 2

Classroom Management: Prevention

INTRODUCTION

Understanding the topics you teach and planning and implementing effective lessons are crucial abilities. However, another is so essential that, without it, the carefully laid plans and strategies cannot work. This is the ability to effectively manage the learning environment.

Well-managed classrooms support learning. In them, students are orderly but not rigid, and they feel safe from both physical harm and the fear of ridicule. They speak freely but understand limits. The classroom operates smoothly and productively, and the teacher seems to be taking little effort to manage it. In contrast, poorly managed classrooms can become seas of chaos. The students are inattentive and disruptive, the teacher is frazzled and exhausted, and little learning takes place.

Research indicates that effective teachers organize their classrooms and design learning activities so that most management problems are prevented rather than stopped once they occur. That's what this chapter is about.

LEARNER OBJECTIVES

After completing your study of Chapter 2, you should be able to do the following:

- Identify prerequisites to effective management
- Describe the relationships between effective management and effective instruction
- Plan for effective management
- Design and teach rules and procedures

APPLYING EFFECTIVE STRATEGIES FOR PREVENTING CLASSROOM MANAGEMENT PROBLEMS

Following is a case study in which a middle school teacher is working with her students in a math lesson. As you read the case study, consider the following questions:

- What has the teacher done prior to class to prevent management problems?
- How has the teacher organized her classroom to prevent management problems?
- How are effective classroom management and effective instruction related?

Sheryl Poulos is a seventh-grade math teacher whose class is involved in a unit on converting fractions to decimals and percents. She has 32 students in a room designed for 24, so the students are sitting within arm's reach of each other across the aisles.

As Ginger comes into the room, she sees a series of fractions with the directions, "Convert each to a decimal and then to a percent," projected high on the screen at the front of the room. She quickly slides into her seat just as the bell stops ringing. Most of the students have already begun working the problems.

Sheryl is finished taking roll by the time the bell stops ringing, and she hands back a set of papers as students busy themselves with the task. As she hands Jack his paper, she touches him on the arm and points to the overhead, reminding him to return from his window gazing.

She waits a moment for the students to finish and then begins. She writes the fraction 7/12 on the chalkboard, and as she says, "Let's think about this fraction. Let's estimate what percent 7/12 will be . . . Donna?," she sees Scott, who sits behind Veronica, stick his foot forward and tap Veronica's leg. She also notices that Ellen is whispering something to Kristen at the back of the room.

In response to the tap, Veronica whispers loudly, "Stop it, Scott."

Sheryl moves down the aisle as Donna responds, "It would be . . . mmm . . . about 60, maybe . . . I think."

Sheryl stops at Scott's desk, leans over, and whispers softly but firmly, "We keep our hands and feet to ourselves in here," and then says, "OK, good, Donna. . . . Explain why Donna's estimate is probably good . . . Jeremy?"

As Jeremy begins, "Well, 7 is over half of 12 . . . yeah . . . so, it would have to be more than 50%," Sheryl moves to the back of the room and stands by Ellen and Kristen.

CLASSROOM MANAGEMENT: AN OVERVIEW

From the 1960s until the present, national Gallup polls have consistently identified classroom management as one of teachers' most challenging problems. In the 2007 poll, it ranked second only behind lack of financial support as the most important problem schools face (Rose & Gallup, 2007). It has historically been the primary concern of beginning teachers, and disruptive students are an important source of stress for beginners and veterans alike (Bohn, Roehrig, & Pressley, 2004; Public Agenda, 2004). It is a major reason that teachers leave the profession during their first 3 years, it is a primary cause of teachers leaving urban classrooms (Weiner, 2002); and colleges of education are being asked to address the issue more carefully (Johnson, 2005).

In spite of concerns about school violence, it is the day-to-day job of establishing and maintaining orderly, learning-focused classrooms that requires so much effort. Management is particularly difficult for preservice and beginning teachers who often feel ill prepared to deal with issues related to classroom management and often find that their university preparation is incomplete (Kher-Durlabhji, Lacina-Gifford, Jackson, Guillory, & Yandell, 1997).

The reasons can be traced to changes in both schools and society at large. Unquestioned respect for authority figures has been replaced by attitudes of questioning, doubt, and hesitancy. Faith in schools as instruments of socialization has been replaced by criticisms of education. Attitudes toward child rearing have changed, and these attitudes have found their way into the schools.

The student population has also changed. Learners will not sit quietly through dull presentations, and motivation is an important consideration in both management and instruction. Students spend a great deal of time in front of television sets, and many urban classrooms have a majority of students with native languages other than English (Kent, Pollard, Haaga, & Mather, 2001; U.S. Department of Education, 2000). An alarming number of students come to school with home environments and experiential backgrounds that place them at risk of not succeeding (Slavin, Karweit, & Madden, 1989).

Classroom Management Versus Classroom Discipline

In this chapter, we will emphasize the concept of **classroom management** instead of the commonly used term **classroom discipline.** Management refers to teachers' strategies that create and maintain an orderly learning environment, whereas discipline involves teacher responses to student misbehavior, such as talking inappropriately, leaving desks without permission, making hostile or sarcastic remarks, or, more seriously, fighting and assaults.

Outcomes of Effective Management

Teachers who effectively manage their classrooms achieve two important outcomes:

- Increased student achievement
- Increased student motivation

Increased Achievement.   The relationship between management and achievement is well documented (Blumenfeld, Pintrich, & Hamilton, 1987; Evertson, 1987). Purkey and Smith (1983) identified effective management as one of the four key characteristics of an effective school. Wang, Haertel, and Walberg (1993), in a comprehensive review of the literature on factors influencing learning, conclude, "Effective classroom management has been shown to increase student engagement, decrease disruptive behaviors, and enhance use of instructional time, all of which results in improved student achievement" (p. 262). In short, effective management is an essential ingredient of effective teaching.

Increased Motivation.   Order and safety are necessary to promote student motivation (Radd, 1998). Brophy (1987a) identified classroom management as an "essential precondition for motivating students" (p. 208). Classroom management is a foundation the teacher builds on in creating motivated classrooms. In addition, by seeking student input on instructional and management issues, the teacher can promote student ownership and involvement, both of which positively influence student motivation (McLaughlin, 1994).

PREREQUISITES TO EFFECTIVE MANAGEMENT

Orderly classrooms do not magically happen. They must be carefully planned, and teachers who are caring, firm, and committed to the students and their learning are less likely to have management problems than their less professional peers (Marzano, Marzano, & Pickering, 2003). In this section, we examine three prerequisites to effective management:

- Classroom climate
- Teacher characteristics
- The relationship between management and instruction

Classroom Climate

Think back to your experiences in elementary and secondary school. Were you comfortable in some classes and uncomfortable in others? Did you look forward to some because they were interesting and stimulating, while you dreaded others and watched the clock in them as the minutes dragged by? The answer for virtually all of us is "yes."

In some classes, the emotional feeling is healthy, positive, and supportive of learning. The environment that supports these feelings represents the **classroom climate.** In classes with a positive climate, students feel capable, included, and secure. A balance is maintained between teacher direction and student choice, students have freedom within well-defined limits, and learner responsibility is emphasized over rigid adherence to rules. The development of learner self-regulation is an overriding goal (Alexander & Murphy, 1998).

Positive climates do not automatically happen, however. They depend on the teacher and the kind of learning experiences students have.

Teacher Characteristics

We have all seen students go from one class in which they are disruptive and out of hand to another in which they are orderly and on task. The difference is the teacher. Effective

Scott Cunningham/Merrill

Providing for student success and safety fosters a positive classroom climate.

managers cover a spectrum of personalities. Some appear quiet and unassuming; others have voices like a drill sergeant. Although one type is not necessarily better than another, effective managers usually have several important characteristics, including the following:

- Caring
- Firmness
- Modeling and enthusiasm
- High expectations

Let's consider each of these characteristics.

Caring: The Foundation of Positive Classroom Climate.   It is virtually impossible to manage a classroom or succeed in any part of teaching without genuinely caring about students and their learning. In one study, researchers asked fourth graders how they knew whether their teacher cared (Rogers, 1991). They described a caring teacher as one who did the following:

- Listens and tries to see things from a student's perspective
- Creates a safe and secure learning environment
- Helps with school work by making sense of learning tasks

The importance of **caring** is captured in this comment by another fourth grader: "If a teacher doesn't care about you, it affects your mind. You feel like you're a nobody and it makes you want to drop out of school" (Noblit, Rogers, & McCadden, 1995, p. 683).

Wentzel (1997) offers an additional student perspective. She asked middle school students, "How do you know when a teacher does and does not care about you?" The students reported that attentiveness to them as human beings was important, but perhaps more striking was their belief that teachers who care make serious efforts to promote learning and hold students to appropriately high standards. This finding suggests that caring is more than warm, fuzzy interactions with students. In addition to understanding how students feel, caring teachers are committed to their students' growth and competence (Noddings, 1995, 1999; Wentzel, 1997).

Savage (1991) describes caring a bit differently. He suggests that caring teachers both respect students and attempt to earn students' respect. He offers the following suggestions for doing so:

- Plan carefully so that you thoroughly understand the topics you are teaching
- Announce tests, be clear on what tests will cover, and avoid tricking students
- Provide genuine encouragement and praise and avoid sarcasm
- Learn students' names quickly and use them regularly
- Provide appropriate rewards for good work

Stipek (2002) offers an additional comment related to the issue of respect:

> One of the best ways to show respect for students is to hold them to high standards—by not accepting sloppy, thoughtless, or incomplete work, by pressing them to clarify vague comments, by encouraging them not to give up, and by not praising work that does not reflect genuine effort. Ironically, reactions that are often intended to protect students' self-esteem—such as accepting low quality work—convey a lack of interest, patience, or caring. (p. 157)

This leads us to the concept of firmness.

Firmness: Helping Students Develop Responsibility.   **Firmness** means viewing students as capable of exercising responsibility and holding them accountable for their actions. A teacher who does not stand firm when a student breaks a rule communicates that the rule has no real purpose and that actions do not necessarily have consequences. These messages confuse students who are trying to make sense of the world. It is essential that a teacher follows through in making students responsible and accountable for their actions (Stipek, 2002).

Modeling and Enthusiasm.   Teachers' beliefs about teaching and learning are communicated through modeling. A positive classroom climate is virtually impossible if teachers model distaste or lack of interest in the topics they teach. Statements such as the following detract from an orderly and learning-oriented environment:

"I know this stuff is boring, but we have to learn it."

"I know you hate proofs."

"This isn't my favorite topic, either."

In contrast, even routine and potentially uninteresting topics are more motivating to students if teachers model interest in them.

By **modeling enthusiasm,** teachers communicate their own genuine interest in the topic. It does not include pep talks, theatrics, or efforts to entertain students. Rather, as shown in the following quotations, it is intended to induce in them the feeling that the information is valuable and worth learning (Good & Brophy, 2008).

High Expectations.

> "This idea is new, and it probably will be challenging, but I know you can all do the assignment. I want you to start right in while the ideas are still fresh in your mind. I'll be around in a moment, so don't be afraid to ask questions if you have any."

> "This material is hard, but we've got to learn it. I want everyone to start right away, and no fooling around. Some of you will have problems with this, and I'll be around as soon as I can to straighten you out. No messing around until I get there."

Teacher expectations for student behavior and achievement are communicated subtly (and not so subtly) every day. The first teacher acknowledged that the assignment was difficult, but she expected students to successfully complete it. The second implied that some students were less able than others and presented the entire assignment with a negative tone.

How Expectations Affect Teacher Behavior.   Research indicates that teachers treat students for whom they have **high expectations** much better than those for whom their expectations are lower. They call on high-expectation students more often, and their interactions are more positive. They give high-expectation students clearer and more thorough explanations, require more complete and accurate answers, and are more enthusiastic in their instruction. They praise high-expectation students more often and give them more complete feedback.

Students are sensitive to this differential treatment, and children as young as first grade are aware of unequal treatment of high and low achievers (Stipek, 2002). In one study, researchers concluded that

> after ten seconds of seeing and/or hearing a teacher, even very young students could detect whether the teacher talked about or to an excellent or a weak student and could determine the extent to which that student was loved by the teacher. (Babad, Bernieri, & Rosenthal, 1991, p. 230)

TEACHER EXPECTATIONS: IMPLICATIONS FOR MANAGEMENT AND INSTRUCTION

What does this research suggest to teachers? First, when teacher expectations are realistic, such as those based on student performance, they pose little problem. When they are based on something other than student performance, however, or are lower than past performance warrants, they can reduce achievement and detract from classroom climate.

Second, expectations tend to be self-fulfilling:

> Such low expectations can serve as self-fulfilling prophecies, that is, the expression of low expectations by differential treatment can inadvertently lead children to confirm predictions about their abilities by exerting less effort and ultimately performing more poorly. (Weinstein, 1998, p. 83)

Our purpose in writing this section is to increase awareness. Expectations are subtle and often out of teachers' conscious control; teachers often do not realize that they hold different expectations for their students. With awareness and effort, teachers will do their best to treat all students as fairly and equitably as possible.

Management and Instruction

Commonly overlooked in discussions of classroom management is the role of effective instruction. Research indicates that it is virtually impossible to maintain an orderly classroom in the absence of effective instruction and vice versa (Doyle, 1986).

In addition to the questioning skills that were discussed in Chapter 6, we want to examine some additional instructional factors that contribute directly to orderly classrooms. They are illustrated in Figure 2.1 and discussed in the sections that follow.

Organization. Let's look back at Sheryl Poulos's class in our chapter-opening vignette. When students walked into the room, they found problems displayed on the screen as Sheryl started her beginning-of-class routines. The class began working on her warm-up activity without being told, and Sheryl moved quickly and smoothly from it to her lesson for the day. She demonstrated four important characteristics of effective **organization.** They are outlined in Table 2.1 and discussed in the sections that follow.

Starting on time and having materials ready can eliminate the "dead time" at the beginning of classes, which is one of the times when management problems are most likely to occur (Emmer, Evertson, & Worsham, 2006; Evertson, Emmer, & Worsham, 2006). Careful organization maximizes opportunities for student involvement and learning and minimizes downtime that can lead to management problems.

Teachers who use several minutes at the beginning of class to take roll and complete other routines and who fumble with papers and demonstrations create the impression they are not sure of what they are doing and are not fully in control of their classes. These teachers are inviting management problems.

Transitions are particularly important in orderly classrooms, and effective managers also help students make transitions from one activity to another quickly and smoothly. Often,

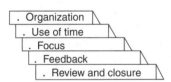

- Organization
- Use of time
- Focus
- Feedback
- Review and closure

Figure 2.1 Instructional Factors That Contribute to Classroom Order

Table 2.1   Characteristics of Effective Organization

Characteristic	Example
Having materials and demonstrations prepared in advance	Sheryl's problems were prepared and waiting when the students came into the room.
Starting on time	Sheryl was finished calling the roll before the bell stopped ringing.
Having well-established routines	Sheryl had a warm-up activity every day.
Making transitions smoothly and quickly	Sheryl moved quickly from her warm-up-activity to her formal lesson.

teachers have a clear idea of where they are going, but they do not communicate this transition to the students. A great deal of confusion can be prevented by using the following techniques:

- Waiting until the whole room is quiet and attentive before making the transition
- Clearly stating what transition is to be made
- Writing important directions on the board if any aspects of the transition might be confusing
- Carefully monitoring the transition as it occurs

Certain times during the school day or year are problematic; during these times, management problems are more likely to occur. Effective managers are aware of these possibilities and are more carefully organized during these times. In addition to the beginning of class periods and transitions, some other problematic times are the following:

- The last period of the day (particularly on Friday)
- The few minutes just before lunch
- Days before big events or holidays
- Beginnings of periods following a rally, school assembly, or fire drill
- Times before, during, and after report cards are distributed

How these times are handled depends on your professional judgment, but some ideas include selecting strongly organized or highly motivating activities, giving seat work or tests, and simply discussing these times with the students to make them aware of what you are doing and why.

Use of Time.   The way teachers use their time is essential for effective management. Time is a valuable resource; efforts at reform have suggested lengthening the school year, school day, and even the amount of time devoted to certain subjects (Karweit, 1989).

Unfortunately, teachers do not always use time effectively. Research indicates that a great deal of class time is spent on noninstructional activities, often more than a third of teachers' scheduled time (Karweit, 1989). Further, some teachers seem unaware of the value of time as a resource, thinking of it as something to be filled or even "killed" rather than an opportunity to increase learning (Eggen, 1998; Wiley & Harnischfeger, 1974).

Sheryl did not fall victim to this tendency. For instance, she had an exercise the students were to complete waiting for them on the board as they came into the room, eliminating any "dead" time that might have existed as she took roll and handed back papers. By the time they finished the exercises, she was ready to begin. The combination of her organization and use of time eliminated the opportunity for management problems to occur.

Lesson Focus.   Effective managers also use the chalkboard, overhead projector, charts, displays, and demonstrations to attract and maintain student attention. Called **lesson focus** (Kauchak & Eggen, 2007), this approach provides two functions. First, it promotes learning by helping maintain attention. Second, since students should be looking at the information display, inattentive students are easy to identify. In some of the lessons from Chapter 4, we will see that teachers used sentences displayed on the overhead, hierarchies written on the chalkboard, and even string and rulers as types of focus. Sheryl's exercises written on the chalkboard were a form of focus.

Student Involvement.   With careful planning, you ensure that your lessons communicate an internal logic and structure to students. The questioning skills and instructional strategies discussed in chapters 6 and 7 can then be used to promote student involvement. At the same time that involvement increases learning, it also helps prevent management problems. It is virtually impossible to be effective at one without the other.

Feedback.   The importance of **feedback,** which gives students information about the accuracy or appropriateness of a response in promoting learning, is well documented (Brosvic & Epstein, 2007; Hattie & Timperley, 2007). Feedback gives learners information about the accuracy of their understanding, and it is also important for student motivation because it helps satisfy their need to know how they are progressing and why (Clifford, 1990).

Effective feedback has four essential characteristics:

1. It is immediate.
2. It is specific.
3. It provides corrective information.
4. It has a positive emotional tone (Brophy & Good, 1986; Murphy, Weil, & McGreal, 1986).

To illustrate these characteristics, let's look at three examples:

Mr. Hill: What kind of figure is shown on the overhead, Jan?

Jan: A square.

Mr. Hill: Not quite. Help her out . . . Karen?

Mrs. Frank: What kind of figure is shown on the overhead, Jan?

Jan: A square.

Mrs. Frank: No, it's a rectangle. What is the next figure, . . . Albert?

Ms. Baker: What kind of figure is shown on the overhead, Jan?

Jan: A square.

Ms. Baker: No, remember we said that all sides have the same length in a square. What do you notice about the lengths of the sides in this figure?

We see that the feedback is immediate in each case, but Mr. Hill gave Jan no information about her answer other than it was incorrect; it was not specific and provided no corrective information. Mrs. Frank's feedback was specific, but it gave Jan no corrective information. Ms. Baker, in contrast, provided specific, corrective information in her response to Jan.

The examples give us no information about the emotional tone of the teachers' responses. Positive emotional tone means that teachers are supportive in their responses to student answers. Harsh, critical, or sarcastic feedback detracts from motivation, achievement, and classroom climate (Pintrich & Schunk, 2002).

Praise is probably the most common and adaptable form of teacher feedback. Research reveals some interesting patterns in teachers' use of praise:

- Praise is used less often than most teachers believe—less than five times per class.
- Praise for good behavior is quite rare, occurring once every 2 or more hours in the elementary grades and even less as students get older.

- Praise tends to depend as much on the type of student—high achieving, well behaved, and attentive—as on the quality of the student's response.
- Teachers praise students based on the answers they expect to receive as much as on those they actually hear (Brophy, 1981).

Using praise effectively requires sound teacher judgment. For example, it must be perceived as sincere to be credible. Effusive praise after every answer loses its credibility even if the teacher is sincere. This is particularly true with older students, who tend to discount praise they perceive as invalid and interpret praise given for easy tasks as indicating that the teacher thinks they are not intelligent. On the other hand, young children tend to take praise at face value and bask in praise given openly in front of a class, whereas junior high students may react better if it is given quietly and individually (Stipek, 2002). High-anxiety students and those from low–socioeconomic status (SES) backgrounds tend to react more positively to praise than their more confident and advantaged counterparts.

Some suggestions for praising effectively include the following:

- Praise genuinely
- Praise immediately
- Praise specifically
- Praise incidental answers
- Praise effort

While much of the feedback students receive is verbal—praise is a common example—teachers also provide valuable feedback through their notes and comments on student work. Because writing detailed comments is time consuming, written feedback is often brief and sketchy, giving students little useful information (Bloom & Bourdon, 1980).

One solution to this problem is to provide model responses to written assignments (Eggen & Kauchak, 2007). For instance, to help students evaluate their answers to essay items, teachers can write ideal answers and share them with the class, allowing students to compare their answers with the model. The model, combined with discussion and time available for individual help after school, provides valuable feedback yet is manageable for the teacher.

Review and Closure.   Lessons are more coherent when review and closure are used to summarize and pull ideas together. A **review** summarizes previous work and helps students link what has been learned to what is coming. It can occur at any point in a lesson, although it is most common at the beginning and end. Effective reviews emphasize important points and help students elaborate on their understanding. Effective reviews involve more than having students recall facts about the lesson; they shift the learner's attention away from verbatim details to deeper conceptual connections in the material being studied (Dempster, 1991).

Closure is a form of review occurring at the end of a lesson; in it, topics are summarized and integrated. The notion of closure is common and intuitively sensible; it pulls content together and signals the end of a lesson. When concepts are being taught, for example, an effective form of closure is to have students state a definition of the concept or identify additional examples. This leaves them with the essence of the topic, providing a foundation for later lessons.

EXERCISE 2.1

We have identified several teacher characteristics and strategies to help prevent management problems. Among them are organization, use of time, focus, interaction and involvement, feedback, and review and closure. For each of the following, identify the teacher strategy best illustrated in the example and defend your answer.

1. "OK," Mr. Izillo begins. "Let's think back to yesterday for a minute. Why did we say the Battle of Gettysburg was the turning point of the war? . . . Teresa?"

2. "Take a look at the chart," Mrs. Moran directs, displaying a chart comparing a frog and toad, their characteristics, what they eat, and where they live. "How do the characteristics compare?"

3. "What part of speech is 'running' in this sentence? . . . Richard?" Mrs. Suarez asks, referring to the sentence "Running is a very good form of exercise."

   "A verb," Richard responds.
   "Take another look," Mrs. Suarez continues. "What is the sentence about?"
   ". . . Running?" Richard continues hesitantly. "It . . . must be . . . a noun."

4. "All right," Mrs. Evans announces. "Our math period is nearly over, and it's time for language arts. Quickly put your math papers away and get your language arts books out." Mrs. Evans watches as the students put their papers away and get their books out. In 2 minutes, they are ready to start language arts.

5. Mrs. Lynch's students are involved in a discussion of the geography of Europe. As the students examine a map showing the Pyrenees Mountains between France and Spain, she asks, "Now, what effect might these mountains have had on the history of the two countries? . . . Jack?"

PLANNING FOR EFFECTIVE MANAGEMENT

Nowhere in teaching is planning more important than in classroom management. Orderly classrooms do not magically occur; they are the result of careful and systematic planning—even for teachers who appear to be "naturals."

Preventing problems involves anticipating potential situations, such as during the problematic times we discussed earlier, and consciously planning for them. This idea is not new, as reflected in maxims such as "Keep your students busy so they won't have time to get into trouble" or "Don't smile until Christmas."

The first step in the planning process is creating a well-designed system of rules and procedures. Once the rules and procedures are in place, teachers should then plan for teaching and monitoring them.

Classroom Rules

Classroom **rules** establish standards for student behavior. They are essential for effective management, and research consistently documents their value (Emmer et al., 2006; Evertson et al., 2006). Rules that are clearly stated and consistently monitored can do much to prevent management problems. Some guidelines for preparing rules are outlined in the following sections.

Keep Class and School Rules Consistent.   This suggestion is self-evident. Teachers cannot develop rules for their classrooms that are inconsistent with the policies of the school or the district. Before preparing and presenting rules to the students, teachers should review district and school rules and then develop their own accordingly. For instance, if the school has a dress code, individual teachers are professionally obligated to enforce it. Teachers who feel strongly that the rule is inappropriate should work to get it changed, not subvert it.

State Rules Clearly.   Rules must be understandable, or they will not have any impact on students' behavior. Also, vague rules need to be constantly interpreted, and this disrupts the flow of learning. For example, a rule that says "Always come to class prepared" has an uncertain meaning, while "Bring needed materials to class every day" is much clearer. Even the second rule will need to be carefully discussed, reviewed, and reinforced to be effective.

Provide Rationales for Rules.   Explaining why a rule exists is important, particularly for classroom climate and the emotional impact it has on students. When rationales are provided, students learn that the world is rational and sensible, and it helps satisfy their need for order. Rules presented without rationales leave the impression of an authoritarian world, perhaps even an arbitrary and capricious one. This is true even for young children. While they may not fully comprehend the rationale at the time it is presented, it is still important to state it. Doing so promotes a climate in which students learn that the world makes sense and provides the sort of experience that helps promote development.

State Rules Positively.   "Wait to be recognized by the teacher before answering" is preferable to "Don't blurt out answers." Rules stated positively create positive expectations and student responsibility. Further, negatively stated rules do not help students understand desirable behaviors; they only specify undesirable ones.

Keep the List Short.   This suggestion is pragmatic. Students commonly break rules because they simply forget. If rules are to be effective, the students need to be constantly aware of their existence, and this is possible only if the list is short. Teachers should be judicious about their rules and include only those that they intend to enforce fully. Superficial or peripheral rules left unenforced detract from the credibility of all the rules on the list.

Solicit Student Input.   Research indicates that the need for control is innate in humans (Ryan & Deci, 2000). One way to give students some control over their classroom environments is to solicit their input as rules are developed. Further, Lepper and Hodell (1989) have identified control as one of the sources of intrinsic motivation. Developing rules in the format of a classroom meeting also helps develop social responsibility in the students, which has been linked to both improved student behavior and increased student achievement (Wentzel, 1991).

Classroom Procedures

While rules provide standards for student behavior, **procedures** establish the routines the class will follow in their day-to-day activities. They address activities such as the following:

- Beginning the school day
- Dealing with absences and tardiness
- Entering and leaving the classroom
- Making transitions from one activity to another
- Turning in work
- Sharpening pencils
- Asking for help

   Procedures for dealing with these activities need to be so well established that students follow them without having to be told. This frees teachers to devote their energies to instruction. If procedures are poorly established, teachers must spend time and energy reminding students, for example, how to turn in their work, to wait for help until they are finished with another student, or to avoid disrupting the discussion to go sharpen a pencil.

Rules and Procedures: Developmental Considerations

As we all know, the behavior patterns of kindergartners and first graders are not the same as those for junior high students. The needs and development of the two age-groups are very different, and these differences should be considered as teachers plan their rules and procedures. In this section, we consider the developmental characteristics of four different age-groups and the implications these characteristics have for management. The stages are somewhat arbitrary, but they will give you a frame of reference as you make decisions about your rules and procedures (Brophy & Evertson, 1976).

Stage 1: Kindergarten Through Grade 2.   Young children are compliant and eager to please their teachers. However, they have short attention spans and often break rules because they forget them. Rules and procedures need to be carefully and explicitly taught, practiced, monitored, and reinforced.

Stage 2: Grades 3 Through 6.   Middle elementary students are becoming more independent, but they still like the attention and affection of teachers. They understand and accept rules and enjoy participating in the rule-making process. Rules need to be monitored and consistently and impartially enforced.

Stage 3: Grades 7 Through 9.   Students at this stage are experiencing a mixture of social, physical, emotional, and sexual feelings, and as a result they can be capricious and perhaps even rebellious. They need a firm foundation of stability in the classroom. Rules need to be clearly stated, administered, and predictably enforced.

Stage 4: Grades 10 Through 12.   Older learners communicate effectively adult to adult. Their behavior has stabilized compared with the previous stage, and they respond well to clear rationales for rules. At this point, students respect teachers for their expertise and ability to communicate. Effective instruction is at least as important as effective management at this stage.

Planning the Physical Environment

The physical environment is an often-overlooked dimension of both management and student achievement. An attractive, well-lit, comfortable, colorful classroom contributes to positive behaviors, which lead to increased achievement; a dim and drab one can have the opposite effect.

Other factors, such as materials and the arrangement, are also important. Students respond positively to attractive learning materials, and you should consider this when choosing among the vast array of already prepared materials or when preparing your own. A positive reaction to learning materials decreases the probability of management problems.

In designing the physical layout of the classroom, at least three factors should be considered (Evertson, 1987):

- Visibility. Can students see the board and other visual displays? Does the teacher have a clear view of all instructional areas to allow monitoring?
- Accessibility. Do high-traffic areas (e.g., pencil sharpener or doorway) allow for efficient movement in the classroom? Are these high-traffic areas designed so that they minimize disruption in the classroom?
- Distractibility. Are potentially noisy areas separated from other areas? Do doors or windows invite students to drift off?

With these general considerations in mind, let's look at some different ways to arrange desks.

The traditional setting with rows of desks and the teacher's desk at front, shown in Figure 2.2, focuses attention on the teacher and tends to detract from communication among students. This is effective when a teacher is presenting a lesson to the entire class, but it can make group work difficult. Students at the rear of the room tend to be physically separated from the teacher and are most likely to be the ones causing problems.

Figure 2.2   A Traditional Seating Arrangement

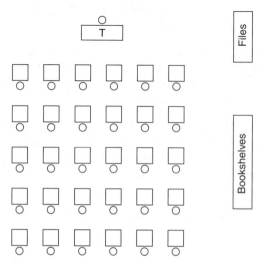

Some classrooms use tables for seating, with the teacher's desk located somewhere on the periphery, as in Figure 2.3. An arrangement in which students are provided their own work space with as little distraction as possible is often used for individualized instruction, as shown in Figure 2.4. Access to materials and the teacher is maintained, and the side-by-side seating is not as distracting as across-table seating.

In considering seating arrangement, factors such as students feeling that they belong to the class are important. Belonging is a basic need; a physical arrangement that promotes a sense of belonging increases feelings of well-being and helps prevent management problems. Again, when considering the physical arrangement of your classroom, consider management and academic objectives. What type of learning is required? Will students need to interact with one another? Will contact be primarily between the teacher and the individual students? Is communication among students desired? Are spaces for individual work as well as group activity important?

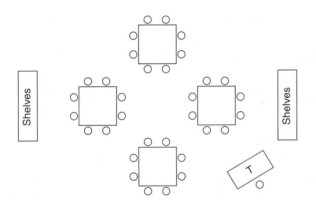

Figure 2.3   An Alternative Seating Arrangement

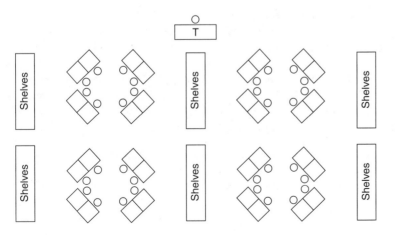

Figure 2.4   An Individualized Seating Arrangement

TEACHING RULES AND PROCEDURES

Rules and procedures will not automatically work just because they exist and have been presented to the students. They should be treated as concepts and explicitly taught with examples just as you would do for teaching any concept (Dowhower, 1991).

Let's see how one teacher accomplishes this.

Jim Gallagher and his first-grade class have established the rule "Leave your seat only when given permission," and Mr. Gallagher is now attempting to help his students fully understand the rule.

He begins, "Suppose that you're working and you break the lead in your pencil. What are you going to do? Selinda?"

". . . I . . . I'll raise my hand and wait for you."

"Yes, precisely," Mr. Gallagher smiles. "And why would Selinda do this? . . . Grant?"

". . . The rule says stay in my seat."

"OK, good. Why did we decide that rule was important? . . . Joyce?"

". . . If people get up like out of their chair, . . .'er seat, it will, will make it so we can't learn as much," Joyce responds haltingly.

"That's right, Joyce. Getting up can disrupt the class, so we won't learn as much. Very good. . . . Now suppose that you made a mistake on your work and you want to start over on a new piece of paper. What will you do with the old paper? . . . Joe?"

". . . Keep it, . . .' til lunch," Joe answers.

"Good, Joe. What will you not do?" Mr. Gallagher continues, raising his voice for emphasis.

". . . Crumple it up and go throw it away in the wastebasket."

"Excellent, Joe! Very good thinking."

The teacher then deals with another example and moves on to the lesson for that period.

In this brief episode, we see how Jim taught the rule. He gave specific, concrete examples of compliance, and he also dealt with cases of noncompliance. If rules are explicitly taught in this way, the likelihood of students breaking them is significantly decreased.

Now let's see how Kathy Francis, a first-grade teacher, taught her students a classroom procedure.

I have a folder for each student and myself on a worktable at the front of the room. I put the students' names in large letters on the front of them. They are told that when they finish a worksheet, they are to take it to the front of the room and put it in the folder without having to ask my permission to do so.

I then showed them what I want them to do by completing a short worksheet and taking it and putting it in my folder. We discussed what I did, and I then gave them a short assignment so they could practice putting their work away. I had them practice a couple times each day for the first week, and now I almost never have to remind them about putting their work away.

Just as Jim did with his rule about remaining in their seats, Kathy explicitly taught her procedure by modeling it and having her students practice it. As with teaching rules, this significantly increases the likelihood that the students will follow the procedure.

The Beginning of the School Year

To be most effective, teaching and reinforcing rules and procedures must begin immediately. During the first few days, the patterns—desirable or undesirable—will be established for the entire year (Emmer et al., 2006; Evertson et al., 2006). Some guidelines for beginning the year include the following (Kauchak & Eggen, 2007):

- Make an effort to create a positive classroom climate by making explicit positive statements about your expectations, such as "I have heard that you're all good kids, and I know you will be very well behaved in this class."
- Begin teaching rules and procedures the first day. With young children, actively practice procedures. With older students, carefully illustrate and discuss rules and procedures.
- Monitor and enforce rules with complete consistency during this period. Intervene immediately when rules are broken or procedures are not followed. Follow through to ensure compliance. You want to make the environment completely predictable for the students during this time.
- Plan your instruction during the first few days for maximum control. Use large-group instead of small-group activities. Stay in the classroom at all times.

Monitoring Rules and Procedures

Merely presenting rules will prevent misbehavior from some students, and carefully teaching rules and procedures will eliminate even more problems before they get started. In spite of these efforts, however, incidents will periodically come up, and effective teachers continuously monitor their rules and procedures to prevent the incidents from expanding into problems (Emmer et al., 2006; Evertson et al., 2006). These teachers react to off-task behavior immediately, stop it, and refer students to the rule, as Sheryl Poulos did by going to Scott and saying, "We keep our hands and feet to ourselves in here." The combination of the rules and procedures, together with careful monitoring, will eliminate most management problems before they get started.

EXERCISE 2.2

The following example illustrates a teacher presenting the class rules at the beginning of the school year. Assess each of the teacher's rules and the way the teacher presented them based on the criteria outlined in the chapter. In your assessment, identify both the positive (if any) and the negative (if any) features of both the teacher's rules and the way the teacher presented them.

Jim Harkness is working with his students in establishing the rules that will govern the students' behavior for the school year. He begins the process by saying, "In order for us to learn as much as we can in this class, we need some rules that will provide guidelines for our behavior. So, I have prepared a list for our class, and I want to discuss them with you this morning."

He then displays the following list:

1. Always come to class ready and prepared to work.
2. Don't touch other students with your hands, feet, or any other part of your body.
3. Speak only when recognized by the teacher.

Establishing rules and procedures on day one, and reinforcing them, are critical if a management plan is to succeed.

Anthoney Magnacca/Merrill

4. Don't leave your desk without permission.
5. Treat the teacher and your classmates with respect.

"Now," he continues, "Let's look at the first one. Why is a rule like this necessary?"

". . . If we aren't prepared to work, we won't learn as much as we could," Karen volunteers.

"OK, good. Can anyone give us another reason?"

Mr. Harkness continues his discussion of the first rule and then leads a similar discussion of each of the others in succession. Finally, he reviews each and then moves to his instruction for the day.

COMMUNICATING WITH PARENTS

No classroom management system will be effective if parents are not involved in their children's education. Learning is a cooperative venture, and teachers, students, and parents are in it together. In a review of factors affecting student learning, researchers concluded that

> because of the importance of the home environment to school learning, teachers must also develop strategies to increase parent involvement in their children's academic life. This means teachers should go beyond traditional once-a-year parent-teacher conferences and work with parents to see that learning is valued in the home. Teachers should encourage parents to be involved with their children's academic pursuits on a day-to-day basis, helping them with homework, monitoring television viewing, reading to their young children, and simply expressing the expectation that their children will achieve academic success. (Wang et al., 1993, pp. 278–279)

Communication with parents or other primary caregivers is not an appendage to the teaching process; it is an integral part of teachers' jobs.

Benefits of Communication

Research indicates that students benefit from parental involvement in at least four ways:

- Higher achievement
- More positive attitudes
- Better attendance rates
- Greater effort on homework (Cameron & Lee, 1997; López & Scribner, 1999)

These outcomes result from parents' increased participation in school activities, their more positive attitudes about schooling, and teachers' increased understanding of learners' home environments (Weinstein & Mignano, 1993). Teachers who encourage parental involvement report more positive feelings about teaching and their school. They also rate parents higher in helpfulness and follow-through and have higher expectations for parents (Epstein, 1990).

Strategies for Involving Parents

Virtually all schools have formal communication mechanisms, such as open houses, which usually occur within the first 2 weeks of the year; interim progress reports that tell parents about their youngster's achievement at the midpoint of each grading period; parent–teacher conferences; and, of course, report cards. Although these processes are schoolwide and necessary, as an individual teacher, you can enhance existing communication processes. Let's look at some ways to do this.

Early Communication. This suggestion can hardly be overstated; parental involvement should start immediately and continue throughout the year. For example, one teacher worked with the students to create the letter that outlined the teacher's commitment to the students' learning, described the teacher's rules and procedures, and included the school phone number and teacher's e-mail address.

The letter was sent home with the students the second day of the school year, signed by the parents and students, and returned by the end of the first week.

While signatures cannot ensure that parents and students will totally honor the intent of the contract, the signatures symbolize a commitment to work with the teacher. This commitment increases the likelihood that parents and students will attempt to honor the contract (Katz, 1999). Also, because students had input into the content of the letter, they felt ownership of the process and encouraged their parents to work with them in completing their homework.

A final point is important. Teachers sometimes send communications home with spelling, grammar, or punctuation errors in them. Do not do it. First impressions are important and lasting. Parents' perceptions of the teacher will be based on this first letter, and a letter that contains errors detracts from a teacher's credibility, which may be necessary later in soliciting parental support.

Maintaining Communication. Just as early, positive communication helps get the year off to a good start, continuing communication can help maintain the momentum. For example, many teachers send packets of students' work home each week, requiring that parents sign and return them. This maintains a tangible link between home and school and gives parents an ongoing record of their children's learning.

Calling Parents.   One of the most powerful ways to maintain communication is to call parents. It is significant for at least two reasons. First, it strongly communicates caring. Everyone has 24 hours a day, and choosing to allocate some of a teacher's personal time, usually in the evening, to calling a parent about an individual student communicates caring better than any other way.

Second, talking to a parent allows teachers to be specific in describing a student's needs and strengths, and it also gives the teacher the opportunity to further solicit parental support. For example, if a student is missing some assignments, the teacher can ask why and at the same encourage the parents to monitor their child's study habits more closely.

TECHNOLOGY IN THE CLASSROOM

Facilitating Communications

As it continues to expand, technology will provide another channel for improving communication. Two simple yet powerful forms of communication now exist that did not only a few years ago. They are voice mail and e-mail.

Voice Mail.   Voice mail can result in improved quality and quantity of teacher–parent communication (Cameron & Lee, 1997). It creates a round-the-clock communication link, and parents feel more comfortable and involved in their children's education knowing that they can contact a teacher any time. Teachers report that parents rarely abuse the system by calling more frequently than is appropriate.

E-Mail.   E-mail affords an additional communication link, and it provides the opportunity to increase communication by conveniently sending class newsletters and other written materials home as simple attachments. One teacher offered the following comment:

The kids create a weekly class newsletter, which I e-mail to all the parents each week. We have a class meeting on Thursday afternoons where we decide what should be in the newsletter, we rotate the tasks among the students, they submit the information to me electronically by Friday noon, and I send it out Friday afternoon. I have the parents' e-mail addresses in a group, so I simply attach the newsletter, and with about four keystrokes it's out to everyone. We have it down to such a routine that it is really quite simple and effortless.

A dilemma exists, however. If some parents do not have e-mail access, the process is not so simple. This teacher commented that she simply printed some copies of the newsletter and asked the kids to hand deliver them to the parents. As more people acquire e-mail capability, the problem will be less and less significant.

DIVERSITY IN THE CLASSROOM

Communications with Parents

Classrooms with large numbers of students from cultural minorities present unique communication challenges. Research indicates that parents of cultural minorities tend to participate in school activities to a lesser extent than do other parents (Griffith, 2002). In general, diversity tends to make encouraging parental involvement more challenging.

Economic, Cultural, and Language Barriers.   Research indicates that economic, cultural, and language barriers can limit the school involvement of minority and low-SES parents.

Involvement takes time, and economic commitments often come first. For example, half the parents in one study indicated that their jobs prevented them from helping their youngsters with homework (Ellis, Dowdy, Graham, & Jones, 1992). Often parents lack economic resources (e.g., child care, transportation, and telephones) that would allow them to participate in school activities. Parents want to be involved in their children's schooling, but schools need to be flexible and provide help and encouragement.

Differences between home and school cultures can also create barriers (Delgado-Gaitan, 1992; Harry, 1992). Parents may have experienced schools that were very different from the ones their children attend, and some may have had negative school experiences. These parents require a great deal of encouragement and support to become involved (Kaplan, Liu, & Kaplan, 2001).

Language can be another barrier. Parents of bilingual students may not speak English, which leaves the child responsible for interpreting communications sent home by teachers. Homework poses a special problem because parents cannot interpret assignments or provide help (Delgado-Gaitan, 1992).

Involving Minority Parents.   Many parents from cultural minorities feel ill prepared to assist their children with school-related tasks, but when teachers offer parents specific strategies for working with their children, the home–school gap is narrowed (Gorman & Balter, 1997; Porche & Ross, 1999). Let's look at an example.

Nancy Miller, an eighth-grade English teacher, had students who spoke several different native languages in her class. Before school started, she prepared a letter to parents, and on the first day she had her students help her translate it into each of their native languages. The letter began by describing how pleased she was to have students from varying backgrounds in her class, saying that these backgrounds would enrich all her students' educations.

She continued with a simple list of procedures and encouraged the parents to support their children's efforts by doing the following:

1. *Asking about school and school work each night*
2. *Providing a quiet place to study*
3. *Limiting television until homework assignments were finished*
4. *Asking to see samples of their children's work and grades they have received*

She told them the school was having an open house and the class with the highest attendance there would win a contest. She concluded the letter by reemphasizing that she was pleased to have so much diversity in her class. She asked parents to sign the letter and return it to the school.

The day before the open house, Nancy had each of her students compose a handwritten letter to their parents, asking them to attend the open house. Nancy wrote "Hoping to see you there" at the bottom of each note and signed it.

Nancy's letter accomplished at least three goals. First, writing the letter in the students' native languages communicated caring, and while communicating caring is important for all students, it is essential for students who come from diverse backgrounds. These students and their parents are sometimes more sensitive to perceived slights or condescension from teachers. On the other hand, they also react strongly to displays of warmth and caring.

Second, the letter included specific suggestions. Even parents who cannot read a homework assignment can become more involved if they ask their children to share and explain their work with them. The suggestion also lets parents know they are needed. Third, by encouraging parents to attend the school's open house, Nancy increased the likelihood that they would actually attend. If they did and the experience was positive, their involvement would likely increase.

EXERCISE 2.3

Look at the following letter sent home by a middle school geography teacher. After reading the letter, identify at least five ways in which it is an effective form of early communication with parents.

August 3, 2006

Dear Parents,

I am looking forward to a productive and exciting year in all my classes, and I hope you are too! I am writing this letter to encourage your involvement and support. You always have been and still are the most important people in your youngster's education. We cannot do the job without you.

In order for us to work together most effectively, some guidelines are necessary. They are listed below. Please read carefully through this information and sign on the line at the end of the letter. If you have any questions or comments, please feel free to call Lakeside Middle School at 213-2980 ext. 2622 any time. My voice mail is active 24 hours a day, and I check it every afternoon before leaving for the day, and I check it again about 7:00 p.m. I will return your call shortly. You may also reach me via e-mail at jawest@mail.clay.k12.fl.us. I also check my e-mail each afternoon and evening and will respond as soon as I can.

Two copies of this letter are being sent home. Please keep one for your reference; your sons and daughters will keep the other in their notebooks throughout the year.

I also want to invite all parents to attend an Open House at Lakeside scheduled for Monday, August 28, at 7.00 p.m. Thank you for your cooperation and help in making this year the best one ever for our junior high students.

SCHOOL SUPPLIES

The students need the following supplies:

1. Loose-leaf notebook and paper
2. Set of tab dividers
3. Set of colored pencils for map work
4. Pen (blue or black ink) and pencil

CLASS GUIDELINES AND PROCEDURES

The following guidelines will help make all classes run smoothly:

1. It is imperative that you take the responsibility for getting organized and staying on top of your workload this year. SUCCESS comes with HARD WORK and DEDICATION.

I'm here to teach, to guide, and to counsel; if you need help, please see me as soon as possible. I WANT YOU TO SUCCEED!

2. Our motto in this class is: I WILL ALWAYS TRY AND I WILL NEVER GIVE UP!
3. Homework and other projects are due as assigned in class. Late homework (unless you are absent) will not be accepted (I have 150 students, and it is very difficult to monitor and keep track of late assignments).
4. Locker passes will not be given to retrieve homework, books, or other materials.
5. Tests will be announced 3 or more days in advance.
6. The policy for makeup work is explained in the student planner.
7. Since developing responsibility is one of the goals of our class, if you're absent when a test is given, it is YOUR responsibility to schedule a makeup test.
8. I will be available for help sessions in the mornings and after school each day.

CLASS RULES

1. Be in the classroom and quiet when the bell rings.
2. Follow directions the first time they're given.
3. Bring covered textbooks, notebook, pen, pencils, and planner to class every day.
4. Raise your hand for permission to speak or leave your seat.
5. Keep hands, feet, and objects to yourself.
6. Leave class only when dismissed by the teacher.

Please see me if you have questions about any of these items.

Student Signature _____

Parent Signature _____

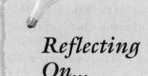

CLASSROOM MANAGEMENT: PREVENTION

INTASC Principles 5 and 10

Think about the discussion of classroom management in this chapter with respect to preventing classroom management problems before they begin.

Reflecting On...

SUMMARY

Classroom management includes the actions that create and maintain an orderly learning environment. Well-managed classrooms result in higher achievement and increased learner motivation.

Enthusiastic, caring, and firm teachers who have high expectations for their students create classroom environments where the focus is on learning and the students are orderly.

Management and instruction are interdependent. Effective teachers are well organized, use their time efficiently, involve students in learning activities, and provide effective feedback. In the absence of effective instruction, creating an orderly classroom is extremely difficult.

Planning for effective management involves creating clear rules and procedures, taking the developmental characteristics of students into account, and arranging the physical environment to avoid disruptions.

In any management system, communication with parents is essential. In addition to schoolwide activities, such as open houses and interim progress reports, sending a letter of introduction home at the beginning of the year and maintaining communication is important for keeping parents involved.

KEY CONCEPTS

PREPARING FOR YOUR LICENSURE EXAMINATION

Read the following two examples and, using specific information from this chapter, answer the questions that follow.

1. Deborah Martin is preparing her handouts on the first day of class. Her eighth graders come into the room; some take their seats, while others mill around, talking in small groups. As the bell rings, she looks up and says over the hum of the students, "Everyone take your seats, please," and she turns back to finish preparing her handouts.

2. Maria Novelo is waiting at the door for her eighth graders with handouts in her hand. As students come in, she distributes the handouts and says, "Take your seats quickly, please. You'll find your name on the desk. The bell is going to ring in less than a minute, and everyone needs to be at his or her desk and quiet when it does. Please read the handout while you're waiting."

   She is standing at the front of the room, surveying the class as the bell rings. When it stops, Maria begins, "Good morning, everyone."

   1. Describe specifically what Maria did that would likely prevent management problems that Deborah failed to do.

   2. Of the teacher characteristics of effective managers described in the chapter, for which is the difference between Maria's and Deborah's behavior most evident? Explain.

   3. Which of the instructional factors described in the chapter is best illustrated by what Maria did? Explain.

VIDEO EXERCISE

Go to MyEducationLab and select the topic "Classroom Management" and watch the video "Arranging Furniture and Materials." Respond to the questions that follow the video episode.

 DEVELOPING YOUR PORTFOLIO

The purpose of this activity is to encourage you to think about organizing your classroom and planning your instruction to prevent management problems before they begin.

- Prepare a list of rules you believe would be effective for the age of children or content area that you want to teach.
- Describe the procedures you will want your students to follow to keep your class running smoothly.
- Create a letter to parents that you might use to begin the communication process with them.

 QUESTIONS FOR DISCUSSION

1. Helping learners develop responsibility and self-control is viewed as an important goal. Do classroom rules and procedures help students reach that goal, or do they detract from that goal? Provide a rationale for your view.

2. Why is it virtually impossible to maintain an orderly classroom if instruction is ineffective? Give an example to illustrate your description.

3. Why do orderly classrooms increase learner motivation? Explain based on your understanding of factors that increase the motivation to learn.

4. Explain how a teacher can be simultaneously caring and firm.

5. Many experts feel that teachers' willingness to give learners their time is the best indicator of caring that exists. Explain why this would be the case.

 SUGGESTIONS FOR FIELD EXPERIENCE

1. Interview a teacher. Some questions you might ask are the following:
   a. How do you organize your classroom to prevent management problems?
   b. What are your rules and procedures? How did you arrive at them?
   c. How did you present your rules and procedures to your students? Did you solicit input from them in preparing the rules and procedures?
   d. How did you "teach" your rules and procedures? Was "teaching" them necessary, or did you merely present them?
   e. How did you communicate your rules and procedures to your students' parents?

2. Observe in a classroom. Identify and describe the classroom management procedures you see. Ask the teacher how the procedures are taught.

3. As you observe in a classroom, look for evidence of classroom rules. For example, are rules displayed? Did the teacher give the students a sheet with the rules written on it? Do the students have rules in a notebook?

4. Observe a teacher conducting lessons. Describe how the teacher's instruction does or does not prevent management problems. Explain why you believe the teacher's instruction is effective or ineffective.

TOOLS FOR TEACHING

Print References

Emmer, E. T., Evertson, C. M., & Worsham, M. E. (2006). *Classroom management for middle and high school teachers* (7th ed.). Boston: Allyn & Bacon. A widely respected text that provides detailed suggestions for designing effective classroom management systems in middle and high schools.

Evertson, C. M., Emmer, E. T., & Worsham, M. E. (2006). *Classroom management for elementary teachers* (7th ed.). Boston: Allyn & Bacon. A widely respected text that provides detailed suggestions for designing effective classroom management systems in elementary schools.

Good, T. L., & Brophy, J. E. (2008). *Looking in classrooms* (10th ed.). Boston: Allyn & Bacon. This well-known and widely used text includes a chapter specifically devoted to the prevention of classroom management problems.

Marzano, R. J., Marzano, J. S., & Pickering, D. J. (2003). *Classroom management that works: Research-based strategies for every teacher.* Alexandria, VA: Association for Supervision and Curriculum Development. This research-based resource provides specific strategies for organizing classrooms to prevent management problems.

Web Sites

www.honorlevel.com/hls_intro.xml Provides strategies for developing an honor system approach to classroom management.

www.nea.org/classmanagement/ifc070814.html Offers a series of strategies for getting the school year off to a good start and keeping your classroom running smoothly throughout the year.

www.nea.org/classmanagement/ifc061212.html Provides suggestions for establishing routines that help create an orderly classroom environment.

www.nea.org/classmanagement/begtk030828.html Includes a series of Web sites that provide classroom management tips for new teachers.

Classroom Management: Interventions

INTRODUCTION

In Chapter 2, we discussed classroom management and the interdependence of effective management and effective instruction. We also noted that expert managers prevent as many management problems as possible instead of eliminating them once they occur.

In spite of teachers' sincere efforts to prevent management problems, however, they will still periodically occur. It happens to every teacher, and it will happen to you, particularly as an intern or a beginning teacher. How you deal with these problems is the subject of this chapter.

LEARNER OBJECTIVES

After completing your study of Chapter 3, you should be able to do the following:

- Describe sources of management problems as emotionally caused, teacher caused, or student caused

- Identify appropriate interventions for different management incidents
- Identify theoretical approaches to management as cognitive or behaviorist
- Describe the characteristics of assertive discipline

APPLYING EFFECTIVE CLASSROOM MANAGEMENT INTERVENTIONS IN THE CLASSROOM

Following is a case study in which an elementary teacher is working with her first graders to create an orderly learning environment. As you read the case study, consider the following questions:

- What does the teacher do to eliminate her management problems?
- What is the theoretical foundation of her intervention?
- How might you apply similar principles in your classroom?

Cindy Daine's first graders are sometimes frustrating. Although she tries "alerting" the groups and having the whole class make transitions at the same time, each one takes 4 minutes or more.

In an effort to improve the situation, she makes some "tickets" from construction paper, buys an assortment of small prizes, and displays the items in a fishbowl on her desk the next day. She then explains, "We're going to play a little game to see how quiet we can be when we change lessons. . . . Whenever we change, such as from language arts to math, I'm going to give you 2 minutes, and then I'm going to ring this bell." She rings the bell as a demonstration. "Students who have their books out and are waiting quietly when I ring the bell will get one of these tickets. On Friday afternoon, you can turn them in for prizes you see in this fishbowl. The more tickets you have, the better the prize will be. If you don't have your books ready, you will lose one of your tickets. Let's see how many tickets we can get."

During the next few days, Cindy moves around the room, handing out tickets and making comments such as "I really like the way Merry is ready to work," "Ted already has his books out and is quiet," and "Thank you for moving to math so quickly."

She knows it's working when she hears "Shh" and "Be quiet!" from the students. She moves from the prizes to allowing the students to "buy" free time with their tickets to finally holding Friday afternoon parties as group rewards when the class accumulates enough tickets. She is gradually able to space out the group rewards as the students' self-regulation develops.

SOURCES OF MANAGEMENT PROBLEMS

To be an effective manager, you must first understand what is meant by the term *management problems*. Management problems are any situations in classrooms that detract from learning or that cause distress to either students or the teacher (Marzano, Marzano, & Pickering, 2003). These problems can be as simple as students sharpening their pencils during a class discussion or as serious as fighting. Some common management problems are the following:

- Talking without permission
- Inattention
- Leaving seat without permission
- Passing notes
- Failure to bring needed materials to class
- Students making unkind remarks to each other

Other, less common problems include students refusing to comply with a request, combing hair and other forms of grooming (particularly in junior high); or even fighting.

In this chapter, we examine ways of dealing with problems that disrupt the teaching-learning process. While drugs, fighting, and attacks on teachers receive widespread publicity, the primary sources of management problems are the relatively minor but chronic disruptions students cause, such as being inattentive, talking without permission, or frequently leaving their seats.

The label *management problem* is sometimes a misnomer because what we typically describe as problems may in fact be symptoms rather than problems themselves. Behaviors that teachers view as problems primarily come from one of three sources: (a) teachers themselves, (b) emotional problems, and (c) casual or capricious student actions. For example, a child's constant daydreaming or talking to friends during a class discussion may indicate that the teacher is not involving students in the learning activity, which is the teacher's problem. The disruption is merely a symptom. This again illustrates the interdependence of management and effective instruction. On the other hand, a student who is frequently fighting may have an emotional problem. And a child walking by a friend, thumping the friend on the shoulder, and being hit back may demonstrate nothing more than children's tendency for horseplay.

Understanding the source of misbehavior is important because it allows us to make better decisions about intervening. For example, you would not treat simple horseplay in the same way as an emotional problem. In the first case, you might simply separate the students, and the second may suggest a call to parents or consultation with a school counselor or psychologist. Further, if you recognize yourself as a possible cause, you can plan your learning activities more carefully or redouble your efforts to create better examples of the topics you teach and ask more questions to involve your students.

As we saw in Chapter 2, many problems, including those with emotional causes, can be prevented. If clear expectations for acceptable behavior are established at the beginning of the year and rules are enforced fairly and consistently, the management of virtually all students is possible.

Casual or capricious actions are the most common sources of management problems. As a regular classroom teacher, you will have, at most, a handful of students who have emotional problems. The most aggravating management problems for a well-prepared teacher are the "kids-will-be-kids" type. The main portion of our discussion focuses on these problems.

EXERCISE 3.1

Identify the following behaviors as coming from an emotionally caused (e), teacher-caused (t), or student-caused (s) source.

1. Getting out of seat without permission
2. Saying negative things to peers
3. Looking out the window during discussion
4. Writing on desks
5. Chewing gum when it is forbidden
6. Blurting out responses without raising hand
7. Throwing temper tantrum when told to wait to respond
8. Being noisy around peers but quiet around teacher
9. Continually using obscene language (although not in front of the teacher)
10. Refusing to respond to questions

CHARACTERISTICS OF EFFECTIVE INTERVENTIONS

The first step in solving management problems is as much prevention as it is treatment. The teacher and students should be clear about what behaviors are acceptable. This is the reason for establishing, teaching, and monitoring rules and procedures, which we discussed in Chapter 2. In addition, you should be clear about available options to management problems. Being clear allows you to act and communicate decisively when problems occur.

Intervening in the case of management problems is never easy. If it were, classroom management would not remain among the teachers' most intractable problems. Research has identified some characteristics of effective intervention. They include the following:

- Withitness and overlapping
- Consistency and follow-through
- Brevity, clarity, and firmness
- Preserving student dignity

Withitness and Overlapping

Jacob Kounin (1970) analyzed the classroom practices of effective and ineffective classroom managers and attempted to isolate variables that differentiated the two. One of the most important is a concept he called **withitness,** which refers to the teacher knowing what is going on in all parts of the classroom all the time and to communicate this awareness to students. Related to withitness is the variable called **overlapping,** which is the teacher's ability to do more than one thing at a time. Both involve dealing with individual problems while maintaining the attention of the class as a whole.

To see these concepts illustrated, let's look again at Sheryl Poulos's work with her students in the chapter-opening case study of Chapter 2. For example, as Sheryl asked the question "Let's think about this fraction. Let's estimate what percent 7/12 will be . . . Donna?" she saw Scott stick his foot forward and tap Veronica's leg. In response, Veronica whispered loudly, "Stop it, Scott." She also noticed Ellen whispering to Kristen at the back of the room.

These behaviors are typical of seventh graders. Scott did what fun-loving seventh graders will do, as did Ellen and Veronica. No evidence of an emotional problem existed, and Sheryl's learning activity involved the students. So, she was dealing with a "kids-will-be-kids" problem.

How did she handle it? First, as Donna responded to her question, Sheryl moved down the aisle, stopped at Scott's desk, and said simply and firmly, "We keep our hands and feet to ourselves in here."

Sheryl demonstrated withitness in three ways. First, she intervened immediately. She caught Scott in the act and moved to prevent further disruption before the incident expanded. Second, she caught the "right one." She saw that Scott was the cause of the incident, so she ignored Veronica's comment. And third, she dealt with the potentially worst problem first. She first stopped Scott's disruption and then moved near Ellen and Kristen. Her proximity then stopped their whispering.

Sheryl quickly stopped the disruptions without interrupting the flow of her lesson and in this way demonstrated overlapping. Most of the students in the class probably were not even aware that an incident was occurring. These abilities are characteristic of effective managers.

If teachers are not "withit"—if they do not know what is going on in their classrooms—then maintaining an orderly learning environment is difficult.

Consistency and Follow-Through

You hear about the need for consistency so often that it is nearly a cliche, but it remains essential (Emmer, Evertson, & Worsham, 2006; Evertson, Emmer, & Worsham, 2006). The need for consistency is obvious, but achieving complete consistency in the real world of teaching is virtually impossible. In fact, research indicates that interventions should be contextualized; they depend on the specific situation and student (Doyle, 1986).

For example, most classrooms have a rule something like "Speak only when recognized by the teacher." Suppose that, as you are monitoring seat work, a student innocently asks a work-related question of another student and then quickly turns back to work. Do you intervene to let that student know that you are "withit" and that talking is not allowed during seat work? Failing to do so is technically inconsistent, but you do not intervene, and you should not. A student who repeatedly turns around and whispers, though, becomes a disruption. A withit teacher knows what is going on, discriminates between the two behaviors, and knows when to intervene.

Effective managers follow through on all interventions to be certain that the undesirable behavior has completely stopped (Good & Brophy, 2008). Take two students who are whispering, for example. They are asked to stop but only reduce their whispering and are soon back at their former level, beginning a new disruptive cycle if the teacher does not follow through.

Brevity, Clarity, and Firmness

Keep encounters as brief, firm, and clear as possible. Long interventions disrupt the flow of the lesson and detract from time devoted to instruction (Crocker & Brooker, 1986).

Clarity describes the precision of the teacher's communication with respect to the desired behavior. For example, "Jenny, we listen quietly when others are talking" is clearer than "Don't, Jenny." It communicates to both Jenny and the rest of the class what the problem is and what is expected.

Firmness means the ability to communicate that the teacher means it and intends to follow through to be sure the behavior stops. "Class, there's too much noise. Please settle down, NOW!" is more effective than "Let's try to settle down and get quiet." A firm response better communicates that the teacher means what is said. The teacher's ability to communicate intent verbally and nonverbally is essential.

While clarity and firmness are effective, roughness, which consists of noisy expressions of anger, frustration, or hostility, is not. Kounin (1970) found that roughness was correlated with increased management problems. Rough and disruptive management interventions tend to have a ripple effect (Kounin, 1970), meaning that the disturbance spreads to the rest of the class when an individual is reprimanded. The ripple effect is more pronounced if teachers use criticism or sarcasm in the reprimand (Rosenshine & Furst, 1971). Prolonged criticism of students wastes instructional time and disrupts students who are working.

Teachers need to be clear and firm when communicating and enforcing acceptable classroom behaviors.

Preserving Student Dignity

Preserving a student's dignity is a basic principle of any intervention. Your emotional tone when you interact with students influences both the likelihood of their compliance and their attitudes toward you and the class. Loud public reprimands, public criticism, and sarcasm reduce students' sense of safety, create resentment, and detract from a productive learning environment. When students break rules, simply reminding them, telling them why the rule is important, and requiring compliance is as far as an incident should go.

Avoid arguments with students. Once a directive is made, follow it through without argument. If students feel they have been treated unfairly, invite them to talk to you about it before or after school or at some other time when you and the students can meet.

Threats and ultimatums can put you in a no-win situation. Because they are usually impossible to carry out, they can eliminate the possibility of follow-through and consistency.

DIVERSITY IN THE CLASSROOM

Effective Intervention

Learner diversity can become a factor when the issue of intervention arises. This diversity exists in at least two areas.

The first is culture and ethnicity. Research indicates that cultural minorities are referred to school authorities for management incidents at a rate that is disproportionate to their numbers in the school population (Slavin, Karweit, & Madden, 1989). At least two reasons are offered for this disproportion.

One suggests that a mismatch exists between home and school cultures. A principal's experience working with Pacific Island students (Winitzky, 1994) is an example. The principal had been invited to a community awards ceremony at a local church to honor students from her school. She gladly accepted, arrived a few minutes early, and was ushered to a seat of honor on the stage. After an uncomfortable (to her) wait of over an hour, the ceremony began, and the students proudly filed to the stage to receive their awards. Each was acknowledged, given an award, and applauded. The children returned to their seats in the audience, and the principal had an eye-opening experience:

> Well, the kids were fine for a while, but as you might imagine, they got bored fast and started to fidget. Fidgeting and whispering turned into poking, prodding, and open chatting. I became a little anxious at the disruption, but none of the other adults appeared to even notice, so I ignored it, too. Pretty soon several of the children were up and out of their seats, strolling about the back and sides of the auditorium. All adult faces continued looking serenely up at the speaker on the stage. Then the kids started playing tag, running circles around the seating area and yelling gleefully. No adult response—I was amazed, and struggled to resist the urge to quiet the children. Then some of the kids got up onto the stage, running around the speaker, flicking the lights on and off, and opening and closing the curtain! Still nothing from the Islander parents! It was not my place, and I shouldn't have done it, but I was so beyond my comfort zone that with eye contact and a pantomimed shush, I got the kids to settle down.

> I suddenly realized then that when these children . . . come to school late, it doesn't mean that they or their parents don't care about learning . . . that's just how all the adults in their world operate. When they squirm under desks and run around the classroom, they aren't trying to be disrespectful or defiant, they're just doing what they do everywhere else. (Winitzky, 1994, pp. 147–148)

In other words, students bring with them ways of acting that may differ from what is expected of them in school (Trawick-Smith, 2000). John Ogbu (1992, 1999) offers another example of cultural differences. He suggests that some cultural minorities, because of a long history of separatism and low status, defend themselves through a process he calls cultural inversion, or "the tendency for . . . minorities to regard certain forms of behavior, events, symbols, and meanings as inappropriate for them because these are characteristic of white Americans" (Ogbu, 1992, p. 8). To become a good student is to adopt white cultural values and "become white." Students who study and become actively involved in school risk losing the friendship and respect of their peers. Ogbu believes that in many schools, students in these groups either do not support school learning or directly oppose it; they form what he calls "resistance cultures" (Ogbu & Simons, 1998). Low grades and misbehavior are symptoms of this conflict.

Gender is a second area in which diversity exists. As with cultural minorities, boys vastly outnumber girls in discipline referrals in spite of their essentially equal numbers in schools. Again, the reasons offered vary. Some researchers suggest that boys are genetically inclined to be more aggressive than girls (Berk, 2006) and that this aggressiveness sometimes manifests itself in misbehavior. Others argue that boys and girls are treated differently from birth and that this different treatment results in different patterns of behavior (Biklen & Pollard, 2001).

When teachers become aware of these differences and the potential issues they raise, the characteristics of effective intervention become even more important. Withitness, consistency, brevity, and preserving student dignity, for example, are important for all students. For members of cultural minorities, who may be extra sensitive to perceived condescension, slights, and favoritism, they are essential.

THEORETICAL APPROACHES TO INTERVENTION

Theories of learning can also provide some guidance in dealing with incidents of inappropriate behavior. In this section, we examine two: cognitive and behaviorist approaches.

Cognitive Interventions

Cognition refers to thinking and processes in people's heads, such as perception, belief, and expectation. We are all cognitive beings. Both teachers and students come to school with sets of beliefs about the way school functions, they have perceptions of fair and unfair treatment, and they acquire expectations about appropriate behavior. A cognitive management system focuses on these processes in an effort to maintain orderly classrooms (Singh et al., 2007).

The concept of consistency illustrates this idea. For example, in the previous section, we noted that achieving complete consistency in interventions is virtually impossible. A cognitive approach to intervention assumes that students can accommodate minor inconsistencies because they understand the difference between a minor and innocent question compared to chronic and disruptive talking. Learner understanding is at the core of cognitive approaches to management.

In this section, we examine three factors that influence the way learners understand and respond to our interventions:

- Congruent communication
- "I" messages
- Logical consequences

Congruent Communication.   If students are to develop understanding and responsibility, our classrooms and the communication in them must make sense to them.

Karen Wilson's 10th graders are working on their next day's English homework as she circulates among them. She is helping Jasmine when Jeff and Mike begin whispering loudly behind her.

"Jeff. Mike. Stop talking and get started on your homework," she says, glancing over her shoulder.

The two slow their whispering, and Karen turns back to Jasmine. Soon, though, the boys are whispering as loudly as ever.

"I thought I told you to stop talking," Karen says over her shoulder again, this time with irritation in her voice.

The boys glance at her and quickly resume whispering.

Isabel Rodriguez is in a similar situation with her ninth-grade algebra class. As she is helping Vicki, Ken and Lance begin horsing around at the back of the room. Isabel quickly excuses herself from Vicki, turns, and walks directly to the boys. Looking Lance in the eye, she says pleasantly but firmly, "Lance, we have plenty to do before lunch, and noise disrupts others' work. Begin your homework now," and then, looking directly at Ken, she continues, "Ken, you too. Quickly now. We have only so much time, and we don't want to waste it."

She waits until they are working quietly, and then she returns to Vicki.

Cognitive approaches to intervention focus on students' understanding—that is, they must understand the way they are supposed to behave in the classroom. In our first example, Karen's communication was confusing; her words said one thing, but her body language said another, leaving the students unconvinced about how committed she was to stopping their inappropriate behavior. As a result, follow-through, one of the characteristics of effective intervention, was virtually impossible.

When messages are inconsistent, people attribute more credibility to nonverbal communication, which includes the tone of voice and body language people use to convey unspoken messages (Mehrabian & Ferris, 1967).

To follow through effectively, communication must be clear and consistent, which was the case in Isabel's intervention. She responded immediately, faced her students directly, emphasized the relationship between classroom order and learning, and made sure that they were on task before she went back to Vicki. Isabel's verbal and nonverbal behaviors were consistent, so her communication made sense to the students. If we expect students to take responsibility for their own behavior, our message must be consistent and understandable, or learner comprehension and compliance will suffer.

Essential elements of nonverbal communication are illustrated in Table 3.1.

Eggen, Paul D.; Kauchak, Donald, *Educational Psychology: Windows on Classrooms*, 7th Edition, Copyright 2007. Reprinted by permission of Pearson Education, Inc., Upper Saddle River, NJ.

Table 3.1   Characteristics of Nonverbal Communication

Nonverbal Behavior	Example
Proximity	A teacher moves close to an inattentive student.
Eye contact	A teacher looks an off-task student directly in the eye when issuing a directive.
Body orientation	A teacher faces a student directly rather than looking over the shoulder or sideways.
Facial expression	A teacher frowns slightly at a disruption, laughs at a humorous incident, and smiles approvingly at a student's effort to help a classmate.
Gestures	A teacher holds up a hand (Stop!) to a student who interjects as another student is talking.
Vocal variation	A teacher varies the tone, pitch, and loudness of voice for emphasis and displays energy and enthusiasm.

"I" Messages.   To begin this section, let's look at a brief encounter between a teacher and student.

Joanne Bass's students are expected to come to class every day with their texts, notebooks, and pencils or pens.

Joanne begins her Wednesday lesson by stating, "Look in your text at the pictures of the different groups found in the Middle East. Can someone describe the different types of people in the pictures on page 79?"

The students begin describing the pictures, and then Ms. Bass asks, "Ron, what can you add?"

Ron replies haltingly, "I didn't bring my book today."

Joanne replies, "Ron, when you don't bring your materials, I have to stop the discussion, the class is disrupted, and I get frustrated."

Let's look specifically at how Joanne handled the incident and see why her approach was cognitive. She helped Ron understand that not bringing his materials to class caused a problem while at the same time being careful to not suggest a weakness in his character or personality.

She began the encounter with what Thomas Gordon (1974) calls an **"I" message.** In reacting to Ron not having his notebook, she did the following:

- Described the behavior (the missing book)
- Identified the consequences of the behavior (disrupting the class)
- Stated her feelings (frustration)

Her goal was understanding; she wanted Ron to understand that not bringing his materials detracted from the learning activity. Cognitive approaches to intervention are based on the idea that the better students understand rules and procedures, the more likely they are to obey them.

Logical Consequences.   Logical consequences treat misbehaviors as problems and help learners see a link between their actions and the consequence.

Let's look at an example.

Ryan, an active sixth grader, is running down the hall toward the lunchroom.

"Hold it, Ryan," Matt Papuga, who is monitoring the hall, says as Ryan runs by. "Go back to the door, start over, and walk back down this hall."

"Aww."

"Go on," Matt says firmly.

Ryan walks back to the door and then returns. As he approaches, Matt again stops him and says, "Now, why did I make you do that?"

". . . Cuz, we're not supposed to run."

"Well, sure," Matt says pleasantly, "but more important, if people are running in the halls, somebody might get hurt, and of course, we don't want that to happen. . . . Plus, I want you to understand that, so the next time you'll realize that you don't want to hurt yourself, or anybody else, and you'll walk whether a teacher is here or not."

In this incident, Matt helped Ryan see the relationship between his behavior and the consequence. The consequence itself is not cognitive; an understanding of the link between the behavior and the consequence is. Again, the goal is the development of learner understanding.

EXERCISE 3.2

Read each of the following brief statements and then submit your responses online:

1. A teacher sees a seventh grader spit on the door to the classroom. Based on the information in this section, which is the more appropriate response—putting the student in after-school detention (which is part of the school's management policy) or having the student wash the door? Explain.

2. A teacher sees a student talking, and the following exchange takes place:

   Teacher: Janet, what are you doing?

   Janet: Nothing.

   Teacher: Yes you were. Speak up so that everyone can hear.

   Janet: [Silence]

   Teacher: You were talking. What's the rule about talking without permission?

   Janet: [Silence]

   Teacher: Let's hear it. I want to hear you say the rule.

   Janet: We don't talk until we're recognized.

   Teacher: That's right. Do you understand that?

   Janet: . . . Yes.

   a. Assess the teacher's handling of the incident based on the characteristics of effective intervention discussed in the previous section.
   b. Describe an "I" message that would have been more effective than the way the teacher handled the incident.

Research indicates that children who understand the effects of their actions on others become more altruistic and are more likely to take action to make up for their misbehavior (Berk, 2006).

Behaviorist Interventions

Cognitive and behaviorist approaches to management have the same goal—the development of desirable classroom behaviors and the elimination of inappropriate behaviors. The emphasis, however, is different. Whereas the focus in cognitive approaches is on thinking and understanding, the focus in behaviorist approaches, as the name implies, is on the behaviors themselves.

Cognitive approaches are the ideal; teachers want students to understand rules and the reasons for them and to accept personal responsibility for obeying them. Unfortunately, however, we sometimes face situations in which learners seem either unable or unwilling to accept responsibility for their behavior (Fabiano, Pelham, & Gnagy, 2007). In addition, time or safety concerns may suggest more direct approaches to management. In situations such as these, behavioral interventions can be effective (Reynolds, Sinatra, & Jetton, 1996).

Behaviorist approaches to management identify specific behaviors that are desirable, and when students display those behaviors, they are rewarded. When they display undesirable behaviors, they are punished (Murphy, 2007).

Cindy Daine's work with her first graders in the chapter-opening case study is an example. Her tickets, free time, and Friday afternoon parties were all intended as rewards for making quick and quiet transitions. In addition, comments such as "I really like the way Merry is ready to work" and "Ted already has his books out and is quiet" were intended to vicariously reward the rest of the children. Losing their tickets for not following the rules was a form of punishment. Research indicates that a behaviorist system such as Cindy's can be effective in initiating new behaviors (McCaslin & Good, 1992).

Systems that focus on rewards are preferable to those that use punishment (Alberto & Troutman, 1999), but focusing exclusively on positive behaviors will not always work. If all punishers are eliminated, some students actually become more disruptive (Pfiffer, Rosen, & O'Leary, 1985; Rosen, O'Leary, Joyce, Conway; & Pfiffer, 1984). It is unrealistic to think that punishment can be totally avoided; it is probably necessary in some cases (Axelrod & Apsche, 1983; Maccoby, 1992). We offer some examples of punishers in the section on assertive discipline later in the chapter.

Some guidelines for using punishment effectively include the following:

- Use punishment as infrequently as possible to avoid damaging the classroom climate
- Apply punishment immediately after the behavior occurs
- Only use punishment severe enough to eliminate the behavior
- Avoid using seat work as a form of punishment
- Apply punishment logically and dispassionately—never in anger

Some approaches to management systematically use reinforcers and punishers in attempts to promote desirable behaviors in classrooms. Assertive discipline is the best known of these systems.

Assertive Discipline: A Systematic Approach to Consequences   During the 1980s, an approach to classroom management, called **assertive discipline,** became enormously popular. The approach is controversial; critics argue that it is punitive and stresses obedience and conformity over learning and self-control (Brophy, 1999; McLaughlin, 1994). Others argue that it is inherently destructive (Kohn, 1996). Proponents disagree and contend that its emphasis on positive reinforcement is effective (Canter, 1988).

We neither support nor condemn its use. While its popularity has waned in recent years, it continues to be well known. It is a rare school district that has not had at least some experience with the program; estimates suggest that more than 750,000 teachers have been trained in the program (Hill, 1990). For this reason, we discuss it in this section.

Assertive discipline was developed from Lee and Marlene Canter's work in the area of assertion training. As they attempted to help their clients become more assertive, they encountered three characteristic patterns of reactions to conflict. Passive people were unable to express their wants or feelings or back up their words with actions. At the other end of the continuum, hostile people were able to express their wants and feelings but often did so by abusing others. An assertive response style, in contrast, clearly communicated wants and feelings but did so without harming other people. As they worked with teachers, they saw these response patterns in classrooms. Let's look at some examples:

Johnny has been told several times to keep his hands to himself in the classroom. The teacher turns around and sees Johnny poking at a student walking by his desk.

Passive Response: Johnny, I don't know what to do with you. Why can't you keep your hands to yourself?

Hostile Response: Johnny, there is something wrong with you; you just won't listen! I've told you a million times to keep your hands to yourself.

Assertive Response: Johnny, you've been warned before, and now you've made the choice to leave the room. Pick up your books and come with me.

Assertive discipline encourages teachers to use assertive rather than passive or hostile responses. It is based on the premise that teachers have three rights:

1. The right to establish a classroom structure that is conducive to learning
2. The right to determine and expect appropriate behavior from students
3. The right to ask for help from parents, the principal, and other professionals to produce order in the classroom

Using these rights as a foundation, assertive discipline advocates create a management system that is based on behaviorist views of learning. Rules and procedures are clearly laid out at the beginning of the year and are enforced with reinforcers and punishers. Reinforcers can include the following:

- Praise
- Awards
- Notes or phone calls to parents (additional forms of praise)
- Special privileges, such as being able to play games or do puzzles
- Material consequences, such as food or prizes

Some punishers include the following:

- Time-out (isolating students from the rest of the class, such as behind a bookshelf)
- Removal of a privilege, such as working on the computer or going to physical education
- Before- or after-school detention
- Being sent to the principal's or dean's office
- Notes or phone calls home specifying misbehaviors

Reinforcers and punishers are made clear to students from the beginning and are administered with names on the board or some other checklist.

Canter and Canter (1992) emphasize a final aspect of assertive discipline called the *broken record*. In dealing with problems, teachers can become sidetracked. To avoid doing so, teachers are encouraged to use a "broken-record" technique, in essence repeating their request until the message is delivered. Here is what this technique sounds like in practice:

Ms. Jackson: Tom, you must stop fighting on the playground.

   Tom: But they're always calling me names.

Ms. Jackson: That's not the point. What gets you in trouble is your fighting. This has to stop.

   Tom: But they pick on me first.

Ms. Jackson: I understand. But still your problem is fighting. You must stop fighting.

If not overused (three repeats is the recommended maximum), this technique helps the teacher maintain focus in the middle of a management problem without becoming distracted from the objective.

Assertive discipline promotes the teacher's right to establish and enforce a positive learning climate in a classroom environment.

While most veteran teachers do not use a management system as rigid as assertive discipline can be, some researchers have recommended it particularly for beginning teachers (Wolfgang & Glickman, 1986). Its structure and clear delineation of alternatives simplifies the management task for teachers. The hope is that teachers use it as a foundation for growth, expanding their repertoire to more complex and truly educational alternatives, as the issue becomes not so much order but learner growth.

Designing and Maintaining a Behavioral Management System.   Designing a management system based on behaviorism typically involves the following steps:

- Prepare a list of specific rules. The rules should represent observable behaviors, such as "Speak only when recognized by the teacher."
- Specify punishers for breaking rules and reinforcers for obeying each rule.
- Display the rules and procedures and explain the consequences to the students.
- Consistently apply consequences.

A behavioral system does not preclude providing rationales or creating the rules with learner input. The focus, however, is on the clear specifications of behavioral guidelines and application of consequences, in contrast with a cognitive system, which emphasizes learner understanding and responsibility.

In designing a comprehensive management system, you will likely use elements of both cognitive and behavioral approaches. Behavioral systems have the advantage of being immediately applicable. They are effective for initiating desired behaviors, particularly with young students, and they are useful for reducing chronic misbehavior. The results of cognitive systems take longer to appear, but they are more likely to develop learner responsibility.

Keeping both cognitive and behavioral approaches to management in mind, let's consider a series of intervention options.

AN INTERVENTION CONTINUUM

Disruptions vary widely, from an isolated incident (such as a student briefly whispering to a neighbor during quiet time) to chronic infractions (such as someone repeatedly poking, tapping, or kicking other students). Because infractions vary, teachers' reactions should also vary. To maximize instructional time and minimize disruptions, our goal is to keep interventions as unobtrusive as possible. A continuum designed to reach this goal is described in Figure 3.1(Eggen & Kauchak, 2007).

Figure 3.1   An Intervention Continuum

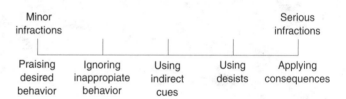

Minor infractions				Serious infractions
Praising desired behavior	Ignoring inappropiate behavior	Using indirect cues	Using desists	Applying consequences

Praising Desired Behavior

Increasing reinforced behaviors is a principle of behaviorism. Since our goal in any classroom is to promote as much desirable behavior as possible, praising desired behavior is a sensible beginning point.

Praise occurs less often than we might expect, so efforts to "catch' 'em being good" is a worthwhile goal, especially as a method of prevention. Elementary teachers praise openly and freely, and middle and secondary teachers often quietly comment to students after class, "I'm extremely pleased with your work this last week. You're getting better and better at this stuff. Keep it up." Making an effort to acknowledge desired behavior and good work can significantly contribute to a productive learning environment.

Ignoring Inappropriate Behavior

A second principle of behaviorism says that behaviors that are not reinforced become extinct, so one way of eliminating undesirable behaviors is to simply ignore them, which eliminates any reinforcer we as teachers might be inadvertently providing (Alberto & Troutman, 1999). This is appropriate, for example, if two students whisper to each other but soon stop. Combining praise and ignoring misbehavior can be effective with minor disruptions (Pfiffer et al., 1985; Rosen et al., 1984).

Using Indirect Cues

Teachers can use **indirect cues** such as proximity, methods of redirecting attention, and vicarious reinforcers. These strategies are appropriate when students are displaying behaviors that cannot be ignored but can be stopped or diverted without addressing them directly (Jones & Jones, 2001). As an example, let's look again at Sheryl Poulos's work with her students in the case study at the beginning of Chapter 2. In response to Scott tapping Veronica with his foot, Sheryl moved down the aisle and stood next to him, using proximity to stop his "foot tapping." She then did the same thing with Ellen and Kristen. Proximity is an indirect cue.

Using Desists

A **desist** occurs when a teacher tells a student to stop a behavior (Kounin, 1970). "Jasmine, we don't leave our seat without permission," "Jasmine!," a finger to the lips, or a stern facial expression are all desists. These are the most common teacher reactions to misbehavior (Humphrey, 1979; Sieber, 1981).

Clarity and tone are important in the effectiveness of desists. For example, "Randy, what is the rule about touching other students in this class?" or "Randy, how do you think that makes Willy feel?" are clearer than "Randy, stop that" because they link the behavior to a rule or the consequences of the behavior. Students react to these subtle differences, preferring rule and consequence reminders to teacher commands (Nucci, 1987).

The tone of desists should be firm but not angry. Research indicates that kindergarten students handled with rough desists actually became more disruptive and that older students were uncomfortable in classes in which rough desists were used (Kounin, 1970). By contrast, gentle reprimands, together with the suggestion of alternative behaviors and effective questioning techniques, reduced time off task by 20 minutes a day (Borg & Ascione, 1982).

Clear communication (including congruence between verbal and nonverbal behavior), an awareness of what is happening in the classroom (withitness), and the characteristics of effective instruction are essential in effectively using desists to stop misbehavior. However, even when these important elements are used, simple desists alone do not always work.

Applying Consequences

Careful planning and effective instruction will eliminate much misbehavior before it starts. Some minor incidents can be ignored, and simple desists will stop others. When these strategies do not stop disruptions, however, you must apply consequences that are related to the problem.

Logical consequences are preferable because they treat misbehaviors as problems and demonstrate a link between the behavior and the consequence. Classrooms are busy places, however, and it is not always possible to solve problems with logical consequences. In these instances, behavioral consequences offer an alternative:

> Jason is an intelligent and active fifth grader. He loves to talk and seems to know just how far he can go before Mrs. Aguilar gets exasperated with him. He understands the rules and the reasons for them, but his interest in talking seems to take precedence. Ignoring him isn't working. A call to his parents helped for a while, but soon he was back to his usual behavior—never quite enough to require a drastic response, but always a thorn in Mrs. Aguilar's side.
>
> Finally, she decides that she will give him one warning. At a second disruption, he is placed in time-out from regular instructional activities. She meets with Jason and explains the new rules. The next day, he begins to misbehave almost immediately.
>
> "Jason," she warns, "you can't work while you're talking, and you're keeping others from finishing their work. Please get busy."
>
> He stops, but five minutes later, he's at it again. "Jason," she says quietly as she moves back to his desk, "I've warned you. Now please go back to the time-out area."
>
> A week later, Jason is working quietly and comfortably with the rest of the class. (Eggen & Kauchak, 2007, pp. 452–453)

Jason's behavior is common, particularly in elementary and middle schools; it is precisely this type of behavior that drives teachers up the wall. Students like Jason cause more teacher stress and burnout than threats of violence and bodily harm. His behavior is so disruptive that it cannot be ignored; praise for good work helps to a certain extent, but much of his reinforcement comes from his buddies. Desists work briefly, but teachers burn out constantly monitoring him. Mrs. Aguilar had little choice but to apply consequences.

The key to handling students like Jason is consistency. He understands what he is doing, and he is capable of controlling himself. When he can, with absolute certainty, predict the consequences of his behavior, he will quit. He knew that his second infraction would result in time-out, and when it did, he quickly changed his behavior. There was no argument, little time was used, and the class was not disrupted.

SERIOUS MANAGEMENT PROBLEMS:
VIOLENCE AND AGGRESSION

Class is disrupted by a scuffle. You look up to see that Ron has left his seat and gone to Phil's desk, where he is punching and shouting at Phil. Phil is not so much fighting back as trying to protect himself. You don't know how this started, but you do know that Phil gets along well with other students and that Ron often starts fights and arguments without provocation. (Brophy & Rohrkemper, 1987, p. 60)

This morning several students excitedly tell you that on the way to school they saw Tom beating up Sam and taking his lunch money. Tom is the class bully and has done things like this many times. (Brophy & Rohrkemper, 1987, p. 53)

What would you do in these situations? What would be your immediate reaction? How would you follow through? What long-term strategies would you employ to try to prevent these problems from recurring? These questions were asked of teachers identified by their principals as effective in dealing with serious management problems (Brophy & McCaslin, 1992). In this section, we consider their responses, together with other research examining violence and aggression in schools.

Problems of violence and aggression require both immediate actions and long-term solutions. Let's look at them.

Immediate Actions

Immediate actions involve three steps: (a) stop the incident (if possible), (b) protect the victim, and (c) get help (Smith & Bondy, 2007). For instance, in the case of the classroom scuffle, a loud noise, such as shouting, clapping, or slamming a chair against the floor, will often surprise the students enough so that they will stop. At that point, you can begin to talk to them, check to see if Phil is all right, and then take them to administration where you can get help.

If your interventions do not stop the fight, immediately send a student to the main office for help. Unless you are sure that you can separate the students without danger to yourself or to them, attempting to do so is unwise.

You are legally required to intervene in the case of a fight. If you ignore a fight, even on the playground, parents can sue for negligence on the grounds that you are failing to protect a student from injury. However, the law does not say that you are required to physically break up the fight; immediately reporting it to the administration is an acceptable form of intervention.

Long-Term Solutions

Long term, students must first be helped to understand the severity of their actions. They need to know that aggression will not be allowed and that they are accountable for their behavior (Brophy, 1996; Limber, Flerx, Nation, & Melton, 1998). In the incident with the lunch money, for example, Tom must understand that his behavior was reported, is unacceptable, and will not be tolerated.

As a preventive strategy, students must learn how to control their tempers, cope with frustration, and negotiate and talk rather than fight. One approach uses problem-solving simulations to help aggressive youth understand the motives and intentions of other people. Research indicates that these youngsters often respond aggressively because they misperceive others' intentions as being hostile (Hudley, 1992). Following problem-solving sessions, aggressive students were less hostile in their interpretation of ambiguous situations and were rated as less aggressive by their teachers.

Other approaches to preventing aggression include teaching students to express anger verbally instead of physically and to solve conflicts through communication and negotiation rather than fighting (Burstyn & Stevens, 1999; Lee, Pulvino, & Perrone, 1998). One form of communication and negotiation is learning to make and defend a position—to argue effectively. Students taught to make effective arguments—emphasizing that arguing and verbal aggression are very different—become less combative when encountering others with whom they disagree. Learning to argue also has incidental benefits: skillful arguers of any age are seen by their peers as intelligent and credible.

Experts also suggest the involvement of parents and other school personnel (Brophy, 1996; Moles, 1992). Research indicates that a large majority of parents (88%) want to be notified immediately if school problems occur (Harris, Kagay, & Ross, 1987). In addition, school counselors, school psychologists, social workers, and principals have all been trained to deal with these problems and can provide advice and assistance. Experienced teachers can also provide a wealth of information about how they have handled similar problems. No teacher should face persistent or serious problems of violence or aggression alone.

EXERCISE 3.3

Read the following vignette and answer the questions that follow. (The paragraphs in the vignette are numbered to make referring to it easier.)

1. Dan Rogers is a fourth-grade teacher. He began his year by first getting to know his students and establishing the rules and procedures for his class.

2. On the first day, he said, "In order to learn the most, we must have some rules that we all want to follow carefully." With that, he displayed a large poster board on which were clearly printed a list of rules for the class during the year. He then asked, "Do all the rules seem fair? Are there others we should add?"

3. The class read the rules and after a short discussion agreed that the rules were OK as he presented them. Mr. Rogers then went on with his class work.

4. A few days later, during an explanation of a math problem, Susan was turned around talking to Shirley. Mr. Rogers ignored the talking for a moment, but it continued. As the rest of the class was working on a problem, the teacher went back to Susan and asked, "Susan, do you know why I've come to talk to you?"

5. Susan hesitated and then said, "Shirley and I were talking."

6. "Yes," Mr. Rogers continued. "Talking disrupts the class, and I get upset when class is disrupted. Remember, we made a rule about talking while someone else is talking. Do you know what that rule is?"

7. Susan nodded.

8. "Now I want you to suggest some way that you can help yourself stay within the rules we agreed on. Let me know after school."

9. Mr. Rogers then continued with the lesson, and Susan stopped in at the end of the day and simply said she would not talk anymore. The teacher asked if she understood why this was important, and she said, "Talking disrupts the learning for the other kids, and learning is what we're here for."

10. The next day during the same class, as Mr. Rogers was discussing another problem, Susan again turned around and began talking. Mr. Rogers went to her after he had the rest of the class involved in an activity and said evenly, "Susan, this is the second infraction of the rules, so I'm going to have to put a check by your name. This means you won't be able to take part in our free-play activity this afternoon. Please try to obey the rules from now on."

11. With that, he again went back to his regular classroom activity.

1. Which paragraphs best illustrate Dan attempting to apply a cognitive intervention in his classroom?
   a. 1–2
   b. 3–4
   c. 8–9
   d. 10–11
   Explain your answer.

2. Which paragraph best illustrates Dan using a behaviorist intervention?
   a. 2
   b. 4
   c. 6
   d. 10
   Explain your answer.

3. Which paragraph best illustrates two different points on the intervention continuum?
   a. 2
   b. 3
   c. 4
   d. 6
   Explain your answer.

4. Dan's response to Susan in paragraph 10 best illustrates which point on the intervention continuum? Explain.

5. With respect to assertive discipline, what does Dan's statement to Susan in paragraph 10, "This means you won't be able to take part in our free-play activity this afternoon. Please try to obey the rules from now on," best illustrate?
   a. A passive response
   b. A hostile response
   c. An assertive response
   Explain your answer.

In conclusion, we want to put problems of school violence and aggression into perspective. Although they are possibilities—and you should understand options for dealing with them—the majority of your management problems will involve issues of cooperation and motivation. Many can be prevented, others can be dealt with quickly, and some require individual attention. We all hear about students carrying guns to school and incidents of assault on teachers in the news. Statistically, however, considering the huge numbers of students who pass through schools each day, these incidents remain infrequent.

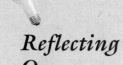

Reflecting On...

CLASSROOM MANAGEMENT: INTERVENTIONS

INTASC Principle 5

Think about the discussion of classroom management in this chapter with respect to intervening in incidents of inappropriate student behavior.

SUMMARY

Management problems can be the result of casual and capricious student actions ("kids will be kids"), emotional problems, or teachers themselves. Regardless of the source, effective interventions can reduce the impact of the misbehavior.

Effective teachers know what is going on in their classrooms at all times, they are consistent in their interventions, and they follow through to be sure the disruptions are eliminated. They keep interventions brief, firm, and clear, and they avoid arguments, threats, and ultimatums.

Cognitive approaches to intervention focus on student understanding and incorporate congruent communication, "I" messages, and logical consequences. Behaviorist interventions focus on the elimination of undesirable behavior and the reward of appropriate behavior.

Interventions include praising desired behavior, ignoring inappropriate behavior, using desists, and applying consequences.

Violence and aggression require both immediate action and long-term solutions. Immediate action requires that all students are safe and that help is obtained. Long-term solutions involve helping students learn to control anger and develop appropriate ways to handle hostility and anger.

KEY CONCEPTS

Assertive discipline   80
Clarity   73
Cognition   75
Desist   83
Firmness   73

"I" message   77
Indirect cues   83
Overlapping   71
Withitness   71

PREPARING FOR YOUR LICENSURE EXAMINATION

Read the following case study and, using specific information from this chapter, answer the questions that follow.

"You did quite well on the assignment," Joel Clarke comments to his geography students while he hands back a set of papers. "Let's keep up the good work. . . . Doris and Candy, please stop talking while I'm returning the papers. Can't you just sit quietly for 1 minute?"

The girls, who were whispering, turn back to the front of the room.

"Now," Mr. Clarke continues after returning to the front of the room, "we've been studying the Middle East, so let's review for a moment. Look at the map and identify the longitude and latitude of Cairo. Take a minute and figure it out right now."

"Stop it, Kent," he hears Melissa blurt out behind him.

"Melissa, we don't talk out like that in class."

"He poked me, Mr. Clarke."

"Did you poke her, Kent?"

". . . Um."

"Both of you stop it," Mr. Clarke warns. "Another outburst like that, Melissa, and your name goes on the chalkboard."

As the last students finish the problem, the teacher looks up from the materials on his desk to check an example on the overhead. He hears Doris and Candy giggling at the back of the room.

"Are you talking, Candy?"

"Yes," Candy answers.

"Well, be quiet then until everyone is done," Mr. Clarke directs and goes back to rearranging his materials.

"Quiet, everyone," he again directs, looking up in response to a hum of voices around the room. "Is everyone finished? . . . Good."

Mr. Clarke collects the papers, puts them on his desk, and then begins, "Now, what did we find for the latitude of Cairo?"

"Thirty," Miguel volunteers.

"North or south, Miguel? . . . Wait a minute. Doris . . . Candy, this is the third time this period that I've had to say something to you about your talking, and the period isn't even 20 minutes old yet. Get out your rules and read me the rule about talking without permission. . . . Doris?"

". . . Um . . ."

"It's supposed to be in the front of your notebook." (Still no response.)

"Candy?"

"'No speaking without permission of the teacher,'" Candy reads from the front page of her notebook.

"Doris, where are your rules?"

"I don't know."

"Move up here," Mr. Clarke directs, pointing to an empty desk at the front of the room. "You've been bothering me all week. If you can't learn to be quiet, you will be up here for the rest of the year."

Mr. Clarke then continues with the lesson.

1. Would Joel Clarke's response to Doris and Candy, "Doris and Candy, please stop talking while I'm returning the papers. Can't you just sit quietly for 1 minute?" best be described as passive, assertive, or hostile? Explain why you think so.
2. Assess Joel's "withitness" in his intervention with Kent and Melissa. Provide evidence from the case study to support your assessment.
3. Using the characteristics of effective intervention as a basis, assess Joel's intervention with Doris and Candy when he said that this was the third time he had to talk to them. Provide evidence from the case study to support your assessment.

VIDEO EXERCISE

Go to MyEducationLab and select the topic "Classroom Management" and watch the video "Modeling Mutual Respect, Routines, and Transitions" and answer the questions that follow the video episode.

DEVELOPING YOUR PORTFOLIO

The purpose of this activity is to encourage you to begin to design a system for dealing with misbehavior in your classroom when it occurs.

Look again at the list of rules that you prepared for the "Developing Your Portfolio" section in Chapter 2.

- Prepare a set of reinforcers that you might offer students for their compliance with the rules.
- Prepare a set of punishers that you would apply in the event of misbehavior. Describe the consequence for the first incidence of misbehavior, the second incidence of misbehavior, and so on.
- Construct an "I" message that you might use in the event of a misbehavior, such as speaking or leaving a seat without permission or failing to bring needed materials to class.

QUESTIONS FOR DISCUSSION

1. What proportion of the management problems that teachers face are "their own fault"? What could these teachers do to prevent those problems?

2. Are classrooms harder to manage, easier to manage, or similarly difficult to manage compared with 5 years ago? Ten years ago? If you believe they are harder to manage, why do you think so? If you believe they are easier to manage, why do you think so?

3. How important a problem is violence in schools? Why do you think so?

4. How significant a problem for learning is the threat to students of physical harm? Is this problem being described accurately in the public media and in professional journals? Explain.

5. To what extent are classroom management problems detracting from students' ability to benefit from instruction? Explain.

6. In some schools, management problems seem to be very serious, whereas in others they do not seem to be a major problem. To what would you attribute the difference?

SUGGESTIONS FOR FIELD EXPERIENCE

1. Interview a teacher. Ask the following questions:
   a. How do you typically handle management incidents? Would you offer two specific examples?
   b. What do you feel are your most chronic problems?
   c. Is this class harder or easier to manage than your other classes (or last year's class)? Why is this class harder or easier to manage?
   d. Have you ever had a serious incident, such as an attack on you or a fight between students? What did you do in response to the incident?
   e. What do you feel are the differences between effective and ineffective managers?
   f. Do you call parents about behavior problems with your students? If you do, how effective do you believe it is in intervening?
   g. Do you ever take points away from a student's average for misbehavior? If so, how effective is this practice?
   h. Do you ever give students extra points on their averages for desirable behavior? If so, how effective is this practice?

2. Observe in a classroom. Look for the following in your observation:
   a. Describe specifically how the teacher intervenes when a management incident occurs.
   b. Describe the differences in the way the teacher responds in the case of a minor incident compared with a more serious incident.
   c. How consistently does the teacher respond in cases of management incidents?
   d. How much emphasis does the teacher place on the development of learner responsibility compared with maintaining control of the students' behaviors?

TOOLS FOR TEACHING

Print References

Emmer, E. T., Evertson, C. M., & Worsham, M. E. (2006). *Classroom management for middle and high school teachers* (7th ed.). Boston: Allyn & Bacon. A widely respected text that provides detailed suggestions for responding to classroom management problems in middle and high schools.

Evertson, C. M., Emmer, E. T., & Worsham, M. E. (2006). *Classroom management for elementary teachers* (7th ed.). Boston: Allyn & Bacon. A widely respected text that provides detailed suggestions for responding to classroom management problems in elementary schools.

Evertson, C. M., & Weinstein, C. S. (Eds.). (2006). *Handbook of classroom management research, practice, and contemporary issues.* Mahwah, NJ: Lawrence Erlbaum Associates. This handbook provides a comprehensive overview of research and effective practice in classroom management.

Good, T. L., & Brophy, J. E. (2008). *Looking in classrooms* (10th ed.). Boston: Allyn & Bacon. This well-known and widely used text includes a chapter specifically devoted to effective responses to disruptive behavior.

Marzano, R. J., Marzano, J. S., & Pickering, D. J. (2003). *Classroom management that works: Research-based strategies for every teacher.* Alexandria, VA: Association for Supervision and Curriculum Development. This research-based resource provides specific strategies for responding to classroom management problems.

Web Sites

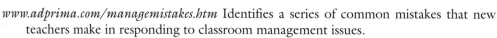

www.adprima.com/managemistakes.htm Identifies a series of common mistakes that new teachers make in responding to classroom management issues.

www.adprima.com/managing.htm Offers suggestions for responding to classroom management issues as well as other suggestions for creating an orderly classroom.

www.4faculty.org/includes/images/solutionstable.pdf Identifies a series of classroom management issues and suggests possible solutions to each.

www.kde.state.ky.us/KDE/Instructional+Resources/Career+and+Technical+Education/ Classroom+Management.htm Offers one state's approach to offering suggestions to teachers about dealing with classroom management issues.

Standards and Planning for Instruction

Standards and the Goals of Instruction

INTRODUCTION

All teachers have goals when they teach, but the goals that teachers select differ in their value to students. For example, some teachers have as their goal keeping students busy and quiet until the bell rings; other teachers have as their goal getting through a textbook or covering a chapter in the following week. The value of these goals is questionable at best and is hard to defend from a professional standpoint because they fail to identify important learner outcomes. This chapter is designed to help you formulate meaningful goals for the students you will teach.

LEARNER OBJECTIVES

After completing your study of Chapter 4, you should be able to do the following:

- Describe major sources of goals for the school curriculum

- Explain similarities and differences among the three domains—affective, psychomotor, and cognitive
- Describe the different levels of the affective, psychomotor, and cognitive domains
- Describe differences between abstractions and facts

APPLYING STANDARDS AND GOALS IN THE CLASSROOM

Following is a case study in which an elementary school teacher presents a science lesson. As you read the case study, consider the following questions:

- What are the goals of this lesson?
- How does the lesson address the affective, physical, and/or intellectual needs of the students?
- Is the teaching focused more on facts or ideas in this lesson?

Traci Connell, a first-grade teacher, begins her science lesson by asking her children, "What have we been talking about this week that ticks . . . Danielle?"

"Our hearts."

"Yes. Our hearts are in our bodies, and they make a ticking sound. Now today we are going to talk about something else that ticks. I'm going to give you two clues, and I want you to look up at the board. Your first clue is a poem. I'll read the first verse, and then I want you to read the next verse, and then I'll finish up. The poem is called 'Big Gears, Little Gears.' OK, I'll start."

Traci reads the first verse and then assists the class with reading the second one. After concluding, she says, "We have been talking a lot about gears, and this poem is clue number 1. Remember, we are looking for something that is not our heart but ticks. Here is clue number 2. Watch very carefully as I turn this handle and see what happens to the pointer."

Traci then moves about the room so the children can clearly see the demonstration, which involves a handle turning gears that then moves a pointer.

"This represents something, and I would like for you to raise your hand and tell me if you think you know. [Pause.] What do you think this represents? What is it . . . Deymon?"

"A clock," Deymon says hesitantly.

"Good thinking," Traci replies enthusiastically. "This is a clock, a machine that tells time. Now, when this handle goes around one time, how many times do you think the pointer is going to go around . . . Bing Jie?"

"Halfway."

"So, you think it will go from the top to the bottom?" Traci asks.

"Yes," Bing Jie answered.

"OK, let's watch and see what happens." Traci then proceeds to turn the handle slowly as the children observe both the handle and the pointer.

"Now, think about what you saw. We'll come back to this question, but now I want to ask you about something else. We were talking about gears in science, and, with what you have seen, what do you think is inside a clock . . . Frank?"

"Gears," Frank says.

"Right, and later on this morning I am going to show you what is inside that big clock against the wall. Today we are going to start working on time, and you are going to be able to tell time and show time by drawing the hour hand and the minute hand. You can be as creative as you want as long as you have the hands in your drawing. Later on we're going to talk about whether or not you like clocks with hands or clocks with numbers, but first I need to ask you a question. How is the heart like a clock . . . Laura?"

"It beats and it ticks."

"What happens if the clock stops ticking? Will it still continue to tell time?"

"No," Laura replies.

"Why not?"

"Because the gears inside don't move the point."

"Very good. Now, what makes your heart beat or move? [Pause.] What do you need to take into your body to make your heart work?"

"Air," Atiya says.

"And what's in the air that your heart needs?"

"Oxygen," Atiya replies.

"Great," Traci continues, "and we can call that energy. Now, what kind of energy does a clock need, Bryan?"

"The gears."

"Yes, but what makes the gears turn? [Pause.] What if we use the word power *for energy?"*

"Oh, batteries," Bryan replies.

"Sure, batteries, or we could plug it in the wall," Traci adds. "Good thinking. Now let's hold on to that thought; we'll return to it in a little bit. For now I have several activities I'd like you to work on in your groups."

Traci spends the remainder of the class involving the children in a variety of hands-on activities involving time and clocks.

SOURCES OF GOALS

The purpose of this chapter is to help you think about your own teaching goals, or what you want students to learn in your classroom. We discuss the different types of goals found in our schools today, providing you with the conceptual tools necessary to select and analyze goals for your own teaching. These goals then will serve as the starting point for the construction of specific learning objectives, which is the focus of Chapter 5. In subsequent chapters, we discuss the process of translating objectives into teaching and assessment strategies that can be implemented in elementary and secondary classrooms.

Before we launch into our discussion of goals, we need to mention basic differences between goals and objectives. Goals are broad statements of educational intent. Typically, they are described in general, abstract terms. Examples are the following:

To understand the importance of the Civil War in U.S. history

To appreciate the importance of good study habits

To know basic principles of proper nutrition

Objectives, by contrast, are typically stated using more specific behavioral terms in an attempt to define educational outcomes precisely. Examples are the following:

Students will identify examples of participles, gerunds, and infinitives.

Students will match major historical events with appropriate U.S. presidents.

Students will apply the Pythagorean theorem to various word problems.

Verbs like *identify, match,* and *apply* specify what is expected of students as they learn and attain the objective. In the next chapter, we discuss the relationship between goals and objectives and how teachers can use goals as the beginning point in the planning process.

Standards as a Source of Goals

As discussed in Chapter 1, states have the responsibility for educating its citizens and use standards to focus our educational efforts on specific kinds of content. In turn, school districts incorporate these **standards** into their curricula. In terms of state standards, these goals become content standards, and objectives become benchmarks (Wiggins & McTighe, 2005).

For example, in the chapter-opening case study, Traci Connell introduced an interdisciplinary science lesson by referring to an earlier lesson that focused on the heart as a foundation for a teacher-led discussion on clocks. If Traci teaches in Nebraska, she would be facilitating a first-grade science standard or goal that states that "science as inquiry requires students to combine processes and scientific knowledge with scientific reasoning and critical thinking to develop their understanding of science." With regard to benchmarks or objectives, she would be addressing the need of students to develop the abilities needed to do scientific inquiry by doing the following:

- Asking questions about their surroundings
- Collecting scientific information from careful observation
- Using simple equipment and tools to extend their senses
- Sharing findings with classmates, families, and community members

Teachers in all states are expected to address standards and benchmarks such as these and use them as guidelines for establishing goals and objectives for their units and lesson plans.

The Child as a Source of Goals

Effective teachers ask two basic questions in considering their individual goals for instruction: What are schools for? and How does my class fit into the larger picture? One pair of answers to these questions is that schools are for people, and the function of both the school and its classrooms is to help young people develop to the fullest extent of their potential. In other words, one source of goals for instruction can be found in the **child** or students themselves (Armstrong, 2003). In tapping this source of curriculum goals, the teacher is basically asking the question, How can the knowledge and skills I possess as a teacher help my students develop into healthy and functioning adults? The answer to this question depends on many factors, such as the students, their cultural backgrounds, their developmental levels, and the subjects being taught.

Society as a Source of Goals

Another way to approach the task of establishing teaching goals is to examine the **society** in which students live and will ultimately function and decide how schools can help students meet the challenges of that society effectively (Armstrong, 2003). Proponents of this view of the curriculum believe that the role of the school is to prepare students for life and that classroom content should be matched to the demands of everyday living. The value of goals established by this approach is measured in terms of their usefulness to the individual in functioning in today's world. A major focus of this emphasis is helping students to understand how basically abstract processes like math have potential utility for functioning in the worlds of work and play. More specifically, when thinking in terms of society goals, the place of mathematics in the curriculum is determined by the extent to which it can help students solve problems through the application of math skills in 21st-century America (Marquez & Westbrook, 2007).

The Academic Disciplines as Sources of Goals

A final way to generate goals for instruction is to examine the various **academic disciplines** and determine which knowledge in these disciplines is most important or central to

Standardized tests often focus on classical information found in the academic disciplines.

T. Hubbard/Merrill

understanding these different content areas (Armstrong, 2003). Proponents of this approach to goal setting contend that the function of the schools is not so much to help students adjust to society or to give them short-range skills that will quickly become outmoded in today's rapidly changing world but rather to transmit to students knowledge that has stood the test of time. These same people call attention to the immense number of changes that have occurred in the past 20 or 30 years and point out that anything other than an academically oriented curriculum that transcends these changes would soon be outmoded. In addition, they believe that a number of other institutions, like the family and the church, are much better suited to teach learner-oriented or life-adjustment skills and that the schools should focus on basic knowledge and intellectual or cognitive skills.

Sometimes goals are selected for inclusion in an academically oriented curriculum because they form the foundation or basis for other goals. For example, teaching young children the concepts of right and left, up and down, big and little, and square and circle is justified in terms of the future value of those concepts in the teaching of reading in addition to their more immediate utilitarian value. These goals are called *readiness skills*.

EXERCISE 4.1

Examine the following goals and try to determine whether their primary focus is the child (c), society (s), or the academic disciplines (a).

1. Junior high social studies students will know the 13 states of the Confederacy.
2. First-year high school math students will understand how to compute cost per unit when given aggregate costs.
3. Fifth-grade science students will understand the concept of an ecosystem.
4. First-grade students will understand that they have rights and responsibilities.
5. Sixth-grade health students will understand how to care for cuts and abrasions.
6. Senior high civics students will understand the voting system in their city, state, and country.
7. Junior high health students will know the causes, symptoms, and means of preventing venereal disease.
8. First-year biology students will know the characteristics of monocotyledons and dicotyledons.
9. Senior high driver education students will know the driving regulations in their state.
10. Fifth-grade math students will know how to convert fractions into decimals.

DIVERSITY IN THE CLASSROOM

Sources of Goals

If one of our goals is to meet the learning needs of every child, then student diversity raises important questions about the sources of our goals. In this section, we use the concept of diversity to examine different sources of goals. We contend that each of these perspectives alone provides an inadequate and distorted view of education and that teachers need to consider all sources of goals when trying to meet the needs of the diverse students in their classrooms.

Currently, the political pendulum is swinging in the direction of academic disciplines and society as primary sources of goals (Casserly, 2002; Mathis, 2003). Accountability, high-stakes testing, and the federal No Child Left Behind Act emphasize content and skill acquisition. In essence, these movements place primary emphasis on every child learning basic content and skills and minimize the importance of individual differences. In fact, some of the major controversies surrounding the current testing movement involve the ways that testing procedures should accommodate learners with exceptionalities and English-language learners, which represent major dimensions of diversity (Abedi, Hofstetter, & Lord, 2004; Olson, 2004).

Critics of this narrow focus on academics contend that it ignores important individual differences and standardizes the curriculum in ways that are unhealthy for children (Hatch, 2002). A more moderate position contends that the emphasis on academic standards only suggests what to teach, not how (Tomlinson, 2000). Under the guidance of academic goals and standards, teachers are free to differentiate instruction in terms of materials (e.g., different reading levels of the same text), learning tasks (e.g., listening versus reading), and the amount of support or scaffolding provided by the teacher.

The society as a source of goals also poses problems from a diversity perspective. Given the considerable student diversity in terms of backgrounds and abilities and the tremendous number of possible niches and roles to fill in our complex and multifaceted society, is it possible to define essential skills that all members of society should possess? In addition, how should the world of work be defined? Some critics question whether schools should have as their primary mission preparing students to work for corporations (Bracey, 2003). Should not schools have broader purposes, such as helping each child achieve maximum personal growth and happiness?

The child as a source of curriculum goals also creates controversies. While few would argue with trying to help students develop into healthy and happy adults, critics question whether this orientation provides a realistic structure for curriculum development (Ravitch, 2000). Individualization, once popular in the 1970s and 1980s, has proven logistically difficult to implement in most classrooms (Good & Brophy, 2008). In addition, critics of a child-centered curriculum question whether we are not doing a disservice to students by not providing a uniform knowledge base for all students (Marzano, 2003). Others contend that a child-centered curriculum need not ignore essential knowledge and skills. Deborah Stipek (2004), an expert in the field of learning and motivation, contends, "There is no reason why attention to young children's intellectual skills needs to come at the cost of health care and opportunities to develop socially and emotionally" (p. 52).

Where does this leave the classroom teacher? Each teacher is faced with the daunting task of balancing these three sources of goals as they attempt to design curricula to meet the diverse learning needs of their students. A challenging task? Yes, but it is not impossible, as thousands of sensitive and effective teachers demonstrate on a daily basis in their classrooms.

THE THREE DOMAINS OF LEARNING

When teachers think about what to teach, they also need to consider the nature of the learning experiences that students will encounter. Just as goals can be differentiated in terms of

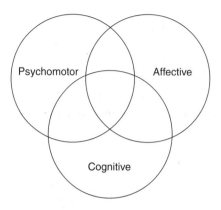

Figure 4.1 The Three Domains of Learning

their sources, goals can be described in terms of the type of learning experiences intended. In this respect, we can describe goals as being concerned primarily with three domains: the development of muscular skills and coordination (psychomotor), the growth of attitudes or values (affective), or the acquisition of knowledge and intellectual skills (cognitive).

Understanding differences between goals in the different domains helps clarify teachers' thinking about what they are trying to teach or accomplish. These differences, then, have implications for planning, implementing, and assessment. The more clearly teachers understand what they are trying to accomplish, the greater the chance that they will achieve those goals (Marzano, 2003).

As we examine the three domains of learning, remember that they do not occur in isolation but rather work together to influence one whole being. Some goals are easily classifiable into one of the three domains, while others seem to overlap a great deal. This overlap appears in Figure 4.1. One example of an integrated behavior that incorporates all three domains of learning in school is handwriting. Children must have the small-muscle coordination to make the necessary intricate movements (psychomotor), they must know what movements are used to form the letters (cognitive), and they must want to perform these enough so that proficiency can be developed through practice (affective).

Now let's consider each of these three domains and examine ways to classify goals and objectives at different levels.

The Psychomotor Domain

Developing muscular strength and coordination is the primary function of goals within the **psychomotor domain.** Although this domain is the least emphasized in our schools, its impact varies according to the age level of the students and the subject. Greater emphasis is given to the psychomotor domain at lower grade levels, and an increased emphasis is found in subjects such as physical education, vocational education, and music. Now let's examine each of the levels in this domain. Note that as the levels progress, the student outcomes become more complex and integrated (Harrow, 1972; Jewett & Mullan, 1977; Moore, 1992).

Levels of the Psychomotor Domain.

Reflex Movements.   Reflex movements or actions are elicited in response to some stimulus without conscious volition on the learner's part. They are not voluntary movements but may be considered as an essential base for movement behavior.

Fundamental Movements.   Basic fundamental movement patterns occur in the learner during the first year of life. The common basic movement behaviors include visually tracking an object, reaching, grasping, manipulating an object with the hands, and progressing through the developmental stages of crawling, creeping, and walking.

Perceptual Abilities.   Although this level appears to suggest cognitive as well as psychomotor behaviors, it is included in the psychomotor domain because many investigators claim that perceptual and motor functions are inseparable. These abilities assist learners in interpreting stimuli, thus enabling them to make necessary adjustments to their environment.

Physical Abilities.   Physical abilities include endurance, strength, flexibility, and agility and are essential to the efficient functioning of the learner. Proper functioning of the various systems of the body enable learners to meet the demands placed on them by their environment. These physical abilities are in fact an essential part of the foundation for the development of skilled movements.

Skilled Movements.   Skilled movement can be thought of in several ways. It can mean proficiency in performing a task. Skill can also connote the economy of effort a learner displays while perfecting a complex movement or signify that an integration of learner behavior regarding a specific task has occurred. In other words, proficiency at this level includes a degree of efficiency in performance of a specific, reasonably complex movement behavior.

Nondiscursive Communication.   Nonverbal communication plays a central role in everyday life and is an important aspect of the learner's psychomotor development. At this level, each learner develops a style of moving that communicates his or her feelings about his or her affective self to the perceptive observer. Accurately interpreting these communicative movement behaviors heightens an educator's perceptions of the learner's feelings, needs, and interest, thereby enabling the educator to make more meaningful selections of learning strategies for that particular learner.

Examples of Goals in the Psychomotor Domain.

- For 10th-grade physical education students to increase their ability to play volleyball so that, when given a practice situation, students will be able to correctly serve (clear the net in the appropriate quadrant) the ball 7 out of 10 times
- For ninth-grade health students to become more familiar with the cardiovascular system so that, without aid, they will be able to discuss three methods developing cardiovascular strength and endurance
- For 12th-grade swimming students to increase their swimming abilities so that, when given a competitive situation, they will undertake the 100-yard butterfly in less than 1 minute, 20 seconds.

As you can see from these examples, the psychomotor domain involves not only the development of strength and endurance but also the teaching of skills and the development of coordination.

The Affective Domain

The **affective domain,** which deals with attitudes, feelings, and values, is probably the most pervasive in terms of implicit inclusion in the curriculum. It is implicit in that virtually all teachers want their students to go away from their classes with more positive attitudes toward the subjects they study, themselves, and other students, but it is seldom made explicit and then consciously translated into teaching procedures.

The primary focus of the affective domain is the development of attitudes and values. We can have attitudes about educationally unimportant things like spinach and baseball or more educationally important things like cultural minority groups or the environment. Like most aspects of human behavior, attitudes are learned and result from experiences. The fact that attitudes are formed through experiences is fortunate in the sense that it allows teachers to positively influence them, but it also places a burden of responsibility on teachers not to contribute to the development of negative attitudes toward various aspects of schooling.

A second major goal in the affective domain is the development of values. Values differ from attitudes in that they are more global, referring not to specific objects such as school or a school subject but instead to aims of existence or ways of leading a life. Some typical values taught in our schools are honesty, self-respect, respect for others, and broad-mindedness. In teaching these values, we hope that they will become character traits that influence the ways students act. Now let's see how the development of values and attitudes works at the different level of the affective domain (Krathwohl, Bloom, & Masia, 1964).

Levels of the Affective Domain.

Receiving.   The lowest level of the affective domain is receiving. The key element at this level is that students exhibit a degree of open-mindedness to new ideas, for without this trait they may not be receptive to the new information under study. The critical factor at this level is that students are open to different ideas. Some examples of behaviors at this level include being willing to listen to others' points of view and being receptive to new information about a controversial topic.

Responding.   The significant difference between responding and receiving is that the former assumes a somewhat positive attitude, whereas the latter implies neutrality. At the responding level, students exhibit some interest, involvement, or even commitment. Some examples of behaviors at this level include being willing to dialogue about a controversial topic or being willing to participate in a new activity introduced in physical education class.

Valuing.   This level of the affective domain implies that students perceive an attitude, value, or belief as having worth and that these have become internalized in terms of behavior and reflected on a continual basis. Unlike the two previous levels of the affective domain, at the valuing level the teacher does not initiate the behavior. Instead, it is initiated by the student, who is committed to a particular position and is willing to discuss and support that position openly. Some examples of behaviors at this level include voluntarily going to an art museum after a presentation on artists displayed at this museum or arguing for a particular position on a controversial topic.

Organization.   The organization level builds on the valuing level in that the latter is singular and the former implies an organized and integrated system. In other words, organization implies a comprehensive and integrated commitment to a specific belief or position. Examples here include integrating something learned at school, such as racial tolerance, into a more comprehensive view of people and how we should all treat each other.

Characterization by a Value or Value Complex.   The previous levels of the affective domain make it possible for the student to integrate different attitudes and values into a comprehensive worldview. This level allows students to develop personal yet global views about such things as the nature of the universe or a philosophy of life. For example, in a health class, students operating at this level integrate attitudes and views about healthy lifestyles into a coherent and comprehensive plan for living.

As teachers work with these different levels of the affective domain, their goal is to help students internalize positive attitudes and values so that they will ultimately guide student behavior.

The Cognitive Domain

The most common types of instructional goals found in our schools are cognitive. This is because the **cognitive domain** focuses on the transmission of knowledge and strategies, which is the most prevalent view of the role of the school both today and in the past. We estimate that anywhere from 80% to 90% of the average elementary and secondary student's school time is devoted to the attainment of cognitive goals. This emphasis can be seen in federal and state standards, in the goals that teachers set in their lesson plans, in the kinds of tests teachers give, and in the standardized tests used to hold both teachers and students accountable.

The cognitive domain is sometimes confused with the affective domain. One way of differentiating between the two is to think of the cognitive domain as involving rational and analytical processes, whereas the affective domain deals with feelings and likes and dislikes. Like the affective and psychomotor domains, the cognitive domain is hierarchical, meaning that successful performance at a higher level is dependent on success at lower levels.

The current cognitive taxonomy (see Figure 4.2) is an updated version of the classic one that was widely used in education since 1956 (Bloom, Englehart, Furst, Hill, & Krathwohl, 1956). The current taxonomy breaks educational goals into six processes, or different ways of dealing with information. We describe these six processes next.

In addition to processes, the taxonomy also separates goals into four knowledge dimensions: factual, conceptual, procedural, and metacognitive. We describe the first two of these later in the chapter; we discuss the latter two in Chapters 8 and 9 when we disucuss specific instructional strategies. Now let's look at the different levels of the cognitive taxonomy.

Levels of the Cognitive Domain.

Remembering.   Remembering important names, dates, and terms is a foundational level for the ones that follow. This area is sometimes referred to as "low level" because it does not call

Figure 4.2   A Taxonomy for Learning, Teaching, and Assessing

The Knowledge Dimension	The Cognitive Process Dimension					
	1. Remember	2. Understand	3. Apply	4. Analyze	5. Evaluate	6. Create
A. Factual knowledge						
B. Conceptual knowledge						
C. Procedural knowledge						
D. Metacognitive knowledge						

for the processing or manipulation of information. However, learning experts remind us that knowledge is one of the basic building blocks for all subsequent learning (Bruning, Schraw, Norby, & Ronning, 2004). Simply stated, the remembering level involves recall or recognition of previously learned material, such as remembering that George Washington was the first president of the United States. Remembering differs from the other levels of the cognitive domain because the act of retrieving different types of information, such as facts, does not require us to do anything with the information. The other levels of the cognitive domain require us to alter or employ information in our thinking.

Understanding.   Understanding is the next level in the domain and requires students to demonstrate comprehension by altering or manipulating information. It represents a step beyond remembering because it asks students to transform information into a form that is understandable to them. Students can do this in several ways.

Restating information in one's own words is perhaps the most basic form of understanding. Translation is another form of understanding that requires a change in format so that the information can be presented in a different way. Students regularly accomplish this task when taking arithmetic problems in the form of words and changing them into numerical symbols. Students can also demonstrate that they understand something by interpreting it from presented material. For example,

given a bar graph representing the major crops grown in the United States (see Figure 4.3), the students will orally name the most widely produced crops.

The major focus of goals involving understanding goals is for students to be able to demonstrate their basic grasp of ideas in some way.

Applying.   Applying, the next level in the cognitive domain, requires using information in some type of problem solving. Two critical characteristics are involved at the application level. The first is that the situation confronting students should be original, or one that has not been encountered before or practiced previously. Otherwise, students would simply be recalling the desired answer or solution.

Figure 4.3   A Bar Graph Handout

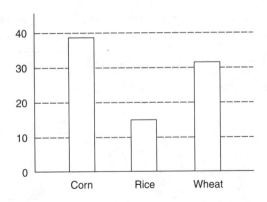

The second characteristic is that the students must select an appropriate tool, solution, equation, or algorithm that in turn is correctly applied to the problem at hand. For example,

> given a drawing of a house and yard (see Figure 4.4), the students will correctly determine the area of the backyard.

The first thing students must do is determine the nature of the problem—that is, one involving the area of a rectangle. Then they must recall the appropriate formula and apply it to the data to solve the problem. Again, it is assumed that the students have not been confronted with this specific problem at a prior time, or only a remembering-level operation would be involved.

Analyzing.   In its basic form, analysis involves the process of taking a whole entity or phenomenon and breaking it down into its separate parts, or determining its particular characteristics. A common laboratory exercise involving analysis occurs when a chemistry student is provided with a substance and is asked to determine its constituent elements. This might involve weighing, dissolving, splitting, flaming, and testing with various chemicals and compounds. In most academic situations, however, it is more common to analyze printed materials in the form of essays, speeches, editorials, poems, and books.

In working at the analysis level, students engage in activities such as identifying the following:

- Assumptions
- Implications
- Fallacies
- Central themes
- Persuasion
- Consistency

In each of these, students are breaking a complex phenomenon into simpler, constituent parts.

Evaluating.   This next level of the cognitive domain requires students to make a value judgment about some product or project. However, the judgment in and of itself is

Figure 4.4   A House/Yard Handout

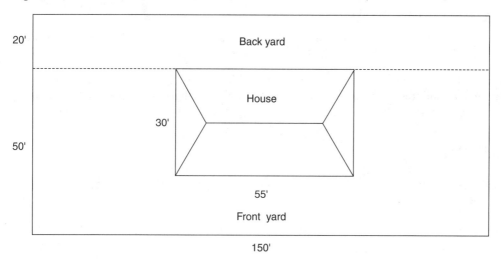

insufficient; it must be supplemented with a reasoned explanation for the evaluation. For example, if a teacher asks his elementary students, "What is the best type of dog for a pet?" and the children respond excitedly with examples such as labrador, boxer, cocker spaniel, and poodle, at this point the children are merely expressing a feeling or an opinion and therefore are operating in the affective domain.

Although making a judgment is important, when considering the evaluating level, we need something in addition—a criterion. A critical process necessary at the evaluating level is the intellectual support or defense of judgment. For example, the teacher might facilitate the development of criteria for the dog question by encouraging students to consider ones that might include the following:

1. The best dog should be under 50 pounds, or it will cost too much to feed.
2. The best dog should have a gentle disposition.
3. The best dog should be short haired if in a warm climate.
4. The best dog should be short eared because a moist climate would promote ear infections.

Having established some criteria, the teacher can then help students apply the criteria to the list of four dogs mentioned. The children would then be operating at the evaluating level because they used criteria in constructing their responses.

Creating.   Creating involves the integration of elements into the synthesis of a unique entity. Creating is more or less the opposite of analyzing. Whereas analyzing requires us to take something apart, creating involves the process of putting things together to produce a new and unique whole. There are two critical considerations when assigning students creative-level activities. The first is that the finished product must be new and unique to the student, not to the world. The second point is that a criterion must be present in order to allow us to apply a standard of success. For example,

given the use of any materials of their choice, wood-shop students will design and build an original table that will be stable and have a finished surface.

The fact that the finished product may resemble other tables is immaterial; the students designed it, and it is theirs. In that it is a creative exercise, there is room for subjective evaluation regarding excellence, but clear-cut criteria (e.g., stability and a finished surface) are used to determine whether the task has been accomplished successfully.

EXERCISE 4.2

Read the following goals and place an *r* in front of those written at the remembering level, a *u* in front of those written at the understanding level, an *ap* in front of those written at the applying level, an *a* in front of those written at the analyzing level, an *e* written in front of those at the evaluation level, and a *c* in front of those written at the creating level.

_____   1. Given appropriate materials, the student will construct a model of an airplane that clearly reflects a set of preexisting specifications.

_____   2. Algebra students will be able to differentiate between quadratic and nonquadratic equations.

_____   3. Given any materials of her choice, the homemaking student will create a dress that is sleeveless and below knee length and that contains at least two different kinds of material.

_____   4. Kindergarten students will be able to tell the names of different farm animals.

_____   5. Given photographs of three fashion designs, the student will determine which is the best and support the selection by addressing issue of cost, style, and availability.

_____   6. Without aid, the student will identify one assumption found in the article "Why French Fashion Wins Out!"

_____   7. Given an amount of energy consumed and the rate per consumed unit, the student will correctly determine the total amount due on an electric bill.

CONTENT IN THE COGNITIVE DOMAIN

Another way to analyze the cognitive domain is to examine the different kinds of content found in that area. The basic idea is that not all content within the cognitive domain is of equal worth; some types of content are more valuable than others in helping students understand the world around them. These ideas are called *abstractions*. In this section, we examine abstractions and analyze how teachers help students learn this important form of content.

Abstractions

Abstractions are the ideas people use to describe, understand, and simplify the world. They are, in a sense, the mental templates we use to perceive and understand our environment. Abstractions form an important part of the curriculum at every grade level. To begin this discussion, examine the following lessons and see if you can identify the abstraction being taught.

Tanya Harris was trying to teach her kindergarten students the basic shapes. She did this by cutting out squares, circles, and rectangles from felt and putting them in a paper bag. Students took turns coming up to the front of the class, pulling one piece of felt out of the bag, and putting it in the correct circle on the board.

Kim Lawson wanted his fifth-grade students to understand basic differences among amphibians, reptiles, and mammals. They read paragraphs about different animals and looked at pictures of them and then tried to classify them into the correct area.

Sean Harris introduced the topic of Elizabethan sonnets by placing several on a handout. He distributed this handout to his 10th-grade literature class without an introduction and asked the class to analyze them for similarities and differences.

Abstractions describe regularities or patterns in the world around us, such as the characteristics of amphibians, reptiles, and mammals in Kim Lawson's lesson. The power in understanding patterns or abstractions is enormous. They greatly simplify the world for us because we need only remember the pattern, not the individual examples that fit it. Understanding abstractions allows students to categorize future examples, such as the basic shapes and Elizabethan sonnets referred to in Tanya Harris's and Sean Harris's lessons, respectively, and act strategically when encountering additional new ones.

As an example of the power of abstract patterns, consider the spelling rule "*i* before *e* except after *c*." Academic rules are another form of pattern. Knowing this academic rule allows a learner to spell individual words, such as *retrieve, believe, conceive, conceit,* and *perceive*. Admittedly, the learner must know the pattern's exceptions, but the pattern makes it unnecessary for the learner to remember how to spell all words individually.

One classical way to think of education is to view it as the process of transmitting existing knowledge and culture to the next generation (Jacobsen, 2003b). For example, social studies education is concerned with teaching students to understand abstractions such as democracy, socialism, and social stratification. Another example of a social studies abstraction is the principle that the more economically diverse an economy, the more stable it is when economic changes occur or that when supply stays constant, price is directly related to demand.

In a similar manner, science teaching involves the teaching of abstractions such as *mammal, ion,* and *magnetism*. Students learn that acids neutralize bases and that the more recent animal phyla have more complex systems.

English or language arts classes also teach abstractions, such as *adverb, metaphor,* and *Elizabethan sonnet*. Students learn that when the subject is singular, they add an *s* to the verb. And, when several adjectives modify a noun, the article goes first. Similar analyses could be done for each of the subject matter areas.

Abstractions form a central core for most subjects taught in schools and constitute a major way of organizing standards and benchmarks. We now turn our attention to the two major types of abstractions taught at the elementary and secondary levels: concepts and generalizations.

Concepts

Concepts are ideas that refer to a class or category in which all the members share some common characteristics (Eggen & Kauchak, 2007). Many abstractions previously mentioned are concepts. For example, *democracy, ion,* and *adverb* are all concepts.

We use defining characteristics to decide whether a particular example belongs in the concept. In addition to the essential or defining characteristics, examples of concepts also contain irrelevant or nonessential characteristics. In the case of the concept *adverb*, irrelevant characteristics include the length of the word, its sound, and the number of consonants or vowels in it. These irrelevant characteristics tell us nothing about whether a word is an adverb. In trying to learn a concept, these nonessential characteristics represent noise that the learner must filter out to focus on the essential characteristics. Essential characteristics are important to remember because they make up the rule for class membership; they help determine whether something is a positive or a negative example of a concept.

Typically, we think of concepts as being single words that represent ideas. Another way of representing concepts is by a definition; for example, a democracy is a form of government in which the power to make decisions resides in the governed. However, experts caution against confusing concepts with vocabulary terms (Marzano & Kendall, 2003). The major difference is the way they are approached instructionally and what we expect students to learn and know. If *democracy* were approached as a simple vocabulary term, we would expect students to have a general understanding of what the term meant. By contrast, if the term *democracy* were approached as a concept, we would want students to know the history of the idea, some examples and nonexamples of the concept, and the concept's place in the larger picture of government. Consequently, concepts encompass much more than the narrow range covered by vocabulary. Some additional examples of concepts from various disciplines are found in Table 4.1.

Notice that as we have discussed abstractions in general and concepts in particular, we have consistently referred to examples. Research strongly supports the value of examples and nonexamples in concept learning (Bruning et al., 2004; Eggen & Kauchak, 2007). By analyzing the positive examples and noting what they have in common and by contrasting these with negative examples, learners are often able to figure out the essential characteristics for themselves. Effective teachers often make this task easier by explicitly identifying these when they introduce a concept. In addition to providing the student with data from which to extract important characteristics, examples also provide concrete referents in the world. In a sense, they make abstract ideas less abstract.

Another way of teaching someone about a concept is by relating it to other concepts (Medin, Proffitt, & Schwartz, 2000). For example, if you were to ask someone what a bird is, a typical reply would be that it is a kind of animal. In a similar way, a social studies teacher might define a democracy as a form of government. In both instances, the concept being explained was related to a larger, more inclusive or superordinate concept. Superordinate relationships can be illustrated either through the use of conceptual hierarchies or through the use of Venn diagrams, as shown in Figure 4.5.

Knowing that a concept is a member of a larger concept is useful because it allows us to infer characteristics of the larger category to the smaller. For example, if a person knows that a lemur is a mammal, a superordinate concept, then the person could infer that lemurs have mammalian characteristics, such as having fur, being warm blooded, giving live birth, and nursing their young. In a similar manner, if someone tells you that cilantro is an herb, then you know that it is a plant used for seasoning. Superordinate concepts help make concepts

Table 4.1 Concepts from Various Disciplines

Language Arts	Science	Mathematics
Homonym	Nucleus	Set
Antonym	Mitosis	Rational number
Syllable	Evaluation	Lowest common denominator
Alliteration	Mesoderm	Quadratic equation
Quatrain	Metamorphosis	Exponent
Inference	Acid	Base
Tragedy	Base	Tangent
Gerund	Algae	Angle
Plot	Fruit	Axiom
Prefix	Energy	
	Plant	

Social Studies	Music	Art
Federalism	Melody	Line
Climate	Rhythm	Texture
Tax	Syncopation	Batik
Inflation	Harmony	Realism
Boycott	A cappella	Cubism

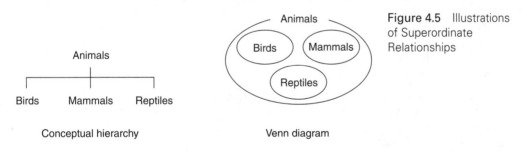

Figure 4.5 Illustrations of Superordinate Relationships

Conceptual hierarchy

Venn diagram

more meaningful by contributing their characteristics to the definition. This is why most dictionaries define concepts in terms of a superordinate one. For example, if you were to look up the term *wok*, you would find it described as a pan for cooking Asian food dishes. The superordinate concept *pan* allows you to infer that this object is probably made of metal, is concave, and is meant to be heated.

In addition to allowing us to infer characteristics, superordinate concepts also show relationships between concepts. For example, in the case of the concept *birds*, linking this concept to animals reestablishes the fact that birds are related to other concepts, like mammals or reptiles. Linking concepts in our teaching is important so that students will see the larger relationships between ideas and learn them as cohesive wholes.

Another one of these linking relationships is between coordinate concepts. Coordinate concepts are abstractions that are subsumed by the superordinate concept and that are different from the concept under consideration. In the previous examples with birds, mammals and reptiles would be coordinate concepts to birds because they are types of animals that are different from birds. To integrate ideas, knowing the coordinate concepts of a given concept is important because coordinate concepts are not only closely related to the target concept but also most easily confused with the concept under study. For example, in a lesson involving the concept *reptiles*, students are most likely to get examples of this concept confused with examples of coordinate concepts, such as amphibians or mammals, rather than unrelated concepts, such as cars, balls, or books.

A third type of relationship that exists between concepts is a subordinate relationship. A subordinate concept is a subset or subcategory of a concept. If you understand superordinate concepts, subordinate concepts are easy to understand because they are reciprocal relationships. For example, in the case of animals and birds, *animal* is superordinate to *bird*, and *bird* is subordinate to *animal*. In a similar manner, the concept *noun* is superordinate to the subordinate concept *proper noun*.

Superordinate, coordinate, and subordinate concepts are discussed again in Chapters 8 and 9 when we describe different instructional strategies. Those wanting to read more about concept teaching in the classroom are referred to Bruning et al. (2004) and Mayer (2008).

EXERCISE 4.3

In answering the following questions, note that more than one response may be correct.

1. Consider the concept *horse*. Which of the following could be superordinate to the concept?
   a. Cow
   b. Domestic animal
   c. Shetland
   d. Beast of burden
   e. None of the above

2. Consider the concept *radio*. If *electrical instructional tools* is superordinate to *radio*, which of the following is coordinate to *radio*?
   a. Encyclopedia
   b. Overhead projector
   c. Textbook
   d. Teacher
   e. None of the above

3. Consider the concept *bread*. Which of the following could be subordinate to the concept?
   a. Rye
   b. Wheat
   c. Meat
   d. White
   e. Vegetable
   f. Food

4. Which of the following could be superordinate to *bread*?
   a. Banana
   b. Rye
   c. Food
   d. Fruit
   e. Vegetable

5. If *fried bacon* and *hot oatmeal* were coordinate to *bread*, which of the following could be superordinate?
   a. Banana
   b. Food
   c. Cooked food
   d. Raw food
   e. Prunes
   f. None of the above

Generalizations

Generalizations are the second major type of abstraction taught in our schools. **Generalizations** are statements about patterns in the world that are either correlational or suggest a causal relationship (Eggen & Kauchak, 2007). Other terms used to refer to these patterns are *rule*, *principle*, or *law*. For our purposes, we will consider these terms synonymous in that all of them describe patterns in the ways that objects and events in our environment operate.

Formulating generalizations promotes students' abilities to understand cause and effect relationships.

"The first one is longer," says Juan.

"The second one has a plural subject," offers Maria.

"Isn't the verb in the first sentence in the past tense?" asks Kathy.

"But so is the verb in the second sentence. And we're supposed to be looking for differences," corrects Jamahl.

After writing these ideas on the board, Ken comments, "Those are all good ideas. Let me give you another example of the first kind of sentence and see if you can narrow your ideas down." To his list he adds the following:

The children ate the oatmeal cookies.

"Look at the sentences again," Ken directs, "and tell me how the first and the third are similar."

The lesson continues until students see that both the first and the third have direct objects. Then Ken discusses the idea of transitive verbs, relating this idea to the examples the students have used.

   a. What kind of abstraction was Ken trying to teach?
   b. What kind of data did the teacher use for examples?

2. Thelma Jones, another English teacher, is also trying to teach her sixth-grade students about verbs. She starts the lesson by saying, "All of you remember what verbs are. We've been working with them all year. Now we're going to learn about a special kind of verb called an *intransitive verb*. Intransitive verbs are verbs that can't take a direct object. Who remembers what a direct object is? Johnny?"

"I think they are words that receive the action of the verb," Johnny responds. "Like, 'He hit me.' *Me* is the direct object."

"Fine, Johnny," Thelma encourages. "Now remember, intransitive verbs are verbs that can't take a direct object. Some examples of intransitive verbs are different forms of the verb *be*, such as *am*, *were*, *was*, and *has been*. I'm going to put a sentence on the board. See if you can tell me whether the verb is intransitive or not."

He was late.

"Yes," offers Saritha, "because it's a form of *be* and can't have a direct object."

"Good," Thelma replies, "and how about this one?"

The woodsman chopped the tree down.

"That can't be intransitive," Rashad says.

"Why not?" Thelma asks.

"Because it has a direct object. *Tree* is the direct object."

"Good, Rashad."

The lesson continues until Thelma feels assured that the students understand intransitive verbs.

   a. What kind of abstraction was Thelma trying to teach?
   b. What kind of data did the teacher use for examples?
   c. How were the two teachers' instructional approaches different? How were they the same?

3. Dave Black wants his fourth-grade students to know biodegradable objects so that they will know what kinds of things can be thrown away and not cause litter. He begins the lesson by

saying, "Today I'm going to teach you about biodegradable objects. Everybody say, 'biodegradable objects.'" He then writes *biodegradable* on the board. "Orange peels and cigar butts are biodegradable. However, bottles and cigarette filters are not. Neither are aluminum foil or bottle caps. Can you tell me what *biodegradable* means?"

Jerry says, "It must be something to do with plant products."

Chris adds, "Or it could be things that are soft."

"Well, let me give you some more information to help you decide," Dave offered.

With that, he takes out a container that is filled with moist dirt and other objects. In the container are a number of biodegradable objects like wood chips and paper that have already started to disintegrate, along with other objects like plastic cups and pop tops. As he takes each of these objects out of the pail, he labels them as either biodegradable or not. On the basis of this information, the class is able to come up with a definition.

a. What kind of abstraction was Dave trying to teach?
b. What kind of data did the teacher use for examples?

Facts

Facts are a second type of content taught in schools. They are statements about the world that are directly observable and typically singular in occurrence, occurring either in the past or in the present. Some examples of facts are the following:

Johnson was one of Lincoln's vice presidents.

Emil von Behring discovered how to control diphtheria.

Japan bombed Pearl Harbor on December 7, 1941.

Each of these statements is a factual report of what happened at a particular place and time in the past. This differentiates them from abstractions in that abstractions are statements about general patterns. Concepts describe categories that are, in a sense, timeless in that what was an adverb yesterday will be an adverb tomorrow. Generalizations describe patterns that were not only valid in the past but also valid now and should also be valid in the future. **Facts**, by contrast, occur only once. This characteristic of facts places severe limitations on their utility to students, as we will see shortly.

Let's look now at a series of facts and their relationship to abstractions. Consider the following:

F.D.R. was from New York.

Richard Nixon was from California.

Both President Bushes were from Texas.

Each of these statements is a fact. Consider also the fact that each state mentioned has a large population. We might then suggest the pattern "Presidents tend to come from populous states." While there are obvious exceptions to this pattern, it tends to be generally valid. Our point in this example is to illustrate the relationship between facts and abstractions. Abstractions are formed by having learners process facts into recognizable patterns. This is one reason for including facts in the curriculum.

The other major reason for learning facts is that some facts are valuable to know in and of themselves and, apart from any relationship to abstractions. Examples of these kinds of facts are the following:

The Declaration of Independence was signed in Philadelphia on July 4, 1776.

Alexander Graham Bell invented the telephone.

Herman Melville wrote *Moby Dick*.

The reason facts such as these are considered inherently valuable is that they make up part of the general store of knowledge shared by most Americans and are considered one of the marks of an educated person. In his book *Cultural Literacy*, Hirsch (1987) equates cultural literacy with knowledge of a certain number of key facts and concepts. However, relative to their utility and importance in the curriculum, facts probably receive an undue amount of emphasis in most classrooms.

Facts and Abstractions: Their Value in the Curriculum

If our biases have not already crept through in our writing, let us make them explicit. We feel that the major amount of time and effort spent in the classroom on cognitive goals should involve the teaching of abstractions rather than facts. The reason for this is that abstractions can be used to summarize large amounts of information, can be used to explain phenomena, and can be used to predict the future.

Abstractions serve a summarizing function in that they can describe large amounts of information in a statement that is easier to remember than all the individual facts. An example from mathematics helps illustrate this point. One of the authors was helping his son with his 9s addition facts. The son was having trouble remembering each of the separate facts, so the father taught him the generalization "When you add 9 to any number, your last number is always one less than the original." (For example, in adding 6 and 9, you get 15, the 5 of which is 1 less than the original 6.) By understanding this generalization, the boy was able to bypass the need for memorizing each of the combinations that 9 could make. Instead, he remembered a general pattern that could apply to all instances. The earlier illustration with the spelling rule "*i* before *e* except after *c*" is another example of the benefits of learning patterns as opposed to isolated facts.

A major argument against learning many isolated facts is that their sheer number makes them hard to remember, as anyone who has taken a course that consisted primarily of the rote memorization of facts can attest. Typically, in courses like this, students memorize the facts for a test and forget them shortly after since these facts are not integrated with other ideas and are seldom ever used again.

A second reason abstractions have particular value in the curriculum is that we can use them to explain phenomena. For example, lower insurance rates for married people and nondrinkers can be explained by generalizations linking these categories of drivers and accident rates. An additional example from teaching further illustrates this explanatory function.

Two elementary teachers taught geometric shapes to their classes. Teacher A pointed out different kinds of circles, squares, rectangles, and triangles around the room, while

Teacher B prepared shapes from cardboard and used these as examples. The students in Teacher B's class seemed to learn the concept faster, but on a posttest the students in Teacher A's class did better at identifying shapes that were embedded in complex designs.

Both of these results can be explained by referring to generalizations that psychologists have found in research on concept learning (Eggen & Kauchak, 2007; Mayer, 2008). The fact that Teacher B's class learned the concept more quickly could be explained by the generalization "Simplifying examples when initially teaching a concept speeds up the learning process." Because of the simple shapes provided by Teacher B, that class had less difficulty in seeing essential characteristics of the concepts in the examples. The fact that Teacher A's class performed better on the embedded figures task can be explained by the generalization "The closer the criterion task is to the learning situation, the better the score on the task." Because Teacher A's class had already had practice in finding shapes embedded in other shapes (like a circle in a clock), they did better on this aspect of the posttest.

A third use of abstractions that makes them valuable in the curriculum is that we can also use them to make predictions about the future. To illustrate this process, analyze the following facts in Table 4.3 and make a prediction about the tides on June 7.

Three generalizations can be formed from the facts in Table 4.3:

High tides and low tides are 6 hours apart.

There are 12 hours between occurrences of high tides and 12 hours between occurrences of low tides.

High and low tides occur 45 minutes later each subsequent day.

On the basis of these generalizations, we can predict that high tides would occur on June 7 at 4:15 a.m. and p.m. and low tides at 10:15 a.m. and p.m. This type of information is valuable to fishermen, sailors, or people just wanting to walk on the beach and not get wet. Note that on the basis of the facts alone, you cannot make this prediction. These facts first need to be processed into abstractions, after which predictions can be made.

The process of making predictions from abstractions is a common and often unconscious everyday occurrence. For example, what time do you expect it to get dark tonight, and where will the sun be when it sets? In addition, how do you expect the temperature this

Table 4.3 High and Low Tides

Date	High Tides	Low Tides
6/4	2:00 a.m.	8:00 a.m.
	2:00 p.m.	8:00 p.m.
6/5	2:45 a.m.	8:45 a.m.
	2:45 p.m.	8:45 p.m.
6/6	3:30 a.m.	9:30 a.m.
	3:30 p.m.	9:30 p.m.

evening to compare to the temperature during the day? Your answers to these questions were predictions based on generalizations that you have formed either consciously or unconsciously about the environment.

Several final comments should be made about the teaching of facts. As already mentioned, one rationale for the inclusion of facts in a curriculum is that some facts constitute a body of knowledge that is generally considered to be necessary for life in modern-day America (e.g., knowledge about our country's history or governmental operations). A second justification for their inclusion in the curriculum is that they are a means of teaching abstractions by serving as the raw material that students process into abstractions. Unless one of these criteria can be applied to a particular fact, we question its inclusion in the curriculum. All too often, a proliferation of facts in the curriculum indicates that teachers do not know the difference between facts and abstractions and, consequently, treat all content the same. When this is done, students are inundated with minutiae, and their ability to discern and learn the major ideas in a discipline is severely hampered.

EXERCISE 4.5

Now let's see if you understand the difference between facts and abstractions well enough to differentiate between examples of each. (By the way, the ideas of a fact and an abstraction are both abstractions themselves.) We tried to teach essential characteristics of these ideas and provided you with several examples. Now let's determine if you have learned these two abstractions by asking you to classify additional positive and negative examples of them.

Classify the following statements as either fact (f) or abstraction (a).

_____ 1. A geometric figure with four equal sides is called a *rhombus*.

_____ 2. Extinction is the cessation of responding caused by lack of reinforcement.

_____ 3. The gravitational pull between two bodies is directly related to their mass and inversely related to the square of the distance between two objects.

_____ 4. When asking a question in the English language, the verb comes before the subject.

_____ 5. Pavlov discovered the phenomenon of classical conditioning.

_____ 6. The older a musical piece or composition, the fewer instruments in it.

_____ 7. Questions placed before a text increase learning directly related to the questions but decrease incidental learning (content not directly related to the question).

_____ 8. There are five national parks in Utah.

_____ 9. A novel is a form of literature that narrates a story.

_____ 10. Community helpers are people who perform important jobs in their neighborhoods.

_____ 11. Water boils at a lower temperature at higher elevations.

_____ 12. Sentences that state a fact or give information are called *declarative*.

_____ 13. Antibodies are body globulins that combine specifically with antigens to neutralize toxins and other harmful substances in the body.

_____ 14. *Adagio* refers to a way of playing music in an easy, graceful manner.

_____ 15. The United States invaded Iraq for the second time in 2003.

TECHNOLOGY IN THE CLASSROOM

Using Technology to Help Students Reach Diverse Cognitive Goals

Technology can be a powerful tool to help teachers reach different cognitive goals. It can assist teachers in helping their students learn facts, understand abstractions, and reach goals at the upper ends of the cognitive taxonomies (Roblyer, 2006).

Helping Students Learn Facts

While facts are often overemphasized in the curriculum, teachers often find that some facts are important for students to learn and that students encounter difficulties remembering them. Technology offers one vehicle to provide practice in the learning of facts.

Software programs are available to teach students important facts, such as the following:

- Math facts
- Important names and dates in social studies
- Chemical symbols in science
- Authors' names and works in literature

Software programs are effective for reinforcing facts such as these because they can be individualized, providing extra practice on items that students are struggling with (Roblyer, 2006). In addition, these software programs free up the teacher to work with students on other educational goals.

Teaching Abstractions

Technology can also be used to teach abstractions by bringing the real world into the classroom. Let's see how this happens in two classrooms.

An American history class is studying the civil rights movement in the United States. Because it occurred more than 30 years ago, the class is experiencing difficulties understanding the human struggle and sacrifice involved in this movement. To help students, the teacher brings in the videodisc Martin Luther King, *which contains video clips of civil rights marchers being attacked by water hoses and dogs, sit-in demonstrators being arrested, and the march on Washington, D.C., capped by Martin Luther King's "I Have a Dream" speech.*

A biology class is studying mammals, and most characteristics like fur and live birth are easily identifiable. However, others, like a four-chambered heart, are harder to illustrate. The teacher uses a videodisc called The Living Textbook *to help students visualize what a four-chambered heart looks like, how it operates, and why it is more efficient than the three- and two-chambered hearts of reptiles, amphibians, and fish.*

Technology can play a powerful role in helping teachers represent abstract ideas for learners, bringing the faraway and remote world into the classroom (Mayer, 2001). Videotape, computer simulations, and videodiscs all provide convenient ways to bring the outside world into the classroom. Videodiscs, with their capacity to store 108,000 razor-sharp images along with theater-quality sound, are especially powerful presentation tools

(Roblyer, 2006). For example, the *National Gallery of Art* videodisc by Videodisc Publishing contains a vast array of works by great artists, information that would be inaccessible in any other way. *Windows on Science*, a collection of still-life and moving images, allows science teachers to illustrate hard-to-imagine ideas and structures. In addition to commercially prepared videodiscs, teachers can also construct their own, blending photographs, diagrams, and videotapes into high-quality images and sounds to supplement their presentations.

Teaching Higher-Level Cognitive Goals

Technology can also be a powerful tool to help students reach goals at the upper ends of the cognitive taxonomy (Forcier & Descy, 2005). Technology can be used to teach students to do the following:

- Gather and organize information
- Store and manipulate data
- Locate and extract information from a variety of sources
- Record information in appropriate ways
- Draft and edit materials being prepared for presentation
- Give and receive information
- Problem solve with software games and simulation programs

Experts believe that the greatest long-term potential for technology in the classroom is as a "mind tool" to expand learners' ability to solve problems in the real world (Jonassen, Howland, Moore, & Marra, 2003).

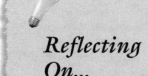

Reflecting On...

THE AFFECTIVE, PSYCHOMOTOR, AND COGNITIVE DOMAINS

INTASC Principles 1, 3, and 4

Think about the different levels of the affective, psychomotor, and cognitive domains. Then think about how you will incorporate the domains in your classroom, with a specific emphasis on the cognitive domain.

SUMMARY

Educational goals originate from one of four sources: standards, the child, society, or academic disciplines. A particular goal can be defended from several of these sources or perspectives. For example, knowing how to compute the areas of different geometric shapes could have a strictly academic focus or could be presented as practical content with real-world applications. Knowing how to compute the area of a rectangle could be used to tell how much fertilizer to buy for a garden plot, and knowing how to compute the area of a circle could be used to adjust a pizza dough recipe for a 9-inch-diameter pan to an 18-inch pan. (Hint:

You do not just double the recipe.) In addition, teaching students about the biological changes that occur during puberty could be defended from all three perspectives. From a student-oriented perspective, this knowledge helps developing adolescents understand and deal with changes occurring in their bodies. From a societal perspective, this information is essential for young people who will soon attempt to assume adult roles in society. And from an academic viewpoint, these changes are interesting in and of themselves, as they illustrate the functioning of complex systems within our bodies.

Proponents of different orientations could claim this content area as their own, and a particular goal could serve several orientations and could be philosophically defined from a number of perspectives. What is important is that you understand the major sources of teaching goals and that you be able to intelligently defend your choice of goals in terms of a well-thought-out rationale.

A second area of study in this chapter involved a discussion of the three domains. The purpose here was to introduce you to the psychomotor, affective, and cognitive domains with a heavy emphasis on the cognitive domain. This is not because we believe that domain to be the most important but because it is the primary focus in so many educational programs. Although objectives involving the affective domain are fewer in number, we are convinced that they should play a critical role in the development of youngsters. This is particularly true at the primary level, where socialization and learning to work and cooperate with others is such an important goal.

Regarding the psychomotor domain, experts throughout the country have become increasingly disturbed with obesity in children, partially caused by children who are not engaged in a constant, sequential physical education program (Lafee, 2005; Schibsted, 2006). In addition, the drive toward academics in the upper grade levels has clearly limited the amount of time spent in physical activities.

As stated early in the chapter, we believe that all three domains have to come into play to promote the healthy growth of children. Even though we have presented only a brief overview of the affective and psychomotor domains, we urge you to incorporate them in your curriculum whenever possible.

Finally, we summarize our discussion of facts and abstractions by referring to Table 4.4.

Probably one of the biggest differences between facts and abstractions is in terms of how they are taught. Facts can be thought of as stimulus–response connections in which the stimulus is a question and the response is the answer. The major way of strengthening this bond is through repetition, which can be accomplished by repeating a fact (Now remember, students, there were 13 states in the Confederacy), by asking a question (How many states were there in the Confederacy?), or by encouraging students to study their notes or reread the text. In contrast to facts, abstractions are learned by presenting a number of different examples that either the teacher or the students analyze for commonalities.

A second major way that facts and abstractions differ is in terms of how they are measured. Facts are typically measured as they were learned, with one part of the fact acting as the stem (Who was the first president of the United States?) and the second part serving as the answer. Abstractions, by contrast, are measured by asking students either to recognize examples of the abstraction (in the case of the concept verb, What do the underlined words have in common?) or to provide new examples (List three verbs not

Table 4.4 Comparison of Facts and Abstractions

Examples	How Taught	How Measured	Uses
Facts The closest planet to the sun is Mercury.	Question/answer S–R	Question/answer S–R	Can be formed into abstractions.
There were 13 states in the Confederacy.	(The stimulus is the question, and the response is the answer.)	(Either the S or the R is presented, and the student has to provide the missing term.)	(Cannot be used to summarize, explain, or predict.)
Abstractions People who exercise regularly have lower pulse rates.	Examples/abstractions	S S–R S	Can be used to summarize, explain, and predict.
The stopping distance of a car is inversely related to its speed.	S S–R S	(New examples are provided, and the student generates the correct classification.)	
An herbivore is an animal that eats only plants.		(Abstraction is given, and the student provides new examples.)	

discussed in class). In both instances, it is important that new examples are used to ensure that the abstraction learned generalizes to new situations. (Note how we did this in the exercises in this chapter.)

 KEY CONCEPTS

PREPARING FOR YOUR LICENSURE EXAMINATION

Read the following case study and, using specific information from this chapter, answer the questions that follow.

> Henry Myers, a middle school social studies teacher, is sitting in the teachers' lounge, gazing out the window. Phyllis Burbank, his neighbor on the second-floor hallway, walks in and asks, "Daydreaming again?"
>
> "Not really. Just trying to figure out what to do with this unit on U.S. politics and elections."
>
> "What's so hard about that? Give them the old tried and true. Like who is running for office this year, what is a senator and representative, and what are the advantages of being an incumbent?"
>
> "Yeah, they'll learn all that, but I also want them to start to develop some personal responsibility for their role in government. So when they get old enough, they'll vote."
>
> "Hmm. That's a tough one. They are only 13, and it'll be 5 years until they get to vote."
>
> "Well, I did think about connecting all this stuff to our school elections. They are interested in that, and if I can get them excited about that, maybe it will help them see how they fit in all this other, more abstract stuff."

1. Identify in the scenario where facts, concepts, and generalizations were mentioned.
2. Each of the different sources of goals was mentioned as a rationale for different approaches to the unit. Identify these and explain how they reflected these different sources of goals.
3. Identify in the scenario hints at the cognitive and affective domains.

VIDEO EXERCISE

Go to MyEducationLab and select topic "Curriculum" and watch the video "The Indirect Instruction Model." After viewing the video, respond to the questions on the video.

DEVELOPING YOUR PORTFOLIO

The purpose of this activity is to encourage you to think about the content you will be teaching in terms of the different kinds of content in the cognitive domain.

Select a general topic for a possible unit that you would teach in your first year in the profession.

■ Using this topic as a general heading, identify two facts, two concepts, and two generalizations that would be included in the unit.
■ Briefly describe how these different forms of content would be connected in the unit.

QUESTIONS FOR DISCUSSION

1. How should the relative importance of the sources of goals—content standards, the child, society, and academic disciplines—change in terms of grade level?

2. Which content areas stress the following sources of goals the most: the child, society, or academic disciplines? The least? Why?

3. How should the relative importance of the affective, psychomotor, and cognitive domains change over the course of the K–12 curriculum?

4. Which of the three areas—affective, psychomotor, or cognitive—should receive more emphasis in today's schools? Less?

5. What are the most important abstractions at your grade level or in your content area? Why are they important?

6. What are some possible reasons why facts are overemphasized in schools?

7. How should the optimal mix of facts, concepts, and generalizations (e.g., 50% facts, and 25% concepts, 25% generalizations) change over the K–12 continuum? Defend your position with a specific content area or discipline.

 SUGGESTIONS FOR FIELD EXPERIENCE

1. Interview teachers at the grade level and/or in the content area in which you plan to teach and ask them about the importance of different sources of goals in their classrooms.
   a. Which is most important? Why?
   b. Which is least important? Why?
   c. Does this order change with different types of students (e.g., gifted and talented or at risk)?
   d. Does this order change with different topics (e.g., Revolutionary War versus voting in elections in social studies)?

2. Interview a teacher and ask him or her about the relative importance of the three domains in the classroom. Ask what factors influence this ranking.

3. Examine a teacher's edition of a textbook or a state or district curriculum guide. Identify an example of a goal or objective in each of the three domains. What domain receives the most emphasis? Why?

4. Use the cognitive taxonomy to analyze the goals or objectives of a chapter in a text or a unit in a curriculum guide.
   a. Identify an example at each level if possible.
   b. At what level are most of the goals or objectives?
   c. Is this an optimal mix? Why or why not?

5. Examine a chapter from a textbook at your grade level or in your content area. Identify several of the following:
   a. Facts
   b. Concepts
   c. Generalizations

   What proportion of the chapter is devoted to each? Is this an optimal mix?

6. Examine a chapter from a textbook at your grade level or in your content area. Select two concepts and describe how well the text identifies the concepts:
   a. Characteristics
   b. Examples
   c. Superordinate concept
   d. Subordinate concept

   Using this information, evaluate how well the book does in teaching concepts.

7. Identify a concept from a unit that has just been completed. Interview a student to see how well that student understands the concept. Specifically, ask the student to describe the following:
   a. Characteristics
   b. Examples
   c. Superordinate concept
   d. Subordinate concept

   What does the student's response tell you about the depth of learning and the quality of teaching?

8. Examine a test a teacher has administered. What proportion of the exam focused on the following:
   a. Facts
   b. Concepts
   c. Generalizations?

   Comment on this mix.

TOOLS FOR TEACHING

Print References

March, C., & Willis, G. (2007). *Curriculum: Alternative approaches, ongoing issues* (4th ed.). Upper Saddle River, NJ: Prentice Hall. Provides an excellent overview of curriculum issues.

Marzano, R. (2003). *What works in schools.* Alexandria VA: Association for Supervision and Curriculum Development. An excellent summary of the research on effective schools and effective teaching.

Ornstein, A., & Hunkins, F. (2004). *Curriculum: Foundations, principles, and issues* (4th ed.). Boston: Allyn & Bacon. A basic text on curriculum issues from a foundational perspective.

Tanner, D., & Tanner, L. (2007). *Curriculum development: Theory into practice* (4th ed.). Upper Saddle River, NJ: Prentice Hall. Describes the history of curriculum in the United States as well as current controversies in curriculum development.

Wiles, J., & Bondi, J. (2007). *Curriculum development: A guide to practice* (7th ed.). Upper Saddle River, NJ: Pearson. An excellent introduction to the process of curriculum development with valuable chapters on standards and integrating technology into the curriculum.

Web Sites

www.ascd.org Web site for the Association for Supervision and Curriculum Development, the primary professional organization that deals with curricular issues.

www.curriki.org Contains repository of free curriculum materials for educators.

www.funderstanding.com/curriculum.cfm A valuable resource for understanding important curriculum concepts.

www.marcopolo-education.org A favorite resource for teachers that contains hundreds of lesson plans as well as a range of ideas for lessons.

www.rmcdenver.com/useguide/lessons/design.htm? Helps teachers understand how to convert standards into usable lesson plans.

CHAPTER 5

Formulating Goals and Objectives Using Standards

INTRODUCTION

Chapter 1 introduced the organization of this text by presenting a model of teaching described in three interrelated phases—planning, implementing, and assessing. Instructional goals and objectives are useful to teachers in each of these phases (Gronlund & Linn, 2000). During the planning phase, goals and objectives help define and clarify what you are trying to accomplish within the scope of national and state standards, which more often than not provide the sources for the content of a curriculum. During implementation, goals and objectives serve as guides to help you make instructional decisions. During the assessment phase, goals and objectives help determine the form and content of your evaluation instruments. In addition, goals and objectives can aid in communication, conveying instructional intent to other teachers and other school personnel as well as students and their parents.

The planning phase begins when a goal is identified, and we introduced you to the impact of standards in Chapter 1 and different sources of goals and domains of instruction in Chapter 4. We now want to look at goals in more detail and examine how to convert them from standards into operational forms for instruction so that we can use them as guides for teaching. These goals mark the beginning of the planning process, which is more fully developed in Chapter 6.

LEARNER OBJECTIVES

After completing your study of Chapter 5, you should be able to do the following:

- Recognize the influence of national, state, and local goals on what is taught in classrooms
- Discuss the function of goals regarding annual, unit, and lesson planning
- Prepare original behavioral objectives
- Prepare original goals objectives
- Explain the current emphasis on the use of objectives in classrooms

APPLYING GOALS AND OBJECTIVES IN THE CLASSROOM

Following is a case study in which a high school science teacher presents a lesson on water purification and the ways in which water is naturally filtered. As you read the case study, consider the following questions:

- Did Ms. Salazar appear to align her goals and objectives with standards?
- How would Ms. Salazar's objectives facilitate her annual plans?
- How would Ms. Salazar's objectives facilitate her unit plan?

Dolores Salazar began her lesson by asking her students to take out their notes to review yesterday's work. The 27 students enrolled in this high school Chemistry in the Community class were seated in a U-shaped arrangement, with laboratory stations lining the walls of the classroom. She began her lesson with an interactive question-and-answer session designed to review information from previous lessons.

"We have been working on water purification, and we said that back in the 1800s, people obtained their water in three different ways. What was one of those ways . . . Toni?"

"Wells," Toni said.

"I couldn't quite hear you."

"WELLS!!"

"Wells. Good. Rob, a second way?"

"Ponds."

"Good. Along with ponds, what else?"

"Rivers, lakes, stuff like that," Bianca added.

"Great!" Ms. Salazar said. "And a third source?"

"Rain," Paul said.

"Right, so those were basically the major sources of water back then. Now, water also had to be discarded, so what were three ways they got rid of wastewater?"

"Cesspools," Nancy said.

"OK, what are cesspools?"

"Pits."

"Good, and what were they lined with?"

"Stones or rocks," Nancy added.

"OK. Now a second way in which water was discarded . . . Alina?"

"How about just using the ground," Alina said.

"Right. A lot of times people just dumped it outside so it went into the ground. And, finally, a third way?" Ms. Salazar asked, gesturing to Gabe.

"A dry well."

"And what is a dry well, Gabe?"

"A well that doesn't have any water in it."

"Exactly, Gabe. Simply a well that has dried up. Now, what happened if somehow wastewater got into the wells or rivers—in other words the drinking water . . . Josie?"

"It got contaminated," Josie said.

"Which means?"

"If you drank it, you got sick."

"Right. Now, today, what are two things we can do with water to prevent sickness or other negative effects?"

"We can filter it," David replied.

"OK," Ms. Salazar said, "but what does filtering do? When we filter something out, what are we actually doing?"

"Taking stuff out," David said.

"How?"

"By holding back the stuff that is too big to pass through the filter," David added.

"Great . . . so filtering is one method. What is a second . . . Melissa?"

"Chlorinating," Melissa answered.

"Chlorinating. Why do you think we need to chlorinate water . . . Vince?"

"In order to kill bacteria," Vince replied.

"OK, good," Ms. Salazar said. "We also talked about the way nature purifies water if left alone and given enough time. However, we often don't have that kind of time because we are using water quicker than the time it takes to naturally replenish itself. In addition, we talked about hard and soft water and that hard water has an excess of calcium, magnesium, or other minerals. So, water purification can also involve the removal of these excess minerals."

"In today's lab, I am going to give you a sample of hard water, which has an excess amount of calcium ions. Your job is to soften or purify this water using filtering techniques."

Ms. Salazar then provided the students with a filtration procedure handout and demonstrated the placement of filters in funnels and test tubes. She went on to briefly discuss how the test would show whether they had gotten rid of the calcium. For the remainder of the class, Ms. Salazar assisted the students at their laboratory stations.

THE INFLUENCES OF STANDARDS ON CLASSROOM GOALS AND OBJECTIVES

As we saw in Chapter 4, the child, society, and the academic disciplines are sources of goals. From each source, goals and standards are generated at the national, state, and local levels, the former being the most global or general and the latter being the most specific. An example of a **national goal,** as presented at the National Education Summit in 1989, was that American students will be first in the world in math and science by the year 2000. This goal and other national goals became part of the Goals 2000 Proposal (U.S. Department of Education, 1994). A **state goal** such as this becomes more concrete and specific and appears in the form of a standard. For example, Ms. Salazar taught chemistry in Albuquerque, New Mexico, and based her lesson on the following New Mexico Content Standards:

> *The Content of Science:* Standards I (Physical Science)
>
> *9–12 Benchmark I:* Understand the properties, underlying structure, and reactions of matter.
>
> *Performance Standards:* Properties of matter. (3) Know how to use properties to separate mixtures into pure substances.

A **local goal** (or classroom-level goal) is typically described in terms of specific outcomes designed to facilitate a state standard and are found in teachers' lessons plans. An appropriate local outcome for Ms. Salazar's would include the student's ability to identify ways to purify water. Now let's examine how these three levels provide direction for educational planning as we look back at our chapter-opening scenario.

Levels and Perspectives

Dolores Salazar undertook a number of goals in her lesson, ranging from the general to the specific. On a national or more global scale, she was concerned with the need for students to become aware of the critical problem of, and the need for, replenishing the nation's and world's water supply. This topic is one of international concern. It is important for American students to be aware of such an issue and to develop knowledge and understanding of ways to pragmatically address this problem as a participant in tomorrow's scientific community.

Sometimes teachers' goals come from professional organizations at the national level. For example, the National Council of Teachers of Mathematics (NCTM) published the following goals to provide guidance for elementary math teachers.

NCTM Standard 1: Mathematics as Problem Solving

In Grades K–4, the study of mathematics should emphasize problem solving so that students can:

- use problem-solving approaches to investigate and understand mathematical content;
- formulate problems from everyday and mathematical situations;
- develop and apply strategies to solve a wide variety of problems;
- verify and interpret results with respect to the original problem;
- acquire confidence in using mathematics meaningfully. (NCTM, 1989, p. 23)

Anthony Magnacca/Merrill

National and state standards provide clarity for student learning which lessons the potential for management problems.

From a state or regional perspective, in this lesson Ms. Salazar wanted to introduce her students to methods that are commonly employed in state and regional efforts to replenish existing sources of water. Issues such as water shortages, agricultural and industrial use, and the debate between a number of states over river rights (e.g., Wyoming and Nebraska over the use of the Platte River) are common agenda items in many state legislatures, all of which lend support to her teaching of this lesson as part of a unit on water issues.

Similar to New Mexico, most states provide teachers with specific performance standards in the content areas for levels K–12. For example, Colorado has the following goals in elementary social studies:

> Students understand how economic, political, cultural, and social processes interact to shape patterns of human populations, interdependence, cooperation, and conflict. . . . In grades K–4, what students know and are able to do includes . . . identifying the causes of human migration. (Colorado Department of Education, 1995)

Broad goals that also include specific outcomes like these assist teachers in their instructional planning. In addition to national and state influences, teachers' planning is also influenced by district curriculum guides that are designed to facilitate standards.

In her classroom, Ms. Salazar designed a lesson that required students to actually employ a given procedure and successfully filter a sample of water. Notice how concrete and measurable her classroom objective was as opposed to the general and ambiguous nature of goals at the national and state benchmark levels. Clearly, the format and the amount of specificity of goals is determined by the levels at which they are formulated (Marzano & Kendall, 2003).

THE ROLE OF GOALS AND OBJECTIVES IN PLANNING

The Three Operational Levels of Goals

Goals provide direction for educators as they attempt to plan learning experiences for students (Marzano & Kendall, 2003). Goals provide direction for teachers at several levels, including long-term or annual planning, unit planning (which spans several weeks or a month), or daily lesson planning.

The function of goals at the first level, annual or **long-range goals,** is both philosophical and conceptual; these goals provide general direction regarding what knowledge students should acquire over the span of a course or term. Decisions regarding the development of long-range goals require the teacher to determine learner outcomes in a general way. For example, for primary school teachers, reading is critical, and it is their responsibility to focus on ways in which they can develop their students' ability to read. This is one example of a long-term or general goal. At the high school level, an American history teacher realizes the need for students to understand the role that wars played in the growth and expansion of the nation.

Long-range goals become less global and more focused and specific at the second, or unit, level. The purpose of **unit goals** is to provide a focal or beginning point for planning a unit of instruction without being too specific or directly measurable.

Returning to our reading example, at the unit level a teacher might be concerned with word recognition strategies that will facilitate the longer, more global goal of increasing reading ability. Likewise, an American history teacher operating at the unit level might have students become more familiar with the Spanish-American War in terms of expansionism.

The third level of goal specificity is found in **lesson goals**. The focus at this level is specific and concrete. Again, regarding our reading example, the lesson plan might call for the student circling all the words with two syllables in a given list. In doing so, word recognition strategies are enhanced (unit level), and the ability to read is increased (long-range level). Turning to our history example, the teacher might have students write an essay discussing three causes of the Spanish-American War (lesson-plan level), which increases familiarity with the war (unit level) and promotes understanding of the role that war played in the expansion of the United States (long-range level). Note that the examples of the objectives at the lesson-plan level are quite specific; circling words and writing an essay are concrete and observable. This specificity is helpful both for teachers planning the lesson and for students trying to figure out what they should learn.

Decision Making in Preparing Objectives

From these examples, we can see how goals and objectives can assist teachers in their instructional decision making at multiple levels. In this process, they answer two important questions: (a) In both a general and a specific sense, what does the teacher want students to know, understand, or be able to do after completing the units and lessons? (b) How will the teacher determine that the students know, understand, or can perform something? Answering the first question assists in identifying the end product during planning and helps the teacher remain focused on the lesson. Teachers play a key role in determining the curriculum that students actually receive, even when clear curriculum guidelines and materials are in place (Ornstein & Behar-Ornstein, 1999). Regarding the second question, objectives help both the teacher and students assess learning because the objectives at the lesson-plan level identify what students should be able to do in specific terms. Let's now take a look at different ways objectives can be prepared and how they influence teaching and learning.

ALTERNATE FORMATS

The use of goals and objectives as the starting point for instructional planning began with Ralph Tyler's (1949) classic text *Basic Principles of Curriculum and Instruction*. This influential work popularized the use of objectives in education, and the ability to write and use objectives continues to be a major component of teacher preparation courses and programs.

Tyler (1949) suggested that the most useful form for stating objectives was "to express them in terms which identify both the kind of behavior to be developed in the student and the content or area of life in which this behavior is to operate" (p. 46). Thus, behavioral objectives were born.

Another powerful influence on teacher planning followed Tyler's when Robert Mager (1962) first published *Preparing Instructional Objectives*. His highly readable book was popular, and thousands of teachers have been taught his principles for stating behavioral objectives. However, his approach to writing objectives has been criticized as too narrow and confining, and an alternative, called the *goals approach* to preparing objectives, was proposed.

This popular approach to preparing objectives has been suggested by Norman Gronlund (2000). He believes that objectives should first be stated in terms of general goals, such as *understand, appreciate, know, evaluate,* or *apply,* which are then followed by observable behaviors specifying evidence that the learner has met the objective. We examine both of these approaches—Mager's and Gronlund's—in this chapter.

Mager's Behavioral Objectives

Robert Mager was enormously influential in changing how objectives are prepared. In his attempt to focus teachers' attention on concrete, observable outcomes, he suggested that a **behavioral objective** ought to clearly state "what it is that students are expected to be able to do, and that each intended performance be directly visible and/or audible; you can see or hear someone doing it" (Mager, 1997, pp. 51–52). With this type of objective, teachers should be able to see or hear the student actually doing something.

Mager suggests that an effective objective has three parts: (a) an observable behavior, (b) the conditions under which the behavior will occur, and (c) criteria for acceptable performance. The following are examples of objectives written using Mager's format:

1. Given six sentences, fifth graders will identify each that contains a simile.
2. Given 10 addition problems requiring regrouping, second graders will successfully solve eight.
3. Given 15 compounds written with the correct chemical formula, chemistry students will identify the valence of the ions in each.

Mager's system, with its emphasis on observable student behaviors, requires a great deal of initial specificity, thought, and effort on the part of the teacher. Mager contends that the effort required to achieve this specificity is worthwhile, and he has even gone so far as to suggest that students can often teach themselves if they are given well-stated objectives.

Mager's objectives, sometimes called an *outcomes approach*, are criticized as being incomplete, however, in that they are only evaluation statements. In other words, they specify the student outcome or how students will be evaluated but do not identify the educational intent of the teacher or the purpose for which the student is being evaluated. An alternative that addresses this criticism is called the *goals approach to preparing objectives* or, more simply, **goals objectives**. We discuss these in the next section.

Goals Objectives

A goals objective answers two questions for the teacher:

1. What do I want the learner to know, understand, or appreciate (or some other educational goal)?
2. How will I know if the student knows, understands, or appreciates?

Mager's outcomes approach to preparing objectives answers the second question. Answers to both are important, however, particularly if you are a beginning education student developing your understanding of teaching. For this reason, we have adopted the goals approach in this text. This approach combines Mager's objective, which is an evaluation statement, with a goal. Thus, a goals objective is more inclusive since it subsumes Mager's format within it. Keep in mind that from this point on, when we refer to an evaluation statement, we mean a Mager objective. Let's look now at the process of formulating goal statements within a goals objective.

Goal Statements

A major purpose for writing this text is to help you begin to think like an experienced, effective teacher. With this notion in mind, imagine that you are responsible for a class in a certain grade level or subject matter area. You are planning a specific lesson for the next day. Your first step in planning is to ask yourself, "What do I want the students to know, understand, or be able to do?" All your planning—and ultimately your actual work with students—derives from the answer to this question. This question is essential for people who are beginning to study and understand the process of instructional planning. At this point in your professional development, instructional planning is most effective when guided by formally and explicitly stating goals in writing. As your thinking and understanding develop, your goals may become less formal and more implicit.

Planning begins with teachers' consideration of what they want their students to accomplish during one or more lessons. This desired result is called a **goal statement**, which is a statement of educational intent that is usually given in general terms. The goal statement answers the question "What do I want my students to know or understand?" Some examples of goal statements include the following:

1. For kindergartners to know the basic colors
2. For eighth-grade science students to understand Newton's first law
3. For senior trigonometry students to solve written problems involving right triangles

Examining these goal statements, we see that they have three common characteristics. First, each identified the particular student population for which it was designed—kindergartners, eighth-grade science students, and senior trigonometry students, respectively. Second, the learning outcome or task was identified. The kindergartners' task is to know colors, the eighth-graders' task is to understand Newton's first law, and the trigonometry students' task is to be able to solve problems with right triangles. Finally, the goal's attainment in each case is inferred rather than observed. We cannot directly observe "understanding"; we can only infer it, and it can mean different things to different people. The same is true for "know," "appreciate," and other desired educational goals. Later, when we discuss the evaluation component of goals objectives, we will see how we can gather information needed to infer knowledge, understanding, and appreciation.

Goal statements can take different forms, but they should be written as simply and efficiently as possible. They may be simply an introductory phrase, as in the first two examples just cited, or they may be a complete sentence, such as our third example. Let's examine some additional examples in terms of both the learner and the learning task.

1. Senior literature students will understand the impact of personal experience on an author's work.
   Learner: senior literature students
   Learning Task: understand the impact of experience on authors' works
2. Sixth-grade science students will understand the concept of density.
   Learner: sixth-grade science students
   Learning Task: understand the concept of density
3. Second graders will understand the rule for adding *-ing* to words.
   Learner: second graders
   Learning Task: understand the rule for adding *-ing* to words
4. Eighth-grade algebra students will be able to solve simultaneous equations.
   Learner: eighth-grade algebra students
   Learning Task: solve simultaneous equations
5. Seventh-grade geography students will know the locations of the countries of Europe.
   Learner: seventh-grade geography students
   Learning Task: know the locations of the countries of Europe

Note that each of the objectives we have written for this text refers to you as a reader and student, and it has been stated in each case. We have done this so that our objectives can serve as appropriate models for you as you study. Specifically stating the intended learner group is useful when designing curriculum at the school or district level. If a teacher has the same audience (which may be herself in personal planning) for an extended period of time, however, it would not be necessary to repeat the learner component in each objective once the learner is clearly established.

Notice also that although the goals are written in nonobservable terms, such as *know* and *understand*, they are specific. Goals such as the following are too general to be useful:

Students will understand American literature.

Algebra students will be able to solve problems.

Geography students will know about Europe.

Because of their lack of specificity, these goals are not helpful in subsequent instructional decision making. Compare these examples with the first, fourth, and fifth of the preceding examples to see the difference.

EXERCISE 5.1

Identify the learner and the learning task in each of the following goal statements. In addition, suggest one way that student achievement of this goal could be evaluated.

1. Fifth graders will know the parts of the digestive system.
   Learner: _____
   Learning Task: _____
   Possible Evaluation: _____

2. American history students will understand Andrew Jackson's philosophy regarding states' rights.
   Learner: _____
   Learning Task: _____
   Possible Evaluation: _____

3. Seventh-grade life science students will know the different types of bacteria.
   Learner: _____
   Learning Task: _____
   Possible Evaluation: _____

4. First graders will know how to print upper- and lowercase letters.
   Learner: _____
   Learning Task: _____
   Possible Evaluation: _____

5. Kindergartners will be able to walk a balance beam.
   Learner: _____
   Learning Task: _____
   Possible Evaluation: _____

Evaluation Statements

When we introduced goals objectives, we said that they provide the answer to two questions:

1. What do I want the learner to know, understand, or appreciate?
2. How will I know if the student knows, understands, or appreciates?

The goal statement answers the first question, and let's now consider the second, the **evaluation statement**. The answer to how we know if a student understands is a complex one, requiring teachers to make decisions during their instructional planning. To illustrate this process, consider the following goal:

Third graders will understand the concept *noun*.

This is seemingly a simple and straightforward goal. However, when we ask how we will know if they understand nouns, this simple goal becomes more complex. Some possibilities to determine whether they understand the concept include the following:

1. Have them define *noun* in writing from memory
2. Have them write a list of nouns that were not used as examples in class
3. Have them identify examples of nouns from a list of words
4. Have them identify nouns in a series of sentences

Even with a concept as simple as *noun*, we see that the evaluation question requires both thinking and decision making. For instance, if students can define *noun*, does this mean that they understand the concept? Probably not. Memorizing a string of words does not ensure concept learning (Eggen & Kauchak, 2007); other measures must be used to ultimately determine whether students truly understand the concept.

This process becomes more complicated as learning outcomes become more complex. For example, imagine instead that you had the following goals for your students:

Senior English students will analyze a writing sample critically.

or

Junior high math students will learn to problem solve.

Both are worthwhile goals, and deciding how to evaluate them is a complex process with multiple options to consider. These are questions teachers must answer every day, and this is what it means to "think like a teacher."

Let's consider evaluation statements further. For instance, by stating,

Third graders will understand the concept *noun* so that when given a list of sentences, they will underline all the nouns in each

the teacher has decided to infer that students understand nouns if they can underline all the nouns in a series of sentences the teacher provides.

Let's look carefully now at the entire objective. It contains a specific goal that identifies the learner and the learning task, and it includes an evaluation statement that designates (a) the expected performance, (b) the conditions under which the student is to perform, and (c) the standard for the performance. Each of these helps clarify the teacher's thinking while also communicating clearly with students and other professionals. Let's examine different parts of the performance component in more depth.

Specifying Observable Performance

The key feature of the performance is that it is observable by the teacher. In our previous example, we see that students demonstrate their understanding of nouns by underlining the

Objectives for standards-based lesson plans are very specific in terms of learner outcomes.

nouns in a series of sentences. As with all inferences, to conclude that students understand, we must have something observable on which to base this conclusion (Wiles, 1999). This **objective observable behavior** is the performance. When we considered different ways of assessing students' understanding of nouns, alternate performances were *define, write*, and *identify*. In addition, verbs such as the following are also observable and can be useful in performance statements:

state	select	list	label
classify	solve	construct	compare
describe	recite	derive	name
identify	draw	underline	organize

Many more could be added to the list, but this gives you alternative examples of verbs that describe observable performances. Although different approaches to writing objectives exist among educators, most adhere to the need for including an observable behavior in the objective's description. In addition, each objective should contain a single performance; if more than one is desired, a second evaluation statement should be written.

Specifying Conditions

When we specify **objective conditions**, we describe what students will have available to them when they demonstrate their knowledge or understanding. For example, let's look again at our example with the concept *noun*. The four possibilities we listed for evaluating the goal were the following:

1. Have them define *noun* in writing from memory
2. Have them write a list of nouns that were not used as examples in class
3. Have them identify examples of nouns from a list of words
4. Have them identify nouns in a series of sentences

Notice that in both examples 3 and 4, students were asked to identify nouns. In one case, they were asked to identify them from a list of words and in the other case in a series of sentences. The conditions under which the students were to perform the behavior were different. Specifying the evaluation condition helps us clarify our own thinking about what we are trying to accomplish, making it easier to communicate more clearly to students exactly what we want them to learn. Some examples of common conditions used in objectives include the following:

From memory

Without aids

Given a list

Given a compass, volleyball, jump rope, pictures (or other materials needed to demonstrate the performance)

By contrast, conditions such as

After instruction

After exposure to

Given experience with

are not acceptable conditions. Rather than specify the conditions under which the performance will be demonstrated, they describe a learning condition. In addition, conditions such as

Given a test

Given multiple-choice items

When asked

are so vague that they are not useful. They do not provide any specific information about the evaluation condition that can help us with our instructional planning or inform students during learning. The learner is always asked, told, or required to respond.

One way to think about conditions is to consider them as specifying the form of the test item. For instance, "identify nouns in a list of sentences" accomplishes exactly that. A corresponding portion of a test would include a series of sentences, and students would be asked to identify nouns by circling or underlining them. This kind of specificity helps teachers in their planning, directly suggesting learning and teaching activities.

Sometimes the term "Given a multiple-choice item . . ." is used as a condition. Unfortunately, this type of condition lacks specificity both for the teacher and for students. A better alternative would be the following:

American government students will understand different forms of government so that when given a case study describing a political ideology, they will identify the form of government it represents.

The measurement of this objective could be in the form of a multiple-choice item where the stem would illustrate the ideology and choices, such as (a) democracy, (b) monarchy,

(c) communism, and (d) fascism. Written in this more detailed way, both teacher and students know what is expected of them.

Specifying Criteria

As a theme for this chapter, we have been describing the thinking processes a teacher must go through when making professional instructional planning decisions. For example, when the teacher attempts to find out if the student has accomplished the goal, the teacher thinks about different aspects of the student's performance. The performance is critical because different performances tell you different things about learning. We have also seen how the condition under which the performance is demonstrated can have an impact on the goal and assessment process.

Let's take the process one step further and consider **objective criteria.** Examine these three items:

1. Second graders will be able to subtract with regrouping so that when given 10 problems requiring regrouping, they will correctly solve seven.
2. Prekindergartners will know their colors so that when given individually colored shapes, they will correctly identify the color of each.
3. World history students will know what kind of impact the Crusades had on Europe so that without aids, they will list four cultural outcomes resulting from the Crusades.

We see that in the first example, the teacher concluded that solving 7 of 10 correctly was sufficient for students to demonstrate their ability to solve problems with regrouping. However, in the second example, the teacher decided that the children should identify the color of each, and in the third, students could demonstrate their knowledge by listing four outcomes. The teachers specified not only the condition and performance but also how well the students were to perform. Considering the level of performance represents the criteria, and it is the final dimension to be considered as you develop your thinking about goals objectives.

Additional examples of criteria include the following:

With 100% accuracy

With no more than three errors

Within 20 seconds

Four times in 10 seconds

The value of criteria in instructional planning depends on the topic and activity. For example, consider the following objective:

Physical education students will demonstrate upper-body strength so that on a horizontal bar, they will do 10 pull-ups in 20 seconds.

Here the performance is to do pull-ups, but the objective has little meaning until we specify the criterion. Without it, we would immediately ask, "How many?" and "In how much time?" On the other hand, look at this objective:

Language arts students will understand the concept *hyperbole* so that when given examples of figurative language, they will identify 80% of the examples of hyperbole.

This objective reflects two important teacher decisions: (a) that understanding hyperbole is an important goal and (b) that we will infer that the students understand if they can identify the examples of hyperbole from among a number of cases of figurative language. In addition, the teacher has set the criteria at 80%, reflecting a professional judgment that this level would be sufficient to demonstrate mastery of this concept.

In typical classroom practice, teachers rarely set explicit criteria in advance. Instead, they establish grading systems, such as those all of us have experienced as students, and the criteria are implicitly incorporated within the system. However, school districts continue to move toward school accountability through competency testing, and setting criteria is important in these cases. In addition, considering criteria encourages teachers to ask important questions, such as "How important is this content?" and "How well do students need to learn it?"

If you look again at the examples provided, you see that many of them do not have criteria as described in this chapter. There is a pragmatic reason for this. As we have emphasized repeatedly, objectives serve as guides for instructional thinking by requiring you to ask yourself what you want the learner to know or understand and, further, how you will determine this knowledge or understanding. However, the explicit statement of criteria can be difficult to determine without a specific context as a frame of reference. Criteria become meaningful when they are applied to a specific group of students with differing learning capabilities. In other words, we support the practice of not explicitly stating criteria in decontextualized situations, as these become meaningful only when applied to a specific class of learners. Our position is that objectives should guide a teacher's thinking but should not restrict it. However, we believe it is worthwhile for you to understand how to specify criteria if it should ever be necessary.

EXERCISE 5.2

Identify the four components of goals objectives by enclosing each in parentheses and labeling them GS (goal statement), C (condition), P (performance), and CT (criteria).

1. Vocational-technical students will demonstrate carpentry skills so that when given a saw, square, and two two-by-fours, they will make a 90-degree joint in the boards to within 1 degree.

2. Middle school music students will know the fingerings for the recorder so that when given an excerpt of music, they will demonstrate the correct fingerings for each note.

3. Elementary physical education students will demonstrate hand–eye coordination so that when given a basketball, they will dribble it 25 consecutive times in place without losing control.

4. Eleventh-grade oceanography students will know the zones of the ocean floor so that when given an ocean topographic map, they will label each zone correctly.

5. Physics students will understand components of forces so that when given the magnitudes and angles of forces on objects, they will calculate the horizontal components of the forces in each case.

EXERCISE 5.3

You are now ready to analyze the overall quality of goals objectives. Consider each of the following and mark them as follows:

A—Objective is accurate and acceptable as written
GS—Missing or inappropriate goal statement
C—Missing or inappropriate condition
P—Missing or inappropriate performance
CT—Missing or inappropriate criteria

After identifying the problems in the objectives, rewrite each in appropriate form.

_____ 1. Fifth graders will understand the calculation of volume of solids so that after seeing sample problems, they will solve 9 of 10 similar problems correctly.

_____ 2. Vocational-technical students will understand common problems in small gas engines so that when given a stalled lawn mower, they will fix the causes of stalling with 80% accuracy.

_____ 3. Students will demonstrate understanding of figurative language so that when given a series of statements, they will identify the figure of speech in each case.

_____ 4. Prealgebra students will understand order of operations so that when given problems involving the four operations, they will correctly simplify each.

_____ 5. Seventh-grade geography students will know the geographical location of countries in Europe so that when given a map and multiple-choice items, they will answer each correctly.

_____ 6. Ninth graders will appreciate the use of verbals so that when given a series of descriptions, they will know appropriate examples of gerunds, participles, and infinitives for each.

_____ 7. American government students will understand the concept of governmental checks and balances so that on an essay test, they will present a written example of a check and balance.

_____ 8. Biology students will understand genetics so that when given case studies with dominant and recessive traits, they will identify the characteristics of each offspring.

GRONLUND'S INSTRUCTIONAL OBJECTIVES

In the previous two sections, we described Mager's behavioral objectives and the goals approach to preparing objectives. They are similar in that the goals approach is essentially a Mager objective attached to a goal statement.

We now turn to an alternative way of formulating objectives popularized by Norman Gronlund (2000). To introduce this approach, let's examine some examples of **instructional objectives** written according to Gronlund's principles and see how they compare to those we have already illustrated. Consider the following example taken from elementary school language arts:

General Objective: Knows spelling rules for adding suffixes

Specific Behaviors:

1. States rule in his or her own words
2. Distinguishes rule from closely related rule
3. Applies rule to unique example

Now consider a second example taken from algebra:

General Objective: Solves word problems

Specific Behaviors:

1. Describes problem
2. Identifies relevant information
3. Specifies variables
4. Writes solution equation
5. Calculates solution

What do these objectives have in common? Gronlund (2000) suggests that objectives should first be stated in general terms, such as *know, understand, apply, evaluate,* or *appreciate,* which are then followed by specific behaviors providing evidence that the learner has met the objective. In this regard, Gronlund's objectives are similar to the goals approach; he suggests that a general objective that identifies the instructional intent should be stated first. The general objective is similar to the goal statement in the goals approach. "Knows spelling rules for adding suffixes" and "solves word problems" were the statements of intent in our examples. The specific behaviors listed following each general objective provide the evidence that the students have met the intent. This approach differs from Mager's in that his objectives specify the evidence but do not include the intent.

Note, too, that Gronlund's objectives are stated in terms of student outcomes rather than teacher performance. For instance, "teach spelling rules for adding suffixes" is a teacher performance and not a student outcome. Virtually all objectives, regardless of the approach, share this characteristic, and both district curriculum guides and state-level curriculum frameworks state objectives in terms of student outcomes.

Gronlund also recommends that objectives should be stated in terms of learning outcomes rather than the learning process, such as "students learn spelling rules for adding suffixes." "Learns" is a student process rather than a student outcome, and Gronlund discourages this approach. Both Mager's approach and the goals approach share this characteristic.

A major difference from previous approaches is that Gronlund believes that conditions and performance criteria are too specific and limit teacher flexibility. For example, consider the objective "Given a drawing of a flower, the student will label in writing at least four of the five parts shown." By specifying the condition "given a drawing," the teacher has excluded the use of a slide or a real flower in the testing condition. In a similar way, by specifying four out of five, the teacher limits instructional flexibility that might suggest lower standards for slower students and higher ones for brighter students.

Because of this flexibility, Gronlund's approach or modifications of it are probably the most popular ones among curriculum writers today. Its primary advantage is one of economy; his objectives are broader and more inclusive than those written according to other approaches. Course content requiring literally thousands of objectives written according to Mager's approach could be expressed in less than a hundred using Gronlund's.

In achieving this breadth and flexibility, the compromise Gronlund makes is in terms of specificity. He does not identify either the conditions for acceptable performance or the criteria, and he discourages the use of specific subject matter topics. This latter feature is often modified by curriculum writers. They typically include specific topics in their objectives, as we will see in the next section.

EXERCISE 5.4

Consider each of the following objectives and identify those that are inappropriately stated according to Gronlund's criteria. Rewrite each of the inappropriately stated objectives in acceptable form. We are purposely sidestepping the issue of content specificity, so do not evaluate them on that basis.

1. Learns concepts in chemistry
   1.1 Defines concept in own words
   1.2 Identifies examples of concepts

2. Teach students parts of speech
   2.1 Define parts of speech for students
   2.2 Provide students with examples
   2.3 Have students identify parts of speech in context

3. Understands subtraction with regrouping
   3.1 States rule for borrowing
   3.2 Solves problems requiring regrouping

4. Understands geographical terms
   4.1 States definition in own words and writes definition
   4.2 Identifies examples in paragraphs
   4.3 Identifies examples on maps

5. Understands Newton's second law
   5.1 States the law
   5.2 Writes the law mathematically
   5.3 Solves problems using the law

TECHNOLOGY IN THE CLASSROOM

Formulating Goals and Objectives

Just as technology has revolutionized learning in the classroom, it has also changed the way teachers plan. The Internet provides a wide source of resources as teachers formulate goals and objectives. One major source of information in formulating goals and objectives are national professional organizations.

Professional Organizations.   Professional organizations provide a variety of activities designed to help teachers implement an effective curriculum, including the following:

- Producing professional publications that provide up-to-date research and information on trends in the profession
- Providing resources to which teachers can go with questions about professional issues and problems
- Providing information about goals and objectives in different areas of the curriculum

Table 5.1 includes a list of prominent professional organizations, their Web sites, and a description of their mission or goal. We recommend that you visit these sites as you plan for goals and objectives in your classroom.

State Offices of Education.   A second valuable resource for teachers as they construct goals and objectives for their classrooms are state office of education Web sites found in every state. The sites contain curriculum standards in different areas for each state as well as additional resources for teachers as they construct lesson plans to meet those standards. For example, the state of Utah (www.usoe.k12.ut.us) has its entire K–12 curriculum outlined in terms of standards and objectives. A third-grade language arts teacher seeking guidance for specific lessons would find the following information under "Language Arts (third grade)":

Standard 4 Phonics and Spelling—Students apply understanding of phonics and other strategies to decode and spell unfamiliar words while reading and writing.

To further assist teachers in their planning, each standard is followed by objectives, such as the following:

Objective 3 Spell words correctly

  a. Use knowledge of word families, patterns, syllabication, and common letter combinations to spell new words
  b. Spell correctly grade-level compound words, words with plural endings, and common phonograms
  c. Spell an increasing number of high-frequency and irregular words correctly (e.g., friend, square, special)
  d. Learn the spellings of irregular and difficult words (e.g., electric, planet, trapper, rectangle)

Teachers can use these standards and objectives as frameworks or beginning points in the planning process. However, a major task teachers still face is determining whether these standards and objectives are appropriate for their students and their classroom.

DIVERSITY IN THE CLASSROOM

Goals and Objectives in a Standards-Based Environment

Current emphasis on standards and accountability will influence the goals and objectives that you will likely construct when you enter your own classroom. Currently, there is considerable controversy nationally over the role that standards should play in teachers' planning. One of the major issues here is the role that individual differences should play in the

Table 5.1 Professional Organizations for Educators

Organization and Web Site	Organization Mission/Goal
American Council on the Teaching of Foreign Languages: www.actfl.org	To promote and foster the study of languages and cultures as an integral component of American education and society
Association for Supervision and Curriculum Development: www.ascd.org	To enhance all aspects of effective teaching and learning, including professional development, educational leadership, and capacity building
Council for Exceptional Children: www.cec.sped.org	To improve educational outcomes for individuals with exceptionalities, students with disabilities, and/or the gifted
International Reading Association: www.reading.org	To promote high levels of literacy for all by improving reading instruction, disseminating research and information about reading, and encouraging the lifetime reading habit
Music Teachers National Association: www.mtna.org/flash.html	To advance the value of music study and music making to society and to supporting the professionalism of music teachers
National Art Education Association: www.naea-reston.org	To promote art education through professional development, service, advancement of knowledge, and leadership
National Science Teachers Association: www.nsta.org	To promote excellence and innovation in science teaching and learning for all
National Council for the Social Studies: www.ncss.org	To provide leadership, service, and support for all social studies educators
National Council of Teachers of English: www.ncte.org	To promote the development of literacy and the use of language to construct personal and public worlds and to achieve full participation in society through the learning and teaching of English and the related arts and sciences of language
National Council of Teachers of Mathematics: www.nctm.org	To provide broad national leadership in matters related to mathematics education
National Association for Bilingual Education: www.nabe.org	To recognize, promote, and publicize bilingual education
Phi Delta Kappa: www.pdkintl.org	To promote quality education as essential to the development and maintenance of a democratic way of life by providing innovative programs, relevant research, visionary leadership, and dedicated service
Teachers of English to Speakers of Other Languages: www.tesol.org/index.html	To improve the teaching of English as a second language by promoting research, disseminating information, developing guidelines and promoting certification, and serving as a clearinghouse for the field

teaching/learning process. At one end of the continuum, advocates for standards-based curriculum argue that standards represent minimal levels of competency that all students should acquire (Marzano, 2003). In essence, these advocates argue that all students in the United States should learn how to read, write, and do basic math. This is the logic under-girding the No Child Left Behind Act (Mathis, 2003). Critics of this approach contend that a one-size-fits-all approach to education is too rigid and that teachers should have the flex-ibility to adjust goals and objectives to meet the needs of each individual student (Hatch, 2002). These critics contend that developmental needs, individual learning styles, and cultural differences need to be accommodated in teachers' planning.

As the teaching profession continues toward increased teacher accountability for stu-dent learning, some districts are placing descriptions of objectives in teachers' hands, re-quiring that they specify the date when the objective was taught. At the secondary level, language arts teachers are sometimes asked to verify that their students have read certain im-portant works from authors such as Shakespeare and Hemingway. Accountability is chang-ing the ways teachers plan and teach. Earlier we suggested that objectives are a way of life in education today, but each teacher must ultimately decide what is best for his or her stu-dents. There are obvious compromises, but objectives are becoming an integral part of the real world of the public schools. They can function as guides designed to aid teachers in their instruction or rigid prescriptions for teaching. Ultimately, each teacher must make profes-sional decisions about his or her own classroom.

OBJECTIVES AND REFLECTION

In addition to serving as guides for instructional decisions, objectives also can be valuable in promoting professional reflection. Reflective teachers are thoughtful, analytical, and even self-critical about their teaching. They plan lessons thoughtfully and take the time to ana-lyze them afterward.

Reflection is important in teaching not only because it improves our effectiveness as teachers but also because it helps us develop as professionals. By continually thinking about themselves and their work with students, reflective teachers develop a coherent philosophy of teaching that helps them integrate theory and practice and continually refine their prac-tice (Rodgers, 2002).

The process of explicitly considering and writing both goal and evaluation statements at this point in your studies encourages you to focus on student learning, the ultimate goal of all good instruction. Goals and objectives are not only useful for instructional planning but also valuable as a tool for professional reflection. Considering goals and objectives within the planning process provides a concrete frame of reference to later think about the overall effectiveness of instruction from a student learning perspective. In a sense, formu-lating goals and objectives is the starting point for professional reflection. The more thoughtful teachers are about goals and objectives, the better they will be able to reflect on their instructional effectiveness.

GOALS AND OBJECTIVES

INTASC Principles 8 and 9

Think about the different roles and formats that goals and objectives can take in teaching. Then think about how you will use goals and objectives in your own teaching.

Reflecting On...

SUMMARY

The purpose of Chapter 5 is to help you understand different reasons for preparing objectives; to introduce you to the ways in which objectives are influenced by standards at the national and state levels; to help you establish long-range, unit, and lesson-level objectives; and to help you develop your skill in writing them. We presented three different approaches to their preparation. Of those three, we emphasized the goals approach because of the advantages it provides in developing your thinking about connections between teaching and learning.

A goals objective has two primary parts. First, the goal statement describes the teacher's intent in general, nonobservable terms. It identifies the learner and the learning task. The evaluation statement, which is identical to an objective written according to Mager's approach to preparing objectives, includes the condition, the performance, and the criteria. The goal statement answers the question "What do I want the learner to know, understand, or be able to do?" and the evaluation statement answers the question "How will I determine whether the learner knows or understands?"

Gronlund's instructional objectives are similar to goals objectives in that a general statement of intent is first identified, followed by specific behaviors that provide evidence that the general objective has been met. Gronlund's objectives, however, are much more general than goals objectives.

Examples taken from state standards and district curriculum materials indicate that although specific procedures for preparing objectives vary, objectives play an increasingly important role in the "real world" of standards and accountability.

Objectives are critical to the planning and implementation of instruction. They increase effective communication, aid teachers in developing learning strategies, and encourage thinking about assessment and reflecting on whether the objectives were achieved. The importance of objectives is further illustrated when we study their central role in the development of lesson plans in Chapter 6.

KEY CONCEPTS

Behavioral objectives 136	Long-range goals 135
Evaluation statement 140	National goal 133

PREPARING FOR YOUR LICENSURE EXAMINATION

Read the following case study and, using specific information from this chapter, answer the questions that follow.

Sasha Perez often uses her summer break to think about the past year and ways to improve her teaching. This often happens at strange times—driving, exercising, or even cooking. One area of the curriculum keeps bothering her: writing. Her sixth-grade students scored below the state and district averages on the state competency exam, with her boys' performance especially low.

"We need to do more work on writing," she says to herself.

In August, as she prepares her room for the upcoming year, she looks at her planning book and pencils in "Writing—every Monday, Wednesday, Friday." As she gets down to specific planning, she reexamines her class's test scores and discovers that paragraph structure was a major problem area.

"We can fix that!" she thinks.

In October, she introduces the topic of paragraph structure by placing two paragraphs on the overhead. After considerable discussion, her class concludes that one is clearly better than the other, but no one is quite sure why. She uses this as an opportunity to place the following on the board:

Our Goal: To learn to write effective paragraphs with:

a) Effective topic sentence
b) Appropriate supporting sentences
c) Summarizing concluding sentence

Ms. Perez then explains her goal by guiding students through the two paragraphs, pointing out where the different components of an effective paragraph are present or lacking.

1. Identify the three operational levels of goals in the case study.
2. What kind of objective did Sasha share with her students?
3. Rewrite Sasha's objective into a goals objective, identifying the major parts.

VIDEO EXERCISE

Go to MyEducationLab and select the topic "Curriculum" and watch the video "The Indirect Instruction Model." After viewing the video, respond to the following questions:

1. In teaching a lesson on graphing, what could be Ms. Brush's long-range goal?

2. What state standard is Ms. Brush's lesson on graphing facilitating? Note: You can select any state and locate graphing under second-grade content standards for math, or you can use the following: go to www.georgiastandards.org, key word "graphing"; under "Subject," select "Math," under "Grades," check "2," then click on "Search." Be sure to click on "Standard Name" to view details.

3. What could be a unit goal (using the goal statement format) for Ms. Brush's lesson?

4. What could be a lesson goal (using an evaluation format) for Ms. Brush's lesson?

DEVELOPING YOUR PORTFOLIO

The purpose of this activity is to encourage you to begin using objectives in your planning.

- Select a topic for a possible lesson that you would teach during your first year in the profession. This is your long-range goal.
- Refine this topic into a unit goal, which is a general statement of what you want students to learn in the unit.
- Finally, construct three goals objectives that could be the focus for a specific lesson and key them to selected state standards.

QUESTIONS FOR DISCUSSION

1. Of the three levels of influence on objectives (national, state, and local), which do you believe will have the most impact on you as a classroom teacher?

2. What are the key structural differences between annual or term-level objectives, unit objectives, and lesson objectives?

3. What are some reasons for the prevalent practice of providing teachers with prepared objectives in materials such as curriculum guides and textbooks?

4. From a teacher's perspective, what are the advantages and disadvantages of providing teachers with objectives and curriculum guides?

5. Is the process of formulating objectives more useful to beginning or experienced teachers in planning? Why?

6. Why are objectives considered to be the cornerstone of planning?

SUGGESTIONS FOR FIELD EXPERIENCE

1. Interview teachers at the grade level and/or subject matter area in which you plan to teach and ask them about the ways in which national, state, and local goals and objectives influence their curriculum.
   a. Which impacts them the most? Why?
   b. Which impacts them the least? Why?

2. Examine a curriculum guide and a textbook at your grade level or in your academic discipline. Are objectives presented in these materials? Are they
   a. Mager's objectives?
   b. Gronlund's objectives?
   c. Goals objectives?
   d. Other formats?

   How many are there for the entire course? Comment on the adequacy of appropriateness of this number.

3. Locate a textbook at your grade level or in your subject field that does not have prepared objectives. Select a chapter and for the content in that chapter, prepare the following:
   a. Mager behavioral objective
   b. Gronlund instructional objective
   c. Goals objective

4. Interview teachers at your grade level and/or in the academic subject area in which you plan to teach and ask them what formats they employ when writing objectives for their original units and lesson.

TOOLS FOR TEACHING

Print References

Gronlund, N. (2004). *Writing instructional objectives for teaching and assessment* (7th ed.). Upper Saddle River, NJ: Merrill/Prentice Hall. This book contains an updated discussion of Gronlund's perspective on formulating goals and objectives.

Morrison, G., Kemp, J., & Ross, S. (2007). *Designing effective instruction* (5th ed.). Hoboken, NJ: Wiley. Explains how goals and objectives can be used to achieve instructional alignment.

Serdyukov, P., & Ryan, M. (2008). *Writing effective lesson plans*. Boston: Allyn & Bacon. Describes how goals and objectives fit into the essential teaching skill of designing effective lesson plans.

Wiggins, G., & McTighe, J. (2006). *Understanding by design* (2nd ed.). Upper Saddle River, NJ: Merrill/Prentice Hall. Explains how goals and objectives fit into the current emphasis on standards and accountability.

Wiles, J., & Bondi, J. (2007). *Curriculum development: A guide to practice* (7th ed.). Upper Saddle River, NJ: Merrill/Prentice Hall. An excellent introduction to the process of curriculum development, with chapters on standards and integrating goals and objectives into the curriculum.

Web Sites

www.ed.gov/G2K/teachers/appndx5.html Here you will find the eight national education goals and specific objectives for each of the goals.

www.sonoma.edu/users/p/phelan/423/standards/html Here you will find an overview of the standards movement that includes introduction and discussion of the evolution of the standards movement, federal legislation (No Child Left Behind Act), and selected state standards.

www.quasar.ualberta.ca/edit573/modules/module8.html Here you will find a discussion on goals and objectives and the best way to develop and present them.

www.uwsp.edu/education/lwilson/curric/behavior.htm Here you will find the advantages of behavioral objectives and problem-solving and cognitive examples of behavioral objectives.

http://edweb.sdsu.edu/LShaw/f95syll/bloom/behobj.htm Here you will find a definition of behavioral objectives and examples of student behavior and performance criteria.

http://med.fsu.edu/education/FacultyDevelopment/objectives.asp Here you will find a definition and characteristics of behavioral objectives and how to write them.

CHAPTER 6

Planning for Assessment with Standards

INTRODUCTION

Can you imagine a surgeon beginning an operation without specific knowledge of the patient's problem and what he or she will try to do to correct it? Can you imagine an engineer building a bridge without detailed blueprints, knowing what it will cost, and understanding how it will affect the environment? Does a pilot go into the air without consulting weather reports, charts, and maps? In each case, the results would be disastrous. While it does not seem as dramatic, teaching is similar. To facilitate intellectual, emotional, social, and physical growth in students, teachers must carefully plan and prepare, just as the surgeon, engineer, and pilot do. Simply stated, you must plan, and you must plan thoroughly. Planning is the way teachers turn their thinking and decision making into tangible teaching strategies.

The development of preservice teachers' ability to construct, conduct, and analyze a lesson is an essential component in their professional training. Helping you learn to make decisions that will result in as much student learning as possible is the focus of this chapter.

LEARNER OBJECTIVES

After completing your study of Chapter 6, you should be able to do the following:

- Discuss the impact of assessment and standards on long-range planning
- Illustrate ways that unit planning can be used to frame and connect a series of specific lesson plans
- Construct effective daily lesson plans
- Identify the advantages and disadvantages of different lesson plan formats
- Describe modifications in planning for inclusive classrooms

APPLYING PLANNING FOR ASSESSMENT IN THE CLASSROOM

Following is a case study in which a sixth-grade science teacher engages in the planning process at the beginning of the year for the concept *erosion*. As you read the case study, consider the following questions:

- What factors were considered regarding long-range planning?
- How was the unit plan framed and used as a focal point for the lesson plans for erosion?
- How would the lesson plans facilitate the unit plan?
- How would Mr. Armendariz assess the achievement of the students?

Harry Armendariz, a middle school science teacher, sat at his desk at the beginning of the school year and thumbed through the science books spread out in front of him. The study of the causes and prevention of erosion appeared on both the state and the district science curriculum guides, and he was trying to decide what the best way to introduce the concept erosion *would be.*

"Sheesh," he thought to himself. "They're gonna croak when I try this out on them. They aren't too crazy about science to start with, and erosion, for crying out loud. That'll seem about as relevant to a bunch of sixth graders as . . ." His thoughts trailed off.

"This stuff is important. . . . It can help them understand how important it is to try to protect the environment," he muttered almost audibly with an air of determination, continuing to flip through the pages and take notes.

"Exactly what do I want them to know about it?" he thought as he wrote the word erosion *down on his notes.*

"How does it [erosion] fit my unit on landforms?" he continued, jotting down erosion—land forms *in his notes.*

"What can I show them so that they'll understand it? How hard will it be to get the materials?" he continued, talking to himself.

"Now, how can I make them see that it's actually relevant?" he thought and shook his head.

He sat for several more minutes and then wrote sand-table demonstration *in his notes as he thought, "I'll start with that demonstration. It's concrete and actually fairly interesting—it'll give them a good reference point. It's a microexample of erosion at work, and they'll even see little canyons*

and deltas. It's also big enough, so the whole class will be able to see it without being too crowded. . . .
Yeah, that's where I'll start."

Mr. Armendariz then decided to supplement his demonstration with a video that further illustrated
the process of erosion in different locations around the world.

Having planned for his initial illustrations, he thought, "I'll try to get them to see how erosion
relates to volcanoes and earthquakes—other factors that change the landscape." Finally, he identified
relevant pages in the text and made a note to himself to assign them for reading.

"Later on," Mr. Armendariz further mused, "I'll take them down to Black Creek, a local stream in
the area, to see how erosion is working right here in town."

DECISION MAKING AND PLANNING

To begin our discussion of this chapter, refer back to the previous case study. Let's think
about some of the decisions that Mr. Armendariz made as he planned. At least four decisions are significant:

- The first and somewhat obvious decision was that of the need to address, in terms of both
  content and methodology, the benchmarks or standards found in both the state and the
  district curriculum guides.
- He proceeded to make decisions about ways to illustrate or demonstrate the concept
  erosion for his students (his sand-table demonstration, the video, the text, and a field trip).
- He then made a decision about sequence; that is, he decided to start the lesson with the
  sand-table demonstration.
- Finally, he made a decision about relating the lesson on erosion to his unit on landforms.

Returning to the first statement, the initial focus on standards not only lends itself to
decisions regarding content and methodologies but also provides the foundations for assessment considerations. As mentioned in Chapter 1, the assessment phase of the three-phase
model of teaching involves the selection of the evaluation instruments that will be most effective
in determining student achievement with specific regard to the stated goals and objectives.
These objectives that are designed to facilitate state standards help the teacher answer the question "How will I know if the student knows, understands, or appreciates the material under
study?" Additionally, when considering assessments in terms of standards translated into goals,
teachers focus on what they want their students to accomplish at the conclusion of the lesson
or unit. More will be said about the influence of standards later in the chapter.

It is equally important to note that, as stated in Chapter 5 under the discussion on objectives,
teachers do not determine specific criteria at this point. The importance here is to decide what
the students need to learn, as what level they need to learn it, and what assessments tools will be
used to determine student progress. Much more will be said about assessment in Chapter 11.

Decision making affects not only assessments but all aspects of teaching and the three-
phase model as well. By definition, a decision involves a resolution or a conclusion that
requires the professional judgment of the person making it—Mr. Armendariz in this case. He
could have made a different set of decisions. For example, instead of using the sand table and
video, he could have used different representations. He could have chosen to sequence the
lesson differently. Or he could have related the concept to the unit on landforms in a different

way. In making his decisions regarding initial planning, Mr. Armendariz took three important factors into account. First, he considered both short- and long-term goals. In asking himself, "Exactly what do I want them to know about it?" he was establishing a clear short-term goal for himself and the students; in wondering, "How does it [erosion] fit my unit on landforms?" he was considering his long-term goals.

Second, he considered the way students learn—the learning process itself. He asked himself, "What can I show them so that they'll understand it?" and "How hard will it be to get the materials?" He also decided to start with his sand-table demonstration because "it's concrete, and . . . it'll give them a good reference point." These decisions indicated that as Mr. Armendariz planned, he was consciously and systematically taking into account the way students learn.

Finally, he considered student motivation as he made his decisions. His first reaction was, "Sheesh, . . . they're gonna croak when I try this out on them. They aren't too crazy about science to start with." His subsequent decisions involved trying to make his presentation interesting and helping the students see the relevance of the topic.

From this description, we begin to see that planning is a complex process that involves making a number of important decisions, and these decisions must take a number of factors into account. With these ideas in mind, let's reconsider the reasons teachers plan.

EXERCISE 6.1

Using the INTASC and NCATE standards introduced in Chapter 1, reread the opening scenario involving Mr. Armendariz and identify all those he is addressing in his erosion lesson.

REASONS FOR PLANNING

Effective teaching cannot be founded on the hope that exciting and relevant experiences will spontaneously occur in the classroom on a regular basis. There can be no doubt that effective teaching is founded on thorough planning at a number of levels that will be discussed later in the chapter. More specifically, planning provides the following (Manning & Bucher, 2001):

- Continuity of instruction
- Efficient use of time
- Educators keeping in mind the needs of their students
- An adherence to local, state, and national curricular guidelines and standards
- A schedule for resources such as library materials and computer labs
- Possible links across disciplines

In terms of promoting effective teaching, professionals plan for a variety of reasons, which can be classified into four categories:

Conceptual

Organizational

Emotional

Reflective

Conceptual Reasons for Planning

We introduced the chapter by asking about surgeons, architects, pilots, and teachers, suggesting that each must plan carefully to do their work effectively. When architects, for example, make decisions about the best materials to use in designing a building, they are involved in the conceptual aspect of planning. Mr. Armendariz, as another example, made decisions about goals—exactly what he wanted his students to know, what he would use to represent the topic, and how he would sequence the lesson. This conceptual planning allows teachers to present ideas in a coherent and connected way.

Organization and Planning

When a surgeon or pilot makes decisions about schedules in surgery or for a flight, they are involved in the organizational dimension of planning. Teachers, in addition to making conceptual decisions about goals and learning activities, also consider classroom rules and procedures, their own use of time, and the optimal use of the physical environment. These are also part of the organizational concerns of planning.

Emotional Reasons for Planning

A third important reason for planning is emotional. It is common knowledge that careful planning, whether it be preparing a speech, organizing a camping trip, or developing a personal budget, provides a source of security and confidence for all of us. This

Thorough planning provides a blueprint for outcomes, strategies, and assessments in a standards/based curriculum.

certainly extends to beginning teachers who feel the need to "cover their bases" and therefore tend to be quite extensive with their written plans. Even veteran teachers take extra care in planning when they face content that is new to them or difficult for students.

Reflection and Planning

Planning is also important for reflection. It helps teachers make clear decisions about their goals, identify why goals are important, and establish how they will go about trying to help students reach goals. This establishes reference points that allow them to reflect on how appropriate the goals are and how effective they were in helping students reach them. Since research shows that student achievement is related to academic engaged time, planning should include consideration of how to involve students. Through a store of perceptions—ways of looking at students and classroom activities—the teacher can make adjustments during instruction when plans must be adapted to the immediate situation (Ryan & Cooper, 2001). Without careful planning, the process of reflecting becomes murky and uncertain at best.

Having examined decision making in planning and considered different reasons for planning, we turn now to planning at three different levels. We begin with long-term planning, then consider unit planning, and finally examine daily lesson planning.

LONG-TERM PLANNING

Philosophical Considerations

Decision making during planning involves philosophical considerations about the value of different goals and objectives. At a broad level, philosophers concern themselves with that which is "ultimately knowable." Teachers then focus on the subset of "knowable" information considered to be necessary and desirable. By definition, education is not only the acquisition of a wide range of desirable knowledge (i.e., intellectual, moral, and propositional) but also the ability to manifest or employ such knowledge.

As you saw in Chapter 4, the knowledge students are expected to learn is intended to satisfy the needs of the individual, the needs of society, and the need to understand essential bodies of information. We saw these views reflected in Mr. Armendariz's planning. He was considering the needs of individual students when he took the nature of learning and student motivation into account. He considered the needs of society when he decided that an understanding of erosion was important to protect the environment. And the important aspects of the body of knowledge were reflected in the curriculum materials.

Standards and Benchmarks

As presented in the seminal work by Ralph Tyler (1949), *Basic Principles of Curriculum and Instruction,* the curriculum of a school system should embody knowledge bases directed toward the individual, the society, and the classical bodies of knowledge themselves. These three areas serve as the foundation on which educational goals are developed, and for many educators, developmental needs should become the basis for planning developmentally responsive instructional experiences. However, these developmental needs are not the only forces that affect instruction (Manning & Bucher, 2001). As discussed in Chapter 1, national standards put forth by professional associations, accreditation agencies, and federal mandates clearly influence the curriculum of American schools. Additionally, and closer to home, state standards, such as the Colorado Academic Standards presented in Chapter 1 and the designated content found in the Virginia Standards of Learning, clearly affect what will be taught and how students, teachers, and schools will be assessed.

It is increasingly common today for states and school districts to provide these goals in the form of standards or benchmarks. An increasingly popular format teachers use to meet content standards is called *backwards planning*, which includes the following steps (Guillaume, 2004):

- Select content standards or outcomes for mastery
- Unify these outcomes through a theme, an issue, or a "big idea"
- Compose essential questions and develop supporting unit questions as well
- Determine acceptable student performance(s)
- Select activities that lead students toward mastery
- Develop rubrics to assess performance
- Review and revise until each component of the unit supports others

We will say much more about unit planning later in the chapter, but for the moment, although it is recognized that teachers *must* be familiar with standards, it is equally acknowledged that teachers *will* facilitate these mandated learner outcomes. For example, the long form of the Teacher Summative Evaluation for the Albany County School District One in Laramie, Wyoming, includes the following:

Has knowledge of subject-area(s) and teaches to District objectives and/or student IEPs [individual education plans]

The following is how Ms. Sue Demaree, a second-grade teacher, responded to this specific district expectation:

I am comfortable with the District curriculum objectives and am enrolled in classes to continue my education and keep updated with current educational trends. I work to translate the District objectives into positive learning experiences for my students. However, I modify my lessons to accommodate each individual child's academic, emotional, social, and physical needs. I meet with the special education and self-contained teacher on a weekly basis to ensure that all objectives in each student's IEP are being met. I am also self-motivated to enhance my knowledge of all subject areas.

(With permission. Ms. Sue Demaree, Grade Two, Spring Creek Elementary School, Laramie, Wyoming. Ms. Becky Pearce, Principal)

In most cases, the standards have been thoroughly formalized. For example, in the state of Florida in 1996, the state board of education approved standards in four separate grade clusters (pre-K–2, 3–5, 6–8, and 9–12). These Sunshine State Standards have been further defined, and, in the subject areas of language arts, mathematics, science, and social studies, they have been expanded to include grade-level expectations that will eventually become the basis for state assessments. Furthermore, when developing lesson plans, teachers are required to identify the specific Sunshine State Standard(s) that are being facilitated by the goal(s) of that lesson.

Standards and benchmarks often appear in the form of a matrix and might look something like the following:

GRADE 8 LANGUAGE ARTS

Content Standard	Benchmark
1. Reading-Students read a variety of grade-level materials, applying strategies appropriate to various situations	1. Students read classic and contemporary fiction and nonfiction, including materials recognizing cultural differences.
	2. Students use a variety of comprehension strategies, including prediction, sequencing, cause/effect, fact/opinion, main idea, compare/contrast, and making inferences.
	3. Students . . .

Standards may also appear in the form of proficiency statements such as (a) use legends, keys, and symbols to read maps and globes or (b) construct and interpret a bar graph. No matter what the format, the goals and objectives teachers incorporate in their unit and lesson plans will increasingly be founded on standards, which will in turn establish the outcomes for which the students, teachers, and schools will be held accountable because standards and testing go hand in hand. Printed standards set forth what a child should know and be able to do in subjects such as math and reading. In addition to standards and goals for students, recent efforts have also been undertaken regarding the development of benchmarks aimed at strengthening the teaching profession by ensuring that preservice teachers are qualified for entry into the profession. Examples of these benchmarks or performance assessments include the following (Morgan, 1999):

- Reflect ideal instructional practices
- Are motivational
- Allow multiple strategies
- Promote natural curiosity
- Integrate knowledge and processes
- Have relevance
- Have an appropriate level of difficulty

These considerations, among others, provide focal points for the numerous specific decisions teachers make, which serves as our next topic for discussion.

EXERCISE 6.2

Reread the chapter-opening scenario involving Mr. Armendariz's erosion lesson. Then go to the Sunshine State Standards Web site (www.firn.edu/doe) and click on "Resources for Teachers," "Sunshine State Standards," "Florida Course Descriptions," and "Basic Education." Then locate the specific Sunshine State Standard that Mr. Armendariz was facilitating.

Specific Teacher Decisions

Teachers begin to operationalize philosophical goals through long-term planning that includes both the philosophical considerations we just discussed and the four reasons for planning outlined in the previous section. However, its primary focus is more on the conceptual and organizational dimensions than on the emotional and reflective. Probably the most important planning and organizational decision teachers must make is what they are trying to accomplish with their long-term goals and how they are going to link those goals to classroom organization, daily instruction, management, and assessment (Arends, Winitzky, & Tannenbaum, 2001). In the conceptual dimension, for example, it broadly outlines a year or semester of content and serves as a framework for more detailed planning that will come later. During the summer or preplanning—the time in the fall when teachers prepare for the school year but students are not yet attending classes—teachers commonly examine their text and other books, curriculum guides, and district- or state-level curriculum frameworks. On the basis of these materials, they often write lists of broad topics in an approximate sequence. For example, a ninth-grade geography teacher wrote the following:

First Term

1. Basic map skills—latitude, longitude, time zones, map projections
2. What is geography—the five fundamental concepts of geography
3. The earth's resources: geography and the environment
4. World climates

Second Term

5. Biomes, soil, and vegetation
6. Landforms
7. Seasons
8. Culture

Third Term

9. Cultural regions
   a. Western Europe
   b. Eastern Europe
   c. Russia and the former Soviet Union
   d. North Africa and the Middle East
   e. Africa south of the Sahara

Fourth Term

   f. South and East Asia
   g. The Pacific World
   h. Anglo-America
   i. Latin America

In addition to these topics, the teacher also considered available videos, worksheets, possible field trip locations, potential guest speakers, and projects.

We can see three important decisions involved in this simple set of notes. First, the teacher made decisions about what topics would be taught; second, she made decisions about sequence; and third, she considered—in a broad sense—resources and learning activities. Her planning and decision making were similar to Harry Armendariz's, only on a broader scale. During long-term planning, the conceptual dimension of planning remains broad; more specific decisions come later. Even though they are broad, however, these decisions help the teacher by reducing the number that must be made later, helping to simplify the overall planning process. For instance, the teacher can look at her outline and conclude, "Oh, yeah, I'm moving into world climates next, so I need to schedule those videos right away." Her decision about the topic to be covered next has already been made.

In the organizational aspect of long-term planning, teachers also consider at least three additional factors:

- Characteristics of the students.   These include their ability levels, needs and interests, and previous experiences. To gather this information, teachers talk to other teachers and look at cumulative folders.
- The physical environment.   Teachers try to create an environment that will induce positive emotions, and they consider practical arrangements that will allow all students to see the board, screen, and television, as well as traffic lanes and access to facilities, such as storage cabinets and the pencil sharpener.
- Classroom management.   Teachers establish the rules and procedures that will set the patterns for the year.

Classroom management deserves further mention in that teachers must attend to many specific decisions regarding the operations or routines undertaken on a daily basis in classrooms. Some of these routines are outlined in Table 6.1.

As with the conceptual dimension of planning, making decisions about organization and management during long-term planning reduces the number of decisions that must be made later.

UNIT PLANNING

Unit planning is the intermediate step between long-term planning and the process of constructing specific lesson plans. A unit can last anywhere from a week or two to a month or more depending on the topic and the age of the students. As with long-range plans at this stage, teachers also reflect and consider students' progress toward achieving objectives, the availability of materials, the time requirements of particular activities, and other such issues. Some teaching skills that support the (unit) planning function include the following (Cooper, 2003):

- Observing student behavior
- Diagnosing student needs
- Setting goals and objectives
- Sequencing goals and objectives
- Determining appropriate learning activities related to the objectives

Table 6.1   Areas for Establishing Routines in Long-Term Planning

Area	Example
General routines	■ Checking attendance ■ Monitoring tardiness
Room use	■ Teacher's desk and storage areas ■ Student desks and storage of personal items ■ Storage for class materials used by all students ■ Sink, pencil sharpener, wastebasket ■ Learning centers and/or lab stations ■ Distributing and collecting materials ■ Expected behavior during interruptions ■ Class helpers in elementary schools ■ Computer use
Transitions in and out of room	■ Beginning the school day or period ■ Procedures for leaving the room and returning (e.g., drinking fountain, bathroom breaks, lunch, school grounds, library, main office) ■ Ending the school day or period ■ Fire and disaster drills
Group-work procedures Seat work and teacher-led instruction	■ Moving to and from groups ■ Expected behavior in groups ■ Student attention ■ Student participation ■ Procedures for leaving seats ■ Asking for help ■ Activities after seat work is completed

While unit planning is an individual matter and the components of teachers' units vary, units commonly include the components outlined in Table 6.2.

Let's examine these components now.

Unit Title

A unit is a series of interrelated lessons that focus on a general topic. Some examples of unit topics in different content areas are shown in Table 6.3.

If long-term planning has been effective, the decisions about unit topics have, for the most part, already been made because these decisions have been based on an examination of national curriculum guides, state and district guidelines, the text, and other resources.

Table 6.2   Unit Components and Descriptions

Component	Description
Unit title	Identifies the unit topic
Unit goal	Generally describes what learners should accomplish
Rationale	Specifies why the unit is important
Content outline	Identifies and sequences the topics included in the unit
Specific lesson plans	Provide specific guidelines for each lesson within the unit

Table 6.3   Unit Topics in Different Content Areas

Language Arts	Social Studies
Nouns	The Civil War
Punctuation	The colonial era
Short stories	Capitalism and socialism
Paragraph writing	Industrial movement in America

Health	Science
Respiratory system	Reptiles
Drugs	Plants
Nutrition	Electricity
Exercise	Nuclear energy

For instance, from our list of geography topics that appeared in the section on long-term planning, *basic map skills, world climates, landforms,* and *Russia and the former Soviet Union* all could be converted into units.

Chapter divisions in textbooks commonly correspond to approximate unit lengths. This does not mean that teachers should mechanically follow the text as the primary organizer for unit topics, however. In some of their most effective units, teachers take only portions of text chapters, add material that does not appear in the text, or change the sequence of the text topics.

Unit Goal

Having identified the unit topic, the teacher is now ready to consider the overall goal or purpose for the unit. Some examples of **unit goals** are outlined in Table 6.4.

The goals form the core of the unit. In specifying the goal, teachers make decisions about what they want students to understand or be able to do with respect to the topic. In the unit on

Table 6.4   Unit Topics and Goals

Unit	Goal
Word endings (fourth grade)	The purpose of this unit is to help students understand the rules for adding suffixes to words.
Plants (seventh grade)	The purpose in this unit is for students to understand the parts of plants and their functions, the necessary conditions for healthy plants, and the critical role of plants in ecosystems.
Civil War (eighth grade)	This unit is designed to help eighth-grade American history students understand the causes, events, outcomes, and aftermaths of the Civil War.
Solving equations (algebra)	At the end of this unit, algebra students should be able to solve two or more simultaneous equations.

plants, for instance, knowing that understanding "why plants are critical to life" is a component of the goal helps the teacher make decisions about specific objectives and learning activities as specific lesson plans are prepared. Again, as discussed earlier in the chapter, goals generally need to facilitate a standard, and it is appropriate to note that standard as part of your unit goal.

Rationale for the Unit

At no point in the planning process is professional decision making better illustrated or more critical than in considering the **unit rationale.** This decision making is critical for at least two reasons. First, we hear a great deal about the "knowledge explosion," which is reflected in the ever-increasing amount of information included in textbooks. It has become literally impossible to cover, even superficially, all the topics that appear in books, so teachers must make judicious decisions about what topics are most important to teach and in what sequence they should be taught. Teachers must think carefully about the reasons for selecting the topics they teach, promoting more important goals and topics over others.

Second, consciously considering rationales for selecting topics in the planning process provides a framework for reflection that will occur after the unit is taught, making the process of reflection more meaningful.

Content Outline

Having wrestled with the unit goal and its rationale, the teacher is now ready to outline the major ideas in the unit. The **content outline** breaks the general topic down into more specific and teachable subtopics. In introducing the unit, the teacher can provide the outline as a type of advance organizer to help students understand where the unit is going and how the ideas are connected. In addition, as daily lessons are introduced, the teacher can refer to the outline to help students understand the relationship of that lesson to previous and future ones.

Different ways of outlining the content of two different units are illustrated in Figures 6.1 and 6.2. The format you choose will depend on your own preferences and the content being considered.

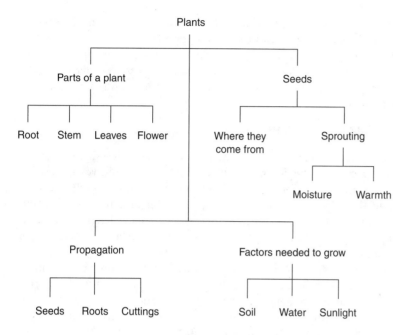

Figure 6.1 An Outline of a Plant Unit Content

Figure 6.2 Outline of Dairy Product Unit Content

Milk and Dairy Products
I. History
II. Nutritional composition of milk
    A. Fats, proteins, carbohydrates
    B. Vitamins
    C. Minerals
III. Processing of milk
    A. Pasteurization
    B. Homogenization
IV. Variety of milk products
    A. Milk
        1. Whole
        2. Skim
        3. Cream
        4. Half-and-half
        5. Buttermilk
    B. Butter
    C. Yogurt
    D. Cheese
    E. Sour cream
    F. Ice cream
V. Storage and care of milk and milk products
VI. Uses of milk in menu planning

Using either outline as a planning guide, the teacher is now ready to consider specific objectives for the unit. The task at this phase of the planning process is to translate content topics into measurable goals objectives. In addition, once constructed, these objectives need to be sequenced in terms of Bloom's taxonomy. This provides a suggested order for teaching as well as a way to clarify the kinds of behaviors expected of students. An example of this process applied to one segment of the plant unit follows.

Integrated Instructional Units (Specific Lesson Plans)

The discipline-centered single-topic approach to planning that we have described so far has at least two advantages, especially for beginning teachers. The first is simplicity; because individual lessons focus on a single topic or skill, it is easier for a beginning teacher to plan learning activities around that topic. A second advantage is that it presents a simpler and clearer picture of the discipline to students. When students leave a math lesson on equivalent fractions, for example, it is hoped that they will have a clear understanding of the topic and how to use it.

However, this approach to planning also has problems and limitations, probably the most serious of which is fragmentation of the curriculum. For example, students study landforms and climate in earth science or geography, and they study historical events, such as the American Civil War, in history. Strong links exist, however, between the geography and climate, economies of the North and South, and causes and outcomes of the war. Studying these topics separately does not help students see connections between different content areas.

However, integrated planning helps students see links between ideas from different content areas by consciously planning learning activities that encourage students to see connections directed toward practical, relevant, global issues.

There are at least three approaches to integrated planning (Wolfinger & Stockard, 1997):

- Combining disciplines
- Identifying themes
- Exploring issues

Let's look at each of these approaches.

Combining Disciplines.   One of the simplest ways to integrate content areas is to start with a topic and explore possible connections in another discipline. For example, a teacher who is planning a social studies unit on different Native American cultures might look to art and music for ways that students could use to describe those cultures. In a similar way, a teacher planning a unit on graphing might look to science or social studies for topics that could be counted, measured, and graphed. A simple way to remind yourself of these opportunities is to pause after you have planned a lesson or unit and ask yourself, "How might I connect this content with other topics and skills my students are learning?" This approach is often referred to as being interdisciplinary in that connections are established between subjects or disciplines even though they clearly maintain their separate knowledge bases. Similar to the "salad bowl theory" in sociology, the salad (instructional unit) is unique, but the ingredients (subject matter disciplines) maintain their characteristics.

Identifying Themes.   A second way to integrate your planning is around themes. Children's common interests at a particular grade level provide one source of themes. For example, children at the lower elementary levels have widely varying interests, such as holidays, their communities, or dinosaurs. Students at the middle school and high school levels are often fascinated by topics such as their changing bodies, interpersonal relationships, and health issues, such as drugs, smoking, and alcohol. Thematic units organized around topics such as these can be used to pull lessons together from different content perspectives.

Exploring Issues.   A third way to integrate planning is through the use of issues or problems. As students study issues such as pollution, terrorism, the arms race, or hunger and poverty, teachers can encourage them to use different disciplines to understand the issues and propose solutions to the problems posed by these issues.

Integrated planning is admittedly demanding. It requires a thorough understanding of content, learners, and goals. However, starting with relatively simple processes, such as the example with graphing information from social studies (Civil War) and science (landforms and climate), is a good beginning point. From there, as you gather experience, you will see more and more opportunities for making connections among the disciplines. Having specified and sequenced the unit topics, the teacher is now ready to prepare specific lesson plans.

EXERCISE 6.3

A fifth-grade teacher is beginning to plan a unit on Native American cultures. Write a unit goal and outline for this general topic.

Unit Goal:

Outline:

LESSON PLANNING

Having specified the unit topic, goal, rationale, and topic outline, the teacher is ready to plan individual lessons. In this phase of the planning process, the teacher is thinking about a single class period. This might be as little as 15 or 20 minutes or as long as 90 or 100 since some middle and secondary schools have gone to block scheduling. It is not uncommon for teachers to do little more than list activities in their lesson plan books, such as "read Chapter 1" or "Handout, Problems 1–3," but in reality, teachers are far more thorough when it comes to the many decisions to be made regarding a specific lesson. Unlike what some refer to as an activity plan, lesson plans tend to be more structured in identifying procedures, questions, and comments. Although still flexible, lesson plans often focus on specific learning and predetermined procedures (Henniger, 2005).

Although there is no one "right" lesson plan, the format we recommend has seven components:

- Unit topic
- Objectives
- Rationale

- Content
- Procedures
- Materials
- Assessment

Each of these components is intended to contribute to teaching effectiveness and student learning. After describing the seven components, we examine different ways of thinking about the planning process.

Unit Title

Individual lessons are not planned in isolation; they should exist in the context of the unit and other lessons that come before and after it. The unit title simply reminds the teacher of the relationship between the individual lesson and the unit as a whole. For example, a lesson on the parts of a flower would exist in the context of the overall unit on plants. A lesson on rules for adding -*ing* endings to words would fit into the overall unit on adding suffixes, and identifying reasons that the South lost the Civil War would be one or more lessons from a unit on the Civil War.

Lesson Objectives

Lesson objectives form the core of the lesson plan. They serve three functions:

- They expand the unit goal by describing it in greater detail.
- They specify what the students should know or be able to do at the end of the lesson.
- They translate the content outline of the unit into measurable outcomes.

In addition, objectives do the following:

- Help teachers plan learning activities with precision
- Help learners become self-regulated because they understand what is expected of them

For instance, the unit goal for the unit on plants was as follows:

The purpose in this unit is for students to understand the parts of plants and their functions, the necessary conditions for healthy plants, and why plants are critical in ecosystems.

Objectives for single lessons within the unit might appear as follows:

1. Life science students will know the parts of a plant so that when given an unlabeled picture of a unique plant (one they have not previously encountered), they will identify and label each part.
2. Life science students will understand the functions of each of the parts of a plant so that when given a list of plant parts, they will describe the functions of each.

As another example, the goal for the unit on suffixes was as follows:

The purpose of this unit is to help students understand the rules for adding suffixes to words.

Objectives for lessons in this unit might appear as follows:

1. Fourth graders will understand the rule for adding -*ing* endings to words so that when given a topic of their choice, they will write a paragraph in which each part of the rule is illustrated.
2. Fourth graders will understand the rule for adding -*ed* endings to words so that given a topic of their choice, they will write a paragraph in which each part of the rule is illustrated.

A rule of thumb in making decisions about the number of objectives is *When in doubt, err on the side of too many.* You have nothing to lose. If you have planned more content than you can cover, you have less planning to do for the following lesson. On the other hand, a lesson completed when half the period remains can lead to uncertainty, classroom management problems, and embarrassment. This is one of the more challenging tasks for interns and beginning teachers.

As a final note, when you are required to key your objectives to a mandated standard, we suggest you note that next to the objective in your lesson plan.

Lesson Rationale

Imagine a visitor to your classroom asking, "Why are you teaching this to your students at this time?" Your answer would be your **lesson rationale.** Typically, it involves a philosophical reason for teaching the lesson. For instance, a teacher might feel that understanding the rules for forming suffixes will make students better writers, which in turn will help them in the world of work. In short, this knowledge satisfies the needs of the individual. Understanding the causes of the Civil War are important in helping students become responsible citizens. This knowledge satisfies the needs of society.

As we noted in the introduction to this chapter, planning helps teachers think about their teaching. In our discussion of unit planning we suggested that the rationale was critical. The same is true at the lesson level; the *rationale* is perhaps the most important part of a lesson plan. If you do not have a clear reason for teaching a topic, maybe it should be eliminated from the unit.

A rationale for knowing the parts of a flower and identifying the reasons the South lost the Civil War might be stated as follows:

- Understanding the parts of a plant is important for understanding how plants and animals interrelate in ecosystems.
- Understanding the reasons the South lost the Civil War helps students see the interrelationships among geography, politics, and agriculture in particular and industrial strength among nations in general.

Rationales also help us get at the idea of *relevance,* one of the most popular and often-used terms in education today. When establishing a rationale, you are considering the applicability of the topic your students are studying. The more applicable the work, the more relevant it is for them.

The rationale can also be viewed as a defense for teaching the content in the lesson. If you can't confidently defend the lesson to yourself, to students, to their parents, and to administrators, you should rethink the objectives for that particular plan. We will return to this idea in the "Planning and Reflecting" section.

Lesson Content

The **lesson content** describes the major ideas you plan to teach. If someone were to walk into the room and ask, "*What* are you teaching?" you would respond by describing the content of the lesson plan.

Having already decided at the beginning of the year what your broad goals are, the content component of the lesson requires you to be more specific. In some cases, the process is simple. If the lesson focuses on a concept, the content is a definition of the concept, its characteristics, examples and nonexamples of the concept, and the relationship of the concept to other concepts. When the lesson involves a generalization or academic rule, it is a statement of the generalization or rule and illustrations and applications of it. For example, in the lesson on adding -*ing* to words, the content is simply the rule with some examples:

When adding -*ing* to a word, you double the final letter if it is a consonant preceded by a short vowel sound, but you do not if it is preceded by another consonant or involves a long vowel sound.

flop	flopping	sing	singing
trip	tripping	jump	jumping
fly	flying	play	playing
read	reading		

On the other hand, if the lesson involves a more complex concept, such as the parts of a flower, the content may exist in outline form:

Pistil (female)
   Stigma
   Style
   Ovary (ripened ovary becomes fruit)
   Ovules (later become seeds)
Stamen (male)
   Anther
   Filament
Petals (add color and attract birds and insects)
Sepals (protect reproductive organs)

The content outline serves as a guide for teachers and helps remind them of what is to be covered. They may refer to it as the lesson progresses to be certain that they have not forgotten anything, and they may even check off the items as they are covered. The outline also allows teachers to emphasize the parts of the lesson that are most important or those parts that may present problems for students.

How much detail should you put in the content section of the lesson plan? This is another illustration of one of this text's themes. It involves a decision made by professionals. Inexperienced teachers or those who are not familiar with the topic may decide to prepare a point-by-point outline, whereas a few key words or phrases might be enough for a tenured educator.

Lesson Procedures

In the content section, you list what you intend to teach. In this section, you consider *how* you intend to teach it. **Lesson procedures** can be viewed as a set of directions or instructions on how to present the lesson. If you were absent from school on a particular day, the substitute should have enough information from the procedures section to teach the lesson as you planned it.

As with the content section, how detailed the procedures section will be involves decisions made by the teacher. The procedures section for novices will probably be detailed; for veterans, it may be quite sketchy.

One effective planning strategy is to write the procedures as a series of steps or directions for a possible substitute. For example, a procedures component for the lesson on adding *-ing* endings to words might appear as follows:

1. Display the following passage on the overhead for the students.

   "Would you like to read the paper?" Latanya's mother asked, handing her the paper.
       "No," Latanya replied, jumping up from her chair, "I've been reading all day."
   "I'm going to jump into the shower."
       "Don't trip on the rug in there. I've been tripping over it every time I go in there," her mother warned.
       "You're flying around the house all the time," Latanya retorted. "I only *fly* around when I'm getting ready for school."
       "Well be sure you lay it down when you leave. I don't want it laying in a heap."

2. Ask the students to get together with their partners.
3. Direct the groups to try and identify any patterns that they find in the underlined words. Give them 5 minutes.
4. Reassemble the class and ask the groups to report on what they have found.
5. Prompt the class if necessary to notice that half the words end in *-ing*.
6. Guide the class to conclude that the final consonant in each root word is doubled if it is preceded by a short vowel sound but is not doubled if it is preceded by another consonant or a long vowel sound.
7. Call on a student to articulate the rule.
8. Write the rule on the board as the student states it.

As another example, the procedures section for the lesson on parts of a flower might appear as follows:

1. Display a transparency showing the parts of a flower.
2. Write the name of each part on the display and link it to the diagram.
3. Describe the function of each part.
4. Show the students an actual flower.
5. Ask individuals to identify verbally the different parts of the flower.
6. After each part is identified, have the students describe the function of the identified part.
7. Give the students a colored drawing of a flower. Have them independently (or in small groups) identify in writing the parts of the drawing and their functions.

Notice how the content and procedures portions of the lesson plan relate. We see that the content is the *what* of the lesson and that the procedures are the *how*. In our example with the flower, when the procedure calls for identifying each part, the content outline provides a reference for the specific parts.

As with other parts of planning, the procedures reflect a great deal of decision making. For example, in the procedures for teaching the rule for adding *-ing* to words, the teacher made three significant decisions. First, she chose a guided discovery approach. (We examine guided discovery in detail in Chapter 7.) She could have decided instead to first state the rule, provide some examples, and explain them, which would have been a more teacher-centered expository approach.

Second, the teacher decided to embed the examples of the rule in the context of a short passage instead of illustrating it in isolated sentences or words, which would have involved a different decision. And third, she decided to first have the students work collaboratively and then as a whole group instead of deciding to conduct the entire lesson with the whole class. As with other parts of planning, the decision-making process is very much a part of selecting procedures.

Lesson Materials

The purpose for listing **lesson materials** in the lesson plan is simple: it reminds the teacher of any special equipment, resource books, illustrations, demonstrations, transparencies, videotapes, computer software, and so on that must be gathered or prepared before the lesson. For instance, the passage illustrating the rule for adding *-ing* to words, the transparency showing the parts of the flower, and the actual flower would be listed in the materials sections of the lesson plans.

By *special*, we mean materials other than textbooks, pencils, notebook paper, and similar items. Although they are technically materials, listing them in a lesson plan is not necessary because they are always available and because students are supposed to have them. Students failing to bring necessary materials is another issue, discussed in Chapter 2.

Lesson Assessment

The **lesson assessment** encourages the teacher to consider—before the lesson—how to evaluate student learning in terms of the stated goals based on standards. This is relatively simple if the objective is complete and includes an assessment statement.

When planning your lesson, try to be as specific as possible in describing what you want students to learn and how you will assess whether this happened. Do not just say, "I'll evaluate on the basis of student responses." Of course you will, but which student responses? Thinking this through will help you be clear about what is targeted and what students will be able to do when you are through.

As examples of the link between objectives and assessment, consider the following:

Objective:

Fourth graders will understand the rule for adding *-ing* to words so that when given a topic of their choice, they will write a paragraph in which each part of the rule is illustrated.

Assessment:

Have the students select a topic and write a paragraph that makes sense in which each part of the rule is illustrated.

Objective:

Seventh-grade life science students will know the parts of a flower so that when given a drawing showing the structure of a flower, they will correctly label each part.

Assessment:

Give the students a handout with a drawing showing the structure of a flower. Have them label each part identified with an arrow.

The point here is that the assessment must be consistent with the objective. If the objective calls for a listening behavior, it would be inappropriate to call for a discussion in the assessment. A detailed discussion of the preparation of items to measure students' attainment of goals is presented in Chapter 11. The assessments in our previous example are summative in that the purpose is to formally ascertain or certify whether the student can perform the desired outcomes. Teachers employ formative evaluations or assessments as part of the learning process and are designed to be nonthreatening. Research suggests that formative evaluations or assessments can raise student performance regarding standards because they promote interactive teaching and learning and because teachers know more about their students' progress and difficulties with learning (Black, 1998).

As a final note, don't confuse the assessment component of the lesson plan with reflection or critique, which is your evaluation of your own teaching performance. Although the critique is not actually a lesson plan component, it is an important step and a critical part of the planning and reflecting process as you evaluate your performance.

THE TOTAL LESSON PLAN

A simple way of organizing all the components of a lesson plan is presented in Figure 6.3. For Exercise 6.4, you will see that we have listed the procedures following the content, whereas in Figure 6.3, they are listed side by side. This arrangement is a matter of personal preference, and no choice is more correct than the other.

Formal paper-and-pencil tests are only one of a wide variety of assessments teachers should employ.

Anthony Magnacca/Merrill

Figure 6.3   Sample Lesson Plan

Unit: Social Classes in America

Objective: For the high school history student to understand social stratification in America so that when given a list of characteristics of a certain family, the student will choose one of the three classes that best represents the family, giving at least three examples of proof. (Colorado Academic Standard—History, 3.2)

Rationale: It is necessary for a history student to understand that America's social stratification is a fluid division of people. It is part of this country's social makeup to have little classification of people, although there are noticeable differences in this country's people.

Content	*Procedures*
I. Upper class	1. Identify characteristics of upper class.
A. Income	2. Discuss relationship of characteristics with each other. Ask "How are education and income related? How about education and occupation?"
B. Education	
C. Occupation	
D. Political affiliation	3. Ask "What characteristics separate them most from other classes?"
E. Residence	
II. Middle class	4. Repeat steps 1, 2, and 3 for middle and lower classes.
A. Income	
B. Education	5. Present case study 1 on overhead. Have class try to identify class in terms of characteristics discussed previously.
C. Occupation	
D. Political affiliation	
E. Residence	6. Present case study 2 on overhead. Discuss characteristics.
III. Lower class	
A. Income	7. If time permits, present case study 3 as a quiz. If there is not enough time, have students prepare for a quiz tomorrow.
B. Education	
C. Occupation	
D. Political affiliation	
E. Residence	

Materials: Dittos of characteristics for each student.

Assessment: Students should be able, in short essay form, to describe why a certain family could fit into one of the social classes studied, giving reasons why and characteristics of that class.

EXERCISE 6.4

Using a topic in your subject matter field or grade level, develop a lesson plan by attending to the areas listed here.

Unit:

Objective:

Rationale:

Content:

Procedures:

Materials:

Assessment:

DIVERSITY IN THE CLASSROOM

Planning for Diverse Populations

As noted frequently throughout the text, today's teachers are experiencing more heterogeneous populations in their classrooms than ever before. As a result, they are expected to teach traditional skills to a nontraditional group of students. In addition, teachers are also expected to diversify their instructional methods in ways that support students' self-esteem, knowledge of technology, and ethnic and language backgrounds (Eby & Herrell, 2005). Therefore, in addition to the standard elements of a lesson plan discussed earlier and summarized in an example in Figure 6.3, many state departments of education and school districts are now directing teachers to address diversity in a lesson plan *accommodations* subhead. Generally, teachers accommodate students by (a) determining backgrounds and prior knowledge, (b) providing sufficient time for students to undertake and complete tasks, and (c) providing appropriate learning materials to ensure student success. Now let's take a look at some plans that provide direction for accommodating students specifically in the area of exceptionalities.

Exceptionalities in Inclusive Classrooms

Increased numbers of students with exceptionalities are being included in regular classrooms in today's schools. As a result, instruction on inclusion is being included in many preservice education programs. One of the most critical of these components involves adapting unit and lesson planning for the needs of students with exceptionalities.

One adaptation uses task analysis, or the process of breaking complex skills down into simpler ones. A sample task analysis is presented in Figure 6.4.

As we see in Figure 6.4, the first task involves assessing the student, which requires identifying the student's level of academic, social, emotional, and physical functioning. Pretests, recommendations, reviews of reports on successive visits, observation, and consultations with external resources such as counselors or physicians can be used for this purpose.

Figure 6.4   Sample Special Education Task Analysis (Unit Plan)

Special Education
Task Analysis (Unit Plan)

Entering Behavior for Each Student: Enrolled in the second grade, Eric is an EMH (educably mentally handicapped) child who is functioning at a 4 to 5 year preschool level in reading and writing. Spelling is slowly being introduced and he is functioning at a kindergarten-level in math. Eric has been diagnosed as having ADD (attention deficit disorder) and is borderline hyperactive. He is currently receiving Ritalin three times a day. He receives his second dose at lunchtime (11:00 a.m.). Approximately 45 minutes before lunch, his frustration level is low, and he has a difficult time maintaining attention to a particular task.

En Route Objectives:

1. Given five pictures of different types of trains, the student will identify the engine, car, and caboose in all five trains (circle the engine, cross out the car, and underline the caboose).
2. Given a worksheet containing 10 words with the *sh, ch, th,* and *wh* diphthongs, the student will identify the diphthongs in all 10 words (circle).
3. Given a worksheet containing 10 compound words, the student will distinguish between the two component words with 80% accuracy (drawing a vertical line).
4. Given a handout of a short train story, the student will identify five of the seven contractions contained within (circle).
5. Given a worksheet with five words and their definitions, the student will identify each word with the appropriate definition with 100% accuracy (match).
6. Given a worksheet comprised of six sentences that describe particular events in the text, the student will state the correct sequence of events with 100% accuracy (by numbering).
7. Given a worksheet containing three short statements, the student will identify the correct statement depicting the main idea (circle).

Terminal Objectives:

Cognitive: For the second-grade EMH student to internalize the use of word-attack skills so that when given a copy of a page from *The Little Engine That Could,* the student will identify all the diphthongs, contractions, and compound words (circle).

Affective: For the second-grade EMH student to know that there are differences in what individuals can accomplish so that when given crayons and drawing paper, the student will describe (drawing) at least one task that is difficult and one task that is easy to accomplish.

This information makes it possible to state a terminal objective for the student. Once you have accomplished this task, you are ready to write *en route objectives,* which are more specific objectives designed to help the student reach the terminal objective.

Next, you will focus on organizing the special education lesson plan designed to facilitate the task analysis. A sample is presented in Figure 6.5.

Figure 6.5   Special Education Lesson Plan Example

Special Education
Lesson Plan

Date   <u>February 23</u>

A.   Enroute Objective #6: Given a worksheet comprised of six sentences that describe particular events in *The Little Engine That Could,* the student will state (by numbering) the correct sequence of events with 100% accuracy.

B.   Methods and Materials:

Materials: *The Little Engine That Could*
Teacher-made trains depicting the numbers 1 to 10
Pictures of sequence of events
Pictures of: the happy little train, the toys, the shiny new engine, the big strong engine, the old and tired engine, the little blue engine
String
Pencils
Crayons
Handouts depicting sequence of events

Methods:

1. Read *The Little Engine That Could* to the class.
   *Early in the morning because of Eric's attention span.
2. Review the numbers 1 to 10 using teacher-made trains and have them put in proper order.
   *Emphasize tactile with Eric using beads to help him to count.
3. Discuss terminology such as *first, then, after,* and *finally.*
4. Hang pictures and have them put in correct order.
   *To avoid confusion, let Eric do the first and the last items.
5. List unfamiliar words and review meanings.
6. Pass out handouts.
   *Eric receives handout with visual cues.

Application of Lesson to Pupil Interests and/or Real Life:

It is important for students to understand the concept that events occur in a particular order in stories as well as in real life. The attainment of this concept will assist them in their communication skills (retelling an event or story) as well as their comprehension skills (recalling a story or event). This concept assists the EMH students in organizing events in their minds, thus enabling a deeper understanding.

C.   Evaluation

Pupil: Teacher-made handout
   *Revised version of handout

Eric: Eric completed the revised handout with 100% accuracy but exhibited a high level of frustration and was restless while doing his work. He also needed teacher assistance.

We see that the lesson plan in Figure 6.5 includes only en route objective 6. In reality, a lesson plan will be prepared for each of the en route objectives listed in the task analysis. In addition, you need to employ a wide and varied selection of classroom methods and learning materials to facilitate the diverse needs of students. Moreover, the focus should not be totally academic but should also employ elements that are applicable, real, and relevant. Evaluations need to be flexible enough to measure both these elements and acceptable individual performance.

As often occurs in individualized education plans, which we discuss in Chapter 10, our examples focused on a single student, Eric. When developing such plans, you will frequently be addressing the needs of three, four, or more students with exceptionalities in your classroom whose instructional needs may or may not overlap. Here is where help from a consulting special education teacher is essential.

English Proficiency

Nationwide, there continues to be a rise in the numbers of children who have a limited English proficiency. This increase has led to the urgent need to provide high-quality education for students in the United States whose native language is not English. Programs designed for teachers range from county or district in-service workshops to university course work and master's degrees. Some of the more common references include English to Speakers of Other Languages, Teaching English to Speakers of Other Languages, and Teaching English as a Second Language. Common objectives include a focus on the following:

- Second-language acquisition
- English-language development
- Communication skills
- Cultural diversity
- Selected theories and practice

In addition to increasing their content and pedagogical knowledge in the area promoting English proficiency, it is equally important for teachers to be sensitive and responsive to the special issues related to educating language-minority children. Too often behaviors and responses from children that fall outside the teacher's expectations are viewed negatively and as culturally and linguistically deficient (Brisk, 1998; Gopaul-McNicol & Thomas-Presswood, 1998). When teachers in regular and special classrooms integrate positive and supportive views with an increased knowledge base, including the examples provided previously, they are in a position to be increasingly effective in promoting learning in students who come to them with limited English proficiencies.

Other Strategies

The effort to ensure an equal education for disadvantaged and minority students also extends to the issue of teaching strategies. In part, this component was placed on the national stage by the Clinton administration when it called for the establishment of Opportunity to Learn (OTL) standards as part of Goals 2000. To date, the focus has been on OTL strategies that are not necessarily viewed as standards but have shown a positive impact on student achievement. Selected strategies that also serve as *accommodation guidelines* include the following (Schwartz, 1998):

- Student access to high-level courses
- Presentations as free as possible from hidden bias
- Strategies for diverse populations and different learning styles
- Respect for diversity and protection from discrimination
- Provision of needed support
- A demonstrated concern for students' well-being
- Logical integration with other course work
- Reflection of the challenges of real-life problems

ADAPTING LESSON PLANNING FOR EVERYDAY USE

The basic formats we have presented here are more detailed than formats you are likely to encounter in schools. Experienced teachers typically use an abridged format that looks something like that shown in Figure 6.6.

Planning books that are blocked out in days and periods are useful tools for keeping track of the week's activities. A quick glance at the page tells the teacher the major activities for that period of that day. This can be helpful after a long weekend or as a means of keeping track on a particularly hectic day. Figure 6.7 shows an example of what a cell commonly looks like.

This brief format and the sketchy information it includes is likely to be misleading. Because we see only a brief outline and do not see objectives, rationales, and procedures, we might conclude that veteran teachers do not think about these things. Nothing could be

	Monday	Tuesday	Wednesday	Thursday	Friday
Period 1					
Period 2					
Period 3					
Period 4					
Period 5					
Period 6					
Period 7					

Figure 6.6 An Abridged Planning Format

Period 1

    Hand back quiz
    Introduce adjective clauses (p. 125)
    Assign exercises (p. 127)
    Begin individual conferences

Figure 6.7 A Completed Cell from an Abridged Planning Format

further from the truth. Master teachers have precise goals in mind, they have clear reasons for teaching the topics they teach, and they know in detail what procedures they will use. Because of their experience, much of this information is not written down. Further, as teachers acquire expertise, some of the procedures are virtually automatic, meaning that they require little conscious thought.

Our goal in writing this chapter is simple. The long-term, unit, and lesson planning we have described in detail is intended to give you concrete illustrations of the *thinking* and *decision making* in which all effective teachers engage. We want you to think and make decisions about content, goals, rationales, procedures, materials, and assessments. As you acquire experience, you too will write down less information. The information in this chapter is intended as a starting point, designed to help you make your thinking clear and systematic. Now, you should be planning in detail and writing down a considerable amount of information. This forces you to be specific and concrete. At this point, if information is not committed to paper, many of the planning decisions tend to be vague and ill formed. As you acquire experience, your thinking will become clearer, more of what you do will be automatic, and you will not have to write as much down.

TECHNOLOGY IN THE CLASSROOM

Facilitating the Planning Process

Planning books often do not provide sufficient space for detailing the information that is critical to implementing an effective lesson. Frequently, a listing of activities becomes the focus in such documents. Obviously, today's teachers are inundated with paperwork, and filing has become a major issue. It is equally obvious that teachers develop hundreds of unit and lesson plans in addition to long-range curricular strategies. The significant benefit of technology here is found in the efficiency of electronically storing plans on templates that are consistent with the formats in a given school district. Among other things, plans are extremely easy to prepare, access, revise, and reproduce for classroom use. In addition, it is a relatively simple and extremely efficient process to engage in reflective thought and undertake revisions immediately. The ability to electronically retrieve a plan instantaneously and revise it while one's thoughts are immediate and fresh provides teachers with a valuable tool in their efforts to continually improve the effectiveness of their instruction and increase their students' achievement.

Planning and Reflecting

You have made a series of decisions about the topics you will teach; what you want the students to know, understand, or be able to do with respect to the topics; why they are important; and how you will help students understand them. After you have taught the topics, you want to consider your thinking and the decisions you have made. This is the reflective aspect of planning. In a basic sense, reflection asks, "How good were the decisions I made?" Specifically, reflection might try to answer questions such as the following:

- How appropriate were the topics (i.e., should they be taught again)?
- Was the sequence of topics appropriate? If not, how should they be sequenced?
- Were my objectives appropriate for my students?

- Was my instruction aligned? Did my lesson plans facilitate my unit plan, and were the procedures and assessments I specified consistent with my objectives?
- Were the procedures I used as effective as they might have been? If not, what procedures might have been better?
- Did the materials I used adequately represent the topic? What representations would have made the topic more understandable?
- Did I adequately accommodate learner needs? What additional procedures and materials should I employ to further ensure student success?
- Could I make the overall environment more conducive to learning?

No one can answer these questions better than you can, but in some ways the answers are less important than developing the inclination to ask the questions. Teaching a topic because it is in the book or because it has been taught before is not an adequate reason for teaching it now. As teachers become reflective, they make more conscious and well-thought-out decisions about the topics they choose to teach and the procedures they will use to teach them. This is the essence of the relationship between decision making and reflection.

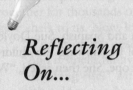

PLANNING FOR LEARNING

INTASC Principles 3, 7, and 9

Reflecting On...

Think about the different levels of planning: long-term planning, unit planning, and lesson planning. Then think about at least three critical considerations for each level.

SUMMARY

Planning exists at three levels: long-range, unit, and lesson planning. Each requires a series of decisions that must be made before instruction begins. Long-range planning, based on state standards, is an overall blueprint within which unit and specific lesson planning occur. Unit planning converts standards and goals into sequences of topics with rationales for teaching those topics. Specific lesson plans then convert the topics into teachable and learnable parts.

Written lesson plans follow a variety of formats. One includes a seven-part sequence, including the unit topic, objectives, rationale, content, procedures, materials, and assessment. Planning for working with students with exceptionalities requires more detailed plans, such as task analysis and individual education plans. Teachers must constantly address the need to accommodate diverse learner needs.

As teachers acquire experience, they are likely to write less information down on paper. This can be misleading, however, because master teachers think carefully about topics, goals and objectives, rationales, procedures, and assessments.

VIDEO EXERCISE

Go to MyEducationLab and select the topic "Planning: Lessons and Units" and watch the video "Civil War Discusssion." After viewing the video, respond to the following questions:

1. What state standard is the lesson on the Civil War facilitating? Note: You can select any state and locate the standards for fifth-grade content standards for social studies or you can use the following: http://doe.sd.gov/contentstandards/social/newstandards.asp. Then click on "Social Studies Standards: By Grade, 3–5."

2. After considering the opening remarks of the teacher, what could be an appropriate unit goal for this lesson?

3. Taking into consideration the unit goal you have identified, what would be two or three lesson plans that would facilitate the unit?

4. What would be an appropriate goals objective for the lesson that was taught on the Civil War?

DEVELOPING YOUR PORTFOLIO

As evidence that you are attaining a working knowledge of the planning strategies presented in Chapter 4, your portfolio task is to develop a unit plan and one lesson plan that facilitates the unit plan in a subject discipline of your expertise, using the formats found in Chapter 6 pp 169–178. In your lesson plan, be sure to cite a standard that your objective facilitates and, in addition to the lesson plan components, cite ways in which you might accommodate exceptional learners.

QUESTIONS FOR DISCUSSION

1. What are some examples of decisions you might make during long-term, unit, and lesson planning? What might be some alternative decisions? Provide rationales for the different decisions.

2. How might administrators and colleagues influence the planning decisions you make? Offer an example in each case.

3. Offer an example that describes how federal, state, and local agencies will influence your planning decisions.

4. Describe the different kinds of knowledge that teachers must possess to make the most effective decisions possible about planning. Offer examples for each of the kinds of knowledge.

5. Would veteran teachers be more effective if they wrote more detailed plans? Provide a rationale for your position.

6. Since veteran teachers typically do not prepare plans in the detail presented in this chapter, is requiring that you go through this process a waste of time? Why do you think so, or why do you think not?

7. An alternative to the planning process we have presented in this chapter might be for you to work as an "apprentice" with a veteran teacher and imitate the process that he or she goes through. How effective would that likely be in helping you learn how to plan? Provide a basis for your thinking with respect to this question.

SUGGESTIONS FOR FIELD EXPERIENCE

1. Interview a teacher. Ask her to describe her thinking when she is involved in long-term, unit, and lesson planning. Ask her to show you some written samples of her plans and describe how she uses them. Ask her what questions she asks herself after she has planned and conducted lessons.

2. Review some curriculum guides and see if you can identify elements of long-term, unit, and lesson planning in them.

3. Assuming that you have been placed at a school site, compare the content of this chapter with the planning you have seen at your school.

4. Given the opportunity, select a goal that appears in a unit plan in your field experience and develop a complete lesson plan for that goal.

5. Given the opportunity, develop and teach a lesson plan to a class or small group of students in your field placement. Then, using the list of questions found on page xxx, reflect on what you did and how you might revise or improve the presentation.

TOOLS FOR TEACHING

Print References

Blackburn, B. (2007). *Classroom instruction from A to Z: How to promote student learning.* Larchmont, NY: Eye on Education. This work presents a wide range of practical chapters, including "Active Learning Is the Focus," "Background Knowledge Is the Foundation," "Choices Add Interest," and "Focus on Your Purpose."

Jalongo, M., Rieg, S., & Helterbran, V. (2007). *Planning for learning: Collaborative approaches to lesson design and review.* New York: Teachers College, Columbia University. This book presents an excellent and thorough discussion on critical components of lesson design and planning.

Slavkin, M. (2004). *Authentic learning: How learning about the brain can shape the development of students.* Lanham, MD: Scarecrow Education. Chapter 6 presents a thorough review of thematic planning/interdisciplinary learning and includes discussions on definitions and benefits of interdisciplinary learning and a step-by-step plan for designing thematic units.

Sotto, E. (2007). *When teaching becomes learning: A theory and practice of teaching* (2nd ed.). New York: Continuum International Publishing Group. Chapter 17 presents a concise discussion on lesson planning, while chapter 21 presents an excellent and unusual chapter that discusses the difficulties and problems teachers may face with "bad lessons."

Utter, B. (2007). *Pick and plan: 100 brain-compatible strategies for lesson design*. Thousand Oaks, CA: Corwin Press. A workbook approach that presents an excellent five-part model for lesson plans that includes (a) engager, (b) frame, (c) activity, (d) debrief, and (e) story and metaphor.

Web Sites

www.sasked.gov.sk.ca/docs/biology/unitplan.html Here you will find a unit plan guide and sample model units.

www.coollessons.org Here you will find a series of educational units and lessons plans.

www.teachers.ash.org.au/bee/plan.htm Here you will find a curriculum exchange that offers unit plans, sample unit plan formats, integrated unit formats, and samples at differing educational levels.

http://school.discovery.com/lessonplans Here you will find a lesson plan library that offers lesson plans for grades K to 5, 6 to 8, and 9 to 12 in all subject matter areas.

www.eduref.org/Virtual/Lessons Here you will find a collection for more than 2,000 unique lesson plans written by teachers from all over the United States.

Standards and Implementing Instruction

In the third unit of this text, we analyze instruction from a learner-centered perspective. The contents of the chapters in this unit—7 through 10—have been influenced by several sources. One of these is the learner-centered principles published by the American Psychological

Association (Presidential Task Force on Psychology in Education, 1993). A summary of these principles highlights the following generalizations about learning and teaching:

- Students' prior knowledge influences learning.
- Students need to think about their own learning strategies.
- Motivation has a powerful effect on learning.
- Development and individual differences influence learning.
- The classroom's social context influences learning.

A second influence on the chapters in this section is student-centered learning and a view that emphasizes four key components (Eggen & Kauchak, 2007):

1. Learners construct their own understanding rather than having it delivered or transmitted to them.
2. New learning depends on prior understanding.
3. Learning is enhanced by social interaction.
4. Authentic learning tasks promote meaningful learning

Like the learner-centered principles, student centeredness refocuses our attention on the learner and reminds us that true learning must ultimately reside within and be influenced by the learner.

As we write about questioning strategies in Chapter 7, teaching strategies in Chapters 8 and 9, and facilitating learner differences in Chapter 10, we try to emphasize the centrality of learners in our instruction. Ultimately our success as teachers is measured in the growth of our students.

Questioning Strategies in an Era of Standards and Accountability

INTRODUCTION

Teaching is basically a combination of art and science. While research tells us in a systematic way differences between effective and less effective teaching strategies (the science of teaching), teachers must practice and apply what is known according to their own personality and to a certain extent their own intuition (the art of teaching). There is no one best way to teach, no super strategy. This chapter and the ones that follow are based on this premise.

We are now beginning the second phase, **implementation**, of our three-step model. You may want to review chapter 1 briefly to refresh your understanding of implementation. Simply stated, having identified goals primarily through the use of state standards, school

district curricula, and No Child Left Behind guidelines, you are now prepared to help learners reach these goals. The specific experiences and learning tasks you design for students to reach or master the goals fall under the umbrella of implementation. Implementation is simply how you teach.

A cornerstone of all effective teaching is that of classroom questioning. In the classroom, teachers ask questions for a variety of reasons. The most common include the follwing (Freiberg & Driscoll, 2000):

- Checking for student understanding of instruction
- Evaluating the effectiveness of the lesson
- Increasing higher-level thinking

Asking questions is an essential teaching strategy that can be used with virtually any subject matter area, grade level, or teacher personality. When done effectively, it can promote involvement, enhance learning, motivate students, and provide both teachers and students with valuable feedback about learning progress (Eggen & Kauchak, 2004). The qualities of effective questions are (Cook, 1999) that they are brief, clear, focused, relevant, constructive, neutral, and open ended.

Questioning also helps promote a student-centered learning environment while maintaining a goal-focused activity. Because of these factors, we discuss questioning specifically first in this chapter and then describe how questioning can be incorporated into complete teaching strategies in subsequent chapters. After completing this chapter and Chapters 8 and 9, we hope you will have the background to begin forming a personally effective way of interacting with your students. The effective use of questioning techniques will significantly improve this interaction by expanding student understanding and getting them actively involved (Henniger, 2004).

We begin our discussion with a description of question level and its influence on learning, followed by explanations and illustrations of specific questioning strategies designed to meet specific goals. We conclude the chapter with a discussion of links between questioning, critical thinking, and motivation.

LEARNER OBJECTIVES

After completing your study of Chapter 7, you should be able to do the following:

- Explain the role of low- and high-level questions in learning
- Understand differences between convergent and divergent questions
- Explain how different questioning strategies (redirection, prompting, and probing) contribute to learning
- Increase your awareness of ways to promote critical thinking through questioning

APPLYING QUESTIONING STRATEGIES IN THE CLASSROOM

Following is a case study in which a high school science teacher presents a lesson on chemical compounds. As you read the case study, consider the following questions (you might want to review the discussion of the cognitive domain in Chapter 4 on pg. 104–108):

- Is the teacher asking questions that simply require students to recall or remember information?
- Is the teacher asking questions that require students to process information at the higher levels of the cognitive domain? If so, what levels?
- Does the teacher involve a number of students in the discussion?
- What does the teacher do if a student does not verbalize a desired response?
- What does the teacher do when she wants more information from a student who has provided a desired response?

A high school physical science teacher begins a lesson on chemical compounds by saying, "In front of each of you are two containers, each with a different substance. Look at the substances carefully and try to make some comparisons between them. How are they similar and different . . . Jim?"

"Well, they're both whitish colored."

"OK, good . . . Nancy?"

"They look sort of grainy. They both look sort of grainy."

"Could you explain what you mean by grainy?"

"Well . . ."

"Would you say they're chunky or powdery, Nancy?"

"Chunky."

"What do you call these chunks . . . anyone?"

Manny answers, "Crystals."

"Good. They're both made of crystals. What else can we say about the two as a comparison . . . Tom? [Pauses several seconds.] Tom, what could we do with the substances besides look at them?"

"Well, we could rub them in our hands."

"OK, let's try that. Here," the teacher says, passing Tom the containers. "How do they feel?"

"This one is finer grained," Tom responds as he holds one up.

"Fine. How could you relate that to what we said about crystals?"

"The crystals of this one are smaller."

"OK, good, Tom. Now, Jacinta, what else could we do with the substances to make comparisons?"

"I'm not sure."

"Well, we've looked at them, and we've rubbed them in our hands to use the senses of touch and sight. What other senses could we use to extend our observations?"

"We could smell them."

"OK, try that," the teacher says, passing the crystals to Jacinta. "What do you smell?"

"I don't smell anything."

"What do you suppose we should try next . . . Anyone?"

"We could taste them," Murray replies.

"Your idea is good, but remember I've said that for safety you should never put anything into your mouth until you're sure what it is. However, I know what these are, and these are harmless substances, so, Juan, you taste this one, and Peter, you taste the other. How do they taste?"

Juan replies first. "This one tastes bitter."

Peter follows quickly with, "This one tastes just the opposite."

"Whoa! Could you clarify that statement, Juan?"

"OK. It tastes like salt."

"How about yours, Peter?"

"It must be sugar."

"OK. So what is the formula for salt . . . Juan? [Pauses several seconds.] Let's try this, Juan. What is salt composed of?"

"Sodium and chloride, I think."

"That's right. What might the formula be, then?"

"NaCl?"

"Right, good! Now, anyone, what is sugar composed of?"

Murray says, "There's carbon in it."

"Yes. What else . . . Nancy?"

Nancy looks confused.

"What is there a lot of in the atmosphere?"

Nancy offers tentatively, "Oxygen?"

"Right! Do you suppose there might be some oxygen in sugar, Nancy?"

"Yeah. There might be."

"You're right; there is. What else might there be? It's the lightest element . . . Tran?"

"Hydrogen?"

"Right. Now, using all this information could anyone guess at the formula for sugar?"

"CHO?" Helene offers.

"Good thinking, Helene. It's consistent with what we said about salt. Suppose, though, that there are twice as many atoms of hydrogen as there are carbon or oxygen in sugar. What might the formula be then?

QUESTIONING LEVELS

Teachers use questions for five major purposes: (a) to involve students in the lesson, (b) to promote students' thinking and comprehension, (c) to review important content, (d) to control students, and (e) to assess student progress (McMillan, 2004). The key to effective questioning is to ask questions that allow you to reach an instructional goal or that facilitates a standard most effectively.

Different types of questions are effective at different times, and teachers ask questions for several reasons, some of which include the following (Brualdi, 1998):

- Asking questions helps teachers keep students actively involved in the lesson.
- While answering questions, students have the opportunity to openly express their ideas and thoughts.
- Questioning students enables other students to hear different explanations of the material by their peers.

- Asking questions helps teachers pace their lessons and moderate student behavior.
- Questioning students helps teachers evaluate student learning and revise their lessons as necessary.

At certain times, questions that establish a knowledge of informational foundation recall are required, whereas at other times we want students to link information and apply it to thinking about our world. For instance, consider these questions:

What is 9 + 6?
What present-day significance does studying the play *Julius Caesar* have for us?

The demands on the learner are obviously much different, but for an elementary school teacher whose goal is for students to know their multiplication facts, the first question is valid and important, as is the second one for a secondary literature teacher who wants students to link or, in this case, analyze moral dilemmas.

Low-Level Questions

In our discussion of the cognitive domain in Chapter 4, we said that the remembering level requires students to recall information that has been learned and stored in long-term memory. **Low-level questions** tap this knowledge. Examples include the following:

What are the three most common tools in a metal shop?

How much is 5 plus 5?

What is the Pythagorean theorem?

Who was the pacifist leader of India after World War II?

How do you spell *anonymous?*

What is one animal that survived the prehistoric age?

Teachers use low-level questions to accomplish several goals:

- To assess students' background knowledge
- To remind students of important information
- To establish an informational base that will be used in higher-level operations, which we discuss in the next section

Often, low-level questions elicit a yes/no response or simply allow for a choice between two alternatives. In that the teacher cannot be absolutely sure the student has truly conceptualized the material, the use of these kinds of questions should be limited. However, when used, the technique of probing, discussed later in the chapter, can be used to check the depth of students' perceptions and knowledge.

High-Level Questions

For certain goals, low-level questions are important and valuable, but at other times we want students to connect ideas and expand their thinking. This leads us to the topic of **high-level questions.** As discussed in Chapter 4, the characteristic that separates a low-level from a high-level question is that the latter requires intellectual processing or the connecting or transforming of ideas by students, whereas the former is limited to memorization with the information being recalled on demand. In terms of the cognitive taxonomy, low-level questions target the remembering level. The remaining five levels (understand, apply, analyze, evaluate, and create) are all considered to be high level.

A high-level question is any question that requires the student to do more than recall previously learned information. Obviously, high-level questions vary in difficulty and demands placed on the students, but the key characteristic they possess is that they require more than mere recall.

Research on the relative merits of high-level and low-level questions underscores the complexity of teaching and the importance of clear goals (Good & Brophy, 2008). While it might seem that higher-level questions are intrinsically better than lower ones because they are more challenging, teachers must also consider the fact that low-level questions can expand and reinforce the students' knowledge base. This suggests the need for teachers to first consider goals or reasons for asking a particular question. If the purpose is to identify or reinforce a particular bit of information, such as math facts, lower-level questions are appropriate. If your goal is to encourage students to *think* about the content they are learning, higher-level questions are more effective at accomplishing that goal. As a final note, research has now established that asking higher-level questions, by itself, does not ensure academic success. Your learners must also have the knowledge base necessary to engage in complex thinking tasks (Armstrong, Henson, & Savage, 2005).

Anthony Magnacca/Merrill

Asking low- and high-level questions is a technique teachers employ to perception check the students' ability to store as well as process information.

Now, let's see how this works in the classroom.

A teacher begins, "In looking at the balance of power arrangements through history, we have seen most such arrangements rarely last more than a few decades. Why do you suppose these arrangements collapse?. . . . Carlos?"

"I think the foreign policies of many countries are changing rapidly, and, as their goals change, the nations have to seek new alliances."

"How about the United States? How does the United States seek out these alliances?. . . . Lavonda?"

"We try to find out who agrees with our position. This would include not only countries who would support us but also those in need of our support."

By asking students questions beginning with phrases such as "why do you suppose" and "how does the United States seek," the teacher extends student thinking beyond rote memory. Both students had to integrate prior information and were therefore working at a high level.

An alternate way to encourage student thinking is to ask students to provide and explain examples of abstract ideas. Consider the statement "Give me an example, that we haven't previously discussed, of a simile." A student responding to this question must generate, on the basis of previous information, a new example of the concept *simile*. Because it requires students to think about content in a deep rather than a superficial manner, it is another excellent way to stimulate higher-level thinking.

Another effective high-level question asks students to state an idea or definition in the student's own words. For example, "Tell me in your own words what we mean by the statement 'Literature reflects the time and society of the authors.'" The answer to this question could be followed by the teacher asking for an example of an author, his or her work, and the characteristics of the society—another high-level question.

Another valuable high-level discussion question is the consideration of author motive, perspective, or reference frame, as in this example: "We've read the column by the noted journalist William F. Buckley. Where do you suppose Buckley is coming from in the column?" The discussion would involve consideration of his conservative orientation, probable motives, and basic philosophical stance.

High-level questions can also require students to provide the solution to a problem, such as "An item originally selling for $20 is marked 20% off. What is the sale price?" The solution to the problem requires a high-level response. We should mention one caution, however. It is a quite common practice in math texts to include a series of problems identical to each other in form. The students solve each as they solved the first, and the level of the task after the first problem is no longer high but, in fact, is merely recall of process. While this occurs more often in assigned work than in an interactive questioning situation, it can occur in both, and teachers may think they are getting a high-level response when the opposite is actually occurring. The solution is simple. Mix up the types of problems, and students will be required to give high-level responses.

EXERCISE 7.1

Using the INTASC and NCATE standards introduced in Chapter 1, reread the chapter-opening scenario that presents a lesson on chemical compounds and identify all those the teacher is addressing.

EXERCISE 7.2

Read the following scenario and identify each teacher statement as being either a low-level (l) or a high-level (h) question.

_____ 1. "On the board are three lists of words I'd like for you to analyze for a minute. What is special about the first two lists . . . Amy?"
"All the words are alike."

_____ 2. "Could you explain what you mean by _are alike?_"
"Well, they're all words that I would use to mean something good about somebody."

_____ 3. "That's right. Does anyone notice anything else about these words . . . Bob?"
"You could use one of them to mean the other."

_____ 4. "Can you give me an example of this?"
"I could say, 'You are a very competent teacher,' or I could say, 'You are a very skill-ful teacher,' and, either way, I'd mean the same thing."

_____ 5. "Good, Bob. So the terms in column 1 are more or less interchangeable with those in column 2, right?" General agreement is evident in students' nods.

_____ 6. "What term do you use to designate this type of relationship?" [No response.]

_____ 7. "OK. Think back to your study of prefixes, suffixes, and root words. Can anybody remember the prefix that means _same_ . . . Sally?"
"_Syn-._"

_____ 8. "Good. Now, can anyone remember the one for _name?_"
"_-onym._"

_____ 9. "So, Sally, when you put them together you get . . ." "_Synonym._"

_____ 10. "Very good. Can you find some relationship between the words in column 1 and those in column 2 . . . Bob?"
"Those in column 2 are synonyms of those in column 1."
Amy adds, "And those in column 1 are synonyms of those in column 2."

_____ 11. "Yes. Now look at column 3. [Pause.] How do these words relate to those in the first two columns?" [No response.]

_____ 12. "OK. Does _odious_ mean the same thing as _pleasant_ . . . Samantha?"
"No."

_____ 13. "Does it mean the same thing as _agreeable_ . . . Jared?"
"No, it's the opposite of _agreeable._"

_____ 14. "Good, Jared. Now, Bob, can you see another set of words in the column that has a similar relationship?"
"Yes, _ugly_ means just the opposite of _pretty_ and _attractive_, and _mean_ is just the opposite of _kind._"

_____ 15. "So can someone tell us the relationship between the first two columns and the third . . . LaDawn?"
"Those in column 3 are opposites of those in columns 1 and 2."

_____ 16. "Good. Do you recall the word that expresses this relationship . . . Kareem?"
"_Antonym._"

_____ 17. "Can someone make up a sentence using words that are antonyms . . . Bob?"
"_Hot_ is the opposite of _cold._"

_____ 18. "Class, is Bob's example correct? If so, why?

QUESTION FOCUS

Convergent Questions

Another way to think about the effects that questions have on student thinking is in terms of convergent and divergent questions. **Convergent questions** are those that generally require one correct answer. Convergent questions are useful for establishing facts or ascertaining answers to problems that have one correct answer. In general, they are questions of fact or recall and are often of a low level, as described in the previous section. For example, the following are convergent questions:

1. What is 6 times 9?
2. What part of speech modifies a noun or pronoun?
3. A turtle is in what animal class?
4. What is the chemical formula for table salt?
5. What is the most populous country in the world?

Note in each of these that there is only one correct answer for each question, and the answer requires recall of previously learned information.

Exceptions to this rule involve convergent questions with a narrow range of correct responses and solutions for problems requiring application or analysis. Regarding the former, asking a student to name a primary color obviously has more than one correct answer, but, the range is very narrow, and therefore the question is still convergent. Regarding application or analysis, if you ask, "I have 400 feet of fence, and I want to enclose the maximum area in a four-sided figure. What should the dimensions be?" this is a high-level question but is still convergent in that only one answer to the problem is correct.

Divergent Questions

While convergent questions require one correct answer, **divergent questions** are just the opposite in that many different answers are appropriate. This allows the teacher to assess student understanding while involving a large numbers of students. For instance, consider the following questions:

1. How are *Julius Caesar* and *Hamlet* alike?
2. Give me an example of a first-class lever.
3. Give me one of the most significant dates in world history.

Notice that each of the questions can be answered in several ways. For example, in the first case, responses might include the following:

1. "They're both written by Shakespeare."
2. "They're both tragedies."
3. "Both have male central characters."

In the second case, responses might include these:

1. "Screwdriver prying open a paint can lid"
2. "Crowbar prying up a rock"
3. "Scissors"

And in the third case, these:

1. "1588—the defeat of the Spanish Armada"
2. "1215—the signing of the Magna Carta"
3. "1066—the Battle of Hastings"
4. "1776—the American Declaration of Independence"

Obviously, many more answers could be given in each case, but the illustrations show how divergent questions can be used to promote student involvement by allowing a number of students to respond to the same question. Additionally, divergent questions can be used to have students explore and reflect on their responses, allowing, from the constructivist point of view, for a refinement of what students think they know. Questions such as "How did you arrive at this answer?" and "How did you approach this problems, " can be used to guide students in a critical exploration process (Parsons, Hinson, & Brown, 2001).

EXERCISE 7.3

As a review for both the level and the direction of questions, label the following statements as low level/divergent (l/d), low level/convergent (l/c), high level/divergent (h/d), or high level/convergent (h/c).

_____ 1. How is architecture influenced by culture?

_____ 2. What were some of the possible economic motives of the United States that added to its conflict with Japan prior to World War II?

_____ 3. What assumptions can you make about a novel that is referred to as a classic?

_____ 4. Name the major organs of the digestive system.

_____ 5. What may have caused Achilles to choose youth and fame over long life?

_____ 6. What are the two elements found in salt?

_____ 7. Put into your own words what effect the philosophies of Aristotle and Plato had on the generations that followed them.

_____ 8. What would be the implications of an average world rate of 5.1 births per woman?

_____ 9. Giving equal weight to all points discussed in the readings, what was the main argument favoring separatism?

_____ 10. You want to get from Jacksonville to Miami, which is 360 miles. The speed limit is 55 miles per hour. If you stay within the speed limit and drive at a steady speed, what is the minimum amount of time the trip will take?

_____ 11. Can anyone give us an example of iambic pentameter?

_____ 12. What fallacies appeared in the theory that the earth was the center of the universe?

_____ 13. List the steps involved in operating a lathe.

_____ 14. Based on three historical events of your choice, to what degree do you believe JFK's "New Frontier" was a success?

_____ 15. In Orwell's *Animal Farm,* what techniques are used to persuade the animals to devote their all to the farm?

QUESTIONING STRATEGIES

Using Open-Ended Questions and Redirection to Increase Student Involvement

A major goal in developing effective questioning strategies is to increase the amount of student participation. Typically, interaction patterns involve a teacher asking a question and a student volunteering a response to the question. As the activity proceeds, more knowledgeable or verbally aggressive students continue to be involved, while others not participating drift away from the activity (Eggen & Kauchak, 2007; Good & Brophy, 2008). These patterns can become well established, with those volunteering being the primary participants and the others rarely responding and often not even attending to the activity. As a result, a teacher often has only a portion of the class paying attention, meaning that only a portion is learning. Furthermore, the teacher should not allow a single response from one of the better students to be the yardstick by which he or she measures if a concept has been mastered. Instead, the teacher should communicate with a representative sampling of all students and demand accurate paraphrasing and summarizing of what was to be learned (Scheidecker & Freeman, 1999).

In general, teachers do not direct questions to particular students but may, more often than not, ask questions of students they believe are higher achievers. An interesting and somewhat ironic aspect of both these phenomena is that teachers are quite unaware of the patterns and will often deny their existence, even to an observer who has pointed them out to the teachers immediately after a lesson.

To create a learning environment that invites the participation of all students, it is crucial that teachers break these patterns. When different interaction patterns are established, powerful results can occur. One effective pattern involves the use of **open-ended questions** coupled with a **redirection** teaching strategy. Open-ended questions are often thought of as questions for which more than one single correct solution is possible. Two other forms of open-ended questions that are easy to ask, quite easy to answer, and excellent for promoting student involvement are descriptive and comparative questions. The first type asks learners to observe and describe an object or event, such as an illustration, a demonstration, a map, a graph, a table, or a statement. Dialogue is initiated by the teacher making a directive such as the following:

1. "What do you notice here?"
2. "Tell me about this."
3. "What do you see?"
4. "Describe the object in front of you."

Descriptive questions provide an effective way to promote involvement, success, and thinking.

The second type, comparative questions, requires the learner to look at two or more objects, statements, illustrations, or demonstrations and identify similarities or differences between them. As students identify similarities, they are moving toward the establishment of a pattern that ultimately results in a concept or generalization. For example, suppose that students are shown the following three sentences:

1. He is quiet as a mouse.
2. He was as large as a mountain.
3. They ran as fast as the wind.

The question "What is similar about the sentences?" requires learners to identify patterns that ultimately specify the characteristics of the concept *simile*. The word *as* appears in each, as does a nonliteral comparison between two objects or ideas.

The second component of the questioning pattern mentioned previously, the redirection teaching strategy, promotes a high level of interaction and thought in a classroom. This strategy involves framing a single question for which there are many possible responses and acknowledging and accepting different responses from several students. The following is an example of how this can occur in the classroom:

"Having completed our overview of the presidents, who do you think was the greatest American chief executive? Tran?"

   "Abraham Lincoln."
   "Sharif?"
   "Woodrow Wilson."
   "José, another one?"
   "George Washington."
   "Those are all excellent choices. Let's talk about them now."

Notice that the teacher does not respond to or discuss the students' replies. Instead, the teacher redirects the original question. In doing so, she eliminates the possibility of a few students dominating the discussion and also quantitatively increases student participation. Other possible benefits of this approach include expanding the scope and elevating the content expressed in the initial responses. Open-ended questions can also be used to elicit high-level thinking. In the next sequence, pay close attention to the ways in which the teacher redirects the question:

"We mentioned different presidents you believe to have been great. Why do you think they were great men? Yes, Betty."

   "I think Lincoln was great because he was able to hold the country together, and Washington was great because he got the country started."

   "Do you have something to add, Daniella?"

   "I think Wilson was great because he was a man of peace and could see the problems beyond his time."

   "Maria, can you add anything else?"

   "They were all great men because they were strong and had the courage to fight for what they believed in."

It is important to note that although the three students may not have been dealing with the same individual, all were responding to a single question posed by the teacher.

Notice in the preceding example that all the redirected questions were divergent. While most redirected questions will be divergent, it is possible to redirect a convergent question as well:

"We have been working on our 5-times tables, children, so my first question is how much is 5 times 2 . . . Myron?"
"5 times 2 is 10."
"What do you think, Suzanna?"
"I think that is right."

Teachers can use convergent redirects to (a) check other students' understanding, (b) involve other students in the lesson, and (c) communicate that the lesson content belongs to students as well as the teacher.

Other questions that are easy to redirect are those that require description and comparison. For example, using the illustration of the concept *simile* provided previously, the teacher could present the sentence "He is quiet as a mouse" and direct a number of individuals to describe the sentence, requesting that each say something different about it. The interaction patterns might appear as follows:

Teacher: What do you notice about the sentence . . . Tim?

Tim: It has six words in it.

Teacher: What else . . . Sue?

Sue: He is the subject.

Teacher: And what else . . . Steve?

Steve: It's about a boy.

This process can go on as long as the teacher desires or until it looks as if the class is ready to move on.

A sensible following step would be for the teacher to present a second example and ask for comparisons. For instance, students now have displayed before them the sentences. "He is quiet as a mouse" and "She was a rock of strength." The teacher could then ask, "What is the same or different about the two sentences" Responses would vary, and the question could be redirected to several students.

In summary, we have defined redirection as any question that is asked of several different individuals. When combined with open-ended questions, it is a powerful strategy to increase student involvement and motivation and also promote achievement.

Prompting

A significant amount of interactive classroom activity is devoted to asking questions in a variety of teacher/student discussions. Questioning can be either positive or negative. **Positive questioning** is operationally defined as questioning that helps the student change a wrong provisional answer into the right final answer. **Negative questioning** occurs when the student shifts from correct to incorrect after questioning. Additionally, what happens when we ask a student a question, and she either fails to reply or she responds incorrectly? Generally, teachers move on to another student in order to maintain interest and momentum (Eggen & Kauchak, 2004). Unfortunately, doing so has problems. The student who was unable to respond often becomes confused, discouraged, and psychologically removed from the discussion. We have stressed desirability of total involvement, but how can we deal with students who cannot answer questions or whose responses are wrong? The following sequence between a teacher and one student illustrates one way to deal with this problem:

"Regarding our discussion on international power patterns, which pattern does this equal arms scale demonstrate? . . . . Pat?" Pat does not respond.

"Any idea?"

"I don't know."

"OK, let's take another look at the scale. If this object is 2 ounces and the one on the other tray is 2 ounces, they are said to be . . . ?"

"Equal."

"Right. Equal in what?"

"Weight."

The teacher nods. "Now, if we have these equal weights, one on each tray, what happens?"

"They balance each other."

"Fine. Let's suppose each weight represents three countries and that the groups are basically opposed to each other. If they are equal in strength or power, they would be . . . ?"

"Balanced."

"Great! Then this demonstration represents what pattern of power?"

"The balance of power pattern."

"Now you've got it!"

The preceding example demonstrates the strategy referred to as **prompting,** which involves the use of hints, or clues, that are used to aid the student in responding successfully. This method can also be employed when a response as incorrect, as in the following example:

"To be specific, the pattern of power called balance is one in which two or more nation-states form a coalition in order to protect themselves from a specific enemy. Coalitions of equal power oppose each other; they are in balance, and peace is preserved. However, once the balance is broken and once coalition tips the power scale in its favor, the likelihood of war is increased. As with our scale, if too much weight is added to one side, the other side will be overpowered. Now, let's examine this idea. Does the United Nations represent a balance-of-power arrangement . . . Marisha?"

"I think it does."

"Let's analyze it and find out. Marisha, does the UN aid and support any group member attacked by an enemy?"

"It's supposed to."

"OK. Is the UN coalition of two or more nations?"

"Yes."

"Is the UN pledged against a specific enemy?"

"I'm not sure."

"Is there another organization of equal size and power with which the UN is locked in mortal combat?"

"No."

"Then what do you conclude?"
"The United Nations is not an example of balance of power."
"Good thinking."

After giving an incorrect response, students benefit most by the teacher asking a series of simple questions that give clues to help them arrive at the correct answer. This is often preferable to merely giving the student the correct answer and moving to another student or asking another student to help immediately after the incorrect response because it makes public the logic behind the correct answer.

Consider one more example. In the previous section, we used the sentences "He is quiet as a mouse" and "She was a rock of strength." The teacher wants the students to identify the first as a simile and the second as a metaphor. She probably has asked a series of divergent questions—descriptions and comparisons—that have been redirected to several individuals. However, let's assume that students do not recognize the sentences as examples of the respective concepts. One way to correct this problem is to prompt students to arrive at the correct answer:

"What do you notice about she and rock in the second sentence . . . Shin?"
    "It says she is a rock."
"Does the sentence mean she really is a rock?"
    "No. Not really."
"So we say this is kind of a comparison?"
    [Pause.]
"Literal or nonliteral?"
    "Nonliteral."
"OK, good. We have a nonliteral comparison of two ideas. The same is true about the first sentence, but there is a special word in it. What word?"
    " As."
"Yes. The word as is added. Otherwise, the two sentences are similar. What are they called?"
    "The first is a simile, and the second is a metaphor."
"Excellent. We have identified the key differences between the two sentences."

As the research literature indicates, prompting is an important technique employed by effective teachers. However, our experience in working with teachers suggests that it can be difficult to implement and is not employed as often as would be desirable. The reason for the difficulty probably is that prompting requires thinking on your feet. While many other teaching procedures and skills can be planned and practiced in advance, prompting can be practiced only in the context of an actual lesson.

Sometimes you simply assume that the student's response will be correct, and you will draw a blank when the student is incorrect. How would you prompt a student who did not know the largest known planet? Would you refer to Roman mythology or perhaps suggest that it begins with a "J"? Would you enlist another student's support or possibly throw in the towel and answer your own question? Regardless of your choice, let us suggest that, assuming that the student did not succeed, you keep that student in mind so that you might be able to facilitate a successful response during the remainder of the session.

Prompting can be enormously rewarding and enjoyable to help learners construct responses they previously could not provide. For these reasons, we encourage you to persevere. With practice, you will become skilled and will reap the intrinsic rewards of feeling that you have had a positive, direct, and tangible influence on student learning.

Careful preparation can be an aid that will help your prompting efforts. For instance, if a teacher knows in advance that she wants the students to identify "nonliteral comparison without *as* or *like*" as the key characteristic of metaphor and "nonliteral comparison using *as* or *like*" for simile, that awareness will help her think on her feet because she knows what she wants from the students. She can then ask whatever questions it takes to get them to the idea.

Probing

At this point, we have discussed ways to increase student involvement through open-ended questions, redirecting, and prompting strategies. The first two involve providing opportunities for complex and creative expression while increasing the numbers of participating students, and the third is a strategy for dealing with incorrect responses in an informative and humane manner. Sometimes, however, the student's reply is correct but possibly insufficient because it may lack understanding or depth. In such a case, it is important for the teacher to have the student supply additional information to ensure comprehensive and complete answers. This strategy is called **probing.** Let's take a closer look at probing in action:

The teacher begins, "Do you think trees are important to the land . . . Carmelina?"
   "Yes."
   "Why, Carmelina?"
   "Because they help hold things together."
   "What do you mean by that?"
   "Well, the roots and all go down into the ground and help the ground stay in one place."
   "That's very good, Carmelina, and as we learned yesterday, when the earth begins to move away to a different place, it's called . . ."
   "Erosion."

Through the process of probing, the teacher attempts to get students to justify or further explain their responses, thereby increasing the depth of the discussion. It also helps to move students away from surface responses. All too often, we do not take our students beyond the simple yes, no, or correct-answer response, and earlier in the chapter we suggested that questions eliciting such responses are not very effective. However, at those infrequent times when such questions are posed, we need to require students to offer a rationale for their choice. We must provide them with increased opportunities to process information—to deal with the why and the how based on the what of their answers.

The function of a probe is to provide an opportunity to support or defend a simply stated position or point of view intellectually. By doing so, students gain experience in dealing with high-level tasks and achieve a greater feeling of success.

EXERCISE 7.4

Read the following anecdote and identify all the teacher's statements that are either redirections (r), prompts (p), or probes.

_____ 1. "Today we're considering the properties of numbers. Here is a list of some numbers." The teacher points to a list on the board. "From the list, identify a prime number . . . Mariko?" "Three."

_____ 2. "Another . . . Shalynne?" "Two."

_____ 3. "Another one . . . Angela?" "Five."

_____ 4. "Now, give me a number that is not prime . . . Pedro?" "Six."

_____ 5. "Another one . . . Rudy?" "Eight."

_____ 6. "OK. Let's try something we haven't done yet. Six can be reduced to the product of two prime numbers. What are they . . . Bob?" Bob does not respond.

_____ 7. "Let me help you, Bob. Now remember your times tables. What times what equals 6?" "Oh, 3 times 2."

_____ 8. "OK, good. Now, from this list, select a number that is a perfect square." Bob adds, "Nine."

_____ 9. "Good, Bob. Another one . . . Sarina?" "Sixteen."

_____ 10. "OK. Another one . . . Ralph?" "Twenty-four."

_____ 11. "Let's check this one. First let's back up a step. A perfect square is some number that can be broken down into the product of another number times itself. What number did we say times itself equals 9?" "Three."

_____ 12. "Good, Ralph. Let me continue to help you with this. What number times itself equals 16?" "Four."

_____ 13. "Now, does any number times itself equal 24?" "Hmmm. No, 24 isn't a perfect square."

_____ 14. "OK. Then can you name a perfect square from this list?" "Twenty-five?"

_____ 15. "That's the way!" Now, why did you pick 25 Ralph?"

_____ 16. "Because 5 times 5 is 25."

_____ 17. "That's great, Ralph. Now you've got it!"

Wait Time

When we ask students thought-provoking questions, we want them to think. One way to do this is through the process of **wait time,** which has been emphasized in the literature through the pioneering research of Mary Budd Rowe (1974, 1986). Wait time can be considered in two ways. The first is defined as the time a teacher pauses after a question. It normally begins when the teacher stops speaking and terminates when a student responds or the teacher speaks again. The second is defined as the time a teacher waits after a pupil responds to either comment or employ prompts or probes.

Researchers found that teachers typically wait 1 second or less for students to answer. Think about that for a moment. Suppose you as a student studying this book are asked in a class discussion, "Under what conditions would it be inappropriate to use prompting as a strategy?" Your instructor gives you less than 1 second to answer before asking another question or turning the question to someone else. This is the situation students face continually. By contrast, if given more time to think, the quality of student answers improve. These are the results that Rowe found in examining the effects of increased "think time." She found that when teachers wait approximately 3 seconds or longer, the quality of student responses improves. This simple process of giving students more time to answer also positively influences learning. When assessing a student's cognitive abilities, the use of controlled, increased wait time following a question or a prompt may well result in more accurate measures of the student's level of functioning.

The implications of this research are obvious. As we question students, we should make an effort to wait a few seconds for them to answer. At first, a period of silence may seem awkward, but both you and the students will quickly get used to it.

However, as with other questioning techniques, this strategy should be implemented with judgment and sensitivity. Imagine, for example, that you call on a student, and she appears to draw a blank. As you wait, she panics. In this case, you would not wait as long as you would in another where the student, appears to be really thinking about the answer. In addition, in asking low-level, convergent questions such as "What is 4 times 7?" or "What city is at the tip of Lake Michigan?" you would not wait as long as you would in asking a more thought-provoking question, such as "Why do you suppose Chicago developed into such a major city?"

In summary, the benefits of wait time include enhanced participation in discussions, increased use of reasoning to justify answers, and more speculative responses. Similar benefits also occur when wait time is used before a teacher comments after a student response (Campbell, Campbell, & Dickinson, 2004). Finally, our primary goal in this discussion is to make you aware of the value of wait time so that you will make an effort to practice it when you teach. None of us employs the technique perfectly, and we are not suggesting that you silently count after every question you ask or do the same after a student responds. However, with effort, you can increase the amount of time you give your students to think, and this will increase your questioning effectiveness.

DIVERSITY IN THE CLASSROOM

Facilitating Needs Through Questioning Strategies

As we have noted throughout the text, students come to school with a wide variety of cultural and learning differences. Effective communication is a critical factor in establishing and reflecting teachers' understanding of their students. Varying groups emphasize storing information as opposed to processing it, individual inquiry versus group processing, active versus passive participation, and attitudinal as well as cognitive exchange of information. The effective use of questioning strategies enables teachers to capitalize on the various strengths of individual students. For example, students who bring differences to the classroom may initially be hesitant to participate in classroom activities, particularly verbal ones. The previous discussion suggested that teachers who employ wait time increase their effectiveness in the classroom. Specifically, when average wait times are longer, learners who have not previously answered questions become more active participants in discussions, and these increased levels of involvement result in teachers' raising their estimations of these learners' abilities (Armstrong et al., 2005).

In addition, recall our earlier discussion of divergent questions, especially open-ended questions. These can be effectively employed at the onset of a lesson to help ascertain individual needs and perceptions by asking children (a) what they already know, (b) what they need clarified, and (c) what questions they need answered. The answers to these questions can provide much helpful information in developing the theme or lesson (Henniger, 2005). Monitoring student responses can also be of use in identifying potentially gifted children who might be disabled, bored, and alienated. Often, such *divergent-thinking* students can develop self-esteem problems when they provide answers that are logical to them but that seem unusual and off-the-wall to their peers (Jarolimek, Foster, & Kellough, 2005).

The appropriate implementation of questioning strategies clearly lends itself to enhancing the quality of verbal interaction, which is a critical factor in meeting the diverse needs of students. Among other things, you should ask yourself, "Am I providing opportunities for the students to interact with one another? Do the students have an opportunity to use (and reflect on) hands-on materials? Are they given a chance to see (and discuss) the practical importance of what they are being asked to learn?" (Eby & Herrell, 2005).

As a final note, teachers should accommodate student needs not only through an awareness of their backgrounds and differences but also in terms of ability levels. Using this information, teachers can then adapt questions to student ability levels, which enhances understanding and reduces anxiety (Powell, 2005).

Ginne Vega/Merrill

Having students raise their hands is one way of employing the questioning technique of wait time.

QUESTIONING SKILLS: THE COGNITIVE DOMAIN AND CRITICAL THINKING

We use questioning strategies in the classroom to help students learn content and to teach them to think more critically and analytically. **Critical thinking** refers to the following characteristics of students (Browne & Keeley, 1990):

- Awareness of a set of interrelated critical questions
- Ability to ask and answer critical questions at appropriate times
- Desire to actively use the critical questions

High-level questions can promote deeper thought and critical thinking through the application of the five process levels of the cognitive domain. Asking questions that require students to apply, analyze, and evaluate information is a major goal in promoting higher-order thinking skills. To accomplish this task, the teacher should pose interesting and challenging questions related to the topic and designed to engage students' thinking. Critical-thinking skills, such as problem identification, classification and categorization, analysis and synthesis, and interpretation, can be enhanced through a structured teacher-led group discussion. Examples of questions and prompts that can be asked to promote critical thinking include the following (Miller, 1998):

- What would happen if . . .
- Predict . . .
- What is similar/different about . . .
- Differentiate between . . .
- Distinguish between . . .
- How would you evaluate . . .
- Rate . . .

Asking such questions, however, is not enough. It is equally important that you establish a classroom climate in which thinking and analyzing are valued (Rodriguez, 1988). A positive classroom questioning environment requires the following:

- Being sincerely interested in what students say
- Being curious about students' ideas
- Building on and paraphrasing students' ideas
- Using divergent follow-up questions that encourage students to expand and "dig" into the problem or subject at hand

As we have seen earlier in the chapter, the use of divergent questions prevents the overuse of factual, yes/no responses that often delimit opportunities for critical thinking. Although recalling facts is sometimes important, both achievement and motivation can be enhanced when teachers ask questions that require students to apply, analyze, synthesize, and evaluate information.

Clearly, using the higher, or process, levels of the cognitive domain, detailed in Chapter 4, will provide you with the foundation to frame and ask questions that promote many of the critical-thinking behaviors cited in this research. Often you will find that just a few such questions strategically interspersed in your lesson plans provide sufficient challenge and stimulation for an entire lesson. We suggest that when you develop a question or discussion lesson plan, you include these key questions under the section of the plan labeled "content." These questions provide a focal point for the intent of your lesson and ensure that your students are engaged in activities that go beyond the recall of data, thereby enabling them to experience firsthand the process of critical thinking.

MOTIVATING STUDENTS THROUGH QUESTIONING

We have to this point discussed different question levels, convergent and divergent questions, and prompting, probing, and redirection. We have illustrated how these strategies can be applied in various teaching situations. However, when they are synthesized and systematically applied to classroom activities, they can also become powerful techniques in motivating students.

Skill in motivating students to learn is central and basic to teacher effectiveness (Good & Brophy, 2008). However, only in the past few years has motivation received systematic attention from educators. Prior to that time, many teachers felt that it was their job to teach, and they argued that they could not also be expected to motivate reluctant learners. In other cases, motivation was a haphazard bag of tricks. Now, all that has changed. Concern about alienated youth, unsuccessful students, and high dropout rates has contributed to this renewed focus.

Conceptually, the process is quite simple, although putting it into practice requires diligence and effort. Essentially, when we use questioning strategies to motivate students, we want to establish two expectations. First, we want to put students in a position where they know with certainty that they each will be called on during the course of a learning activity. Kerman (1979) found impressive results when teachers were trained to call on all students equally. This communicates to all students that they are part of the learning community and that you as a teacher expect all to participate and learn. To accomplish this, call on all students equally, calling on volunteers only 10% to 15% of the time in a learning activity. This means that much of the time, you will be calling on students who do not have their hands raised. This can be accomplished by extensively using open-ended questions and redirection. These can be particularly effective when redirection is combined with divergent questions calling for description or comparison. The type of question, however, is not as important as putting students in a position where they know they will be called on to answer. When they know they will be called on at some point in the process, their attention improves markedly.

"I can't do that," some people might argue. "I put the kids on the spot, and they're worse off than they were before." This brings us to the second expectation: when students are called on, they know you will arrange the question so that they can give an acceptable answer. Notice that we said *acceptable answer*. We did not say that students would give you the answer you want to the original question, but they will give you an answer you can acknowledge as acceptable. For example, consider the following dialogue taken from a lesson on adverbs:

Mrs. Wu is involved in a lesson where her students are learning to identify adverbs in sentences. She goes through a series of examples, calling on the students to analyze the sentences. She continues by writing the following on the board: "Steve quickly jumped over the hedge to get out of sight."

Mrs. Wu continues, "What is the adverb in the sentence . . . Tim?"

"Umm . . . I don't know."

"What did Steve do?"

"He jumped over the hedge."
"Yes, indeed! He certainly did! Good, Tim."

At this point, Tim has given an acceptable answer. He admittedly did not identify the adverb in the sentence, but his answer nevertheless moved the lesson forward and also gave the teacher a chance to praise him. Mrs. Wu could then continue prompting and probing by asking Tim, "How did he jump?" Or she could let him off the hook and continue the process with another student. Either way, Tim has had a successful and positive experience.

For students who are rarely called on and who even more rarely give a correct answer, this experience can be very positive. As a result, they will be less uncomfortable the next time they are called on and will also be more inclined to try to answer. Motivational experts believe that an emotionally safe learning environment is critical to student motivation, and Mrs. Wu helped create a safe environment for Tim (Pintrich & Schunk, 2002).

Obviously, you will not turn a hostile or seriously unmotivated student around immediately with these techniques. However, if the pattern in the classroom becomes one in which all students are called on—and when they are, they can answer—in time you can markedly improve their attention and inclination to participate in class. Good questioning is essential to good teaching and effective motivation. Skillful questioning can arouse student curiosity, stimulate the imagination, and motivate students to solve problems.

Consider also the kind of classroom climate you are establishing with this process. You are communicating to students that all of them are capable of learning, that you expect them to be able to answer, and that you care and are committed to their successes (Scheidecker & Freeman, 1999). Specifically, the implementation of teacher-led discussions can be used to increase student motivation by (a) asking stimulating or thought-provoking questions designed to arouse interest asnd (b) leading the class to answer the questions of why the topic is important, which gives purpose and direction to learning (Miller, 1998). This climate, together with using the strategies of redirection and prompting to help you involve your students and promote success, can do much to enhance their motivation.

TECHNOLOGY IN THE CLASSROOM

Fostering Effective Questioning Strategies

The effective implementation of questioning strategies involves both quantitative and qualitative considerations. Needless to say, in an effort to promote a student-centered, constructivist learning environment, teachers employ a wide range of questions that address both recalling and processing information through the use of low-level and high-level questions. Qualitatively, teachers employ techniques to increase involvement, reflect on inaccuracies, and clarify responses. Although this can be an overwhelming task, the ability to electronically store, arrange, and edit questions can do much to simplify this task. By attaching key questions to the content section of a specific lesson plan stored electronically on a template, teachers can reflect on whether the language used is clear and simple, whether the question or strategy achieved its purpose, and what follow-up questions might be employed to further student achievement. Additionally, when implementing a given lesson, key questions can be highlighted and reproduced in large point sizes on overhead transparencies for use as advanced organizers or to focus on critical considerations during the lesson.

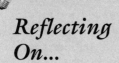

QUESTIONING STRATEGIES

INTASC Principles 3, 5, and 6

Reflecting On... Think about the different questioning levels, focus, and skills discussed in this chapter. Consider how you will use these strategies to address individual needs and challenge students in your classroom.

SUMMARY

We began this chapter by stating that questioning strategies are the cornerstone of effective teaching. The different levels, direction, and strategies contribute to teachers' overall repertoire of instructional strategies. At times, high-level questions are most desirable, and at others low levels are preferable. You will ask both convergent and divergent questions. The levels and direction of your questions will be determined by your goals for the lesson, while the specific goals of questioning techniques are the following (Johnson, 1997):

- To provide every student with an equal opportunity to answer questions
- To increase each student's success rate when answering questions
- To involve the maximum number of students during questioning

Open-ended questions, redirection, prompting, probing, and wait time are all strategies that can be used to promote student involvement, enhance success, and promote a positive and emotionally safe learning environment. As with the levels and direction of your questions, these strategies should be employed to help you reach the goals of your lesson. However, you have additional goals for every lesson—to involve and motivate your students and promote critical-thinking skills. When systematically integrated, questioning strategies can help you reach these goals. Finally, when preparing and implementing questions, consider the following (Kellough, 2000):

- Plan thoughtfully worded cognitive questions and include them in your lesson plan
- Match questions with their targeted purposes
- Ask your well-worded question before calling on student for a response
- Avoid bombarding students with too much teacher talk
- After asking a question, provide students with adequate time to think

KEY CONCEPTS

Convergent questions   202
Critical thinking   213
Divergent questions   202
High-level questions   198

Implementation   194
Low-level questions   198
Negative questioning   206
Open-ended questions   204

PREPARING FOR YOUR LICENSURE EXAMINATION

Let's look now at a teacher who is working with a group of business law high school students. Read the case study and, using specific information found in Chapter 7, answer the questions that follow.

Kana Condon, a business law teacher at Monte Vista High School, began class by sharing with students that she wanted them to gain a better understanding of the democratic process and the rights of citizens to participate in the process. She then asked them what they might want to do in class that would enable them to further their own views on these processes.

"We could take a look at how Congress goes about passing laws," Lee said.

"Yeah . . . and maybe it could be a patent law or something like that," Virginia added.

"That's a good suggestion if we think about our representatives as citizens," Ms. Condon said. "Is that OK?"

"I guess I'd rather just think of everyday people as citizens," Donna replied.

"Me too," Georgia said.

"OK, then," Ms. Condon said. "Keep thinking."

"How about a mock trial!" Claudia said enthusiastically.

"Cool," Lee chimed in.

"All agreed?" Ms. Condon inquired. She then looked around the room and confirmed that the students seemed satisfied with Claudia's suggestion. "Fine," she continued, "but why do you think a mock trial would be beneficial as a learning experience to get you to reflect on democracy and citizens' rights?" Ms. Condon asked.

"We could use it to better figure out some of the things we have been doing in class," Sandi said.

"Fine, any other comments?" Ms. Condon asked.

"I think we could find out more about some areas of the law," Pam added.

"And I guess we would have to learn about how things actually happen in court," Georgia said.

"Such as?" Ms. Condon asked.

"Well, the different procedures, I guess."

"Good guess. What else, Georgia?"

"What people do there," Georgia added.

"Great! So what are some of the roles people play in court?"

"Gotta have a judge," Andrea said.

"And you gotta have a jury," Denisc added.

"Somebody has to go on trial," John said.

"And what do we call that person?" Ms. Condon asked.

"Innocent until proven guilty," John answered.

"That is a major tenet of our legal system, John, but what does that person have to do if put on trial?"

"Defend himself. Oh, I got it. The defendant."

"Good enough, John, and if you have defendants, who else do you need?"

"Somebody who brings a charge against them?" John replied.

"Right. Does anyone know that name?"

"I think it's the plaintiff," Phil responded.

"Right you are, Phil. So we have a judge, jury, plaintiff, and defendant," Ms. Condon summarized. "Do we need anybody else?"

"We can't have a trial without lawyers and witnesses," Donna said.

"Fine," Ms. Condon concluded. "Now let's move on to something else. Do you want to choose a real-life case, or do you want to make one up?"

"Let's make it up; that will be more fun," Pam said with the obvious support of her classmates.

"Sounds good," Ms. Condon said. "Now how about a topic?"

After a lengthy discussion on such things as ethics, social responsibility, and environmental and constitutional laws, the students decided on an employment discrimination case and began their deliberations on how they would organize and present their mock trial.

1. Which of the questioning levels discussed in Chapter 7 did Ms. Condon use?
2. Which of the questioning skills discussed in Chapter 7 did Ms. Condon employ in her lesson?
3. How effective was Ms. Condon's use of the questioning strategies? Explain your answer.

VIDEO EXERCISE

Go to MyEducationLab and select the topic "Questioning Strategies" and watch the video "Higher Order Questioning." After viewing the video, respond to the questions on the video.

DEVELOPING YOUR PORTFOLIO

As evidence that you are attaining a working knowledge of the questioning strategies presented in Chapter 7, your portfolio task is to develop a lesson in a subject discipline of your expertise using the format found on page 178. Your procedure will be a large-group, teacher-led discussion. Under the content section, list a number of key questions that will lend themselves to arousing interest in your selected topic. Try to frame at least one question for each of the following levels and skills presented in the chapter:

- Low-level questions
- High-level questions
- Convergent questions

- Divergent questions
- Redirections
- Prompts
- Probes

QUESTIONS FOR DISCUSSION

1. Should low-level questions always precede high-level ones? Why or why not? In your answer, provide specific examples.

2. Should the mix or ratio of high-level and low-level questions vary with grade level? How does content area influence this optimal mix?

3. Based on your experience in classrooms, should teachers ask more or fewer divergent questions? Why?

4. Some teachers assert that prompting students only further embarrasses those who have failed to respond correctly in the first place. How would you respond to these teachers?

5. How should wait time vary in terms of the following variables?
   a. Type of questions
   b. Age of student
   c. Place in unit (i.e., early or late)
   d. Teacher's goals

6. Think about the most effective teacher you have encountered in terms of questioning. How would you describe the teacher in terms of the concepts in this chapter? What else did he or she do in terms of questioning that was not discussed in this chapter?

SUGGESTIONS FOR FIELD EXPERIENCE

1. Interview a teacher in terms of questioning.
   a. How do they plan for questioning ahead of time?
   b. How do they know who to call on during a lesson?
   c. What do they do to encourage participation from all students?
   d. What do they do when a student can not answer?
   e. What is the hardest part of questioning?

2. Observe an interactive lesson and list the questions the teacher asks. (You may want to record the lesson on an audiotape to make the task easier.)
   a. How many questions were high and low level?
   b. Was there any pattern to the use of high-level and low-level questions?
   c. How successful were students in answering these questions?
   d. What suggestions do you have to improve this aspect of questioning?

3. Take the questions you listed in activity # 2 and analyze them in terms of convergent and divergent.
   a. How many of each have they used?
   b. Was there any pattern to their use?
   c. How did students respond to these different questions?

4. Observe a lesson and, using a watch with a second hand, compute the wait time for different teacher questions.
   a. What was the average wait time?
   b. Did wait time vary with the type of question (e.g., high versus low level)?
   c. Did wait time vary with the type of student?
   d. What suggestions do you have to make wait time more effective?

5. Design a lesson plan for an interactive questioning lesson. In the lesson plan, write specific questions you will ask to reach your goal. Analyze these in terms of the concepts in this chapter (e.g., high versus low level, convergent versus divergent).

6. Teach the lesson you designed in activity # 5.
   a. How well did the questions work in stimulating thinking?
   b. How often did you have to rephrase or explain a question?
   c. How often did you have to change or adapt your questioning plans?
   d. What did you learn about the use of questioning to promote learning?

TOOLS FOR TEACHING

Print References

Gagnon, G., & Collay, M. (2001). *Designing for learning: Six elements in constructivist classrooms.* Thousand Oaks, CA: Corwin Press. This work presents examples and characteristics of questions along with techniques for questions.

Llewellyn, D. (2007). *Inquire within* (2nd ed.). Thousand Oaks, CA: Corwin Press. Chapter 10 presents a thorough presentation on questioning with subheadings on wait time, answering questions, asking questions, and posing reflective questions.

Milner, J., & Graciano, M. (Eds.). (2006). *The act of teaching English: What effective teachers do in their classrooms.* Lewiston, NY: Edwin Mellen Press. Unit III presents discussions on examining questions, questioning patterns, teacher responses and classroom discussion, wrong answers and raised hands, and teacher corrections and student responses.

Morgan, N., & Saxton, J. (2006). *Asking better questions* (2nd ed.). Markham, On: Pembroke Publishers. A thorough presentation of ways to frame better questions with chapters that include questions that promote the six levels of the cognitive domain and fewer questions, better questions, and time to think.

Rief, S., & Heimburge, J. (2006). *How to reach and teach all children in the inclusive classroom: Practical strategies, lessons, and activities.* San Francisco: Jossey-Bass. An excellent source for strategies employed in diverse classrooms.

Web Sites

www.utexas.edu/academic/cte/sourcebook/questioning.pdf Here you will find information on questioning skills and principles that are designed to promote student learning, a checklist for asking artful questions, and benefits of using wait time.

www.criticalthinking.org/resources/articles/the-role-of-questions.shtml Here you will find a discussion of the role of questions, including the kinds of questions teachers need to ask, why thinking is driven by questions, and the need for students to frame questions for themselves.

www.iun.edu/~edujal/e343/m201/questioning.html Here you will find reasons for asking questions, basic types of questions, and questions that promote critical thinking.

http://hsp.myweb.uga.edu/question.htm This site presents types of questions and examples of these questions that promote action learning, including information questions, probing questions, and group processing questions.

http://inquiry.uiuc.edu/ Here you can find out more about what inquiry is and become familiar with a spiral path of inquiry: asking questions, investigating solutions, creating new knowledge, discussing experiences, and reflecting on new found knowledge.

CHAPTER 8

Meeting Standards Through Teacher-Centered Instructional Strategies

INTRODUCTION

We are now at the implementation phase of the general teaching model. In this phase, teachers use different strategies to help students reach goals identified earlier during the planning phase of instruction. In this chapter, we incorporate the questioning strategies described in Chapter 7 and show how these microstrategies can be incorporated into more comprehensive macrostrategies. Effective teachers use a variety of strategies to address standards and meet their learning goals. These instructional strategies vary from teacher-centered ones, in which teachers assume major responsibility for reaching learning goals, to strategies in which teachers play a more facilitative role, allowing students to take a more active part

in learning. This chapter is designed to help you construct and implement teacher-centered instructional strategies in your own classroom.

LEARNER OBJECTIVES

After completing your study of Chapter 8, you should be able to do the following:

- Understand the major characteristics of teacher-centered teaching strategies
- Know how to plan and implement teacher-centered lessons in different content areas
- Explain the role of examples in furthering student understanding in teacher-centered lessons

APPLYING TEACHER-CENTERED STRATEGIES IN THE CLASSROOM

Following is a case study involving a principal in a middle school. As you read the case study, consider the following questions:

- What are the different ways that teachers help students learn?
- Which instructional strategies are most effective in promoting student learning?
- When should teachers play a more active role in instruction, and when should they step back and facilitate student efforts?

Cassie Jones walks through the halls of the inner-city middle school where she is the principal and listens to the sounds coming from the different classrooms. As she walks by Ben Carlson's social studies class, she hears him say, "Yesterday we talked about the strengths and weaknesses of the North and South at the outbreak of the Civil War. Who remembers one of these?"

As Cassie proceeds down the hall, she stops in front of Sarah McCarthy's science class. Sarah is at the front of the room swinging a set of keys from a piece of string. "Hmmm," Cassie thinks, "no wonder her class is so quiet—she's got them hypnotized." As she listens further, she hears Sarah ask, "Class, this is a simple pendulum, just like the one we find in grandfather clocks. Who can tell me what factors influence the rate at which a pendulum swings?"

"Good question," thinks Cassie. "Maybe that's why her kids are so quiet."

When Cassie turns the corner, she is greeted by a steady stream of student voices arguing about something.

"I don't care what you say, stealing is wrong."

"But his family didn't have enough to eat. They were hungry—he couldn't let them starve!"

"What's Hector up to today?" Cassie thinks as she listens more closely to Hector Sanchez's English class.

"Class," Hector breaks in with a booming voice, "it's not enough just to disagree with your partners. You have to explain why. Remember, one of the reasons we read books like Sounder *is to help us understand our own lives. So, you have 3 more minutes in your discussion groups to explain why the father was right or wrong to steal food for his family."*

Cassie chuckles as Hector's class rejoins the battle. "He's sure got them stirred up today. I guess I'm lucky to have such a talented teaching staff that is able to use so many different teaching strategies."

TEACHER-CENTERED AND LEARNER-CENTERED INSTRUCTIONAL STRATEGIES

As Cassie Jones concluded, effective teachers are able to implement a number of teaching strategies, ranging from teacher-centered approaches to more student-centered ones. The teacher-centered strategies discussed in this chapter are direct instruction, lecture-discussion, and guided discovery. In the next chapter, we describe more student-centered approaches, such as cooperative learning, discussion, and problem-based learning, which we illustrate with examples from different disciplines.

Teacher-centered instruction *includes teaching strategies "in which the teacher's role is to present the knowledge to be learned and to direct, in a rather explicit manner, the learning process of the students"* (Shuell, 1996, p. 731, emphasis added), whereas in **learner-centered instruction,** students, with the teacher's guidance, take more responsibility for constructing their own understanding (McCombs & Miller, 2007).

Research shows that students' active involvement in learning is important for both their understanding and their motivation (Eggen & Kauchak, 2007). This might lead some to conclude that the only appropriate approaches to instruction are learner centered. This is not true; for some goals, teacher-centered approaches are more effective, and for others, learner-centered approaches are superior (Fullan, Hill, & Crevola, 2006). The key to effective instruction is twofold: (a) understanding the goals and content being taught and matching the instructional strategy to those goals and (b) actively involving students in learning no matter which specific strategy is employed. In this chapter, we examine different topics for which teacher-centered approaches are more effective.

Content targeted by teacher-centered strategies typically has one or more of the following characteristics:

- It is content that is specific and well defined. For example, many math skills, such as adding, subtracting, multiplying, and dividing, can be clearly identified and defined.
- It is content that all students need to master to ensure success in later learning efforts (Popham, 2007). Like math skills, many reading skills need to be mastered to ensure later success in other content areas.
- It is content that students would have difficulty obtaining on their own.

Making students responsible for constructing their own understanding of math or reading skills, as would be the case in learner-centered instruction, could be inefficient in terms of time and effort and potentially confusing; in these instances, teacher-centered strategies are more effective.

When teachers plan for teacher-centered instruction, they identify standards from state or district curriculum guides, design specific objectives for the lesson, and construct learning activities to help students meet the objectives (Wiggins & McTighe, 2005). During instruction, the lesson is clearly focused on the objectives, and the teacher takes primary responsibility for guiding learning by modeling, explaining, and questioning.

In skills-based lessons, students practice the skill with the goal of developing automaticity; in content-oriented lessons, teachers use questioning to ensure that students understand new content.

Teacher-centered and learner-centered approaches are complementary in the classroom. For instance, the basic skills that students master through teacher-centered approaches are necessary for subsequent problem solving, and problem-solving abilities are often most effectively developed with learner-centered approaches in which students have more freedom and autonomy. Similarly, teachers might use a well-organized lecture-discussion—a teacher-centered strategy—to help students acquire the background knowledge needed to carry on an effective discussion—a learner-centered strategy.

As a teacher, you will likely design and teach lessons that incorporate features from more than one strategy. This is desirable as you develop your own personal teaching style, adapting instruction to the needs of your students. However, we discuss each teaching strategy separately for the sake of clarity and the development of your understanding. As your thinking develops and your teaching evolves, you will make adjustments in these strategies to fit your personality and style and your students' needs.

We begin our discussion of teacher-centered strategies with direct instruction, one of the most widely used instructional strategies

DIRECT INSTRUCTION

Direct instruction is an instructional strategy designed to teach essential knowledge and skills that are needed for later learning (Eggen & Kauchak, 2007), and its effectiveness is well documented by research (Carnine, Silbert, Kame'enui, Tarver, Jongjohann, 2006; Kroesbergen, van Luit, & Maas, 2004). Math and reading skills are examples of essential knowledge, as are students acquiring specific writing strategies, chemistry students learning to balance equations, and geography students using longitude and latitude to pinpoint locations. Direct instruction is useful when skills can be broken down into specific steps and has been found to be particularly effective in working with low achievers and students with exceptionalities (Kroesbergen et al., 2004; Turnbull, Turnbull, Shank, Smith, & Leal, 2007).

Direct instruction ranges from a highly structured, nearly scripted approach (Carnine et al., 2006) to one that is more flexible in its implementation (Eggen & Kauchak, 2007). We discuss the latter here because it provides the teacher with more flexibility to adapt instruction to the specific learning needs of students. To illustrate the characteristics of direct instruction, let's look at the following lesson, which describes a teacher using this strategy to teach math content.

Carl Hite wants his fifth-grade math class to understand the formula for computing the circumference of a circle ($C = \square \times d$). He begins by drawing a large circle on the board and saying, "How big is this circle?" After a short pause, he continues, "How could we find out how far it is around this circle?" gesturing with his hands while pointing at the circle. "Today we're going to learn how to compute the circumference of a circle. When you're finished, you'll be able to find the circumference when you're given the diameter or even the radius. This will help you solve math problems involving circumference,

Figure 8.1   A Circle Handout

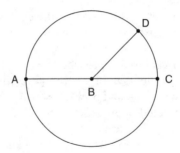

and you'll also be able to apply this to situations in your life" He then writes C = □ × d *on the board and says, "What do we have up here? Go ahead and read this, Antonio."*

"*C equals pi times* d," *Antonio answers.*

"*OK, fine, Antonio," Carl replies with a smile. "Now what is the* C . . . *Jan?"*

"*It's the circumference."*

"*And what do we mean by circumference . . . Derek?"*

"*It's . . . I'm not sure," Derek stammers.*

Carl then draws a circle on the board with both the diameter and radii in it, as shown in Figure 8.1.

"*Derek, look at the circle. What is the circumference?" he asks as he points to the board and makes an imaginary circle in the air.*

"*It's the distance around the circle," Derek says, smiling at Carl's arm movement.*

"*That's right, Derek," Carl grins back. "Now what is the* d *in the formula . . . Sasha?"*

"*It's the diameter."*

"*And where is it on our circle?" he asks, pointing to the circle on the board. "Cal?"*

"*It's the line AC," Cal responds after studying the circle.*

"*All right, good, Cal. Now we have one part left in the formula. What is it . . . Shanda?"*

"*It's that little squiggly thing that is 3.14," she says.*

"*Good, Shanda. What did Antonio say we called that when I wrote the formula on the board? Anyone?"*

"*Pi," three students respond together.*

"*OK, terrific. Now we're all set."*

With that, Carl gives each of the students a ruler, string, and a handout with four circles drawn on it and assigns them to groups of two to work on the problem.

"*Look at the circles on the handout, everyone. I want you to measure the diameter with your rulers and calculate the circumference of the first one. Then check your calculation by measuring the circumference with the string. We'll do the first one together as a group so everyone understands what we're doing. Then I want you to practice on the rest."*

After the class does the sample problem with Carl's guidance, he assigns the remainder of the problems as in-class work. The students go quickly to work, computing the circumference of each circle, and checking their answers by measuring each.

We turn now to a description of the planning and implementing phases of teacher-centered lessons. But before continuing, complete Exercise 8.1.

EXERCISE 8.1

Read the following teaching anecdotes and determine whether they involve teacher-centered instruction (T) or some other type of strategy (O).

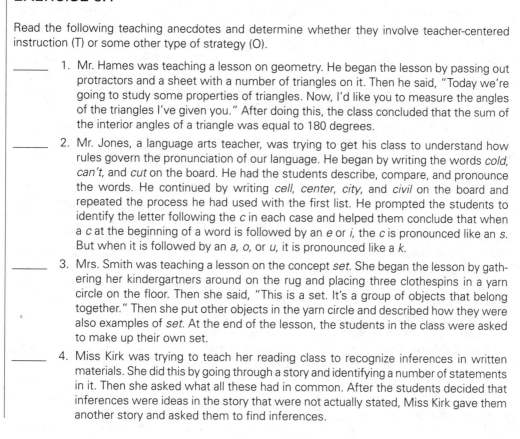

_____ 1. Mr. Hames was teaching a lesson on geometry. He began the lesson by passing out protractors and a sheet with a number of triangles on it. Then he said, "Today we're going to study some properties of triangles. Now, I'd like you to measure the angles of the triangles I've given you." After doing this, the class concluded that the sum of the interior angles of a triangle was equal to 180 degrees.

_____ 2. Mr. Jones, a language arts teacher, was trying to get his class to understand how rules govern the pronunciation of our language. He began by writing the words _cold_, _can't_, and _cut_ on the board. He had the students describe, compare, and pronounce the words. He continued by writing _cell_, _center_, _city_, and _civil_ on the board and repeated the process he had used with the first list. He prompted the students to identify the letter following the _c_ in each case and helped them conclude that when a _c_ at the beginning of a word is followed by an _e_ or _i_, the _c_ is pronounced like an _s_. But when it is followed by an _a_, _o_, or _u_, it is pronounced like a _k_.

_____ 3. Mrs. Smith was teaching a lesson on the concept _set_. She began the lesson by gathering her kindergartners around on the rug and placing three clothespins in a yarn circle on the floor. Then she said, "This is a set. It's a group of objects that belong together." Then she put other objects in the yarn circle and described how they were also examples of _set_. At the end of the lesson, the students in the class were asked to make up their own set.

_____ 4. Miss Kirk was trying to teach her reading class to recognize inferences in written materials. She did this by going through a story and identifying a number of statements in it. Then she asked what all these had in common. After the students decided that inferences were ideas in the story that were not actually stated, Miss Kirk gave them another story and asked them to find inferences.

Planning for Direct Instruction in a Standards-Based Environment

Three essential steps are involved in planning for direct instruction lessons. The first is to identify a topic, which is often suggested by state standards, curriculum guides, or textbooks (Wiggins & McTighe, 2005). The topic in Carl Hite's lessons was computing the circumference of circles. The second planning step is to translate that general topic into specific learning objectives that provide the focus for instruction. The third step is to design instructional and assessment activities that provide students with opportunities to practice the new skill or concept. Let's see how the planning process is influenced by standards.

During planning, teachers identify specific objectives for the lesson and design learning activities to help students meet the objectives. For instance, Carl Hite's objective could be stated as follows:

> Fifth-grade students will understand the formula for computing circumference so that given a ruler and four circles with the diameter drawn in, they will calculate the circumference of each without error.

The specificity of the objective provides direction for both the teacher and students.

During instruction, the lesson is clearly focused on the objectives, and the teacher takes primary responsibility for guiding learning by modeling, explaining, and questioning. In skills-based lessons, students practice the skill with the goal of developing automaticity; in content-oriented lessons, teachers use questioning to ensure that students understand new content.

Standards can have a powerful influence on planning. As we saw in Chapters 4 and 5, **standards** are attempts by states and national organizations to clearly specify what students need to learn and know (Darling-Hammond, 2001). Some standards are stated specifically, whereas others are quite general. Those stated in general terms are often followed by more specific statements called *benchmarks, expectations,* or *indicators*. Your school will be held accountable for helping students meet these standards, so you must be able to design learning activities to reach this goal.

Standards are essentially broad and general statements of learning goals. Because of this generality, you will, in most cases, have to interpret the specific meaning of the standard for your students, which can be more demanding than establishing your own objectives. Carl did this as he planned. He decided that being able to find the circumference of a circle addressed the standard *understands concepts involving basic geometric shapes such as triangles, rectangles, and circles;* then he identified problems students could use to learn this content; and finally he prepared assessment items to provide additional practice and measure the amount his students learned. His planning ensured both that he helped his students meet the standard and that his objectives, learning activities, and assessments were aligned.

One way that Carl used standards to frame his decisions was through a process called **backward design,** an approach to planning that first identifies desired learning objectives, then specifies ways to assess whether these objectives are met, and finally establishes learning experiences to reach the objectives (Wiggins & McTighe, 2005). It really is nothing more than good instructional planning that ensures that objectives, learning activities, and assessments are aligned.

The thinking involved in planning for standards-based instruction is similar to the thinking involved in any planning. The standard begins the decision-making process by presenting an objective in a form with varying degrees of specificity. You then are responsible for making decisions about learning activities and assessments.

The third step in planning for direct instruction involves the selection or preparation of problems or examples. Problems provide opportunities for students to practice the skill; examples allow students to see how the concept applies to the real world. In planning for teaching a skill, the teacher should ensure that the problems provide opportunities for students to both understand and practice the skill. In Carl Hite's lesson, problems allowed students to calculate the circumference and compare their results with a string and ruler. The use of string and rulers was important for learning because it helped make concrete a relationship that would be quite abstract based on calculations alone.

Selecting examples for teaching an abstraction is simple conceptually, but in practice it can be difficult to accomplish. The simple part is recognizing the traits of a good example. A good example includes the important characteristics if you are teaching a concept; it will illustrate the relationship or connection between concepts if you are teaching a generalization. The hard part involves finding examples that accomplish this task. For some simple concepts, the task is straightforward. For instance, the concept *quadrilateral* has the following characteristics: four sided, plane figure, and straight lines. Examples abound and are fairly simple to prepare.

On the other hand, finding examples for more abstract concepts, such as *democracy, socialism,* and *communism,* can be quite difficult. In fact, this concept is rarely illustrated with examples. Instead, it is often only defined, and how well students learn the concept depends on the quality of the definition as well as their background knowledge. As research has shown, the problem with using only a definition is that students often memorize the definition without understanding the concept. Examples are the key to learning both concepts and generalizations (Mayer, 2008).

Both positive and negative examples are necessary to prevent concepts from becoming easily confused with closely related concepts (Eggen & Kauchak, 2007). Positive examples tell the learner what the concept is, while negative ones illustrate what the concept is not. For example, if a teacher wants students to understand the concept of metaphor, the teacher would include similes as negative examples, or nonexamples.

In selecting positive examples to teach concepts, the essential characteristics can be used as a checklist to evaluate the adequacy of the examples in conveying a complete and accurate concept. For example, you are teaching the concept of adverb and have determined that key characteristics of the concept are that it is a word that modifies a verb, an adjective, or another adverb. Examine the following list of positive examples to determine their adequacy:

1. The boy ran quickly across the lawn.
2. The boulder thundered loudly down the mountain.
3. She did not know the answer to the vaguely phrased question.
4. The shark tugged relentlessly at the thin line.

The use of both positive and negative examples enhance student conceptualization when employing teacher-directed lessons.

Anne Vega/Merrill

In the list, there is no example showing an adverb modifying another adverb. Consequently, the concept that students will form from this lesson will be incomplete and inaccurate. By checking examples such as these against a list of essential characteristics, a teacher can avoid these potential pitfalls.

An additional aid in selecting examples is to analyze the concept in terms of coordinate and subordinate concepts. The subordinate concepts can be used to generate positive examples, while the coordinate ones can provide negative examples that can be potentially confused with positive ones. Presenting these as negative examples helps students understand important differences between these closely connected ideas. Negative examples generated in this manner are much more useful to students than other types of negative examples. For example, if a teacher were trying to teach the concept *reptile* to a class, the negative examples of amphibians, mammals, and birds would be much more helpful to the learner than negative examples like car, tree, ball, or boat. These latter examples are so far removed from the concept that they contain few characteristics in common with the concept and consequently provide little valuable information about what the concept is not.

Planning for teaching a generalization is a slightly more complex process because the examples must illustrate the interaction between concepts in the generalization. For example, a psychology teacher trying to teach the generalization "The amount of time between a behavior and its reinforcement is inversely related to the speed with which that behavior is learned" would need to provide examples in which behavior was being reinforced with different time lapses and different related results. This could be done with written anecdotes, live or videotaped examples, or data in a chart or table.

In summary, when teaching abstractions, the planning process amounts to identifying a topic, forming an objective, and carefully selecting examples to illustrate the idea. It is a logical and analytical task, requiring careful thought.

Implementing

Direct instruction occurs in four sequential phases that build on each other and are designed to help students learn abstractions and develop skills:

- Introduction and review
- Developing understanding
- Guided practice
- Independent practice

Introduction and Review

Carl introduced his lesson by drawing a circle on the board. **Introduction and review** is the first part of a direct instruction lesson and is designed to attract students' attention, pull them into the lesson, and remind them of previously learned content. He then had them review terms within the equation. This review served as the springboard for his lesson on finding the circumference of circles. The value of introduction and review is well established by research, and although its importance seems obvious, the majority of teacher lessons begin with little or no attempt to attract attention or activate relevant prior knowledge (Brophy, 2004).

An important component of the introduction phase is to explicitly share with students your learning goals(s) for the lesson. Carl did this when he said, "When you're finished, you'll be able to find the circumference when you're given the diameter or even the radius." Sharing your objectives with students provides them with "achievement targets" that provide them with clear goals for their learning efforts during the lesson (Stiggins, 2007).

Developing Understanding

In this phase of the direct instruction strategy, the teacher models and explains the skill being taught or describes the essential characteristics of the concept. **Developing understanding** is the segment of a direct instruction lesson where the teacher explains new content and is perhaps the most important phase of direct instruction. Ironically, it is the one that teachers often perform least well. Instead of working to develop student understanding, they often emphasize memorization, fail to ask enough questions, or move too quickly to practice.

Carl was very effective in this phase. He carefully walked students through the solution of the first problem, using questioning to make sure that students understood as he proceeded. Let's return to his lesson to see how he did this.

"And what are we trying to find here? What do we call the distance around this circle? Alberto?"

"Circumference."

"Good, Alberto. And what is this line here? Angelica?"

"Umm . . . diameter!"

"Excellent. And what does our formula tell us to do to find the circumference or distance around . . . Kareem?"

"We have to multiple the diameter times pi.*"*

"Fine. Let's go ahead and do that and see what we get. Who has their calculator read? What is 6 inches times pi? *Who remembers what* pi *is . . . Shandra?"*

"3.14."

"Good. So who has an answer for us . . . Katya?"

"18.84 inches."

"Okay? Does everyone else get that?" Seeing nods, Carl proceeds. *"Now, how could we check our answer to be sure it makes sense? Anyone? Octavio?"*

"Measure the circumference?"

"Good answer. Everyone take their string and put it around the circumference like this," he explains, modeling with the large circle. *"Then we need to straighten out the string and measure it with our rulers. Go ahead and do that and see what you get."*

Carl walks around the room, answering questions and helping students. After a minute or so, he continues.

"So, what did you get . . . Sarah?"

"18$\frac{1}{2}$ inches." Carl writes the responses on the board.

"Julia?"

"19 inches."

"Katya?"

"18$\frac{7}{8}$ inches."

"Billy?"

"18$\frac{5}{8}$ inches."

Carl then has the class average these and reminds the class about measurement error, an idea they have discussed before. When the class agrees that the average circumference figure is really close to the one they computed, he next asks students to work on the next one, checking their answers as a whole class before proceeding to additional problems.

Notice that Carl did not have students practice on additional problems until he was confident that most of his students had a thorough understanding of the process. This is essential for the success of the next phase: guided practice (Kauchak & Eggen, 2007; Kroesbergen et al., 2004).

Guided Practice

Guided practice provides students with opportunities to try out the new skill and for teachers to provide feedback about learning progress. Once Carl felt that most students understood circumference and how to calculate it, he assigned three additional problems that required students to find the circumference and asked them to solve the first one. As they worked, he carefully monitored their progress and then provided detailed feedback about the first problem before asking students to solve the second one. Feedback is important to learners because it tells them what they have learned and what they still need to work on (Hattie & Timperley, 2007). He repeated this process with both the second and the third problems. Had students struggled, he would have had them solve additional problems under his guidance until he believed they were ready to practice independently on their own.

Independent Practice

Independent practice is the final phase of direct instruction and is designed to provide additional opportunities for students to practice the new content. In this final phase, Carl helped students make the transition from working under his guidance to working on their own. The goal in this phase is for students' understanding to be developed to the point that they can perform the operation smoothly and automatically with little conscious effort. During independent practice, the teacher reduces the amount of support he gives and shifts responsibility to the students.

Teacher monitoring continues to be important, however. Effective teachers carefully monitor students to assess their developing understanding (Safer & Fleischman, 2005); less effective teachers are more likely to merely check to see that students are on task (e.g., on the right page and following directions).

Homework is one type of independent practice, and when properly used, it can reinforce students' developing understanding and skills (Cooper, Robinson, & Patall, 2006; Marzano & Pickering, 2007). *Properly used* means that teachers assign homework that is an extension of what students have already studied and practiced in class, that is, it is aligned with learning objectives and learning activities (Bransford, Brown, & Cocking, 2000). Although grading homework can be time consuming, teachers should have some mechanism for giving students credit and providing feedback if they are to take it seriously and use it as a learning tool.

Using Direct Instruction to Teach Concepts

In addition to teaching skills, direct instruction can also be used to teach concepts. When using direct instruction to teach concepts, the teacher first writes the abstraction on the chalkboard or displays it on an overhead. For example, if a teacher's topic were the concept of acids, the teacher would write, "Acids are compounds that taste sour and release a hydrogen ion into solution." Writing the abstraction on the board or displaying it on an overhead is important because the written or displayed information gives students something to focus their attention on visually. It also serves as a point of reference as the lesson develops (Eggen & Kauchak, 2007).

When teaching concepts through direct instruction, the teacher follows the same sequential steps as with skills, modifying them to the characteristics of concepts (Eggen & Kauchak, 2007). After defining the concept, the next step is to clarify the terms in the definition and relate the concept to a meaningful superordinate concept. This can be done by asking students to define the terms in their own words or by asking students to cite examples of the terms. During the next phase, the teacher helps students develop understanding by presenting positive examples, linking them to the definition. Negative examples should also be provided to help students understand what the concept is not. In presenting these examples, the teacher should ask students to relate these to the essential characteristics listed in the definition. This ensures that the characteristics are meaningful to students and that they are linked in students' minds to the examples.

Once teachers feel that students understand the concepts they are teaching, they can provide additional examples for students to classify during guided practice. In doing this, they should encourage students to explain their classifications based on the concepts' characteristics. Having students classify positive and negative examples and explain their thinking serves several functions:

- It reinforces the concept.
- It encourages active student participation.
- It helps the teacher assess students' understanding.

If students can successfully classify examples, the teacher can ask them for their own examples; if not, additional examples can be provided for them to classify and explain. Once the teacher feels that students understand the concept, the teacher can reinforce the idea further through independent practice.

These steps are reflected in the lesson plan in Figure 8.2, which is implemented in the following learning activity.

Kathy Hutchins begins her lesson on imperative sentences by saying, "The last few days we've been talking about different kinds of sentences. Yesterday we talked about interrogative sentences, and the day before, we talked about declarative sentences. Today we're going to talk about imperative sentences. When we're all through, you should be able to pick out the imperative sentences from a list of mixed sentences."

Then she draws the following diagram on the board:

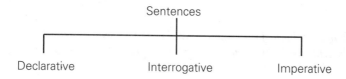

Figure 8.2 Expository Lesson Plan for Imperative Sentences

Unit: Types of sentences

Goals Objective: Fifth graders will understand imperative sentences so that when given a list of sentences, they will identify all those that are imperative.

Rationale: Students need to understand imperative sentences in order to make their writing accurate and expressive.

Content: Imperative sentences are sentences that give a command or order.

Procedures: Present the following outline on the board:

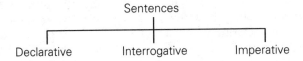

Present a definition of imperative sentences.
Present the examples:

> Don't do that!
> Please pick up your clothes.

Identify the characteristics of imperative sentences.
Relate examples to the definition.
Show the examples:

> He didn't want to go.
> Go or else I'll call the police!
> Don't tell me any more lies!

Have the students identify those that are imperative and explain their reasoning.
Ask students for additional examples.

Materials: Outline of the types of sentences.
            Examples of types of sentences.

Evaluation: Have students identify imperative sentences from a list of sentences.

She continues, "Imperative sentences are a special kind of sentence that gives a command or an order, like these," writing the definition on the board. She then places the following on an overhead:

Don't do that!

Please pick up your clothes.

"Often, the subject of the sentence, 'you,' is understood. In the first example, the word 'you' isn't in the sentence, but we understand that it means, 'Don't you do that.' You can see in both

of these examples that someone is telling somebody else to do something. Also, almost always the verb in imperative sentences is in the present tense. Sometimes imperative sentences have exclamation marks in them to show that someone really wants something done. An example of this would be, 'Stop, or I'll shoot!' You would put an exclamation point at the end of this sentence. Also, note that the verb is in the present tense, and 'you' is understood."

Then Kathy writes the following on the board:

He didn't want to go.
Go or else I'll call the police!

"Now look at these two sentences and tell me if they are imperative . . . Jenny."

"I think the second one is, but the first one isn't, because the second one gives a command, and the first doesn't."

"Also," adds Tom, "the second one is in the present tense, and the first isn't."

"Anything else . . . Francesca?"

"Yes, you can see the subject in the first sentence. It's 'He.' But in the second, the subject is understood because we can't see it."

"Excellent."

Kathy then writes an additional sentence on the board:

Don't tell me any more lies!

"How about this sentence? Is it an example of an imperative sentence . . . Cal?"

"Yes, because it gives a command. Also, the subject is understood, and there's an exclamation point at the end."

"Good. Now who can give me some additional examples of imperative sentences?"

From this example, we see that Kathy closely followed the steps in direct instruction. Note, too, that she made her objective clear at the beginning of the lesson and told students what they should be able to do when the lesson ended. In addition, she made the content organization clear by illustrating the relationship between this new concept and the old ones with a diagram. All these help make the logic of the lesson more apparent to students, resulting in better initial learning and better retention.

Using Direct Instruction to Teach Generalizations

Because generalizations are so similar to concepts in that both are abstractions, the steps to follow in teaching them are quite similar to those involved in teaching concepts. As you read the following lesson involving a generalization, see if you can identify the four phases of direct instruction.

Shannon Swenson's class had been studying sounds and how they are made. In this lesson, she wants her class to understand factors that influence the pitch of a sound. She prepared for the lesson by gathering together a number of sound-making objects like a bamboo flute, a guitar, and some rubber band instruments.

She begins her lesson by saying, "We've been talking about how sound comes from vibrations. Now we're going to learn how to make different kinds of sounds that are high and low. Today we're going to learn that the longer the vibrating column, the lower the pitch. The shorter the vibrating column, the higher the pitch."

Writing this on the board, she continued, "When we're through, you should be able to tell me how pitch is affected by the length of the vibrating column and show me how this works with different instruments. Who knows what pitch is? [Pause.] No one? It's how high or low something sounds."

Shannon then illustrates the concept of pitch with a pitch pipe, having her students listen to different sounds and identifying these as being high or low in pitch. Once she feels students understand this concept, she continues.

"Look at this pitch pipe closely." She shows how it has different holes in it. "These are the openings for the different vibrating columns. The noise is made here and vibrates through these columns. That's what makes different kinds of pitch."

She next takes the bamboo flute and shows the class how the different holes affect the length of the vibrating column. As her next illustration of the generalization, she goes to the piano and plays the same key hard and softly, as well as fast and slowly, and asks students if the pitch has changed. When they say no, she proceeds to lift up the top of the piano for the class to see. She explains how the hammer hitting the strings causes the sound and explains how strings can also form a vibrating column. Then she asks them to predict which of the strings would make high and low sounds.

As a test to determine whether her class understands the generalization, she brings out a guitar and plucks the strings several times. Then she asks the class what would happen if she held down the strings part of the way down the neck. Some students can answer the question, but others cannot, so she thinks another example might be helpful. She brings out empty soda bottles and has two students blow into them to make sounds. After determining that the class understands what the vibrating column is, she asks them what would happen to the pitch if they put water in the bottles. To conclude the lesson, she passes out a worksheet that has a number of drawings of different paired simple instruments. The students' job is to determine which of the pairs would have a higher pitch and explain why.

Let's pause a second and analyze this lesson in terms of the steps involved in direct instruction. Shannon began the lesson by stating the generalization and determining that students understood the concepts of pitch and vibrating column. This introduction and review defined the abstraction and linked it to ideas that students already knew. During the developing understanding phase, she then illustrated the generalization with a number of positive examples and a negative one. The negative example in this case was hitting the same piano key in different ways so that students could see that this was unrelated to pitch. In teaching abstractions, positive examples are more useful than negative examples in helping students learn the abstraction, but negative examples still help clarify what the abstraction does not include. During guided practice, Shannon followed the presentation of positive and negative examples with additional examples in which the students had to make predictions, which essentially involved classifying examples. The lesson ended when she asked her students to work with additional examples of their own.

DIVERSITY IN THE CLASSROOM

Diversity and Background Knowledge

Diversity comes in many forms. One of the most powerful forms of student diversity affecting student learning occurs in the background knowledge that students bring to the classroom (Bruning, Schraw, Norby, & Running, 2004; Carnine et al., 2006). This previous knowledge not only influences initial learning during a lesson but also affects how well students retain information and transfer it to new situations (Mayer, 2008). A major way that effective teachers deal with this dimension of diversity is through continual and systematic formative assessment.

Formative assessment involves gathering information about student learning progress during instruction to provide students with feedback and aid the teacher in diagnosing learner background knowledge and subsequent adjustments to instruction (Stiggins, 2007). The timing of formative assessment is crucial; it needs to be systematic and continual, providing both teacher and students with constant feedback about learning progress (Popham, 2006). If learning is not occurring, instruction needs to be modified to address the learning problem.

Formative assessment is especially important in direct instruction because the strategy is sequential, with student success at each stage laying the foundation for the next. For example, if students do not understand the basic concepts being revisited during the introduction and review, they are likely to encounter difficulties during the developing understanding phase, where teachers introduce new ideas based on previously learned ones. In a similar way, if students do not understand these new ideas, they will encounter difficulties during guided and independent practice.

Effective teachers use several diagnostic tools during direct instruction to provide them with feedback about their students' readiness for subsequent learning. The first of these is some type of pretest that assesses students' background knowledge in the content area being introduced. A short paper-and-pencil pretest provides the teacher with a quick and efficient snapshot of the entire class's readiness for learning the new material. Then during instruction, effective teachers continually monitor learning progress through interactive questioning that focuses on problems and examples. The problems and examples provide a concrete frame of reference for all students and allows the teacher to probe for learning problems and glitches. During guided practice, effective teachers ask all students to demonstrate their developing understanding by interacting with the new content. Information gathered during independent practice allows the teacher to determine which ideas were understood and retained.

One of the most common mistakes that beginning teachers make is to ask students, "Do you understand?" during lessons. The students who do not understand typically nod along with the ones who do, afraid or embarrassed to admit that they do not understand an idea. Teacher questions that actually ask students to demonstrate that they understand new content avoid this problem. Systematic and continuous formative assessment during direct instruction lessons provides teachers with a powerful tool to deal with background differences that students bring to the classroom.

GUIDED DISCOVERY STRATEGIES

As an alternative to direct instruction, effective teachers often use guided discovery to teach concepts and generalizations. **Guided discovery** is an instructional model designed to teach concepts and relationships among them (Eggen & Kauchak, 2007; Mayer, 2004). When using this strategy, teachers present students with examples, guide them as they attempt to find patterns in the examples, and come to closure when students are able to describe the idea that the teacher is attempting to teach (Clark & Mayer, 2003; Moreno, 2004). During guided discovery, teachers still provide structure and guidance to ensure that the abstraction being learned is accurate and complete.

Guided discovery is often contrasted with "pure," or unstructured, discovery, where learners identify patterns and relationships without guidance from a teacher. Research indicates that unstructured discovery is less effective than guided approaches because time is not used efficiently, and, without help, students often become lost and frustrated, and this confusion can lead to misconceptions (Clark & Mayer, 2003; Mayer, 2002, 2004). As a result, unstructured discovery is rarely seen in today's classrooms, except in student projects and investigations.

When done well, guided discovery's effectiveness is supported by research: "Guided discovery may require more or less time than expository instruction, depending on the task, but tends to result in better long-term retention and transfer than expository instruction" (Mayer, 2008, p. 310). When using guided discovery, teachers spend less time explaining and more time asking questions, so students tend to be more cognitively active, promoting both learning and motivation (Moreno & Duran, 2004).

As with direct instruction, guided discovery exists in four phases, which are outlined in Table 8.1 and illustrated in the following lesson.

Helen Cane wants to teach her third-grade students a generalization to help them with their word attack skills. To begin the lesson, she puts the following words on the board:

beat	*boat*
meet	*main*
beak	

She then says, "Class, today we are going to continue our work on word attack skills. Who remembers the two kinds of letters we were talking about yesterday . . . Consuela?"

"Vowels and consonants."

"Good, Consuela and who can find a vowel in the words up here on the board . . . Hassam?"

"E and a in beat*?"*

"Good, Hassam and how about a consonant . . . Enrika?"

"Um . . . how about b *and* t *in* beat*?"*

"Excellent. Now class, look at these words more closely. Tell me what else you see . . . Henry?"

Table 8.1   Phases of Guided Discovery

Phase	Learning Component
Introduction and Review: The teacher begins with a form of introductory focus and reviews previous work.	■ Attract attention ■ Activate prior knowledge
The Open-Ended Phase: The teacher provides examples and asks for observations and comparisons.	■ Provide experiences from which knowledge will be constructed ■ Promote social interaction
The Convergent Phase: The teacher guides students as they search for patterns in the examples.	■ Begin construction of abstraction ■ Promote social interaction
Closure: A description of the concept or relationship is put into words.	■ Clarify description of new abstraction

"*They all have four letters.*"

"*Good, anything else . . . Pam?*"

"*Some are verbs, and some are nouns, and some are adjectives, like main.*"

"*They could be all nouns,*" interjects Geraldo, "*because* main *could be a noun like* water *main, and* meet *could be a noun like* track meet.*"

"*Good observation, Geraldo. Anything else? How about you, Jimmy?*"

Jimmy pauses.

"*Say the word* beat, *Jimmy.*"

"*Beat.*"

"*And what do you notice about the sound?*"

Jimmy doesn't respond.

"*Say it to yourself again and tell me which letters you hear.*"

"*Three—the* b, *the* e, *and* t.*"

"*Excellent, Jimmy. And was the sound of* e *long or short . . . Pam?*"

"*Long.*"

"*And what other letter is in the word . . . Will?*"

"*A.*"

"*What do you notice about the* a *. . . Stephanie?*"

"*You don't hear it at all.*"

"*Good, so we say it's . . .*"

[Tentatively.] "*Silent.*"

"*Yes! Super, everyone. Now look at the other words and compare them to* beat *. . . Mike?*"

"*They all have two vowels.*"

"*And what about the sound of the vowels, Javier?*"

"*The first one is long in each case.*"

"*Can anyone describe the pattern we see in all these words? [Pointing to the words on the board.] Missy, you have your hand up.*"

"*If you have two vowels together, the first one is long.*"

"*What about the second vowel?*"

"*Oh, yeah, you don't say it.*"

"*That's correct. It is silent. How about the rest of you? Does what Missy says agree with the words that we have on the board? Do all of you agree? Listen again, and I'll say it while I write it on the board for all of us to think about, 'When two vowels go together, the first is long, and the second is silent.' Does that sound accurate . . . Anne?*" *[Anne nods.]*

"*Tell me why, using a word on the board.*"

"*Well,* boat. *It has a long* o *and a silent* a.*"

"*Can you do the same with the last word on the list . . . Jason?*"

"*Yes, in that word, the* a *is long, and the* i *is silent.*"

"*Excellent, now I'm going to give you some more words to see if they follow the rule we wrote on the board.*" Helen writes the following on the board:

> pain
> beet
> meat
> man

"Some do, like pain, *because the* a *is long and the* i *is silent," Abdul offers.*

"Also, beet, *because the* e *is long and the second* e *is silent," Jess adds.*

"What about man . . . *Antonio?"*

"It doesn't fit the rule," Antonio says hesitantly. "It only has one vowel in it."

"Good, Antonio. The rule doesn't apply in this case. Now, give me another example from our list that fits our pattern. Anyone? Go ahead, Katalina."

"How about meat?*"*

"OK. Does Katalina's example fit, Kim?"

"Yes."

"Why do you say so?"

"We hear the sound of a long e, *and we don't hear the* a *at all."*

"Excellent, Kim! Good thinking!"

Helen then reviews the rule and closes the lesson by giving an assignment for the next day.

Let's pause now to consider this lesson, which involved a teacher using a guided discovery approach to help students learn abstractions. In it, students learned a phonetic generalization about word patterns. We call lessons such as these *guided discovery* because students are provided with information, and through the guidance of their teachers they "discover" the abstraction the teacher targeted in her objective (Mayer, 2008).

Planning

Many teachers have the misconception that guided discovery lessons do not require planning and that teachers only need to turn their students loose to discover things about the world. While it is true that children are capable of discovering abstractions about the world on their own, this process is often inefficient and frustrating for students (Mayer, 2008). A far more effective way of ensuring that students will learn an abstraction is to explicitly plan for such learning and to provide enough guidance to be sure it takes place. Guided discovery provides this instructional scaffolding.

A comparison of direct instruction and guided discovery reveals that the planning phases for each are nearly identical. As with direct instruction, planning for guided discovery lessons also begins with identifying a topic and forming an objective. A consideration of students' background knowledge is also critical in both approaches to instruction. However, the selection of examples is all the more important in guided discovery lessons because students must rely on the data or examples to form the abstraction being taught. In direct instruction lessons, the teacher can make allowances for the lack of adequate examples by explaining the abstraction more thoroughly, though the dangers of excessive teacher talk are a continual problem. If the examples are inadequate in guided discovery lessons, learning the abstraction becomes much more difficult.

An essential question the teacher should ask in planning for guided discovery is, What illustrations can I provide to help students understand the concept or generalization? This amounts to selecting good examples that offer observable characteristics for concepts or that illustrate an observable relationship for generalizations. For instance, a picture of a cow is much better than the word *cow* for teaching the concept *mammal* because the characteristics of the concept are more observable in the picture. The same criteria for selecting examples for direct instruction lessons—the extent to which they illustrate essential characteristics or relationships—apply to selecting examples for guided discovery lessons.

The next step in the planning process is to order the examples. Placing obvious examples of an abstraction first will lead to quicker attainment of the abstraction, whereas placing less obvious examples first provides students with more practice in analyzing data and forming hypotheses. The sequence of examples can also be varied to match the difficulty level of the task with the ability of the students. A more difficult sequence might be used to challenge brighter students, while an easier one might be used to help less academically talented students.

One final consideration in planning for guided discovery lessons is time. Because students do not have a definition or generalization written down to focus on, their initial responses will tend to be more divergent than those in teacher-directed lessons. Therefore, the lesson may take longer than a direct instruction lesson covering the same material. The extra time is often well spent in terms of motivation and the possibilities for incidental learning, but time is a factor the teacher should consider in planning guided discovery activities.

Implementing

While the planning phases for direct instruction and guided discovery lessons are essentially the same, the implementation phase is markedly different. In a direct instruction lesson, the abstraction is defined or described for students, whereas in guided discovery teaching, it is not. In a guided discovery lesson, students construct the abstraction themselves using the examples and the teacher's guidance.

Anthony Magnaccal/Merrill

Facilitating the student's ability to form an abstraction is a critical step in the Guided–Discover process.

As students use the examples to construct the abstraction, teacher guidance is essential (Mayer, 2008). Teachers should have a clear content goal in mind as they implement the lesson and use questioning strategically to guide students in their efforts to discover the abstractions. Let's see how this process is reflected in the lesson plan in Figure 8.3 and the lesson involving Helen Cane in the case study at the beginning of this section.

Figure 8.3   Guided Discovery Lesson for Word Pronunciation

Unit: Rules for pronouncing words

Goals Objective: Third graders will learn the rule "When two vowels are together, the first is long and the second is silent," so that when given a list of words, they will pronounce each correctly.

Rationale: Students need to understand rules in order to pronounce words correctly.

Content: When vowels are placed together in words, the first is long (says its name), and the second is silent.

Procedures:
Display the following words on the board:

> beat   boat
> meet   main
> beak

Have the students describe the words.
Have a student pronounce one of the words.
Ask the student what he or she hears.
Ask if it is a long or short sound.
Prompt the students to notice that the other vowel is silent.
Have the class compare the other words to the first one.
Identify the generalization (rule).
Show the students the following words:

> pain
> late
> meat
> man

Ask them which ones follow the rule and why.
Ask them how *boat* would be pronounced if it were spelled b-a-o-t.

Materials: List of words

Evaluation: Have students pronounce a series of words based on the rule

Table 8.2   Steps in Guided Discovery Teaching

Teacher:	1. Present example
Students:	2. Describe example
Teacher:	3. Present additional examples
Students:	4. Describe second example and compare to first example
Teacher:	5. Present additional examples and nonexamples
Students:	6. Compare and contrast examples
Teacher:	7. Prompt students to identify characteristics or relationship
Students:	8. State definition or relationship
Teacher:	9. Ask for additional examples

First, we see that she displayed five examples of the generalization she was trying to teach rather than one (see Table 8.2). This provided opportunities for students to analyze the examples for commonalities.

Then Helen conducted a short review of consonants and vowels—background information students would use in the lesson. During the open-ended phase, Helen asked her students to describe the examples, accepting a variety of answers. She redirected the question to several students to promote involvement. She did a good job of prompting when students could not identify the pattern in the examples immediately. Consider also how Helen's questioning strategies were designed to motivate learners by encouraging them to participate in the lesson. Typically, teachers ask questions that have one right answer, and the same bright students are the quickest to answer these questions. This leaves a significant part of the class without the opportunity to participate, and, consequently, their interest wanes. This is a natural reaction; it is not much fun to sit back all the time and watch others get reinforced for giving the right answers. Guided discovery lessons provide opportunities for students to make observations with little fear of being wrong. This approach encourages nonparticipants to join in the discussion. By asking students to make observations, all of which are correct at that time in the lesson, the teacher invites everyone in the class to participate with a minimum danger of failing.

During the convergent phase, Helen asked for comparisons of the examples, guiding the class toward the generalization she was trying to teach. As students discovered the patterns with Helen's assistance, she asked them to relate the generalization to additional examples. Finally, note how Helen placed the abstraction on the board for the class to see and think about during closure. This is important for several reasons. It provides a concrete record of the lesson for the class to consider. This is crucial because most classes are composed of students of different interests and abilities, and even the best-prepared lesson can leave some students behind. Placing the abstraction on the board or on an overhead allows all students to see it and provides them with the opportunity to relate it to the examples. Writing the abstraction somewhere for all the students to see also provides an alternate channel for learning, thus accommodating different learning styles.

EXERCISE 8.2

Examine the following lesson, which describes a teacher using guided discovery, and then answer the questions that follow.

Peggy Steiner was trying to teach her kindergarten students the concept of set equality. She prepared to do this by gathering together objects from around the room and asking small groups of students to come work with her in a small group on the floor. She began her lesson by saying, "Today I've got some things for us to look at and talk about. I'm going to show you some of them, and I want you to tell me what you see."

With that, she brought out two books and two blocks and put them in two separate piles beside each other. Then she said, "Who can tell me what you see?"

"There are two blocks over here."

"One of them is blue."

"The other is red."

"There's the book we read the other day, Mrs. Steiner."

"Right, and what else do you see?"

"The other book is about animals."

"And it has a picture of an elephant on the cover."

"And how many books are there altogether . . . Jamie?"

"Two."

"And how many blocks do we have here . . . Ahmad?"

"Two."

"Good. Now I want you to look at some more things."

She then moved the two groups of objects to the side, placing each group inside a circle of yarn, and brought out three trucks and three spoons, which she placed in two distinct groups. Next, she asked the class to tell what they saw.

"All the trucks are red."

"And there are three spoons over there."

"One of the trucks has a wheel missing."

"And how many trucks are there?" Peggy asked. "Let's count them together—1, 2, 3. Are there more trucks or more spoons . . . Shelly?"

"They're the same."

Next Peggy brought out six beanbags and six pieces of chalk and asked the class to make additional observations. With prompting, the class decided that the numbers in each group were the same. She repeated this procedure with several other equal sets of objects until a student finally noticed that the numbers in the matched sets were always the same. With that, Peggy introduced the term equal to them. She wrote the symbol on the board and used toothpicks for equal signs to show the students how the matched sets were always equal. Then she mixed up the objects, formed new sets, and asked students to tell whether the sets were equal. Some were, and some were not. Then she had the students form their own equal sets from the objects in front of them.

1. Identify the following steps in the lesson:
    a. Introduction and review
    b. Open-ended phase
    c. Convergent phase
    d. Closure

2. Peggy told students the term for "the same number" was *equal*. Is this advisable in a guided discovery lesson? Explain your reasoning.

LECTURE-DISCUSSION

A third widely used type of teacher-centered instruction is lecture-discussion. **Lecture-discussion** is an interactive instructional strategy designed to help students acquire organized bodies of knowledge (Eggen & Kauchak, 2007). **Organized bodies of knowledge** are topics that connect facts, concepts, and principles and make the relationships among them explicit (Rosenshine, 1987). For example, when students examine relationships among plot, character, and symbolism in a novel such as *Moby Dick* in literature; study landforms, climate, and economy in different regions of the world in geography; or compare parasitic and nonparasitic worms and how differences between them are reflected in their body structures in biology, they are acquiring organized bodies of knowledge.

Lecture-discussions are modifications of traditional lectures. Let's begin by looking at these prevalent but ineffective instructional strategies.

Lectures

The prevalence of the lecture as a teaching method is paradoxical. Although it is the most criticized of all teaching methods, it continues to be the most commonly used (Cuban, 1993). Its popularity is due in part to its ability to do the following:

- Help students acquire information not readily accessible in other ways; lectures can be effective if the goal is to provide students with information that would take them hours to find on their own.
- Assist students in integrating information from a variety of sources.
- Expose students to different points of view.

  Lectures provide one way to accomplish these goals.

  Lectures have three other advantages. First, since planning time is limited to organizing content, they are time and energy efficient. Second, they are flexible; they can be applied to virtually any content area. Third, they are relatively simple compared to some other teaching strategies. The demands on the teacher are relatively low, allowing teachers to concentrate on organizing and presenting content. Even beginning teachers can learn to deliver acceptable lectures.

  Despite their ease, efficiency, and widespread use, lectures have several important disadvantages:

- They are ineffective for attracting and maintaining attention. All of us have sat through mind-numbing lectures with a goal of simply getting the time to pass more quickly.
- Lectures do not allow teachers to check students' perceptions and developing understanding. Teachers are unable to determine whether students are interpreting information accurately.
- While relatively easier for teachers, they impose a heavy cognitive burden on learners, so information is often before students can encode it in long-term memory.
- Lectures put learners in passive roles. This is inconsistent with cognitive views of learning and is arguably the primary disadvantage of the strategy.

  Lectures are especially problematic for young students because of their short attention spans and limited vocabularies, and they are also ineffective if higher-order thinking is a goal.

Overcoming the Weaknesses of Lectures: Lecture-Discussions

Lecture-discussions help overcome the weaknesses of lectures by interspersing short periods of presenting information with systematic teacher questioning.

Lecture-discussion is an instructional strategy designed to teach organized bodies of information in an interactive manner and occurs in four phases:

- Introduction and review
- Presenting information
- Comprehension monitoring
- Integration

These phases and their relationships to student learning are outlined in Table 8.3.

Let's see how a 10th-grade American history teacher implements these phases with her students.

Diane Anderson wants her students to understand the events leading up to the American Revolutionary War. She begins with a review, "So, where are we now in our study of U.S. history?" as she points to a time line above the chalkboard.

"About there," Adam responds, pointing to the middle of the 1700s.

"Yes, good," Diane smiles. "We're almost to the Revolutionary War—a major event in our country's history. However, I would like for us to understand what happened before that time, so we're going to back up a ways, actually, all the way to the early 1600s. When we're finished today, we'll see that the Revolutionary War didn't just happen; there were events that led up to it that made it almost

Table 8.3   The Relationships Between Lecture-Discussion Phases and Student Learning

Phase	Student Learning Outcome
Introduction and review: The teacher begins with a form of introductory focus and reviews previous work.	■ Attracts attention ■ Helps students remember previously learned knowledge
Presenting information: The teacher presents information. Presentations are kept short to prevent overloading learners' working memories.	■ Students acquire knowledge about the topic.
Comprehension monitoring: The teacher asks a series of questions to check learners' understanding.	■ Puts students in active roles and checks whether they are understanding new content ■ Begins process of constructing new organized body of knowledge
Integration: The teacher asks additional questions to help learners integrate new and prior knowledge.	■ Students connect new ideas into a coherent body of information

Note: The use of both positive and negative examples enhance student conceptualization when employing teacher-directed lessons. Facilitating the student's ability to analyze is a critical step in the inquiry process.

inevitable. . . . That's the important part of history . . . to see how events that happen at one time affect events at other times and even all the way to today.

"For instance, the conflicts between the British and the French in America became so costly for the British that they began policies in the colonies that ultimately led to the Revolution. That's what we want to begin looking at today. . . . Here we go."

She then begins, "We know that the British established Jamestown in 1607, but we haven't really looked at French expansion into the New World. Let's look again at our map. "Here we see Jamestown, but at about the same time, a French explorer named Champlain came down the St. Lawrence River and formed Quebec City, here." She points again to the map. "Over the years, at least 35 of the 50 states were discovered or mapped by the French, and they founded several of our big cities, such as Detroit, St. Louis, and New Orleans," she continues pointing to several locations she had marked on the map.

"Now, what do you notice about the location of the two groups?"

After thinking a few seconds, Alfredo offers, "The French had a lot of Canada, . . . and it looks like this country too." He points to the north and west on the map.

"It looks like the east was . . . British, and the west was French," Troy adds.

"Yes, and remember, this was all happening at about the same time," Diane continues. "Now, these were two important differences between the French and English settlers. Also, the French were friendlier with the American Indians than the British were. Also, the French had what they called a seigniorial system, where the settlers were given land if they would serve in the military. So, . . . what do these two differences suggest about the military power of the French?"

"Probably powerful," Josh suggests. "The people got land if they went in the army."

"And the American Indians probably helped because they were friendly with the French," Tenisha adds.

"Good thinking—remember those points; they're important. Now, what else do you notice here?" Diane asks, moving her hand up and down the width of the map.

"Mountains?" Danielle answers uncertainly.

"Yes, exactly," Diane smiles. "Why are they important? What do mountains do?"

". . . The British were sort of fenced in, and the French could expand and do as they pleased."

"Good. And now the plot thickens. The British needed land for new settlers and wanted to expand. So they headed west over the mountains and guess who they ran into . . . Sarah?"

"The French?" Sarah responded.

"Right! And conflict broke out. Now, when the French and British were fighting, why do you suppose the French were initially more successful than the British . . . Dan?"

"Well, they had that sig . . . seigniorial system, so they were more eager to fight because they were fighting for their land."

"Other thoughts . . . Bette?"

"I think that the American Indians were also part of it. The French got along better with them, so they helped the French."

"Okay, good thinking everyone. So now we have two advantages for the French settlers. Now let's think about the British. . . . Let's look at some of their advantages." (adapted from Eggen & Kauchak, 2007, pp. 427–428)

Let's look now at Diane's efforts to help her students acquire and understand an organized body of knowledge. She introduced the lesson with a review and attempted to capture students' *attention* by explaining how events in the past influence the way we live today. Then she *presented information* about Jamestown, Quebec, and French settlements in the present-day United States, using a map to illustrate the geographical connections of ideas in her presentation. Research shows that maps, diagrams, and other forms of visual representations can have a powerful positive effect on student learning during teacher presentations (Nesbit & Adesope, 2006; Reed, 2006). After this brief presentation, she used questioning to involve her students in the *comprehension monitoring* phase. To illustrate the process of checking student understanding, let's review a brief portion of the lesson.

Diane: Now, what do you notice about the location of the two groups?

Alfredo: The French had a lot of Canada, . . . and it looks like this country too. [Pointing to the north and west on the map.]

Troy: It looks like the east was . . . British, and the west was French.

Diane's questions were intended to put students in cognitively active roles, check to see if their background knowledge was accurate, and assist them in understanding and organizing the new information. Satisfied that they understood the new content, she returned to presenting information: "Yes, and remember, this was all happening at about the same time." She continued by briefly describing the French seigniorial system and pointing out the friendly relations between the French and American Indians.

Then she again turned back to the students.

Diane: So . . . what do these two differences suggest about the military power of the French?

Josh: Probably powerful. The people got land if they went in the army.

Tenisha: And the American Indians probably helped because they were friendly with the French.

The two questioning segments appear similar, but there is an important distinction. In the first, Diane was *monitoring comprehension;* students' responses to the question "Now, what do you notice about the location of the two groups?" helped her assess whether they understood what she had presented in the first segment. In the second segment, she attempted to encourage the integration of ideas by helping students connect the seigniorial system, the relationship between the French and the American Indians, and French military power.

After completing this cycle of *presenting information, monitoring comprehension,* and *integration,* she would repeat the process, with the second integration being broader than the first. Diane's goal for the entire lesson was the development of complex, interconnected ideas of the cause-and-effect relationships between the French and Indian wars and the American Revolutionary War.

The effectiveness of lecture discussions depends on the quality of the discussions during the lesson. These discussions allow the teacher to continually assess whether students are understanding new content and helps them connect new ideas into integrated and organized bodies of knowledge. This is the primary reason that lecture discussion is a more effective instructional model than is traditional lecture.

TECHNOLOGY IN THE CLASSROOM

Using Technology to Enhance Instruction in the Classroom

This chapter has emphasized the need for teachers to supplement their verbal presentations with continual feedback and examples, problems, figures, and diagrams that provide learners with opportunities to see abstract ideas connected and represented in concrete, tangible form (Nesbit & Adescope, 2006; Reed, 2006). Technology can be used to enhance teacher-centered instruction in two major ways:

- Using PowerPoint to present information in interesting and interactive ways
- Providing opportunities for practice with quality feedback that is both immediate and responsive about student performance

Let's examine these uses.

PowerPoint: Presenting Information in Dynamic Ways

Presenting new information is an important instructional role in teacher-centered instruction. Teachers are often faced with the problem of explaining information in clear and motivating formats (Donovan & Bransford, 2005). Microsoft's PowerPoint format provides one effective alternative.

Jokingly referred to as "an overhead projector on steroids" (Cuban, 2005), PowerPoint is actually a versatile presentation format. Once mastered, it allows teachers to include the following in their presentations:

- Written text
- Photographs
- Samples of student work
- Charts and graphs
- Video clips
- Voice-overs

Students can also learn to use PowerPoint in their presentations, and these options can encourage them to think more deeply about the material they are presenting and its effect on their audience (Saltpeter, 2005).

PowerPoint does not have to be one-way presentation of information. As teachers present information, they can—and should—check whether students understand and are connecting ideas. PowerPoint can also be used to present quizzes that provide both teachers and students with immediate feedback about learner progress (Finkelstein, 2005).

Drill and Practice

When educators recognized that computers and other forms of technology could perform tasks quickly and systematically, they began to search for ways to use these innovations to imitate the functions of human teachers (Roblyer, 2006). For instance, students often use worksheets and flash cards to practice basic skills, such as word recognition and phonetic analysis in reading and addition and multiplication facts in math. Could computers be used to provide an improved form of practice, educators wondered? This question led to the development of drill-and-practice programs, software designed to provide extensive practice with feedback (Lever-Duffy, McDonald, & Mizell, 2003).

Because students can use drill-and-practice programs on their own, teachers do not have to be directly involved. However, they do not substitute for teachers' expertise, and developers of these programs assume that students have had previous instruction related to the facts or concepts. For example, when students first learn about multiplication, effective teachers help them understand that 6×9 means 6 sets of 9 items, or 9 sets of 6 items, and they present several concrete examples to illustrate the concept of *multiplication*. Drill-and-practice programs are used after this initial instruction to help students practice until the skill becomes automatic—that is, until they know the facts essentially without having to think about them.

Some drill-and-practice software programs use a "game" format to increase student motivation. For example, instead of typing in the correct response to $6 \times 9 = ?$, students might aim a laser blaster at an alien emblazoned with 54.

The best drill-and-practice programs are adaptive, matching the demands of the task to a student's ability. For example, in a program designed to improve knowledge of multiplication facts, an adaptive program begins by pretesting to determine what multiplication facts students already know. Problems are then strategically presented to ensure high success rates. When students fail to answer or answer incorrectly, the program prompts by providing the answer and then retests that fact. More difficult problems are introduced only when students have reached a certain skill level. Because the ultimate goal is for students to be able to recall math facts automatically, the amount of time given to answer is shortened as they become more proficient. This also increases motivation by challenging students to become quicker in their responses.

What are the benefits of drill-and-practice programs? First, they provide practice with effective feedback, informing students immediately of what they have mastered and where they need more work. Research supports the effectiveness of this process (Attewell, 2001). Second, they are often motivating for students turned off by paper-and-pencil exercises (Gee, 2005). Third, they save teachers' time since they do not have to present information and score students' responses.

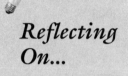

Reflecting On...

TEACHER-CENTERED TEACHING STRATEGIES

INTASC Principles 3 and 4

Think about the different instructional strategies that you learned in this chapter. Then think about how you will incorporate these strategies in your own classroom, with a specific emphasis on the level of the students that you will teach and the content areas for which you will be responsible.

Researchers caution, however, that more time on computers does not necessarily equal more learning (Roblyer, 2006). More important are the quality of the learning experiences and the extent to which they are linked to the teacher's goals.

 SUMMARY

This chapter describes three teacher-centered instructional strategies. All are designed to teach students important content that is essential to future learning. In addition, they all ask the teacher to play a central role in guiding and directing student learning during the lesson. They differ in terms of the specific steps of each strategy and the demands placed on learners.

Direct instruction is a strategy used to teach concepts, generalizations, and skills. Skills are forms of learning that have a specific set of operations, can be illustrated with large numbers of examples, and are developed through practice. Concepts are categories that are illustrated through positive and negative examples. Generalizations are composed of concepts and describe general patterns in our world.

Concepts form an important part of the curriculum. When we teach concepts, we want students to understand (a) the concept's essential characteristics, (b) how these relate to positive and negative examples, and (c) the relationship of the concept to other ideas. This last function is accomplished by linking the concept to superordinate, coordinate, and subordinate concepts.

Direct instruction lessons begin with an introduction and review, which is followed by the teacher presenting and modeling or explaining the concept or skill; this second phase is aimed at developing understanding. Then students practice the new content, first under the supervision of the teacher (guided practice) and then on their own (independent practice). The goal in direct instruction lessons is to develop the new content to the point of automaticity so that it transfers to a variety of contexts.

Guided discovery is an instructional strategy designed to teach concepts and relationships among them. When using the strategy, teachers specify learning objectives, present students with information, and guide them to the objectives with questioning.

Guided discovery is grounded in constructivism, a view of learning that suggests that learners develop their own understanding of the topics they study rather than receive understanding in already organized form. New learning develops in the context of current understanding and is facilitated by social interaction as learners work with real-world tasks, problems, and questions.

Planning for guided discovery lessons begins with identifying topics and then proceeds with specifying clear and precise learning objectives, selecting examples and nonexamples, planning for social interaction, and making decisions about assessment.

Guided discovery lessons begin an open-ended phase in which students observe and describe the examples they encounter. This is followed by a convergent phase, as the teacher guides students toward the learning objective; closure, when the topic is summarized; and application, where new understanding is applied through additional examples.

Organized bodies of knowledge are interrelated connections of facts, concepts, generalizations, principles, and academic rules. A significant portion of the school curriculum focuses on these forms of content. Theories, which describe precise relationships among concepts, are specialized subsets of organized bodies of knowledge.

When lecturing, teachers present information to students in an organized way. Lectures are flexible and easy to plan and implement. They can be effective for helping students acquire information not readily accessible in other ways, but they put learners in passive roles, can easily overload students' memories, and do not allow teachers to assess learning progress.

Lecture-discussions combine the flexibility and simplicity of lectures with the benefits of interactive teaching and are effective for teaching organized bodies of knowledge.

Effective lecture-discussions begin with an introduction that is designed to attract and hold students' attention and are followed by the teacher presenting information in a minilecture. Comprehension monitoring and integration follow the presentation.

Lecture-discussion lessons are developed when one cycle of presenting information, monitoring comprehension, and integration is linked to earlier cycles. With each succeeding cycle, the process of integration becomes broader and deeper.

KEY CONCEPTS

PREPARING FOR YOUR LICENSURE EXAMINATION

Read the following case study and, using specific information from this chapter, answer the questions that follow.

Margaret Fontini looks over the yearlong plans she has laid out for her sixth-grade language arts curriculum and discovers notes from her previous teaching year:

Students have trouble with summarization. Don't know where to start.

"I remember that unit. It was like pulling teeth. I just didn't know how to get the idea across. I've got to do better this time," she mumbles to herself as she opens several language arts teacher editions that she has on her bookshelf. On Monday, Margaret begins her language arts class by saying, "Okay, class please put your math away. If you haven't finished your problems, be sure to take them home and have them ready for class tomorrow."

After pausing for a few moments while students put their math books away, Margaret continues, "Today in language arts we're going to learn a new comprehension skill that will help us when we read. It's called summarization. It will help you learn in language arts, and it should be helpful in other content areas as well. I'd like everyone to look up here on the overhead. I've got a definition for you.

A GOOD SUMMARY RESTATES THE MAIN IDEA OF THE PASSAGE, DELETES UNIMPORTANT AND REDUNDANT INFORMATION, AND, SOMETIMES, INVOLVES SUPERORDINATION.

After pausing for a few moments to allow her students to read the definition, Margaret continues.

"Let's see what a good summary looks like. I'd like you to read this passage, and then I'm going to show you two summaries. Your job is to see if you can tell me which is the better summary for the paragraph. Here we go."

In the desert there are no clouds to stop the sun's burning rays. So the sun heats up the earth. As a result, it gets very hot, the temperature easily reaching 120 degrees. And rainfall is slight in the desert. Most deserts get less than 10 inches of rain per year. Years may pass between showers. Sometimes 5 or 10 years may go by without a drop of rain falling on the desert.

"Has everyone had a chance to read the paragraph? Now, let's look at two possible summaries that I've created. Look up on the overhead and tell me which is better.

1. The desert is a hot and dry place.
2. The sun in the desert is merciless.

"Who has an idea? Which do you think is better . . . Tanya?"

"I think number 1 is better. It . . ."

"Good Tanya, I agree with you. Number 1 is definitely better. Let's try another one. Again, read the paragraph, and then I'll give you two possibilities to choose from.

The heat doesn't bother the seeds from plants and they can do without water for an extended period. After a rain, the seeds sprout, and flowers bloom. Then the desert is covered with many brightly colored flowers. The desert is a beautiful place when there are red, yellow, orange, and blue flowers everywhere. But soon the ground begins to dry up. As the ground dries, the flowers produce new seeds and then die. These new seeds fall to the ground and wait for the next rainfall. When it rains, they grow, blossom, leave new seeds, and then die.

"Has everyone had a chance to read this and think about a summary? Okay then, which of these do you think is the better summary? Look up here on the overhead."

1. Desert flowers bloom only after a rain.
2. Seeds are perfectly suited to the desert.

"Ricardo, do you have an answer?"

"I think number 2 is better because the paragraph is more about seeds than flowers."

"Good, Ricardo. Does everyone agree? Any questions? If not, I have several more paragraphs about the desert that I'd like you to summarize on your own, and we'll compare our answers tomorrow."

With that, she hands out a piece of paper that has four paragraphs on it.

"Remember class, you're supposed to write a summary for each of these paragraphs. Get busy, and I'll be around to help."

As students start on their assignment, Margaret circulates around the room. As she does this, a number of hands go up, asking for help. As she works with each student, she notices that they are all having trouble knowing where to start.

"Hmm, I guess I better do more work on getting started writing a summary. I'll do that first thing in class tomorrow."

1. How effective was the introduction and phase of the lesson? How could Margaret's introduction be improved?

2. How effective was the developing understanding phase of the lesson? How could it be improved?

3. How effective was the guided practice phase of the lesson? Explain, making direct reference to the case study in your assessment.

4. Analyze the quality of the independent practice phase of the lesson. How could the independent practice phase of the lesson be improved?

VIDEO EXERCISE

Go to MyEducationLab and select the topic "Direct Instruction" and watch the video "The Direct Instruction Model." After viewing the video, respond to the questions on the video.

DEVELOPING YOUR PORTFOLIO

The purpose of this activity is to encourage you to think about different ways that you can use teacher-centered instructional strategies in your classroom. Think about the grade level and kinds of students you will likely be teaching in your first year in the profession.

- Which of the teaching strategies in this chapter will be most useful to you in the grade level you will be teaching? Why?
- Which of the teaching strategies in this chapter will be most useful to you in terms of the different kinds of content you will be teaching? Why?
- In addition to the teaching strategies you listed in the first two questions, what other teaching strategies will you employ? What will these other teaching strategies accomplish?

QUESTIONS FOR DISCUSSION

1. How do the following factors influence the importance of skills in the curriculum?
   a. Grade level
   b. Subject matter
   c. Ability level of students (i.e., high versus low)

2. Teachers often have to make professional compromises: You've just begun a direct instruction lesson and find out that, because of a changed school schedule, you have only half as much time as you had planned. How will you adjust your teaching with respect to the four phases of the direct instruction model? Why?
    a. Introduction and review
    b. Developing understanding
    c. Guided practice
    d. Independent practice

3. Identify several topics you believe can be effectively taught using lecture-discussions. Identify other areas where you believe the strategy would be inappropriate. How are the two areas different?

4. How might lecture-discussions be adapted for working with students in the lower elementary grades? How might they be adapted for working with students who are not native English speakers?

5. How do the following factors influence the optimal length of one lecture-discussion cycle?
    a. Age of students
    b. Difficulty or complexity of material
    c. The students' prior knowledge
    d. Student motivation
    e. The teacher's presentation skills

6. As technology becomes increasingly prominent in schools, will guided discovery be a more or a less important teaching strategy? Explain why you think it will or will not be.

 SUGGESTIONS FOR FIELD EXPERIENCE

1. Observe a teacher implementing a teacher-centered lesson.
    a. Outline the major points in the lesson.
    b. What was the teacher's primary content focus?
    c. How specifically did the teacher illustrate abstract ideas?
    d. How did the teacher involve students in the lesson?
    e. What suggestions do you have to improve the lesson?

2. Direct Instruction: Concept Teaching. Observe a teacher teaching a concept (or teach one yourself) and critique the lesson in terms of the following criteria:
    a. Characteristics clearly defined
    b. Examples and nonexamples linked to characteristics
    c. Superordinate concept familiar to students
    d. Coordinate concept clearly differentiated from the target concept

    How could the lesson be improved?

3. Interactive Skills Teaching. Observe and either audio- or videotape a skill-oriented lesson. Analyze it in terms of the following:

a. Introduction and review
b. Developing understanding
c. Guided practice
d. Independent practice

How could the lesson be improved to increase student learning?

4. Interactive Skills Teaching: Trying It Out. Plan for, teach, and tape a skills lesson using the basic skills model. Listen to or watch your tape and address the following questions:
   a. Was your introduction clear? Did it include the following?
      1) What the skill was and how it related to other skills already learned
      2) How it can be applied
      3) Why it is useful
      4) When it should be used
   b. Did you state a goal or an objective for the lesson?
   c. Did you relate the skill to material previously covered?
   d. Did you think aloud while modeling the skill?
   e. What did student success rates during the following suggest about your pace during the following?
      1) Guided practice
      2) Independent practice
   f. How did the amount of teacher talk vary throughout the lesson?
   g. What percentage of the class can perform the skill at an acceptable level? How do you know? Define what this level is and explain why this level is acceptable.

What would you do differently next time?

5. Examine a textbook, curriculum guide, or state standard and identify several possible topics for a lecture-discussion lesson.
   a. What do these topics have in common?
   b. What kinds of background knowledge would students need to participate in the lesson?
   c. What kinds of questions would you use to (a) begin the lesson, (b) monitor comprehension, and (c) integrate information?

If possible, teach and critique the lesson.

6. Observe a teacher (or professor) using a lecture-discussion format. Try to determine beforehand that the lesson will not be entirely lecture. Analyze the lesson in terms of the following:
   a. The length of each lecture-discussion cycle (i.e., how long the teacher talks before asking a question).
   b. What kinds of questions did the teacher ask? (Jot these questions down in order, with times attached to them. Later determine whether these were comprehension or integrative.) What could the instructor have done to make the lesson more effective?

7. Plan, teach, and videotape a lesson using the lecture-discussion format. Analyze the taped lesson in terms of the following variables:

a. Introduction/overview
b. Organizational aids
c. Average length of one lecture-recitation cycle
d. Comprehension checks in each cycle
e. Integrative links in each cycle

In hindsight, what could you have done differently to make the lesson more effective?

TOOLS FOR TEACHING

Print References

Beers, B. (2006). *Learning-driven schools.* Alexandria, VA: Association for Supervision and Curriculum Development. An excellent introduction to applying the latest research to standards and accountability.

Carnine, D., Silbert, J., Kame'enui, E., Tarver, S., & Jongjohann, K. (2006). *Teaching struggling and at-risk readers: A direct instruction approach.* Upper Saddle River, NJ: Prentice Hall. Provides a comprehensive overview of direct instruction applications for the teaching of reading.

Marzano, R., Norford, J., Paynter, D., Pickering, D., & Gaddy, B. (2005). *A handbook for classroom instruction that works.* Upper Saddle River, NJ: Pearson. Provides a comprehensive and readable overview of the research on effective instruction.

Mayer, R. (2008). *Learning and instruction.* Upper Saddle River, NJ: Pearson. Describes different approaches to instruction as well as their psychological underpinnings.

Wiggins, G., & McTighe, J. (2005). *Understanding by design* (2nd ed.). Upper Saddle River, NJ: Pearson Education. Explains how to design instruction around standards and goals.

Web Sites

www.nwlink.com This site provides a historical look at the use of discovery learning in classrooms.

www.rmcdenver.com/useguide/lessons/design.htm? This site has valuable information about designing standards-based lessons.

www.secondaryenglish.com/approaches.html Although this site focuses on English instruction, it also contains useful information about teacher-centered instruction in general.

www.secondaryenglish.com/approaches.html This site describes an interesting experiment comparing teacher-centered versus learner-centered instruction in a high school class.

www.nctm.org This site for the National Council of Teachers of Mathematics, while it focuses on math instruction, also contains valuable information about controversies involving teacher-centered versus learner-centered instruction.

CHAPTER 9

Meeting Standards Through Learner-Centered Instructional Strategies

INTRODUCTION

In Chapter 8, we posed the question, "What is the best way to teach?" In that chapter, we found that effective teachers utilize a variety of instructional strategies, matching these to their objectives and the students they teach. Sometimes more direct, teacher-centered strategies are more effective; at other times, effective teachers stand back and allow their students to play a more active role. This chapter is designed to help you construct and implement learner-centered instructional strategies in your own classroom.

Learner-centered instruction describes teaching strategies in which teachers facilitate rather than direct student learning (McCombs & Miller, 2007). In learner-centered

strategies, teachers consciously place more emphasis on student involvement, initiative, and social interaction. Goals that are most effectively reached through learner-centered strategies include the following:

- The development of communication skills processes, such as tolerance for dissenting views, being able to work in groups, and the critical examination of our own and others' positions
- The development of deep understanding of topics, such as identifying relationships among Marco Polo's visit to the Orient, the Portuguese explorers' trips around the tip of Africa, and Columbus's discovery of the New World
- The development of inquiry and problem-solving skills (Cornelius-White 2007; Li et al., 2007)

   These goals are complex, high level, and less able to be "mastered" in the same sense that students master basic skills. This chapter is designed to help you plan for and implement learner-centered instructional strategies in your own classroom.

LEARNER OBJECTIVES

After completing your study of Chapter 9, you should be able to do the following:

- Explain the major characteristics of learner-centered instructional strategies
- Explain how to plan and implement cooperative learning strategies
- Understand how to plan and implement discussions
- Explain how to plan and implement problem-based lessons

APPLYING CHARACTERISTICS OF LEARNER-CENTERED INSTRUCTION

Following is a case study of several teachers using learner-centered instructional strategies to teach their students. As you read the case study, consider the following questions:

- What do these different lessons have in common?
- How are they different?
- What roles do students play as they attempt to learn new content?
- What role does the teacher play in promoting learning?

Sasha Harris, a sixth-grade math teacher, has a problem. Her students vary dramatically in their math skills, and she does not know where to start in introducing multidigit multiplication. She begins by breaking students into small groups, making sure that each group has both good and struggling math learners.

   Jon Davis, a high school social studies teacher, wants his students to understand presidential and congressional rights as defined by the U.S. Constitution. He begins by showing them a short video that provides a brief overview of the issues involved. Then he leads a lively discussion in which students debate the pros and cons of increased powers for each of these government branches.

Maria Sanchez, a middle school science teacher, wants her students to understand basic principles of healthy nutrition. To capture her students' interest, she asks them to focus on the school lunches they eat, analyzing them for both desirability and taste as well as nutritional content. In doing this, they interview the school dietitian as well as other students in the school.

CHARACTERISTICS OF LEARNER-CENTERED INSTRUCTION

All the lessons you just read about were learner centered in that students played a major and active role in reaching the lesson's objectives. Learner-centered instruction includes the following characteristics:

- Students are at the center of the learning process; teachers encourage them to be responsible for their own learning.
- Teachers guide student learning and intervene only when necessary to prevent them from heading down "blind alleys" or developing misconceptions.
- Teachers emphasize a deep understanding of both the content and the processes involved.

Students at the Center of the Learning-Teaching Process

The expanding influence of cognitive learning theory, research examining the thinking of experts, and criticisms of more teacher-centered instruction have resulted in increased emphasis on the role of students in learning. This emphasis requires teachers to design learning activities in which students assume more responsibility for their own learning and interact with each other while learning new content (Cornelius-White, 2007).

Teachers Guide Learners

A second characteristic of learner-centered instruction is that teachers *guide* learners rather than directly instructing them (Mayer, 2008). To put this into perspective, let's look back to Carl Hite's work with his fifth graders in Chapter 8. In that lesson, Carl wanted his students to understand how to compute the circumference of a circle. Carl made *himself directly responsible* for students' learning by modeling and explaining a specific procedure for finding the circumference of a circle and being sure that students successfully followed it. In learner-centered instruction, teachers make *students responsible* for their own learning by giving them a task and intervening only when they flounder.

Teaching for Deep Understanding

A third major characteristic of learner-centered instruction is its emphasis on deep understanding (Bransford, Derry, Berliner, & Hammerness, 2005). The phrase "teaching for understanding" seems like a paradox; no teacher consciously teaches for lack of understanding. However, understanding does not always result from instruction, and "teaching for understanding" is not as simple as it appears. Understanding involves thought-demanding processes, such as explaining, finding evidence, justifying thinking, providing additional examples, generalizing, and relating parts to wholes. Students need opportunities to practice these skills while wrestling with new content; learner-centered instruction provides these opportunities.

Misconceptions About Learner-Centered Instruction

Teachers sometimes misinterpret learner-centered instruction when they attempt to apply it in their classrooms. Some misinterpretations include the following:

- Clear goals and careful preparation are less important in learner-centered than in teacher-centered approaches.
- If students are involved in discussions and other forms of interaction, learning automatically takes place.
- Teachers play less important roles in student-centered learning than in traditional instruction.

Because students are responsible for constructing their own understanding, teachers might mistakenly conclude that clear goals are less important when using learner-centered approaches. Nothing could be further from the truth. Clear goals are as—or even more—important because they give teachers focal points as they design lessons and assist their students. Teachers may modify their goals as the lesson develops, but they begin with clear goals in mind.

Concluding that discussions and other forms of social interaction automatically lead to learning is equally inaccurate. We want students to become self-regulated and construct understandings that make sense to them, but their understandings must be valid. If students head down blind alleys or develop misunderstandings about the topic, teachers must intervene and redirect the discussion (Ding, Li, Piccolo, & Kulm, 2007).

Finally, because teachers are not lecturing and directly explaining, it might appear that they have a less important role in learner-centered than in teacher-centered instructional approaches. However, their role is both more subtle and more sophisticated. If they understand a topic, most teachers can learn to adequately explain it. Guiding learners so that they develop a deep understanding of the topic is much more difficult.

In this chapter, we examine three learner-centered strategies: cooperative learning, discussions, and problem-based learning. We begin with cooperative learning in the next section.

COOPERATIVE LEARNING STRATEGIES

Recent research reveals that the vast majority of time (91%) spent in elementary classrooms consists of either teacher-led whole-group instruction or individual seat work, leaving little time for students to interact with each other (Pianta, Belsky, Houts, & Morrison, 2007). **Cooperative learning** is a general term for a collection of teaching strategies designed to foster group cooperation and interaction among students. Common to all these strategies is students working together in small groups on common learning goals. These strategies are designed to eliminate the competition found in most classrooms, which tends to produce "winners and losers." The resulting competitive classroom pecking order discourages students from helping one another (Johnson & Johnson, 2006; Madrid, Canas, & Ortega-Medina, 2007). Cooperative learning strategies are specifically designed to encourage students to work together and help each other learn common goals. Because of this, they have been found to be successful in not only learning content but also fostering positive intergroup attitudes in diverse and multicultural classrooms (Banks, 2006b). Let's see how cooperative learning might accomplish these goals in a middle school classroom.

As Sasha Harris examines the pretest she has administered at the beginning of her sixth-grade basic math class, she shakes her head. Not only are her students ethnically diverse, they are also diverse in terms of their math backgrounds. Some can do decimals and fractions, while others are struggling with basic math operations like multiplication and division.

To make the most of this diversity, she divides her students into groups of four, based on pretest scores and cultural backgrounds. In addition to teaching math, she also feels strongly about the need to help her students know and get along with different student groups.

The next day, Sasha begins class by reviewing the procedures for multidigit multiplication. She knows that, for some, this would be an easy review, while others would struggle. After her initial presentation, she forms students into teams, gives each group worksheets, and explains how the performance of each team would be determined by the test scores of each member of the team. When some students groan, she explains that the teams were specially designed for balance and that the students would be evaluated on personal improvement and not direct competition with each other.

As the groups work on their problem sheets, Sasha circulates around the room, encouraging cooperation and giving students hints on how to help their teammates learn. At the end of the period, each student takes a quiz, which she grades and returns the next day. She incorporates the grades into the team scores.

Cooperative learning can be used to accomplish many different but compatible goals. It can be used to teach traditional academic goals, basic skills, and higher-level thinking skills. It also can be an effective strategy to teach interpersonal skills and to help different racial and ethnic groups learn together. Cooperative learning has also been used to foster acceptance of special education students mainstreamed into the regular classroom (Johnson & Johnson, 2006).

Whatever the goals, five essential elements undergird all effective cooperative learning strategies (Johnson & Johnson, 2006):

- Social interaction is used to facilitate learning.
- Students work together in groups on clearly assigned tasks.
- Learning objectives create group goals that direct learning activities with the group.
- Teachers hold students individually accountable for their learning.
- Students develop collaboration skills while also learning content objectives.

Face-to-face social interaction between students has several benefits. It encourages students to put their sometimes fuzzy thoughts into words. This is a cognitively demanding task (as anyone who has tried to write something will attest) that promotes clear thinking and learning. Social interaction also allows for the sharing of alternate perspectives, helping students view ideas in different ways. Face-to-face interaction also allows students to coconstruct knowledge, building on the ideas of others (Eggen & Kauchak, 2007).

Learning objectives focus students' energy on an agreed-on and shared learning task. The objective in Sasha Harris's class was for all members to learn how to perform multidigit multiplication. This clear objective provided direction for both Sasha and the groups as they worked together.

Group goals motivate students to help each other, in turn giving them a stake in one another's success. In support of this view, researchers found that successful groups had extensive interactions focusing on content and that group goals encouraged students to explain content to their teammates (Webb, Farivar, & Mastergeorge, 2002). Group goals also encourage students to ask for and give help. Teachers can promote group goals by setting up grading systems that reward students for the whole group's performance. The reward for team performance can be anything that is important to students, such as free time, certificates of achievement, or bonus points for grades.

Student accountability means that each individual in the group is held responsible for learning essential content through quizzes, tests, or individual assignments. Individual accountability can also be combined with group goals when the group grade or reward is based on the average of individual members' quiz scores. Without individual accountability, the most able students in the group may do all the work, with teammates being ignored or given a "free ride."

A final essential characteristic of cooperative learning is that students learn both content and social interaction skills. These social interaction skills include turntaking, listening, learning to disagree constructively, giving feedback, reaching consensus, and involving every member in the group. These collaborative skills are some of the most important outcomes learned in cooperative learning activities and often must be taught and developed (Blatchford, Baines, Rubie-Davies, Bassett, & Chowne, 2006; Li et al., 2007). Group processing after a cooperative learning activity encourages members to reflect on the effectiveness of their group. This makes the group more effective and helps individuals understand how their actions contribute to the workings of the group.

EXERCISE 9.1

Explain how Sasha Harris applied each of these essential characteristics of cooperative learning in her class.

1. Group goals

_____

2. Individual accountability

_____

3. Development of social skills

_____

Getting Started

"What are we supposed to do?"

"I don't know either."

Learner–centered instruction allows students to assume more responsibility for their own learning.

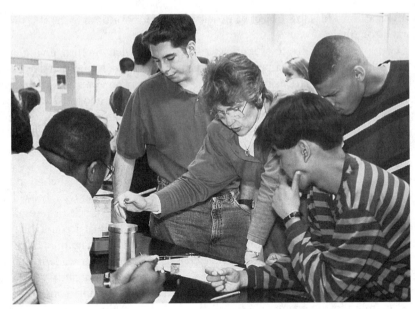

Anne Vega/Merrill

"Be quiet! You never listen to me!"

"I can't hear. It's too noisy."

Successful cooperative learning activities do not just happen. Instead, they are the result of thoughtful planning and preparation (Evertson, Emmer, & Worsham, 2006). When students have had limited experience with these instructional strategies, the teacher needs to make a special effort when introducing cooperative learning to students (Blatchford et al., 2006).

Teachers implementing cooperative learning strategies in their classes identify the following potential problem areas:

- Off-task behaviors
- Failure to get along
- Misbehavior
- Ineffective use of group time (Vaughn, Bos, Candace, & Schumm, 2006)

Let's see how teachers can address each of these potential problem areas.

Off-Task Behaviors.   Off-task behaviors typically result from two factors: unclear task goals and lack of accountability. Before breaking students into groups, the teacher should clearly indicate the goal for the activity and the specific product that should result. In addition, specify the amount of time students have to accomplish the task (and keep it relatively short). When first introducing students to cooperative learning, start with short, simple tasks and make goals and directions clear. This clear description of a product also relates to accountability. When students know exactly what they are to produce, they have a clear target at which to aim.

Failure to Get Along.   Learning to work together effectively does not automatically happen; social skills need to be developed (Berk, 2006, 2007). In many of their learning activities, students sit quietly, isolated from each other. Cooperative learning requires them to talk, listen, and help each other learn. The process is often made more complicated by the group's heterogeneous nature.

Teachers can use the following cooperative team-building exercises to develop students' interactive skills (Johnson & Johnson, 2006):

1. *Name learning.* Allocate some time at the beginning of group formation for students to learn each other's names. Make this a game and give an oral "quiz" where other team members have to name each of their partners.
2. *Interview.* Extend the name-learning exercise to one in which students interview each other about interests, hobbies, favorite foods, or something that no one else knows about them. Have students present these in a short introduction to the rest of the class.
3. *Team name or logo.* Encourage students to develop a name for their group. As they make this choice, stress broad participation, consensus building, and respect for individual rights.

An important goal for cooperative learning in particular and for school in general is for students to learn to treat each other with courtesy and respect. Breaking this rule should be the one cardinal sin in your class. With effort and persistence, you can enforce this rule, and many of the problems associated with students wanting to work only with their friends will disappear.

Misbehavior.   Given the interactive nature of cooperative learning strategies, the freedom and lack of structure may result in increased student management problems (Emmer, Evertson, & Worsham, 2006; Evertson et al., 2006). Solutions to this potential problem are specific task demands and agenda setting, accountability, and careful student monitoring.

Many management problems occur because of unclear student roles and expectations (e.g., "What are we supposed to do?"). Before you break students into groups, make sure that all students know what they are expected to do. Do not just describe student tasks; rather, directly model them with the same learning materials students will be using. Student accountability also helps create structure and minimizes management problems. When students know that a product is expected or that a quiz will be given, their efforts become more focused on the learning task at hand.

Ineffective Use of Group Time.   Once students are in groups, monitor the groups by circulating around the room and helping individual groups. Stand back from time to time and observe the whole classroom. Which groups are working well? Which students are busy, and which ones are dawdling or playing? Spend extra time with those groups that need extra help. Make sure that groups that do work effectively are rewarded with positive comments and make a special effort to call the whole class's attention to effective groups.

Types of Cooperative Learning

Researchers have found that teachers use a variety of hybridized cooperative learning strategies in their classrooms, borrowing elements of different ones to maximize learning (Eggen & Kauchak, 2007; Emmer & Gerwels, 2002). They found the most successful strategies included high levels of individual or group accountability, teacher monitoring, feedback, and the use of concrete or manipulative materials that provided a focal point for students' thinking (Emmer & Gerwels, 2002). In this section, we describe several cooperative learning strategies, differentiating them in terms of goals and procedures.

Group Work.   **Group work** is an instructional strategy that uses students working together to supplement other strategies, such as teacher-centered direct instruction or lecture-discussion. Group work can be used to teach both lower- and higher-level goals. Examples of lower-level goals include the following:

- Basic math facts
- Historical names and dates
- Chemical symbols and terms in science
- Punctuation and grammar in language arts

Group work can also be used to stimulate students' thinking in the same content areas, such as the following:

- Improving students' problem-solving skills
- Helping students understand trends and cause-and-effect relationships in social studies
- Teaching students how to design experiments in science
- Providing feedback about written drafts (Ginsburg-Block, Rohrbeck, & Fantuzzo, 2006; Harris, Graham, & Mason, 2006)

Group work exists in a number of forms depending on the goals of the lesson, the size and composition of the group, and the learning task. The simplest group-work arrangement consists of learning pairs. When they are seated next to each other, students working in pairs can be easily integrated into existing lessons. In this section, we discuss two popular group-work options: think-pair-share and pairs check.

In **think-pair-share,** the teacher asks a routine question, but instead of calling on one student, the teacher asks all students to think about the answer (the think part of the strategy) and discuss it with their partner (the pair-share aspect of the strategy). After a short time, the teacher asks a person in each pair (or several of the pairs) to share his or her thoughts with the whole class. Think-pair-share is most effective when embedded within whole-group, teacher-led instruction.

Four factors contribute to the strategy's effectiveness:

- It elicits responses from everyone in the class and promotes active learning.
- Because each member of the pairs is expected to participate, it reduces "free rides," which are sometimes a problem in group work.
- It is relatively easy to plan for and implement.
- It can help learners make the transition to other, more complex cooperative learning strategies.

A second type of group work popular in schools is **pairs check.** This strategy involves student pairs working at their desks while focusing on problems with convergent answers. The strategy usually follows instruction in which a concept or skill has been taught and provides students with opportunities to practice on the topic by alternating roles between "solver" and "checker." Pairs are given handouts containing convergent problems or questions that have clearly right or wrong answers, such as math problems, spelling words, grammar, or punctuation. One member of the pairs works two or three problems, the second member checks the answers, and then the roles are reversed.

As students work, the teacher monitors the process and encourages students to discuss, when appropriate, the reasons the answers are correct. If they do not, pairs check amounts to little more than individual students checking their work in the back of the book. In addition, time is reserved at the end of the activity to allow whole-class discussion on areas of disagreement or confusion.

Student Teams Achievement Division.   In **student teams achievement division** (STAD), which Sasha Harris used, high- and low-ability students are paired on evenly matched teams of four or five, and team scores are based on the extent to which individuals improve their scores on skills tests (Slavin, 1995). An important feature in STAD is that students are rewarded for team performance, thus encouraging group cooperation.

The steps involved in implementing STAD are the following:

1. Pretest students. This can be an actual pretest or work from previous units.
2. Rank students from top to bottom.
3. Divide students so that each team of four has high-, low-, and medium-ability students and that groups are diverse in terms of gender and ethnicity.
4. Present content as you normally would.
5. Distribute prepared worksheets that focus on the content to be learned.
6. Monitor groups for learning progress.
7. Administer individual quizzes to each student.
8. Assign team scores based on individually gained scores.

STAD is a popular cooperative learning strategy because of its wide applicability across most subject matter areas and grades. For a more detailed description of how to implement it in the classroom, see Slavin (1995).

Group Investigation.

Maria Hernandez was asked by her principal to help purchase new equipment for the gym and playground in her elementary school. She thought this would be a good opportunity to involve her students in a group investigation. When she first posed the problem to the class, all the students blurted out personal preferences, like basketballs and jump ropes, but Maria encouraged them to think beyond their own personal wishes. She broke the class into groups and encouraged each group to think of a way to gather information about the problem. All agreed to search the Internet and library for information. Some decided to poll students at different levels; others visited neighboring schools to check out their physical education equipment and facilities. As each group gathered data, Maria helped them organize it and place it in a form that could be shared with the whole class. At the end of the week, each group presented its findings, and the class discussed differences between the findings.

Cooperative learning can also be used to promote higher-level learning goals. **Group investigation** places students together in teams of three to six to investigate or solve some common problem (Tan, Sharan, & Lee, 2007). Examples might include a science or social studies experiment, a home economics project, or the construction of a diorama or collage in art. Students are responsible for developing specific group goals, assigning individual responsibilities, and bringing the project to completion. Cooperation is fostered through common group goals, and grades are assigned to the total project.

There are six steps in the group investigation strategy:

1. *Topic selection.* Students choose topics to investigate within a general area.
2. *Cooperative planning.* Students, with the help of their teacher, plan how to gather data and other learning activities, such as Internet or library searches.
3. *Implementation.* Students carry out the plan they have devised, using different learning strategies and data sources.
4. *Analysis and synthesis.* Students analyze and organize the information they have gathered to present to other groups.
5. *Presentation of final product.* Students share the information they gathered.
6. *Evaluation.* Students compare findings and perspectives and discuss similarities and differences.

To accommodate diversity, teachers should ensure that groups are heterogeneous and that all group members contribute to the final product.

Jigsaw Strategy.

Felicia Garret's high school biology class was starting a new unit on reptiles. She wanted to actively involve her students in the unit, so she decided to break students into learning teams of four. She strategically placed students on these teams in terms of ability, gender, and ethnic background. Each team had the same topics to learn: similarities and differences with amphibians, reptile subspecies (e.g., snakes, turtles, and lizards), reptilian physiology and anatomy, and reptilian ecological adaptations. Each team member was responsible for learning about one of these and then had to teach the others in the group what they had learned. To assist them, Felicia had special expert groups meet in which the designated expert on a particular topic from each group got together to discuss their findings. After this meeting, the experts taught the other members what they had learned, and this was followed by a comprehensive test for the whole class.

Jigsaw is a cooperative learning strategy that places students in small groups to investigate a common topic (Aronson, Wilson, & Akert, 2005). These topics are typically broad enough in scope (e.g., the country of Mexico in geography, reptiles in science, or contagious diseases in health) that individual members of the team can be assigned specific subjects within the topic. Individuals are then responsible for researching and learning about their area of specialization and teaching this topic to other members. All students are expected to learn all the information on the topic, and comprehensive quizzes can be used to supplement group reports to measure if this happens. These different forms of cooperative learning are summarized in Figure 9.1.

DIVERSITY IN THE CLASSROOM

Cooperative Learning: A Tool for Capitalizing on Diversity

Unfortunately, people tend to be somewhat wary of others who look or act differently than they do or of those who come from backgrounds that are different from their own. This tendency is common in social settings, and it also occurs in schools. Students of a particular ethnic group tend to spend most of their time together, so they do not learn that all of us are much more alike than we are different. As teachers, we cannot mandate tolerance, trust, and friendship among students with different backgrounds, but we can place them in

Strategies	Content Goals	Structure
Peer tutoring	Facts, skills, goals	Drill-and-practice supplement to regular instruction
Student teams Achievement diversions	Facts, skills	Heterogeneous team reinforced for team performance
Group investigation	Group problem solving/inquiry	Heterogeneous, with teams assigned to group projects
Jigsaw	Group investigation of broad topic	Individual team members assigned to facets of large topic

Figure 9.1   Cooperative Learning Strategies

situations where working together results in positive outcomes and healthy relationships (Johnson & Johnson, 2006).

Research supports this strategy. Students working in cooperative groups improve their social skills, increase their acceptance of students with exceptionalities, and develop friendships and positive attitudes with others who differ in achievement, ethnicity, and gender (Vaughn et al., 2006).

The positive effects of cooperative learning on racial and interpersonal attitudes stem from three factors:

1. Opportunities for different types of students to work together on joint projects
2. Equal status roles for participants
3. Opportunity for different types of students to learn about each other as individuals (Vaughn et al., 2006)

Cooperative learning's positive effects on intergroup relations may result from opportunities for friendships and blurring of intergroup boundaries. As students work together, they develop friendships across racial and ability groups, tending to soften and blur well-defined peer group boundaries that lead to other cross-group friendships. To achieve these positive benefits, teachers need to plan carefully and implement strategically (Blatchford et al., 2006).

Effective interaction does not just happen; it must be planned and taught (Blatchford et al., 2006; Ding et al., 2007). "Helping" behaviors can be learned, and these skills are especially valuable for minority students, who are often hesitant about seeking and giving help. Helpful interaction skills include the following (Li et al., 2007):

- Listening and questioning.   Encouraging other students to verbalize their understanding and listening to others' ideas without criticizing them
- Checking for understanding.   Asking for elaboration when answers are incomplete
- Staying on task.   Making sure the discussion remains focused and time limits are met
- Emotional support.   Offering supportive comments for incorrect answers (e.g., "That's OK. I don't always get it the first time either.")

Role playing, teacher modeling, and videotapes of effective groups can all be used to help students learn these skills.

To be successful in promoting acceptance of diversity, learning tasks need to require cooperation and communication. By rotating students through leadership roles, teachers can encourage participation from all group members and help prevent higher-status or more aggressive students from dominating the activity. Other tasks that can be used to encourage communication and cooperation include presenting and checking math problems, practicing spelling and grammar exercises in which students take turns as tutors, and providing open-ended problems (Johnson, & Johnson, 2006; Vaughn et al., 2006).

In addition, groups need constant monitoring and support, especially initially. Student achievement is related to the amount and quality of interaction in groups, which also influences group cohesion and intragroup relations. Teachers should deal initially with interpersonal problems in individual groups. If the problems persist, they can reconvene the class for discussion, additional modeling, and role playing.

DISCUSSION STRATEGIES

Discussions are instructional strategies that use teacher–student and student–student interactions as the primary vehicle for higher-level learning goals. They are characterized by decreased focus on the teacher, increased student–student interactions, and high levels of student involvement. When effectively used, discussions can stimulate thinking, challenge attitudes and beliefs, and develop interpersonal skills (Burbules & Bruce, 2001; Meter & Stevens, 2000). However, if not organized and managed properly, they can be boring for students, frustrating for the teacher, and a general waste of time.

Discussion strategies are different from cooperative learning strategies in terms of both goals and procedures (Keefer, Zeitz, & Resnick, 2000; Meter & Stevens, 2000). They are not designed to teach specific types of content like concepts or generalizations. Instead, they are used to reach other important classroom goals, such as learning the following:

1. To understand the connections and relationships between ideas
2. To become an active listener
3. To develop leadership skills
4. To summarize group opinions
5. To develop self-directed learning skills
6. To develop analysis, synthesis, and evaluative skills
7. To arrive at a consensus
8. To handle controversy and differences of opinion

Students learn these skills by actively engaging in classroom discussions.

A second difference between discussions and student-centered strategies relates to the teacher's role. In discussions, the teacher becomes less a director of learning and more a facilitator. In many ways, this role is more difficult because the teacher has less control over the lesson's direction and pace. Nevertheless, the teacher's role remains critical, for the teacher must ensure the promotion of learning through student interaction and exchange of ideas. This can be accomplished by the teacher carefully initiating, informing, supporting, monitoring, and evaluating the discussion activity. Let's now look at how teachers plan for discussion strategies.

Planning

The bottom line in planning and implementing discussion lessons is organization. It is absolutely critical that teachers carefully organize the activity, or the activity will result in nonlearning at best or disintegrate into chaos at worst. The single biggest problem with discussions is the tendency for students to drift away from the central focus or topic of the lesson. Only careful planning and organization can help prevent this problem.

Five crucial decisions are essential when planning for a discussion activity. First, the teacher carefully considers goals. As noted previously, discussion goals include the acquisition of communication and social skills in addition to content goals.

Second, the teacher needs to decide if the activity would be best implemented in a large-group, teacher-led discussion or in small-group, student-led activity. This decision relates to the teacher's goal. If the primary goal is to develop leadership skills, active listening, or other related interactive skills, small-group activities are more effective. On the other hand, exploring the relationships among ideas and the development of analysis, synthesis, or evaluation skills can probably be facilitated more through teacher-directed discussions.

Third, the teacher should consider the background and experience of students. Young or inexperienced students need structure in the form of explicit directions, a relatively simple task, and a shorter time period. As students acquire experience, they can take on more initiative themselves. Our discussion goals should be developmental; a teacher hoping for success with the strategy needs a full grading period or more for students to develop the skills for effective discussions.

Fourth, the discussion should result in a specific product, such as a summary, list, series of conclusions, or something concrete that can be shared with the class. A clear task that requires students to produce something concrete in a short time period can help considerably with this potential problem.

Finally, the teacher needs to consider the time allotted for the activity. In general, the time allotted for discussions should be short. All of us have had experiences where we were put into groups and discussed the given task for a short time and then talked about everything from our friends to the weather. This tendency to drift away from the task is one of the major problems with small groups. It can be remedied by accountability in the form of specified products and specific time frames.

Implementing

In implementing discussion strategies, teachers use lesson plans to provide structure and use questioning to guide students during the lesson. Examine the lesson plan in Figure 9.2, and then let's turn to a teacher's implementation of the plan.

John Williams wants his students to analyze and evaluate the president's constitutional right to impose a wage and price freeze without congressional approval.

He begins the activity by saying, "Today we are going to analyze the president's right to make executive orders without the approval of Congress. I'm going to show you a video, and I want you to identify in the video the two positions taken and at least one item of information that supports each position. . . . Now tell me what you are going to do first . . . Tom?"

"We're going to identify the two positions on the issue."

Figure 9.2 Lesson Plan Illustrating a Discussion Strategy

Unit: The executive branch of government

Goals Objective: American history students will understand the relationship between conclusions and evidence, so that when given an issue they will take a position and defend it with evidence.

Students will understand leadership roles so that when placed in a position that requires leadership, they will help the group meet its goals.

Students will understand group consensus so that when given an issue, they will arrive at consensus.

Rationale: The ability to assess conclusions with evidence is important in developing analysis, synthesis, and evaluation skills. Leadership and the ability to arrive at group consensus are important skills in the workforce.

Content: The president of the United States can make executive decisions without the approval of Congress only if a national emergency exists. What constitutes a national emergency is controversial and open to debate.

Procedures:

> Introduce the issue of the president's right to make executive orders without the approval of Congress.
> Show film illustrating the two positions.
> Have the class identify the positions in the film and give one item of information that supports each position.
> Break students into groups with the following charge:
>
> > Take a position on the issue and document it.
> > Summarize the information to be reported to the class.
> > Come to group consensus. If consensus is impossible, prepare a minority statement.
>
> Monitor the groups to check their progress toward consensus.
> Have the class present their findings.

Materials: Film illustrating the issue of presidential executive orders

Evaluation: Have students turn in papers that include a position, supporting evidence, and summary.

"Exactly. Very good. Then, what will you do next . . . Maria?"

"We will identify one item of information that supports each position."

"Excellent, Maria. I think we're ready to look at the video."

After showing the video, John continues, "All right, who can tell me what the two positions are?"

Tony volunteers, "Well, they are really simple. One position was that he had the right to impose the controls, and the other was that he didn't."

"OK," John says with a smile. "Now, give me some information that supports each position."

Jasmine raises her hand.

"Jasmine?"

"Inflation was running at a 12% annual rate, and some people on fixed incomes were being squeezed terribly. That supports imposing the controls."

"Hasam?"

"Technically, it's unconstitutional unless a national emergency exists. While the inflation was bad, it really wasn't a national emergency."

"Very good, everyone. Now listen carefully. This is what we are going to do. As you walked into class today, you selected a number from 1 to 6. You also see the numbers 1 through 6 hanging on the walls of the room. When I tell you to move, I want all the people with 1s to group themselves under the 1, those with 2s under the 2, and so on. Now look at your numbers. In each group, all but one of you has the number in numeral form, and one has the number written out. The person with the number spelled out will be the group leader. This was done at random, and during the course of the year you'll each be a leader more than once. Leaders, it's your responsibility to appoint a recorder and lead the discussion. Recorders, you must summarize the information and report to the whole class. Each group's task is to take a position on the issues presented in the film, document the position in writing, and orally report your position to the whole class. Take either side of the issue. You must come to a group agreement. If one of you disagrees strongly, you may make a minority statement when reporting to the class."

John then reviews the task with the class, as he did before showing the film. Finally, he says, "You have 15 minutes, starting now. Begin."

John then moves from group to group and announces the time at 5-minute intervals. At precisely the 15-minute point, he calls the class together.

"We didn't have time to finish," Sharon complains.

"We couldn't come to a consensus," Pam says from another group.

"Hmm . . ." John sympathizes. "Let's discuss both of those problems."

With that, he explains why he gave them only 15 minutes and praises them for their diligence in the groups. He also explains that in time they will become more efficient. He then begins a large-group discussion on ways of reaching a consensus. Finally, he has each group report their results and says that they will analyze the results in greater detail the following day.

Exercise 9.2 analyzes John Williams's lesson and reinforces your understanding of the content of this section.

EXERCISE 9.2

Consider the lesson illustrated in the scenario you just read and answer the questions that follow.

1. John had four goals he wanted to develop in the lesson. Identify the four goals that were implicit in his lesson.

2. John used both large- and small-group techniques. Identify the portion of his lesson devoted to each.

3. Describe how John took the experience and development of his students into account.

4. What provisions did John make to ensure that the discussion was as effective as possible? You should identify at least four factors.

PROBLEM-BASED INSTRUCTION

In this section, we examine **problem-based instruction,** a broad family of strategies designed to teach problem-solving and inquiry skills. Problem-based learning, as its name implies, uses a problem as a focal point for student investigation and inquiry (Gijbels, Dochy, Van den Bossche, & Segers, 2005; Lam, 2004). Included within the family of problem-based learning are inquiry, problem solving, project-based teaching, case-based instruction, and anchored instruction. In this section, we examine two of the more popular forms of problem-based learning: inquiry and problem solving. Common to all these strategies is the active involvement of students in trying to solve some problem or answer some question.

To introduce you to the topic of problem-based learning, let's look at two problem-based lessons:

A high school communications class was studying different forms of media and their influence on American culture. The topic of TV advertising came up, and students had questions about the different kinds, length, and frequency of TV advertising. To answer these questions, teacher Carla Schmidt had students gather data based on hypotheses the class formulated.

Maria Sanchez's middle school science class was studying health and nutrition. During the course of the unit, students continually complained about the cafeteria lunches. After checking with the principal and school dietitian, Ms. Sanchez asked the class if they would like to try to do something about the problem. The class agreed and divided into teams to gather information about monetary and dietary constraints as well as the preferences of students at different grade levels.

How are these problem-based teaching episodes similar? What characteristics do they share, and how do these characteristics contribute to learning? What specific roles do students and teachers play in problem-based learning? We attempt to answer these questions by analyzing the inquiry and problem-solving strategies of problem-based learning.

An Overview of Problem-Based Instruction

Problem-based learning is based on the work of the educational philosopher John Dewey (1923, 1938), who emphasized the importance of learning through experience. Dewey basically believed that children are socially active learners who learn by exploring their environments (Dewey, 1910). Schools should take advantage of this natural curiosity by bringing the outside world into the classroom, making it available and accessible for study. Dewey believed that the knowledge students learn should not be some inert information found in books or delivered in lectures. Instead, knowledge becomes useful and alive when it is applied to the solution of some problem. Dewey's work had a major influence on the progressive education movement in the United States and continues to be felt in areas such as project-based learning, thematic units, and interdisciplinary teaching.

Problem-based learning strategies share the following common characteristics (Gijbels et al., 2005; Lam, 2004):

1. Lessons begin with a problem or question that serves as the focal point for student investigative efforts. In the high school communications class, questions about the type, length, and frequency of commercials provided a focus for students' inquiries. The teacher in the middle school science class used cafeteria lunches to frame her students' investigation.

2. Students assume primary responsibility for investigating problems and pursuing questions. This responsibility is important both instructionally and motivationally because students in problem-based lessons literally learn by doing (Pintrich & Schunk, 2002).

3. The teacher's role in problem-based learning is primarily facilitative. As opposed to more content-oriented models in which the teacher actively disseminates information, problem-based learning requires teachers to assist more indirectly by posing problems or questions and asking helpful, probing questions.

Goals

Problem-based lessons have three interrelated goals. One is to develop students' ability to systematically investigate a question or problem. By participating in structured problem-based activities, students learn how to attack similar problems in a comprehensive and systematic manner. A second goal of problem-based learning is the development of self-directed learning. By assuming responsibility for their own investigations, students learn to regulate and control their own learning (Meltzer, 2007).

A third but less important goal for problem-based learning is content acquisition. Much of the content students learn in problem-based lessons is implicit and incidental in the sense that neither the teacher nor students know exactly where the investigation will proceed. Because of this, problem-based strategies can be less effective for teaching content than more teacher-centered strategies, such as direct instruction or lecture-discussion (Kirschner, Sweller, & Clark, 2006). However, there is some evidence that information learned in this way is retained longer and transfers better (Barak & Dori, 2005).

Let's begin our investigation of problem-based strategies with inquiry, described in the next section.

Inquiry

Inquiry is a process for answering questions and solving problems based on the logical examination of facts and observations (Victor & Kellough, 2004). **Inquiry strategies** use these processes to teach content and to help students think analytically. Inquiry teaching begins by providing students with content-related problems that serve as the focus for the class's research activities. In working with a problem, students generate hypotheses or tentative solutions to the problem, gather data relevant to these hypotheses, and evaluate these data to arrive at a conclusion. Through inquiry lessons, students learn the content associated with the problem along with strategies for solving problems in the future. The planning steps for an inquiry lesson are listed in Figure 9.3 and illustrated in the classroom case study that follows.

Carla Schmidt, a high school communications teacher, is doing a unit on the effect of the media on American life. During the course of the unit, her class has learned about the history of different media forms in America—the long life of the newspaper, the invention of the radio and its growth, and, finally, the recent impact of television on our lives. As they investigate these topics, the role of advertising in each of these media is discussed. From students' comments about advertising, Carla realizes that they do not really understand how advertising functions in the field of media. Therefore, she decides to have her students gather some information about this topic. She begins the activity by saying, "We've mentioned advertising a number of times in our discussion of media. What are some of the things we've found out . . . Jacinta?"

Figure 9.3   Lesson Plan Illustrating an Inquiry Strategy

Unit: The Effect of Media on American Life

Goals Objective: High school communications students will understand the effect of the media on American life so that when given a question about television advertising, they will identify the relationship between programming and types of advertising.
Students will understand the inquiry process so that when given a hypothesis and data, they will identify which items support and which items detract from the hypothesis.

Rationale: Understanding the impact of advertising on consumer spending habits will help students make better purchasing decisions. Understanding the inquiry process will help students learn to make decisions based on evidence instead of emotion.

Content: Television advertising tends to be aimed at the group most likely to watch the type of programming being presented.
The inquiry process involves forming hypotheses to answer a question or solve a problem, gathering data, and using the data to assess the validity of the hypotheses.

Procedures:
>   Introduce questions about how often television ads occur and what kinds of products are most often advertised.
>   Have the students form hypotheses that answer the questions.
>   Break the class into groups and have them gather data that will be used to assess the hypotheses.
>   Have the groups chart and display their data.
>   Have the students discuss the data and assess the hypotheses.
>   Generalize on the basis of the hypotheses and data.

Materials: Television commercials (students watch at home)

Evaluation: Give students a hypothetical sample of television programming. Have them predict the type of advertising they are most likely to see. Give the students a hypothesis and data. Have them identify which items of data support the hypothesis and which items detract from the hypothesis.

"Well, advertising helps manufacturers tell people about their products."

"Also, it helps to pay for the cost of some media, like newspapers and magazines," Chadra remarks. "We don't have to pay as much for them because they have advertising in them."

"And television and radio are almost totally paid for by advertising," adds Jewel.

"Good, now I'd like for us to take a closer look at television advertising and see if we can understand how it works. But first let's see how much we already know about television commercials . . . Shanene?"

"Well, they're too long, and there are too many of them."

"OK, anyone else? . . . No one, hmmm. Well, let's see if we can ask some questions that would help us find out more about television advertising. Pretend that there is a man here from the network to answer questions. What kinds of questions might you ask him? Let's break up into our small groups and see if we can generate a list of questions."

After a period of time, the groups come back together again to share their ideas. As they do this, they find that the following two questions commonly come up: "How often do television commercials occur?" and "What kinds of products are advertised most?"

When Carla asks the class to form hypotheses about the answers to these questions, a heated debate arises. Some people think that commercials come on every 5 minutes, whereas others think they come on every 15 minutes. In addition, the members of the class disagree about the major products advertised on television. Some say they are toys, others say they are beer and cars, and still others claim they are food and detergents. To settle these arguments, Carla says, "A lot of you have different ideas about the answers to these questions. Let's write them on the board and call them hypotheses, and then let's try to gather some information to see which of these are correct."

Hypotheses:

1. *Commercials occur every: (a) 5 minutes or (b) 15 minutes.*
2. *The most commonly advertised products are:*
   a. *toys*
   b. *beer*
   c. *cars*
   d. *food*
   e. *detergents*

Then she adds, "Well, at least we found that we don't all agree about the answers to some of these questions. Now how can we go about finding which of these hypotheses are correct? Any ideas?"

Some members of the class suggest that someone write to the stations for the answers. Others suggest that perhaps the answers could be found in magazines or books, while others suggest finding the answers by actually watching television. After some discussion, they decide to break into teams to gather data by watching television. In organizing for this, the class decides that each team would watch at different times and different stations. They agree to use clocks to time the commercials and to write down what they find in notebooks to share with the class. After a week, they bring their information back to class, and Carla helps them organize the information into a chart, a part of which is shown in Table 9.1.

Carla begins the discussion by saying, "Look at the first three columns of the chart and tell me what you see . . . Antonio?"

"Well, on the same channel there are different kinds of programs during the day."

"Anything else . . . Terry?"

"And there are different kinds of commercials during the day, too."

"Good, and why do you think there are different kinds of programs on at different times of the day . . . Joan?"

"Because different people like to watch different things."

"Anyone else . . . Cassie?"

"Also because people watch television at different times. Like the only time my Dad gets to watch television is at night and on weekends."

"And so what does the information we gathered tell us about our second hypothesis? What is the most commonly advertised product . . . Jim?"

"Well, it depends on when you watch. If it's during the day, the products are for kids and mothers, but at night they're for the whole family and for dads. Also, it depends on what program is on. When I watched a football game, there were lots of commercials for trucks and beer."

Table 9.1   Television Viewing Chart

Time of Day	Type of Program	Product Advertised	Length of Commercials	Intervals of Commercials
Early morning	cartoons	cereal toys	20 sec. 30 sec. 45 sec.	10 min. 10 min
Midday	serials talk shows	detergents food household goods	20 sec. 30 sec. 45 sec.	10 min. 8 min.
Evening	sitcoms specials movies	snacks beer cars	25 sec. 35 sec. 45 sec.	15 min. 12 min.
Weekend afternoon	sports	beer cars	25 sec. 35 sec. 45 sec.	15 min.

The class then continues to analyze the data they have collected, using the hypotheses they formed to guide their discussion.

Let's pause now to see how this lesson was an example of inquiry.

An inquiry lesson consists of four parts. In the first, the teacher presents the class with a problem. Carla initiated this phase by asking the students how advertising functioned in the media.

Hypotheses are formed in the second phase of the activity. In a global sense, hypotheses are tentative notions about the way the world operates; in the classroom, they are tentative answers to the questions or solutions to the problems presented in the first phase of the inquiry activity.

In the third phase, data are gathered to assess the validity of the hypotheses. Carla's students gathered data by watching television and noting the length and kind of commercials that occurred.

In the final phases of an inquiry activity, hypotheses are then analyzed using the data. In Carla's class, this phase began when the students' data were displayed and Carla asked them to look for patterns in the data. As the discussion continued, she guided students' analysis of the hypotheses with questions such as "And what does the information we gathered tell us about our third hypothesis?" These steps are summarized in Figure 9.4.

Inquiry can be a valuable tool in a teacher's instructional repertoire for several reasons. One is that it provides the teacher with a means of teaching students systematic

Figure 9.4 Steps in Inquiry Lessons

Students: (with teacher guidance)	1. Identify problem 2. Form hypotheses 3. Gather data 4. Analyze data and form conclusion

investigative skills. By seeing how questions can be addressed in the classroom, they are provided with a model to follow in framing and answering questions in other areas of their lives. In addition, the stages in the inquiry model provide students with practice in information gathering and analysis and skills with wide application in other facets of life. A third reason for using inquiry is that it provides alternate means of teaching content to students who may already be saturated with more teacher-oriented, teacher-centered techniques. Because students are actively involved in each of the phases, inquiry activities can be a motivating alternative to other approaches (Brophy, 2004; Sungur & Tekkaya, 2006).

Planning Inquiry Lessons

The first step in planning for inquiry activities is to identify a problem. Essentially, this involves examining the different topics you are teaching and determining if any of these can be taught using an inquiry-oriented approach. This is not always possible, but when it is, it allows the teacher to teach both content and inquiry skills at the same time.

Often inquiry questions or problems arise spontaneously in the course of other lessons. For example, one of the authors witnessed an elementary science lesson in which the class was discussing some seeds they had planted weeks earlier. Some of the seeds had sprouted, while others had not. The class was trying to figure out why. The teacher seized on this situation to initiate an inquiry lesson focusing on what factors cause seeds to germinate. The class then generated hypotheses about different factors (e.g., moisture, warmth, and sunlight) and investigated them by germinating seeds under various growing conditions.

In this case, the inquiry lesson followed from a question or a problem that arose naturally in a previous lesson. This is an especially effective way to initiate inquiry lessons for two reasons. One is that students view the lesson as a functional response to a need rather than as an artificial topic imposed by the teacher. In addition, students can see the utility of the inquiry process in solving problems they encounter in their worlds, increasing the likelihood of transfer.

Often, however, inquiry lessons do not arise naturally from problems encountered in class. Or a teacher may have a particular topic that students need to learn. In situations like these, the teacher needs to recognize opportunities when inquiry activities are beneficial and structure the content effectively. Inquiry strategies are most appropriate when some type of causal relationship is involved in the content area. For example, in the science lesson, the inquiry lesson focused on factors that caused or influenced germination. In a similar manner, the lesson on advertising focused on factors that influenced or affected the content of television advertisements. When areas of content are addressed in this way, the first phase of the inquiry lesson, identifying a problem, is already satisfied.

The second task in planning for an inquiry lesson is to arrange for data gathering. Sometimes the materials needed are readily available, as was the case in the lesson on television commercials. At other times, the teacher must plan ahead to make sure necessary materials will be available when needed. For example, the science teacher had to bring pots, seeds, and potting soil to class to allow the students to gather data about germinating seeds. Anticipating these needs ahead of time allows the process of inquiry to proceed with a minimum of wasted time and effort.

EXERCISE 9.3

Examine the following topics and determine whether they could be taught using an inquiry approach (i) or whether a discovery or teacher-centered approach (d/e) would be more appropriate.

_____ 1. An elementary teacher wants students to know factors that affect plant growth.

_____ 2. A language arts teacher wants students to understand the term gerund.

_____ 3. A health teacher wants students to know the relationship between exercising and pulse rate.

_____ 4. A home economics teacher wants students to know the effect that volume buying has on the cost per unit.

_____ 5. A social studies teacher wants students to know the difference between capitalism and socialism.

Implementing Inquiry Lessons

The first phase of an inquiry lesson involves presenting a problem (see Figure 9.4). This problem provides the focus for the remainder of the lesson and gives direction to the next phase: generating hypotheses. The problem can occur as the result of a situation encountered in a previous lesson or can be initiated by the teacher. When teacher initiated, it is sometimes helpful to provide a focusing event that captures students' interest. For example, a teacher wanting to teach a lesson on the factors affecting the preservation of food might bring out two apples that had been cut open at the same time, one refrigerated and one not. The teacher then asks the class to observe the condition of the two and try to explain why differences occurred. The focusing event provides a natural and tangible starting point for the inquiry lesson.

Similar events could be constructed for other types of inquiry lessons. For example, the teacher in the lesson on television advertising might have turned on a television before the lesson and asked the students to observe different commercials. In these examples, the focusing event provides a concrete experience to which students can relate. Focusing events can be motivating if they are eye-catching and can be helpful in getting students to see the relevance of the problem to the world around them (Eggen & Kauchak, 2007). However the problem is introduced to the students, though, a formal statement of the problem should be written on the board or overhead for all to see and consider.

After students have had time to think about the problem, the teacher should encourage them to offer ideas about solutions. Often these hypotheses are produced spontaneously; at other times, it is necessary for the teacher to prompt students to offer them. For example, the teacher who wants students to focus on factors affecting food spoilage and preservation might ask, "What kinds of things do we do in our kitchens to keep food from spoiling?" or "If you were going on a weeklong hike, what kinds of foods would you take?" Answers to these questions help students identify factors that might become hypotheses.

Once hypotheses have been formed, the next task for the class is to gather data to test these hypotheses. The data-gathering process can take place in several ways. It can occur as an in-class group activity or as an individual activity outside of class time; the major factors to be considered here are time and resources. If classroom time is scarce or the equipment needed is unavailable in class, then the data-gathering process can be assigned as an out-of-class activity. Having students gather data outside the classroom can have several advantages. One is that it reinforces the idea that inquiry is not just something that is done in the classroom. In addition, having students gather data at home provides an opportunity for parents to become involved in their children's learning.

The final inquiry phase is data analysis. The major goal of this phase is to examine the hypotheses while analyzing the information gathered to determine if they agree. If they do not, the hypotheses need to be revised and alternative conclusions offered. In essence, this part of the lesson involves summing up the activities of the lesson into conclusions that students can take with them. These conclusions then form the major content outcomes of the lesson. Because of this, these conclusions should be written on the board for all the class to see and record in their notes.

Organizing the data facilitates analysis. This can be done by placing the information in charts or by graphing it. The experience of wrestling with data and attempting to come up with an optimal organizational pattern is an educational experience in itself. Often students have had no previous experience with this process and will experience difficulty. The teacher who first tries to involve students in the analysis of data should not get discouraged; this skill can be taught, and the best way to teach it is through experience.

Problem Solving

Problem solving is a problem-based teaching strategy in which teachers help students learn to solve problems through hands-on learning experiences. As with all problem-based strategies, it begins with a problem that students are responsible for solving with the assistance of the teacher. Let's see how one teacher uses problem solving in her classroom.

Maria Sanchez, a middle school science teacher, uses student interest and concern about school lunches to initiate her problem-solving lesson. When students complain about the quality of the lunches, Maria invites them to do something about it. She structures her lesson around the problem-solving model shown in Figure 9.5, which she shares with the class on an overhead.

Figure 9.5 Problem-Solving Model

Identify the problem

↓

Represent the problem

↓

Select the strategy

↓

Carry out the strategy

↓

Evaluate results

"Everyone, look up here. What's the first thing we need to do to solve this problem we discussed?"
Maria asks. "Rashad?"

"Better food in the cafeteria."

"OK, that's a starting point to identifying the problem, but what exactly does better food mean?
Let's see if we can be a little more precise."

After considerable discussion, the class agrees that it is not the quantity or quality of the food served
but rather the content of the meals. There are too many soggy vegetables and not enough crunchy things
that students like. With some prompting from Maria, the class comes up with the following list:

Foods We Don't Like	*Foods We'd Like More Of*
Peas	*Hamburgers*
Green beans	*Pizza*
Jello	*Fries*
Meatloaf	*Tacos*
Stew	*Hot dogs*

After they compile the list, Maria continues, "How can we know if this list is right for the
whole school? If we're going to try and change something, we need to know if all the grades and
classes agree. Also, why do you think our school dietitian serves the kinds of lunches she does—to
torture you?"

When the class settles down again after laughter and student comments, Maria encourages the
class to think about ways to gather data from other students as well as the dietitian. The class agrees
to break into teams to poll other grades and classes and also interview the dietitian to find out how she
plans her meals.

When the class reconvenes several days later, they hear reports from each of the data-gathering
teams. The class finds out that other classes had similar but not identical food lists, and Maria en-
courages the class to quantify the results in a graph. In addition, the group responsible for interview-
ing the dietitian brings back pamphlets and handouts describing guidelines that she had to follow in
designing lunches. Armed with this new information, the class begins formulating a report that will
address the preferences of the students while still meeting nutritional guidelines. The class agrees to
share this report with the dietitian before sharing it with others.

Problem-solving instruction has the following five steps, which we saw Maria implement in her lesson:

1. Identify the problem
2. Represent the problem
3. Select a strategy
4. Carry out the strategy
5. Evaluate results

These steps were shared on the overhead and guided students' activities during the
lesson.

Problem-solving strategies enable students to solve problems through hands-on learning experiences.

Planning for Problem-Solving Activities

Problem-solving lessons have both short- and long-term goals. A teacher's short-term goals are for the students to solve the problem successfully and understand the content behind the problem solution. This relates to the content component of problem-based learning discussed earlier. In Maria's lesson, she wanted students to understand general principles of nutrition and how they applied to school lunches.

Maria's long-term goals were for students to understand the process of problem solving and to develop as self-directed learners. She helped students understand the process of problem solving by concretely relating what they were doing to the problem-solving model. She helped students develop as self-directed learners by providing them with opportunities to think about what they knew and needed to find out and by encouraging them to reflect on the process of problem solving as they proceeded.

As with all problem-based strategies, the first planning step is to identify a problem that can serve as the focal point for the lesson (see Figure 9.5). Maria used students' dissatisfaction with school lunches as a springboard to get them to think about nutrition and the dietary constraints that a well-balanced diet imposed on lunch construction.

A second planning step is to ensure that data-gathering procedures are logistically feasible. Maria did this when she checked with the principal, dietitian, and other teachers in her school to make sure that students would have access to people to interview.

Implementing Problem-Solving Lessons

Effective problem-solving lessons exist on two levels that correspond to the major goals of this model. At one level, our goal is to teach students to solve a specific kind of problem.

Teachers do this through interactive questioning, which guides students' data-gathering efforts. At another level, we want our students to understand the process of problem solving and become better self-directed learners.

The first step in the problem-solving model is to identify the problem. While this first step may seem self-evident, many students experience problems with this process (Bruning, Schraw, Norby & Ronning, 2004). This is because of several factors, perhaps the most important of which is that students are not provided with sufficient practice with ill-defined problems—the most common kind found in everyday life. Ill-defined problems have ambiguous goals and no agreed-on strategy for solving them. Most of the problems we encounter in real life are ill defined. The best way to teach students how to deal with problems like these is to provide them with lots of practice, including work with defining exactly what the problem is.

Other obstacles to defining the problem include lack of domain-specific knowledge and students' tendency to rush toward a solution (Eggen & Kauchak, 2007). When students lack background knowledge for a problem, they encounter difficulties in clearly identifying what the problem requires. The other problem students encounter at this stage is jumping to a solution before they have considered all the complexities of a problem. Expert problem solvers take more time at the beginning of a problem, evaluating what is given and what needs to be done (Bruning et al., 2004). Students learn to do this through practice and feedback from the teacher.

The second implementation step involves teaching students how to represent problems, which gives them a strategy that bridges the conceptual gap between defining a problem and selecting a strategy. Students are often overwhelmed at this stage of problem solving, and strategies like drawing a picture diagram and listing knowns and unknowns often help. Maria did this when she had her students list the foods they liked and did not like. This helped focus their attention on salient aspects of the problem.

At the third stage of problem-solving lessons, students are assisted in choosing an appropriate strategy for the problem. One problem is the tendency for students to grab on to the first solution that arises without thinking about alternate solutions. This may give them an immediate answer but fails to place this particular problem in a larger context. The result is that students may get the right answer but fail to understand why or fail to relate this problem to the larger context in which it is embedded. Maria helped her students select a strategy that took into account other students' preferences and nutritional requirements.

If the previous steps are systematically pursued, carrying out the strategy allows students to try out or reality test the quality of their thinking. This stage is a natural extension of the previous three and provides opportunities for students to implement and experiment with their ideas. This stage should flow smoothly from the other three, but if it does not, teachers can provide scaffolding through supportive questioning.

In the final stage of the model, teachers encourage students to judge the validity of the solution they produced. Students often have problems with this stage because they are so ego involved with the problem and the work they put into it. Other times, students are eager to wrap up a problem and get on with other things, even if a solution does not make sense. Getting an answer, regardless of whether or not it makes sense, is all too often the students' goal. Young children in particular have trouble at this stage, wanting to rush through, finish the assignment, and get on to the next problem.

Analyzing the Process of Problem Solving

This final step in the problem-solving process—analyzing—may be the most important in terms of our long-term goals in using the model. A primary reason for using this model is to help students become more systematic and analytical problem solvers and more aware of their own thinking as problem solvers. Teachers can encourage this by asking, "What did we learn about problem solving today?" As students think about this question, teachers should encourage students to (a) think about the steps they went through in solving the problem, (b) discuss how well the process worked, and (c) indicate what changes they would recommend.

This concludes our discussion of implementing problem solving. Now complete Exercise 9.4, designed to increase your understanding of problem-based learning.

EXERCISE 9.4

Read the following description of a college instructor using problem-based learning and then answer the accompanying questions.

Jim Hayes's methods class has been talking about factors that influence the effectiveness of textbooks. He begins this new lesson by saying, "Now I'd like to have us take a look at factors that influence the readability of different texts. Let's take a second to think about factors that might influence how easy something is to read. Any ideas . . . Cal?"

"How about the number of pictures?"

"OK, that's an idea. Anyone else?"

"Also, the kinds of words. Longer words are usually harder to understand than shorter ones," adds Leeann.

"And the length of sentences, too. The longer the sentence, the harder it is to understand," Mike contributes.

"Another thing is the number of graphs and charts," offers Cambrey. "These make a book hard to understand."

"That's a good start," Jim responds. "Now does anyone have any suggestions on how we could find whether or not these ideas are correct?"

The class discusses the matter for a while and decides to look at textbooks at different levels in terms of the variables they have mentioned. They select texts at the first-, fourth-, and eighth-grade levels and compare them to high school and college texts. In comparing them, they count the average numbers of the following: syllables per word, words per sentence, illustrations per 10 pages, and graphs or charts per 10 pages. The results of this investigation are then compiled into the chart shown in Table 9.2.

The lesson then continues with Jim asking, "What do the data tell us about our hypothesis linking grade level and number of syllables per word . . . Don?"

"It was correct because we can see that the number of syllables per word increases with each grade level."

"OK, and how about the number of words per sentence . . . Kerry?"

The lesson continues with the class analyzing each of the columns in terms of the hypotheses they have formed.

1. What type of problem-based lesson was this: inquiry or problem solving?
2. Identify the different phases in the lesson using specific information from the text.

Table 9.2   Information on Texts

Level	Syllables	Words	Illustrations	Charts or Graphs
First grade	1.2	6.2	6.0	0.0
Fourth grade	1.3	8.4	5.1	0.0
Eighth grade	1.4	12.8	4.4	2.1
High school	1.6	15.0	3.1	2.4
College	1.7	17.0	2.0	2.5

TECHNOLOGY IN THE CLASSROOM

Using Technology to Teach Problem Solving

Technology can be used to pose realistic problems for students to solve through simulations that allow students to directly participate in activities that are realistically motivating. Let's look at an example.

Jasper has just purchased a new boat and is planning to drive it home. The boat consumes 5 gallons of fuel per hour and travels at 8 mph. The gas tank holds 12 gallons of gas. The boat is currently located at mile marker 156. Jasper's home dock is at mile marker 132. There are two gas stations on the way home. One is at mile marker 140.3 and the other is at mile marker 133. They charge $1.109 and $1.25 per gallon, respectively. They don't take credit cards. Jasper started the day with $20. He bought 5 gallons of gas at $1.25 per gallon (not including a discount of 4 cents per gallon for paying cash) and paid $8.25 for repairs to his boat. It's 2:35. Sundown is at 7:52. Can Jasper make it home before sunset without running out of fuel? (Williams, Bareiss, & Reiser, 1996, p. 2)

The problem you just read is a condensed episode taken from a videodisc-based, problem-solving series called *The Adventures of Jasper Woodbury* (Cognition and Technology Group at Vanderbilt, 1997). The series consists of 12 problems, and each begins with a 15- to 20-minute video episode that illustrates a challenge to the characters in the episode. Researchers developed these video-based episodes because many of the math problems students are asked to solve do not capture the realism and complexity of life-related applications.

The problems in each episode are purposefully left ill defined so that students are given practice in problem finding and separating relevant from irrelevant information. They also acquire experience using means–ends analysis, which requires identifying subgoals, such as finding out how much money Jasper has left. Students work collaboratively with other students over multiple class periods (from several days to several weeks). During class sessions, students share their ideas about problem solving, receive feedback to refine their thinking, and present their solutions to the class. This approach provides opportunities to analyze strengths and weaknesses of different solution strategies.

Research indicates that middle school students using the Jasper series were more successful than students in traditional programs in solving verbal problems and were better at planning for problem solving and generating subgoals. They also understood basic math concepts as well as traditional students, and they had more positive attitudes toward math

(Cognition and Technology Group at Vanderbilt, 1992). Teachers' comments corroborated these results: "The kids would go home so excited and [the parents would say] 'I've got to find out about this Jasper. It is all my kids would talk about'" and "If you have any way of getting to (my) kids in high school, you'll find that they remember those four Jasper episodes. They may not remember anything else that we did that year but they'll remember . . . those episodes because it did hit them and it did make an impact on them this year" (Cognition and Technology Group at Vanderbilt, 1992, p. 308).

Computers can also be used to teach problem-solving and higher-level thinking skills through the use of simulations (Newby, Stepich, Lehman, & Russell, 2006). In the popular program *Oregon Trail*, students attempt to reach Oregon along the trail that pioneers used to travel from Independence, Missouri, to Fort Vancouver, Washington. Students must budget food and supplies and practice their problem-solving skills through a series of simulated crises like bad weather and broken equipment. The goal of reaching Oregon is foremost to students but is incidental to the problem-solving skills and information gained by students as they progress through the program.

As another example, learners can use computer software to simulate a frog dissection rather than cut up an actual frog. While the simulation has the disadvantage of not allowing students the hands-on experience, it has at least three advantages: (a) it is less expensive since it can be used over and over; (b) it is more flexible because the frog can be "reassembled," allowing students to return to and reconsider previous frames; and (c) the simulation avoids sacrificing a frog for science (Roblyer, 2006). As software development improves and expands, technology will become an increasingly powerful tool for providing students with rich and realistic problem-solving experiences.

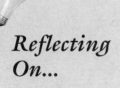

TEACHING STRATEGIES

INTASC Principles 1 and 4

Think about the teaching strategies in this chapter in terms of the particular teaching situation you plan to be in when you begin your professional career (e.g., grade level, content area, or urban versus rural).

Reflecting On...

SUMMARY

This chapter described several different student-centered teaching strategies. These strategies are designed to reach goals involving organization skills, group work, interpersonal communication skills, and the development of affective goals like open-mindedness and willingness to consider others' opinions. Different cooperative learning strategies provide teachers with instructional alternatives to capitalize on social interaction. In addition, discussion strategies can be effective if they are carefully organized and monitored.

Problem-based learning is a family of teaching strategies that actively involves students in investigating questions or problems. Inquiry methods are useful for developing systematic inquiry abilities in students within the context of the content they are learning. Inquiry problems often arise spontaneously during the course of typical learning activities, and alert and creative teachers can seize on opportunities to develop inquiry problems as a natural outcome of other activities. When they do not arise spontaneously, they can be planned in advance and implemented using other activities as the context.

Problem solving encourages students to approach authentic, real-world problems in a systematic way. The teaching strategy begins with identifying and representing the problem and proceeds to selecting and implementing a strategy. In the final stages, students evaluate results and analyze the process.

Technology helps teachers more effectively implement these teaching strategies. High-quality representations can be used in both teacher-directed and discovery lessons to provide examples and information. Technology can be used as an effective platform for simulations and problem solving, providing data and information that students can use in their problem-solving efforts.

KEY CONCEPTS

Cooperative learning   261
Discussions   270
Group investigation   267
Group work   266
Inquiry strategies   275
Jigsaw   268
Learner-centered instruction   258

Pairs check   266
Problem-based instruction   274
Problem solving   281
Student teams achievement
    division   267
Think-pair-share   266

PREPARING FOR YOUR LICENSURE EXAMINATION

Read the following case study and, usin.g specific information from this chapter, answer the questions that follow.

Juanita Escobar, a seventh-grade health teacher, is teaching a unit on the circulatory system and how it works. One of her first lessons focuses on the heart. She begins by saying, "Who knows what your pulse rate is? Lynn?"

"It's how fast your heart goes," Lynn replies.

"Good," Juanita encourages, "and who knows how we can count that . . . Jan?"

"The doctor can do that by listening to your chest," Jan responds.

"Fine. Can anyone think of another way . . . Mary?"

"You can hold your wrist like this and feel the bumps going through your veins."

"That's good, Mary. Let's everyone try and see if you can feel your pulse," Juanita directs.

She then goes around the room helping students find the pulse and showing how to time it using the clock on the wall. After everyone can count their pulse rate, she continues by writing the following question on the board:

What factors influence your pulse rate?

"Everybody look at what I've written on the board," Juanita instructs. "Does anyone have any ideas . . . Andy?"

"Exercise could do it," Andy offers.

"Being scared, too," adds Mary. "When I get frightened, my heart really beats fast."

"Good. Let's look at one of these for now and see what we can find out. Who can give me a hypothesis to test that has exercise in it . . . Juan?"

"Umm. How about this? The harder you exercise, the faster your pulse rate."

"Good," Juanita encourages, "and who has some ideas of how we could test this hypothesis . . . Ken?"

"We could all do some exercises and see what effect this has on our pulse rate," offers Ken.

With that, the class breaks up into groups and measures their pulse rates while sitting. Then they walk around the room for a minute and jump rope for a minute, checking their pulse after each activity. As each group completes their task, they put their results on a poster the teacher has prepared. The next day, the first part of the science period is devoted to graphing the data.

"What can we say about our data in terms of the hypothesis we formed . . . Anita?"

"The graph shows that our hypothesis can be accepted. The more we exercise, the faster our pulse rate goes."

"Good, Anita," Juanita replies. "That was a good answer. Do you think this is true for all people . . . Luisa?"

"I think so, but the graph might look a little different if we just used people who exercised a lot."

"Hmm. That's an interesting idea. Maybe we could investigate that tomorrow when we have science again."

1. Which of the instructional strategies described in this chapter did Juanita Escobar use? Using information from the lesson, explain your answer.

2. Using information from the lesson, identify the major steps or phases of the instructional strategy.

3. How might Juanita teach the same content using a teacher-directed strategy?

 ## VIDEO EXERCISE

Go to MyEducationLab and select the topic "Cooperative Learning and the Collaborative Process" and watch the video "Cooperative Learning." After viewing the video, respond to the questions on the video.

 ## DEVELOPING YOUR PORTFOLIO

The purpose of this activity is to encourage you to think about the different instructional strategies you learned about in this chapter.

- Think about the grade level and select content area for a topic you expect to teach in your first year in the profession.
- Design a lesson using one of the instructional strategies described in this chapter. Using the lesson plan format presented in Chapter 4, construct a lesson plan for this activity.
- Why did you select this particular strategy? Why would it be effective for the students and content area you envisioned?
- How could you teach the same topic using an alternative strategy described in this chapter? What would be the advantages and disadvantages of using this alternative strategy?

QUESTIONS FOR DISCUSSION

1. How does the developmental level of students (i.e., first grade versus high school) influence the value or effectiveness of guided discovery versus teacher-directed strategies such as direct instruction or lecture-discussion?

2. In which content areas are teacher-directed strategies more valuable or effective? In which content areas are student-centered lessons more valuable or effective?

3. In which type of strategy—teacher centered or student centered—are examples more important? Why?

4. How are guided discovery and inquiry strategies similar? How are they different?

5. What are the advantages and disadvantages of whole-class discussions? Small-group discussions?

6. Can discussions be used effectively with lower elementary students? Why or why not? If so, what adaptations are necessary?

7. Should problem-solving lessons occur at the beginning or the end of a unit? Why?

SUGGESTIONS FOR FIELD EXPERIENCE

1. Observe a teacher implementing a student-centered lesson.
   a. Outline the major points in the lesson.
   b. What was the teacher's primary content focus?
   c. How specifically did the teacher illustrate abstract ideas?
   d. How did the teacher involve students in the lesson?
   e. What suggestions do you have to improve the lesson?

2. Design a lesson plan (see Chapter 4) for a student-centered lesson.
   a. Clearly identify your content focus.
   b. Clearly identify the examples you would use to illustrate the abstraction.
   c. What questions would you use to involve students in the lesson?

3. Teach the lesson in activity 3 and then answer the following questions.
   a. Was your introduction clear, and did it draw students into the lesson?
   b. Were your examples effective and adequate in number?
   c. Were students actively involved in the lesson?
   d. Did students achieve your lesson goal? How do you know?
   e. How would you change your lesson to make it more effective?

4. Examine a textbook, curriculum guide, or state standard and identify several possible topics for a discussion lesson.
   a. What do these topics have in common?
   b. What kinds of background knowledge would students need to participate in the lesson?
   c. What kinds of questions would you use to (a) begin the lesson, (b) keep the discussion rolling, and (c) wrap up the lesson?
   If possible, teach and critique the lesson.

5. Design a lesson plan for an inquiry lesson. How in the lesson will you initiate the following phases?
   a. Problem presentation
   b. Hypothesis
   c. Data gathering
   d. Analysis of data
   If possible, teach and critique the lesson.

6. Design a lesson plan for a problem-solving lesson. How in the lesson will you initiate the following phases?
   a. Identity problem
   b. Represent problem
   c. Select a strategy
   d. Implement the strategy
   e. Evaluate results
   If possible, teach and critique the lesson.

TOOLS FOR TEACHING

Print References

Johnson, D., & Johnson, R. (2006). *Learning together and alone: Cooperation, competition, and individualization* (8th ed.). Needham Heights, MA: Allyn & Bacon. This book provides a comprehensive overview of research and issues surrounding cooperative learning.

Kain, D. (2003). *Problem-based learning for teachers, grades K–8*. Needham Heights, MA: Allyn & Bacon. This is an excellent introduction to problem-based instruction in elementary classrooms.

Mayer, R. (2004). Should there be a three-strikes rule against pure discovery learning? *American Psychologist, 59,* 14–19. This review article explains, from a research perspective, why guided discovery is more effective than pure discovery.

McCombs, B., & Miller, L. (2007). *Learner-centered classroom practice and assessment.* Thousand Oaks, CA: Corwin. This provides an excellent introductory overview to issues involving learner-centered classroom instruction.

Slavin, R. (1995). *Cooperative learning: Theory, research, and practice* (2nd ed.). Needham Heights, MA: Allyn & Bacon. This classic in the area of cooperative learning describes different instructional strategies in a direct and straightforward way.

Web Sites

www.ed.gov/pubs/OR/ConsumerGuides/cooplear.html This U. S. government site provides excellent information about cooperative learning strategies.

www.nicic.org/Downloads/PDF/TrainingResources/018534/018534.pdf This site provides useful information on designing learner-centered instructional activities.

www.ncrel.org/sdrs/areas/issues/content/cntareas/science/sc3learn.htm An excellent resource for implementing learner-centered instruction in the classroom.

www.georgetown.edu/crossroads/guide/engines.html Explores different ways to use technology in learner-centered instruction.

http://pblmm.k12.ca.us/PBLGuide/AssessPBL.html Explores issues around assessment in problem-based lessons.

CHAPTER 10

Building on Learner Differences: Instructional Strategies

INTRODUCTION

At one time in our imaginary past, all American children lived in a two-parent, two-child family and attended a traditional American school. In this fictional past, all children who came to our classrooms spoke English, were well scrubbed and dressed, and were eager to learn. Some teachers, in fact, taught as if such a uniform society existed, and all instruction was aimed at a homogeneous class. However, changes have occurred, making both our country and our classrooms more diverse. This chapter is designed to help you teach in our increasingly diverse classrooms.

LEARNER OBJECTIVES

After completing your study of Chapter 10, you should be able to do the following:

- Understand the characteristics of an effective cross-disciplinary multicultural approach to teaching
- Describe different approaches to helping English-language learners succeed in the classroom
- Explain how classrooms can assist students placed at risk
- Describe the essential elements of inclusion
- Explain different ways that technology can be used to address diversity in the classroom
- Differentiate between various types of learning styles and explain how they influence learning

APPLYING INSTRUCTIONAL STRATEGIES: THE CHANGING FACE OF U.S. CLASSROOMS

Following is a short case study of an elementary school teacher preparing for her first year of teaching. As you read the case study, consider the following questions:

- What kinds of diversity did you encounter when you attended K–12 classrooms?
- What kinds of diversity are you likely to encounter when you have your own classroom?
- How will you adapt your instruction to meet the needs of all students?

As Juanita Coleman prepares for her first year of teaching, she looks over the cumulative folders of her fifth graders. "Whew," she thinks, "I've sure got an interesting assortment of kids. They're all over the place on their achievement scores, and previous teachers' comments tell me that they're not all A students. I can't wait to meet them and get the year started. I hope they'll like the curriculum I've got planned. With such a diverse group, I think I'll use lots of group work. It will not only help build cohesiveness in the class but also let some of the higher-achieving students help the others. We'll see how it goes on Monday."

Our classrooms are becoming increasingly diverse, and this diversity occurs in several different dimensions. Recent statistics reveal a number of important changes in the students we teach. The "traditional" American family—a husband who is the primary breadwinner, a mother who does not work outside the home, and two school-age children—made up only 6% of the households in the United States in 2000. Instead, we see the following patterns:

- Families headed by married couples now make up 68% of all households compared to 77% in 1980.
- Twenty-three percent of all children live only with their mother, 5% live only with their father, and 4% live with neither.
- Seven out of 10 women with children are in the workforce.

- The divorce rate has quadrupled in the past 20 years; the number of single-parent families is estimated at 25% and is expected to increase.
- The incidence of poverty among single-parent families is between seven and eight times higher than families headed by married couples (Federal Interagency Forum on Child and Family Statistics, 2005; U.S. Bureau of the Census, 2005).

In addition to changes in the American family, we have also seen dramatic changes in our students' cultural and ethnic backgrounds. More than 14 million people immigrated to the United States during the 1970s and 1980s. While most immigrants during the early 1900s came from Europe, more recent immigrants come from Central America (37%), Asia (25%), and the Caribbean (10%) with only 14 percent of recent immigrants having Europe as their point of origin (U.S. Bureau of the Census, 2003). This has resulted in a dramatic increase in the proportion of students who are members of cultural minorities (U.S. Department of Education, 2005).

By 2020, the U.S. school-age population will see many more changes. Experts predict considerable increases in the percentages of Hispanic students and Asian/Pacific Island students, while the percentage of African American students will remain essentially the same. During this time, the proportion of white students will decrease from 63% to 54% of the total school population (U.S. Bureau of the Census, 2003; U.S. Department of Education, 2002) (see Figure 10.1). By 2020, almost half the U.S. school population will consist of members of non-Caucasian cultural groups. Each of these groups brings a distinct set of values and traditions that influences student learning.

The overall picture that emerges is a rapidly changing, diverse student population that will provide opportunities for learning and present challenges for America's teachers. Traditional teaching strategies like the lecture, which assume that students are homogeneous in terms of background, knowledge, motivation, and facility with the English language, will no longer be effective. Tomorrow's teacher will have to be skilled in a number of teaching strategies that recognize and build on student diversity.

The goal of this chapter is to introduce you to teaching strategies that accommodate and build on students' diversity as strengths.

MULTICULTURAL EDUCATION

The United States has always been a nation of immigrants, but the recognition of how this cultural diversity affects schools and schooling is a fairly recent development. During the late 1800s and early 1900s, the concept of the melting pot predominated; the cultures that immigrants brought to America were expected to blend into and be assimilated into a homogeneous American society. This did not occur, and educators recognized that this diversity both posed problems and offered the potential for enriching the school curriculum. This recognition has resulted in the concept of multicultural education.

Pat Andrews's first-grade classroom reflects the diversity of the neighborhood in which she teaches. Her class of 28 students includes 11 Asian, 7 African American, 6 Hispanic, and 4 Caucasian children. They come from countries as diverse as Vietnam, Cambodia, Guatemala, Puerto Rico, and Mexico.

Figure 10.1   Changes in the School-Age Population, 2000–2020

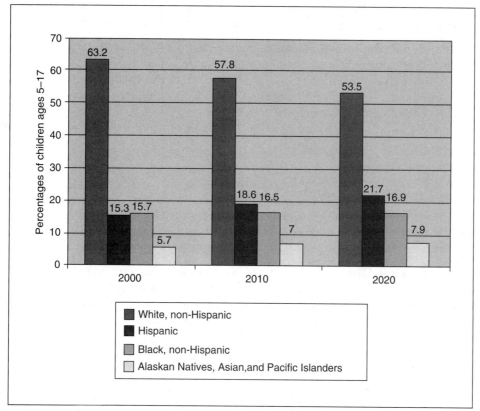

Source: U.S. Bureau of the Census (2003); Eggen, Paul D., Kauchak, Donald, *Educational Psychology: Windows on Classrooms,* 6th Edition, Copyright 2004. Reprinted by permission of Pearson Education, Inc., Upper Saddle River, NJ.

On the bulletin board is a map of the world with strings connecting the names of students to their or their ancestors' country of origin. Above the blackboard, each child has a photograph with a story of his or her background and information about his or her cultural heritage.

Pat began the school year by openly discussing the diversity in her classroom. She described her own cultural background and had the students discuss their own families. Each member of the class took turns coming to the front of the room to a cardboard booth where they could see the most important person in the world—a mirror image of themselves. To conclude the discussion, Pat stressed that despite this diversity, she expected everyone to be the same in one respect—to learn and to grow in her class.

This multicultural approach permeates her curriculum as well, and she tries to reinforce this multicultural approach in the rest of the curriculum. In math, the whole class has learned to count to 20 in Spanish. In reading, she had students dictate a story about their families. The stories were typed and then illustrated by each child. In social studies, the class studies families from a different country *every week, and Pat arranges to have parents and grandparents come in to share pictures, clothes, music, and even native dishes from their countries. The class learns to sing songs from different countries, and their art projects often focus on art forms unique to different students' cultures.*

Multicultural education is a comprehensive term for a variety of strategies schools use to accommodate cultural differences and provide educational opportunities for all students. Instead of trying to create a melting pot, these approaches align with new metaphors that describe America as a "mosaic" or "tossed salad" in which each culture's unique contributions are recognized and valued. Multicultural education seeks to recognize and celebrate cultural differences and contributions to our American way of life. A major way to do this is through culturally responsive teaching.

Culturally Responsive Teaching

Culturally responsive teaching is instruction that acknowledges and accommodates cultural diversity in classrooms (Gay, 2005). Components of culturally responsive teaching include the following:

- Creating a positive classroom environment in which all students are valued and respected
- Communicating positive expectations for learning for all students
- Recognizing cultural diversity in students and integrating this diversity into the curriculum
- Using teaching strategies that build on students' backgrounds and strengths

Teachers in American schools can expect to work in culturally diverse classrooms. Probably the most important response to this diversity is the creation of a classroom environment in which all students are welcomed and in which there are positive expectations that all can learn. The research is clear on the subtle ways that teachers' expectations directly and indirectly influence learning (Good & Brophy, 2008). Teachers who express positive expectations for all students throughout the school year communicate that all students can and will learn, which can powerfully influence learning for culturally diverse students.

Effective multicultural teachers also actively recognize cultural diversity and respond to it in their classrooms. Their curriculum reflects the fact that students come to class with different needs and interests and opportunities to explore. These are built into the curriculum. Home–school connections are forged through active channels of communication using periodic letters to parents and other caretakers, and these adults are encouraged to come into the classroom and contribute to the class (Epstein et al., 2002).

Effective multicultural teachers also recognize the importance of building on students' backgrounds and experiences. Rejecting a compensatory model that views different experiences as a deficit, effective teachers instead build on students' interests and needs (Banks, 2006a, 2006b). Teachers do that when they talk about and celebrate holidays that are important to their students, including the Chinese New Year, Mexican Independence Day, the Tet holiday for Vietnamese students, and Ramadan for Muslim students. Discussion of these holidays motivates students and helps to build valuable school–family connections.

Another way to foster multicultural goals and meet the diverse needs of students is through cooperative learning, which we discuss in the next section.

EXERCISE 10.1

Describe how Pat Andrew's class exemplified the following characteristics of an effective multicultural classroom:

1. Cultural diversity of students valued
2. Positive expectations
3. Cultural diversity in the curriculum
4. Use of students' background knowledge

TEACHING ENGLISH-LANGUAGE LEARNERS

The diversity in languages among students is staggering; the number of English-language learners (ELLs) in the United States increased by 95% between 1991 and 2002 (Gollnick & Chinn, 2006). **English-language learners** are those students for whom English is not their first language. Currently, 329 different languages are spoken in the United States with the most common language groups being Spanish (73%), Vietnamese (4%), Hmong (1.8%), Cantonese (1.7%), and Cambodian (1.6%) (Office of English Language Acquisition, 2004). The number of ELL students is expected to triple during the next 30 years. This language diversity is a challenge for teachers because most of our instruction is verbal.

Schools across the country have responded to the challenge of language diversity in several ways, outlined in Table 10.1. All the programs are designed to ultimately teach English, but they differ in how fast English is introduced and to what extent the first language is used and maintained. **Maintenance language programs** place the greatest emphasis on using and sustaining the first language. For example, in one bilingual program in Houston, Texas, students initially receive 90% of instruction in Spanish and 10% in English (Zehr, 2002). The amount of English then increases in each grade. In contrast with maintenance programs, **immersion language programs** emphasize rapid transition to English, with little or no attempt to preserve the first language. **English-language learning programs**, with their heavy emphasis on content acquisition, are one kind of immersion program. **Transition language programs** maintain the first language until students acquire sufficient English.

Currently, the future of maintenance programs, such as bilingual education, is unclear. The Bilingual Education Act of 1968 gave the federal government a central role in promoting bilingual education. In 2001, as part of No Child Left Behind legislation, Congress passed the English Acquisition Act of 2001, which promoted the principle that the primary objective of U.S. schools should be to teach English without any attempt to preserve minority languages (Spring, 2006). The goal of the English Acquisition Act is for students to develop English proficiency as quickly as possible, and this proficiency is to be tested on an annual basis.

Logistics are often a factor when schools consider which type of program to use. When large numbers of ELL students speak the same language, such as Spanish-speaking students in Los Angeles, transition programs are feasible because one teacher who speaks the students' native language can be hired. When several different first languages exist in the classroom, however, it is not feasible to find teachers who speak all the languages. High

Table 10.1   Different Programs for ELL Students

Type of Program	Description	Advantages	Disadvantages
Maintenance	First language maintained through reading and writing activities in first language while English introduced.	Students become literate in two languages.	Requires teachers trained in first language. Acquisition of English may not be as fast.
Immersion	Students learn to read in first language and are given supplementary instruction in English as a second language. Once English is mastered, students are placed in regular classrooms, and first language is discontinued.	Maintains first language. Transition to English is eased by gradual approach.	Requires teachers trained in first language. Acquisition of English may not be as fast.
Transition	Students learn English by being "immersed" in classrooms where English is the only language spoken.	When effective, quick transition to English. Does not require teachers trained in second language.	Loss of native language. Sink-or-swim approach hard on students.
English language learning programs (ELL)	Pullout programs where students are provided with supplementary English instruction or modified instruction in content areas (also called sheltered English programs).	Easier to administer when dealing with diverse language backgrounds.	Students may not be ready to benefit from content instruction in English. Pullout programs segregate students.

schools, with students going from one content classroom to the next, also present logistical challenges, and ELL programs are more likely to exist at this level.

Because you will likely teach students whose first language is not English, you should add to your teaching repertoire strategies to help ELL students learn both English and academic content. These are based on the following guiding principles:

■ Become familiar with the language backgrounds and capabilities of students
■ Use concrete experiences as reference points for language development
■ Provide opportunities for ELL students to practice language

Let's see how these principles guide Maria Garcia, a second-grade teacher, as she works with her students.

Eight nonnative English speakers are included in Maria's second-grade class of 24 students. During the first 2 weeks of school, Maria makes a point to talk to each of her students and finds out as much about them as she can. During parent–teacher conferences, she uses other teachers to help her communicate with the parent of her students. Throughout the year, she pays particular attention to the progress of her students who are learning English along with the rest of their academics.

As she reads a story to her class from a book liberally illustrated with pictures depicting the events in the story, she shows the pictures and has the students identify the object or event being illustrated, such as a lost cabin in the woods that the boy and girl in the story decided to explore. After finishing reading the story, she continues with a discussion.

"Tell us something you remember about the story . . . Carmela?" she begins.

". . . A boy and a girl," Carmela responds hesitantly.

"Yes, good, Carmela," Maria smiles. "The story is about a boy and a girl," pointing again to the picture of the characters.

". . . Lost . . . house."

"Yes," Maria nods encouragingly. "The boy and girl were exploring a cabin—that's a kind of house—and they got lost." Again she points to the pictures in the book. "Have any of you ever been in a cabin in the woods?" After several students share their experiences with different kinds of cabins, Maria shows the class additional pictures of cabins, discussing them and relating them to the story. She then asks, "What do you think exploring means . . . anyone?"

Scott Cunningham/Merrill

Culturally responsive teachers provide a positive learning environment in which all students are respected and valued.

Let's examine Maria's efforts to implement the guiding principles for teaching ELL students. First, she made it a point to learn as much as she could about all her students and particularly those who were not native English speakers. Teachers can not adjust their teaching to meet the needs of ELL students if they are not aware that these students exist. Talking with counselors, administrators, other teachers, the students themselves, and their parents can help teachers understand their learners' backgrounds. Then teachers can communicate through actions and words that they respect and value this diversity.

Second, Maria used concrete experiences to facilitate language development. ELL students face two learning tasks at the same time—the content they are studying and a new language—so concrete experiences can be particularly useful. Maria did this in at least three ways. First, she constantly referred back to pictures in the book, which provided concrete frames of references for the story and the new vocabulary students were learning. Second, she provided additional examples of concepts, such as *cabins* and *explore*, and linked the concepts to information in the stories. Finally, she encouraged students to share their own personal experiences with the concepts. Research shows that linking new information to existing knowledge, while effective for all students, can be especially effective for ELL students (Echevarria & Graves, 2007).

Third, Maria provided students with opportunities to practice language. In large part, language is a skill, and students learn English by using it in their day-to-day lives. Students in general—and ELL students in particular—need to spend as much time as possible literally "practicing the language" (Peregoy & Boyle, 2005). Teacher-centered instruction, in which the teacher does most of the talking while students listen passively, should be avoided. Instead, students should be provided with concrete experiences and opportunities to talk, write, and read about them. Open-ended questions that allow students to respond without the pressure of giving specific answers are valuable tools for eliciting student responses (Echevarria & Graves, 2007).

Other strategies proven effective with ELL students include the following:

- Modifying speech by slowing down and simplifying vocabulary
- Supplementing words with gestures, pictures, and other forms of visual representation
- Using small-group activities to increase opportunities for students to use and practice English
- Relating new vocabulary to native terms
- Encouraging writing and reading through creative and interactive tasks (Echevarria & Graves, 2007; Peregoy & Boyle, 2005)

These strategies help ELL learners and enrich instruction for all students.

EXERCISE 10.2

You are a kindergarten teacher teaching a social studies lesson about the family. Your students speak several different languages at home. You want them to understand the different names and roles of family members. How could you design a lesson that would (a) provide concrete reference points and (b) provide opportunities for ELL students to practice English?

TEACHING STUDENTS PLACED AT RISK

An increasing number of our students struggle in school. Several background characteristics place them at risk for school failure:

- Lower socioeconomic status
- Inner-city residence
- Family history of transience
- Minority status
- Little or no familiarity with English
- Divorced parents

These background characteristics contribute to a number of education problems listed in Table 10.2.

Students placed at risk are those in danger of failing to complete their education with the skills necessary to survive in modern society (Slavin, Karweit, & Madden, 1989). The term *at risk* is borrowed from medicine, where it refers to individuals who have conditions or habits that make them likely to develop a specific disease. For example, an overweight person with high blood pressure is described as at risk for a heart attack. The term became widely used after 1983, when the National Commission on Excellence in Education proclaimed the United States a "nation at risk," emphasizing the growing link between education and personal economic well-being in today's technological society.

Effective Learning Environments for Students Placed at Risk

What can educators do to minimize the negative effects that these risk factors pose? Research reveals that students placed at risk need supportive learning environments. Effective schools for students placed at risk focus on mutual respect between teachers and students, personal responsibility, and cooperation (Ilg & Massucci, 2003; Pressley, Raphael, & Gallagher, 2004). They emphasize the following:

- A safe, orderly school climate, including the meaning behind and purpose of school and classroom rules
- Academic objectives focusing on mastery of content
- Caring and demanding teachers and high expectations for all students

Table 10.2 Educational Problems of Students Placed at Risk

Low grades	Low self-esteem
Low achievement	Low standardized test scores
Low motivation	High suspension rates
Lack of interest in school	High dropout rates
Poor attendance	Low participation in extracurricular activities
Retention in grade	High rate of drug use
Misbehavior in classes	High criminal activity rates

- Cooperation, sense of community, and prosocial values
- Student responsibility and self-regulation; decreased emphasis on external controls
- Strong parental involvement

Effective schools for at-risk students create a structured and supportive learning environment in which the message is clear: "You can and will succeed if you try."

Effective Teachers for Students Placed at Risk

Well-run and academically focused schools are important, but they are not sufficient. Highly skilled, sensitive teachers are also essential for the success of students at risk of academic failure (Doll, Zucher, & Brehm, 2004). Teachers need to be skilled in making instructional decisions that communicate both challenge and support. This ability is essential in working with students placed at risk because their needs and personal sensitivities make them particularly vulnerable to failure, personal slights, hints of favoritism, and questions about the relevance of school. Alienation from school is a problem for students placed at risk (Barr & Parrett, 2001). Boredom, lack of involvement, and feelings that they are unwelcome keep them on the fringe, prevent them from participating in school experiences, and lower motivation. When bright spots appear, they are usually the result of teachers who care about these students as people and learners (Drajem, 2002; Jordan, 2001).

How can teachers help these students develop academically? Teacher understanding and commitment to student success is one essential element. One high school teacher reported the following:

A graduate whom I had not seen for many years stopped by after school when he saw me working late. His eyes were thick with tears as he spoke: "You never gave up on me. You never ignored me. You always encouraged me to get my work in and pass all of my classes, even when I wasn't nice to you. Thank you." (Barnoski, 2005, p. 37)

Effective teachers go the extra mile to ensure student success.

Less effective teachers are more authoritarian and less accessible. They distance themselves from students and place primary responsibility for learning on them. They view instructional support as "babying students" or "holding students' hands." Lecture is a common teaching strategy, and motivation is the students' responsibility. Students perceive these teachers as adversaries, to be avoided if possible, tolerated if not. They also resent teachers' lack of high expectations and standards:

There's this teacher [over at the regular school] . . . you can put anything down and he'll give you a check mark for it. He doesn't check it. He just gives you a mark and says, "OK, you did your work." How you gonna learn from that? You ain't gonna learn nothing.

Student, JFY Academy
Boston, Massachusetts
(Dynarski & Gleason, 1999, p. 13)

Alienation from school is a problem for students placed at risk. Boredom, lack of involvement, and feelings that they are unwelcome keep them on the fringe, prevent them from participating in school experiences, and lower their motivation to learn. When bright spots appear, they are usually the result of teachers who care about these students as people and learners (Drajem, 2002; Jordan, 2001). But beyond the human element, what else can teachers do?

Effective Instruction for Students Placed at Risk

How should teachers adapt their instruction to meet the needs of students placed at risk? The overall suggestion is to offer more structure and support while still challenging students and emphasizing concrete and real-world applications. Research consistently supports the need for instruction that is challenging, motivating, and connected to students' lives (Corbett & Wilson, 2002; Easton, 2002; Thompson, 2002).

Teachers of students placed at risk do not need to teach in fundamentally different ways; instead, they need to apply effective strategies more systematically (Eggen & Kauchak, 2007). They need to provide enough instructional support to ensure success while at the same time teaching students active learning strategies that allow them to take control of their own learning. Effective instructional practices for students placed at risk include the following:

- High expectations
- Emphasis on student responsibility
- Increased structure and support through clear teacher explanations and modeling
- Using interactive teaching with frequent questions
- Giving frequent feedback
- Ensuring high success rates (Brophy, 2004; Eggen & Kauchak, 2007)

Let's see what these characteristics look like in the classroom.

Jenny Reeder is beginning a new math unit:

"Class, I'd like everyone to look up here at the board. We've got an important new idea today that everyone needs to learn, so I need everyone's attention. Good.

"Now, we've been working on our subtraction, and we're getting pretty good at taking away. Today I'd like to introduce a new kind of subtraction problem that's kind of like the old ones but just a little different.

"Suppose we went to our school bookstore with 27 cents and bought an eraser for 9 cents. How much would we have left? This is a subtraction problem. We've done these kinds of problems before, so let's write it down like this:

$$\begin{array}{r} 27 \\ -\ 9 \\ \hline \end{array}$$

"So, let's see, 7 take away 9. Wait a minute! Nine is more than 7. What are we going to do? Sometimes we'll run into subtraction problems like this, and we'll need to borrow. Borrowing allows us to subtract numbers like this. That's what we're going to learn about today.

"This is an important skill that all of you need to learn and can learn. We're going to work hard at this skill until everyone understands it. To do that, let's take out our play money chips and see if we can figure out this problem.

"OK, now everyone go into your money box and take out two dimes and seven pennies. How much is that . . . Chanille?"

"Twenty-seven cents!"

"Good. Now let's look at our problem on the board again. It says subtract 9 cents from the 7. . . . But, wait! We don't have enough pennies. We can't take 9 from 7 because 7 is already less than 9. Hmm? So we have to borrow from a dime. Let's do that. Let's go into our money boxes and trade a dime for 10 pennies. So, we put a dime away and trade it for 10 pennies [illustrating this with pennies and a dime on the felt board]. Now we put the 10 pennies with the other 7, and we have 17. That's called borrowing. Now we can take away the nine pennies like the problem says. Let's do that.

"Now, let's try another one. Everyone look up at the board and try this one on your chalkboards." [Each student had a chalkboard slightly larger than a piece of notebook paper on which to work the problem.]

$$\begin{array}{r} 33 \\ -\ 7 \\ \hline \end{array}$$

"Hmm . . . 3 minus 7. Can we do that? Why not . . . Jacinta?"

"Because 7 is more than 3."

"Good. So what do we have to do . . . Alicia?"

"Borrow."

"Excellent. Now look at this problem. It's a little different from our first one because we have a 3 in the 10s place. What does that mean . . . Jamal?"

"Thirty."

"Good. Because the 3 is in the 10s place, it means three 10s, or 30, so we have 33. Now, we need to borrow 10 from the 30. Let's do that with our coins."

Jenny continues, "Let's try one more. Kim, Mario, Kareem, and Susan, come up to the board and try this one. The rest of you, work it at your seats and see if they get the right answer." With that, she writes the following on the board:

$$\begin{array}{r} 46 \\ -\ 8 \\ \hline \end{array}$$

As she observes the students at the board, she notices that all have done the problem correctly except Kareem, who is staring at the board. She walks over to him, puts her hand on his shoulder, and says, "Kim, can you give Kareem a hand?"

She does not respond.

"What did you do first . . . Kim?"

"I tried to subtract 8 from 6."

"And what happened?"

"I couldn't."

"Why not, Kim?"

"Because 8 is larger than 6."

"So then what did you do?"

"I borrowed."

"Did everyone hear that? Kim tried to subtract 8 from 6, but she couldn't. So she had to borrow. Show us how you did that, Kim."

"Well, I went to the 4 and crossed it out and made it a 3."

"Why did you do that, Kim?"

When she does not respond, Jenny asks, "What does the 4 in the 10s column represent?"

"Oh, 40."

"So when you crossed out the 4 and made it a 3, what were you doing?"

"Borrowing! Uh . . . I was borrowing 10 from the 40 and making it 30."

"Excellent, Kim. And where did that 10 go? Kareem, do you know?"

"Did we add it to the 6?"

"Good thinking, Kareem. Now can you subtract the 8 from 16?"

"Eight?"

"Good. Write it down. And how much is left in the tens column?"

"Three—I mean 30."

"Write that down, too. So what is the correct answer, Kareem?"

"Thirty-eight."

"Good work, Kareem. Now let's try another one to be sure."

By combining structure with support, Jenny was able to help all her students, including those at risk of developing academic problems; learn this essential skill.

EXERCISE 10.3

Analyze Jenny Reeder's lesson in terms of the following characteristics of effective instruction. Identify where each of the following occurred.

1. Communicating high expectations
2. Emphasizing student responsibility
3. Increased student structure and support through clear explanations and modeling
4. Interactive teaching with frequent questions
5. Frequent feedback
6. High success rates

INCLUSION

Education changed markedly in 1975 with passage of Public Law (P.L.) 94-142, a law affecting people with disabilities. Now named the **Individuals with Disabilities Education Act,** the law requires that children with disabilities be provided with a free and appropriate education (Sack-Min, 2007). Let's see how this law changes the way we work with students with disabilities.

Vicky Harrison was a first-year teacher in a large eastern U.S. city. She spent her first month getting students adjusted to the first grade. Now she was ready to begin what she hoped would be an exciting start on reading and math.

She had parents come in to work with her students on prereading and premath skills. As she analyzed the results, she found that she had some students who could already read first-grade books, while others struggled just to read their names. Math was a similar story; some could count and label groups of objects, while numbers were a mystery to others.

As the school year proceeded, she noticed that three of her students were falling farther and farther behind. She tried extra help, even having them come in after school, but they still were not learning. Vicky was feeling frustrated.

She talked to her principal, who suggested that they ask a special education teacher and the school psychologist for their help. As the team discussed the three children, they decided to involve their parents in the process. In meeting with the parents, the group decided that two of the three children should be tested in both Spanish and English to see if language contributed to the problem. When the results came back, the team sat down with the parents to plan a program of study for each child. For one, this program involved instruction in a pullout program in both English and Spanish. For the other two, the special education teacher teamed up with Vicky to help her adapt her instruction to meet the special needs of these students.

In the past, one way schools accommodated student diversity was to create special classes. Special education classes often existed as separate, self-contained classrooms next to regular classrooms. The majority of the students in these special education classrooms were mildly disabled, needing only minor modifications in instruction to learn successfully (Hardman, Drew, & Egan, 2008).

Research on these separate classrooms revealed that students suffered in several ways (Sapon-Shevin, 2007). First, they did not reach their full learning potential, and, second, they were failing to learn to live in the "regular world." A third negative by-product of separate classes was that other students were not learning how to live with and accept exceptional students.

With enactment of the Individuals with Disabilities Education Act, schools set up what is called a **least restrictive environment.** This concept means that all children have the right to learn in an environment that fosters their academic and social growth to the maximum extent possible. Removal from the regular classroom environment is to occur "only when the nature and severity of the handicap is such that education in regular classes with the use of supplemental aids cannot be achieved satisfactorily" (Sec. 612, [5] [B]). This part of the law requires the integration of students with disabilities into the regular classroom. The rationale for this provision is that academic performance, self-concept, and peer acceptance of students with disabilities all benefit from the contact with regular teachers and students (Hardman et al., 2008).

Initially, this process of placing students with disabilities into "regular" classrooms was called **mainstreaming.** Over time, educators recognized that mainstreaming alone did not meet the total needs of students with disabilities. Out of this came the concept of inclusion. **Inclusion** is a comprehensive approach to educating students with exceptionalities that advocates a total, systematic, and coordinated web of services. The inclusion movement has three components:

1. Placing students with special needs in a regular school campus
2. Creating appropriate support and services to guarantee an adaptive fit
3. Coordinating general and special education services

Inclusion into the regular classroom provides students with disabilities with valuable experiences in dealing with people and problems in the "real world," where they will ultimately live. Perhaps as important, it benefits regular students by providing them with opportunities to learn about exceptional students and develop relationships with them.

Inclusion directly affects the classroom teacher more than any other part of the law (Turnbull, Turnbull, Shank, Smith, & Leal, 2007). It means, for example, that you will have students with mild disabilities in your classroom and will be asked to work with special educators to design and implement special programs for these students. The exact form that these programs take varies with the nature of the disabilities and the capabilities of the students. Different options for placing students in a least restrictive learning environment are found in Figure 10.2. The important idea here is that each child be considered individually in terms of that child's needs and capabilities.

An essential element in doing this is the **individualized education plan** (IEP). An IEP is a comprehensive description of an individualized curriculum designed for each student. It must include the following information:

- Measurable annual goals and short-term objectives that enable the child to participate in the general curriculum
- Special education services and program modifications that allow the student to attain goals and be involved in the regular and extra curriculum
- An explanation of whether and why the student will not participate in regular educational activities
- A description of any modifications in state or district assessments or descriptions of alternate methods of assessment

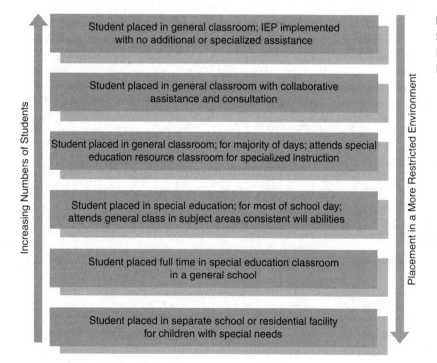

Figure 10.2 Educational Service Options for Implementing the Least Restrictive Environment.

- Projected dates for the beginning of services and frequency, location, and duration
- Methods to inform parents of their child's progress toward annual goals (Vaughn, Bos, Candace, & Schumm, 2006)

See Figure 10.3 for a sample IEP. People required to be at this meeting include the parents, regular and special education teachers who will be working with the child, and an official representative of the school.

A final provision of P.L. 94-142 is the assurance of due-process procedures for children with disabilities and their parents. Procedural safeguards protect students and their families from decisions and procedures that could negatively affect their present education and their futures. These due-process safeguards require that parents be notified in advance of important educational decisions, that they have input into the decision, and that they have an opportunity to be heard if they have grievances. As mentioned previously, parents' attendance at IEP meetings is legally required. An important part of the due-process provision is the requirement that all services for children with disabilities be reviewed annually. This review evaluates the effectiveness of the present educational procedures and examines whether the student should be placed in a less restrictive environment.

How does this affect the classroom teacher? In all likelihood, you will have students with exceptionalities in your classroom. About 6 million students in the United States are enrolled in special education programs, two-thirds of them for relatively minor problems (Heward, 2006). Approximately 14% of students in a typical school receives special education services; 78% are in a regular classroom for a significant portion of the school day. Children with exceptionalities who can benefit from regular classroom instruction will spend part or all of their day mainstreamed into your classroom. In addition, students already in your regular classroom who are not successfully functioning because of some learning problem may also be identified as needing special help. Here the classroom teacher's help is essential. These disabilities may range from speech and language disorders to hearing or visual impairments to mild learning and behavioral differences (Heward, 2006).

A major challenge for the classroom teacher is to create a supportive classroom learning environment for students with exceptionalities. Ways to do this include the following:

- Communicating regularly with students so that adjustments can be made to instructional modifications
- Establishing routines so that students know classroom procedures and expectations
- Providing encouragement and support through supplemental reinforcement strategies
- Communicating frequently with special education support teachers to ensure that the team is working effectively
- Helping students with exceptionalities form positive relationships with other students (Hardman et al., 2008; Heward, 2006)

Efforts such as these help make the classroom environment a supportive and nurturant one for students with exceptionalities.

You will also be asked to alter your curriculum and teaching methods to help meet the needs of these students. Some of these are listed in Table 10.3, while others were introduced to you in the discussion of lesson planning in Chapter 5. As you can see from Table 10.3, these adaptations reflect basic principles of good teaching for all students; their importance to students with mild disabilities is crucial.

Figure 10.3   Sample IEP

INDIVIDUAL EDUCATION PROGRAM

Date ___3-1-05___

(1) Student

Name: Joe S.
School: Adams
Grade: 5
Current Placement: Regular Class/Resource Room

Date of Birth: 10-1-93   Age: 11-5

(2) Committee

		Initial
Mrs. Wrens	Principal	D.Q.W.
Mrs. Snow	Regular Teacher	AS
Mr. LaJoie	Counselor	dlg
Mr. Thomas	Resource Teacher	M.T.
Mr. Ryan	School Psychologist	H.R.R.
Mrs. S.	Parent	J.d.
Joe S.	Student	Joe L.

EP from _3-15-05_ to _3-15-06_

(3) Present Level of Educational Functioning	(4) Annual Goal Statements	(5) Instructional Objectives	(6) Objective Criteria and Evaluation
MATH Strengths 1. Can successfully compute addition and subtraction problems to two places with regrouping and zeros. 2. Knows 100 basic multiplication facts. Weaknesses 1. Frequently makes computational errors on problems with which he has had experience. 2. Does not complete seatwork. Key Math total score of 2.1 Grade Equivalent.	Joe will apply knowledge of regrouping in addition and renaming in subtraction to four-digit numbers.	1. When presented with 20 addition problems of 3-digit numbers requiring two renamings, the student will compute answers at a rate of one problem per minute and an accuracy of 90%. 2. When presented with 20 subtraction problems of 3-digit numbers requiring two renamings, the student will compute answers at the rate of one problem per minute with 90% accuracy. 3. When presented with 20 addition problems of 4-digit numbers requiring three renamings, the student will compute answers at a rate of one problem per minute and an accuracy of 90%. 4. When presented with 20 subtraction problems of 4-digit numbers requiring three renamings, the student will compute answers at a rate of one problem per minute with 90% accuracy.	Teacher-made tests (weekly) Teacher-made tests (weekly) Teacher-made tests (weekly)

(7) Educational Services to be provided

Services Required	Date Initiated	Duration of Service	Individual Responsible for the Service
Regular reading-adapted	3-15-05	3-15-06	Reading Improvement Specialist and Special Education Teacher
Resource room	3-15-05	3-15-06	Special Education Teacher
Counselor consultant	3-15-05	3-15-06	Counselor
Monitoring diet and general health	3-15-05	3-15-06	School Health Nurse

Extent of time in the regular education program: 60% increasing to 80%
Justification of the educational placement:

It is felt that the structure of the resource room can best meet the goals stated for Joe; especially when coordinated with the regular classroom.

It is also felt that Joe could profit enormously from talking with a counselor. He needs someone with whom to talk and with whom he can share his feelings.

(8) I have had the opportunity to participate in the development of the Individual Education Program.
   I agree with Individual Education Program   (✓)
   I disagree with the Individual Education Program ( )

Parent's Signature ___Mrs S.___

Table 10.3 Instructional Modifications for Inclusive Classrooms

Modification	Description
Provide greater structure and support	Objectives need to be clearly laid out and instruction needs to be adapted to ensure success.
Take smaller steps with more redundancy	Break assignments into smaller steps and Provide more opportunities for practice.
Offer more frequent feedback	Monitor student progress through frequent assignments and quizzes.
Allow more time for learning	Accommodate different learning rates by allowing students more time to complete quizzes and assignments.
Emphasize success and mastery, not competition	Design assignments and quizzes to promote success. Grade on content mastery, not competition.

A major help to the teacher in adapting the curriculum to the needs of these students will come from special educators either working in a consulting capacity or as a team-teaching partner in the classroom (Hardman et al., 2008). Before a student with disabilities is mainstreamed into the regular classroom, a multidisciplinary team consisting of administrators, parents, special educators, counselors, school psychologists, and the teacher meets to discuss the needs of the individual child. This team's function is first to assess the student's strengths and weaknesses and then to design an IEP that is compatible with these characteristics and able to be administered by the classroom teacher.

The role of the classroom teacher in these meetings begins with explaining conditions in his or her classroom and exploring how these conditions might help or hinder the student's success in the classroom. In addition, if the teacher has already worked with the student in the classroom, the teacher can be a valuable source of information in the diagnosis of the student's problem. As the IEP is constructed, the teacher can also help to ensure that the demands of the IEP are consistent with classroom practice and realistic in terms of the classroom's resources.

Finally, the teacher has an essential role as implementer of the IEP and evaluator of its effectiveness. As mentioned previously, these plans are reviewed annually to ensure that they are accomplishing the established goals.

EXERCISE 10.4

Read the scenario about Vicky Harrison at the beginning of the section. In this scenario, identify where or how the following concepts occurred.

1. Least restrictive learning environment
2. Mainstreaming
3. IEP
4. Due process

TECHNOLOGY IN THE CLASSROOM

Using Computers to Accommodate Diversity in the Classroom

Computers hold great promise not only to improve teaching in general but also to accommodate instruction to meet the diverse needs of different students. The presence of computers in schools has grown considerably in recent years, and their ability to meet the needs of different students is being developed in such diverse areas as basic skills like math and reading and higher-level skills like problem solving and inquiry. In this section, we examine the growth of computer use in education and analyze how they can be used to meet the needs of all students.

Computer Uses in the Schools

Technology is changing the way we live and the way we learn and teach. Some examples of the dramatic growth of technology in schools include the following:

- Currently, the ratio of Internet-connected computers to students is about 46 students to every computer.
- Nearly 100% of public schools are linked to the Internet.
- Almost every school in the country has at least one television and videocassette recorder (Swanson, 2006).

The most dramatic area of technology growth has occurred with computers (Roblyer, 2006). Initially, computer literacy, or preparing students for life in the age of computers, was the focus of most computer use in the schools. Over time, instructional uses of computers have expanded to include the following:

- Computer-assisted instruction, including drill and practice, tutorials, simulations, and multimedia instruction
- Computer-managed instruction, including student record keeping, diagnostic and prescriptive testing, and test scoring and analysis
- Design of instructional materials, including text and graphics
- Information tools for students, including capabilities for information retrieval, processing, and multimedia learning

Technology in general—and computers in particular—are also being viewed as essential parts of instruction to help students develop critical-thinking skills (Roblyer, 2006). Today's teachers need to be familiar with these technologies.

Adaptive Uses of Computers

Instructional use of computers varies from helping students learn basic facts to teaching them complex thinking strategies. Their value to students at both ends of the learning continuum—mildly disabled or gifted and talented—comes from their ability to adapt instruction to meet the diverse needs of different students. Computer-assisted instruction is designed to develop automaticity, or quick and confident responses, in basic skill areas. Math research reveals that a major problem facing slower students is an overdependence on finger-counting strategies in the computation of math problems (Bruning, Schraw, Norby, & Ronning, 2004). When students have not mastered math facts to the point where they can readily retrieve them to solve math problems, they have to expend an inordinate amount of their attention on remembering basic facts, leaving little time or energy for thinking about or solving the problem.

Computer programs attack this problem in several ways (Roblyer, 2006). They begin by pretesting to determine students' entry skills. Building on existing skills, they then introduce new math facts at a pace that ensures high success rates. When students fail to answer or answer incorrectly, adaptive programs provide answers and then retest that fact. To develop automaticity and discourage finger counting, presentation rates are timed. As students become more proficient, their response times are shortened. Research on these programs is encouraging; they both motivate students through immediate feedback and save teachers time (Roblyer, 2006).

The best drill-and-practice programs are adaptive, which means that they match the demands of the task to a student's ability. For example, in a program designed to improve knowledge of math facts like $6 \times 7 = 42$, an adaptive program would begin by pretesting to determine how many of the 6s and 7s multiplication facts the student already knows. Then, it introduces new facts at a pace that ensures high success rates. When the student fails to answer or answers incorrectly, the program prompts by providing the answer and then retests that fact.

Since our ultimate goal is for students to be able to recall math facts automatically, the amount of time given to answer is shortened as they become more proficient. This also increases motivation by challenging students to become quicker in their responses.

What are the benefits of drill-and-practice programs? First, they provide practice with effective feedback, informing students immediately of what they have mastered and where they need more work. Research supports the effectiveness of this process (Attewell, 2001). Second, they are often motivating for students turned off by paper-and-pencil exercises (Gee, 2005). Third, they save teachers time since teachers do not have to present the information and score students' responses.

Assistive Technology

Technology can be an especially powerful tool in helping students with exceptionalities learn. **Assistive technology**, which includes adaptive tools that help students use computers and other types of technologies, has a particularly important impact on students with exceptionalities. Some, such as those who are blind or who have severe physical impairments, cannot interact with a standard computer unless adaptations are made. These changes occur through either alternative input or output devices (Heward, 2006; Hopkins, 2006).

Adaptations to Computer Input Devices

To use computers effectively, students must be able to input their words and ideas. This can be difficult if not impossible for nonreaders and those with visual or other physical disabilities that do not allow standard keyboarding.

One adaptation includes devices that enhance the keyboard, such as making it larger and easier to see, arranging the letters alphabetically to make them easier to find, or using pictures for nonreaders. Additional adaptations completely bypass the keyboard.

For example, students with physical disabilities that do not allow them to use their hands to input information use switches activated by a body movement, such as a head nod, to interact with the computer. Touch screens allow students to go directly to the monitor screen to indicate their responses. In addition, speech/voice-recognition software can translate speech into text on the computer screen (Silver-Pacuilla & Fleischman, 2006).

Adaptations to Output Devices

Adaptations to the standard computer monitor either bypass visual displays or increase their size. Size enhancement can be accomplished by using a special large-screen monitor or by using a magnification device that increases screen size. For students who are blind, speech synthesizers can read words and translate them into sounds.

These technologies are important because they prevent disabilities from becoming obstacles to learning. Their importance to students with exceptionalities is likely to increase as technology becomes a more integral part of classroom instruction.

Computers have also been used to track students' educational progress. A persistent theme throughout this chapter has been that students learn at different rates and in different ways. A powerful way that computers can be used to improve instruction for students is as data-gathering and tracking tools that help teachers keep track of where students are in the learning cycle. Computers can be used to do the following:

- Plan and construct assessment instruments
- Analyze assessment results
- Maintain and update, on a daily basis, the evidence of student learning progress (Newby, Stepich, Lehman, & Russell, 2006)

Patrick White/Merrill

Computers provide an avenue for meeting the diverse needs of the wide-range of student abilities found in today's classrooms.

A related use of computers is in the construction and monitoring of IEPs, discussed in the previous section on mainstreaming. Computers can be useful in the initial construction of the plan, in periodic monitoring and record keeping, and in writing the final report, which documents progress in meeting the objectives of the IEP.

LEARNING STYLES

Unquestionably, individual students come to us with different ways of attacking the tasks of learning and solving problems. **Learning styles**, also called *cognitive styles*, are students' preferred ways of learning, solving problems, or processing information (Denig, 2003). They influence the ways students perceive and interact with their learning environments.

Jan Healy wanted to make science fun for her second graders, so her class spent an hour every Tuesday and Thursday afternoon investigating different topics in learning centers around the room. Some students planted seeds and measured their growth, while others worked at the computer on simulations of experiments. Some of the time students worked alone, while at other times they worked in groups.

As Jan observed her students over time, she noticed definite patterns. Some students always worked alone, while others were always in a group. Some liked to read. Others were happier doing things with their hands; the bigger the mess, the better—giving new meaning to the term hands-on science. Many were fascinated by the computer, but others avoided it. Jan wondered what these differences meant for her teaching in other areas.

Students with different learning styles interpret and try to solve educational problems in different, relatively stable ways. In this section of the chapter, we look at some different ways that learning styles have an impact on teaching learning.

Learning Styles: The Work of Dunn and Dunn

One of the most popular approaches to learning styles was developed by Ken and Rita Dunn (1992a, 1992b, 1993). These educators found that students differed in terms of their response to three key dimensions of learning: environment (e.g., sound, light, and temperature), physical stimuli (e.g., oral versus written), and structure and support (e.g., working alone or in groups). Some of these key dimensions are listed in Table 10.4.

The existence of these different preferences or styles makes intuitive sense. All of us have heard people say, "I'm a morning person" or "Don't try to talk to me before ten in the morning." In terms of learning modalities, we have also heard, "I'm a visual person. I need to be able to see it," meaning someone learns most effectively through visual representation of concepts and other ideas. Other people tend to be more auditory, learning best through oral presentations. Some are tactile; they have to "feel" it. Each of these preferences can have powerful influences on learning.

To identify students' different learning styles, these researchers developed the Learning Style Inventory (Dunn, Dunn, & Price, 2000). This inventory asks students to respond to statements such as "I study best when it is quiet" and "I like to study by myself" on a Likert scale (i.e., strongly agree, agree sometimes, disagree, or strongly disagree). Teachers can develop their own inventories by focusing on the dimensions in Table 10.4 and can use the information to adapt instruction to individual students, groups of students, or whole classes.

Another promising approach to learning styles distinguishes between deep and surface approaches to processing information (Evans, Kirby, & Fabrigar, 2003). For instance, when you study a new idea, do you ask yourself how it relates to other ideas, what examples of the idea exist, and how it might apply in a different context? If so, you were using a deep-processing approach. On the other hand, if you simply memorized the definition, you were using a surface approach.

As you might expect, deep-processing approaches result in higher achievement if tests focus on understanding and application, but surface approaches can be successful if tests emphasize fact learning and memorization. Students who use deep-processing approaches also tend to be more intrinsically motivated, whereas those who use surface approaches tend to be more motivated by high grades and their performance compared to others (Pintrich & Schunk, 2002).

The idea of *learning styles* is popular in education, and many consultants use this label when they conduct in-service workshops for teachers. These practices are controversial, however. Advocates claim that matching learning environments to learner preference results

Table 10.4 Learning Style Dimensions

Dimension	*Learning Style Differences*
Environment	
Sound	Is a quiet or noisy environment best for learning?
Light	Do students prefer bright or subdued light?
Temperature	Is a warm or cool room preferred?
Seating	Are individual desks or clusters of desks best for learning?
Physical stimuli	
Duration	How does attention span influence the optimal length of activity?
Modality	Does the student prefer to read or hear new information?
Activity	Do students learn best when actively involved, or do they prefer more passive roles?
Time	Does the student work best in the morning or afternoon?
Structure/support	
Motivation	Do students need external rewards, or are they internally motivated?
Monitoring	Do students need constant support and monitoring, or are they independent learners?
Individual/group	Do students prefer to work alone or in a group?

in increased achievement and improved attitudes (Carbo, 1997; Farkas, 2003). Critics counter by questioning the validity of the tests used to measure learning styles (Stahl, 1999), and they also cite research indicating that attempts to match learning environments to learning preferences have resulted in no increases and, in some cases, even decreases in learning (Brophy, 2004; Klein, 2003).

The concept of *learning style* has three major implications for teachers. First, it reminds us of the need to vary instruction since no instructional approach will be preferred by all students (Brophy, 2004). Chris Burnette discovered this when he tried to implement a one-size-fits-all approach to his teaching. As you will see in Chapter 12, effective teachers use a variety of instructional strategies to reach different instructional goals. Second, awareness of learning styles can increase our sensitivity to differences in our students, making it more likely that we will respond to our students as individuals. Third, it suggests that teachers should encourage students to think about their own learning, that is, to develop their metacognition.

Metacognition refers to students' awareness of the ways they learn most effectively and their ability to control these factors (Martinez, 2006). For example, a student who realizes that studying with a stereo on reduces her ability to concentrate and then turns the stereo off is demonstrating metacognition. Students who are metacognitive are better able to adjust strategies to match learning tasks than are their less metacognitive peers, and, as a result, their achievement is higher (Eggen & Kauchak, 2007). By encouraging students to think about how they learn best, teachers provide students with a powerful learning tool they can use throughout their lives.

HOWARD GARDNER'S MULTIPLE INTELLIGENCES

Another way to describe ability differences in the students we teach is in terms of **multiple intelligences,** a view of intelligence that proposes that our intellect is composed of several different kinds or dimensions of intelligence (Gardner, 2006; Gardner & Moran, 2006). The idea behind multiple intelligences makes sense: different people are "smart" in different ways. All of us have encountered students who are talented in math but not in speaking or writing or people who have great interpersonal skills but are not as talented in traditional academic subjects.

Howard Gardner has identified eight different ways that students differ in terms of intelligence (see Table 10.5). Teachers wanting to help students develop these different aspects of intelligence should do the following:

- Create multidimensional classrooms where students can succeed in different ways
- Provide learning tasks that tap different dimensions of learning
- Encourage students to express themselves in different modalities
- Allow students options in demonstrating they have mastered a concept or skill (Gardner & Moran, 2006; Moran, Kornhaber, & Gardner, 2006).

As with learning styles, perhaps the most important message teachers should take from Gardner's work is that students are complex, multifaceted individuals who need to be treated with sensitivity and taught through a variety of teaching methods.

Table 10.5 Gardner's Theory of Multiple Intelligences

Dimension	Example
Linguistic intelligence	
Sensitivity to the meaning and order of words and the varied uses of language	Poet, journalist
Logical-mathematical intelligence	
The ability to handle long chains of reasoning and to recognize patterns and order in the world	Scientist, mathematician
Musical intelligence	
Sensitivity to pitch, melody, and tone	Composer, violinist
Spatial intelligence	
The ability to perceive the visual world accurately, and to re-create, transform, or modify aspects of the world based on ones perceptions	Sculptor, navigator
Bodily-kinesthetic intelligence	
A fine-tuned ability to use the body and to handle objects	Dancer, athlete
Interpersonal intelligence	
The ability to notice and make distinctions among others	Therapist, salesperson
Intrapersonal intelligence	
Access to one's own "feeling life"	Self-aware individual
Naturalist intelligence	
Able to identify relationships in nature	Biologist, botanist

Source: Chekley, K. (1997).

Reflecting On...

LEARNER DIFFERENCES

INTASC Principles 3 and 9

Think about the learner differences you read about in this chapter in terms of yourself and your own classroom.

SUMMARY

Student diversity, always an important dimension of teaching, is becoming increasingly important as the students in our classrooms come to us with different backgrounds and learning histories. This diversity makes teaching both more challenging and more rewarding.

To meet these challenges, teachers need a variety of instructional strategies designed to accommodate this diversity. Multicultural education attempts to build on student strengths to help students from all cultures achieve at their highest level. Cooperative learning, another teaching strategy, teams students of diverse backgrounds and abilities in learning activities. Mastery learning addresses student diversity by providing students with formative feedback, additional time, and alternate learning activities. Inclusion, a comprehensive approach to meeting the needs of exceptional children, integrates these students into the school and classroom with special assistance. Finally, computers provide an additional way to meet the instructional needs of different students.

In the final sections of the chapter, we looked at the way learning styles and multiple intelligences influence instruction. Learning styles remind us of the individuality of each student and help explain the effectiveness of a variety of instructional strategies. Multiple intelligences help us understand that there are many ways to be "smart" and encourage us to design classrooms where different kinds of intelligence can develop.

KEY CONCEPTS

PREPARING FOR YOUR LICENSURE EXAMINATION

Read the following case study and, using specific information from this chapter, answer the questions that follow.

Amy Tran, knowing that her third-grade, inner-city students were fascinated with animals, wants to teach a lesson to capitalize on this interest. She prepares for the lesson by cutting and mounting a variety of pictures taken from wildlife magazines. She begins the activity by saying, "Today we're going to find out something new about animals. It's an important idea that all of you can learn."

She then displays the first two pictures, one of an elephant and the other of an insect nearly hidden inside a flower. She then asks the children to describe the pictures. Initially, they don't see the insect in the flower.

"I see an elephant," Sandra says.

Tommy adds, "It's really big."

"He's standing by a tree," Roberto observes.

"His trunk is wrapped around some leaves," Russ notes.

The teacher smiles and says, "Very good. Now, how about the other picture?"

"Well," Kwan hesitates, "the flowers are yellow."

"There are four flowers in the picture," Ian adds.

The class is silent for a moment. Amy finally prompts by pointing at the picture and saying, "Look closely at this flower."

"Aha!" Sandra jumps up. "There's a bug in there."

"He looks just like the flower," Cindy states.

"What do you mean?" Amy questions.

"He's the same color," Cindy responds.

"He's sort of round, too, just like the flower," Juan adds.

"Do you know a word that describes it when you say he's sort of round like the flower?" Amy asks. When no one responds, she says, "We call that shape. The bug is shaped like the flower."

Amy praises the class: "Excellent, everyone! Let's look at some more pictures." She next shows a picture of a bison standing on the prairie and a small fawn nearly hidden in the bushes and shadows of a forest. These are put next to the elephant and the insect, and again the teacher asks the children to tell what they see. They respond with the following comments:

"The bison is brown."

"He's very big."

"The fawn has spots on his back."

"He's very hard to see."

"There's his nose."

Then Amy continues, "Now I want you to pair up with your partner and compare the fawn and the insect. I want you to find three similarities you can share with the class. I'll give you 5 minutes to do this." After 5 minutes, the class gathers to share ideas.

"They're both animals," offers Terry.

"They both hard to see because they look like the flower and the bushes that they're in," Kanya adds.

"Do you know what we call it when animals are hard to see?" Amy queries. No one responds. "We say that animals that are hard to see because of color or shape are camouflaged. Later we'll learn other ways animals can be camouflaged, but for now we'll concentrate on color and shape."

1. How did this lesson incorporate effective instructional practices for ELL students?

2. How did this lesson incorporate effective instructional practices for students placed at risk?

3. Which of Gardner's dimensions of multiple intelligences did this lesson use?

VIDEO EXERCISE

Go to MyEducationLab and select topic "Diversity: Cultural and Linguistic" and watch the video "Incorporating the Home Experiences of Culturally Diverse Students." After viewing the video, respond to the questions on the video.

DEVELOPING YOUR PORTFOLIO

The purpose of this activity is to encourage you to think about different ways you can use and build on learner differences. Think about the group of students you will likely be teaching in your first year in the profession.

- How will these students differ in terms of the major dimensions of diversity described in this chapter?
- What specific instructional strategies could you use to build upon this diversity?

QUESTIONS FOR DISCUSSION

1. Is multicultural education more important at some grade levels than in others? Why? Is multicultural education more important in some content areas than in others? Why?

2. For what types of students are cooperative learning strategies most effective? Least? Why?

3. How does the responsibility for learning shift in mastery learning? Is this shift a productive one?

4. Experts debate whether teachers should adjust instruction to match student learning styles or teach students to broaden their learning repertoires. Which approach is more desirable? Why?

5. Is technology more valuable at some grade levels than others? In some content areas more than in others? Which ones, and why?

6. How does inclusion benefit the following populations?
   a. Students with exceptionalities
   b. Regular students
   c. The teacher

   What possible undesirable side effects might occur with these three populations? What can be done to minimize these side effects?

SUGGESTIONS FOR FIELD EXPERIENCE

1. Interview a teacher about the diversity in that teacher's classroom. How do students differ in terms of the following?
   a. Culture
   b. Home language
   c. Socioeconomic status

    d. Learning styles
    e. Multiple intelligences

What does the teacher do to accommodate these differences?

2. Observe a classroom and focus on several minority students.
    a. Where do they sit?
    b. Who do they talk to and make friends with?
    c. Do they attend to the class, and are they involved?
    d. Do they participate in classroom interaction?

Ask the teacher what she or he does to build on differences in these students.

3. Ask the teacher to identify several minority students. Interview these students and ask the following:
    a. How long have they been at this school?
    b. What do they like most about school?
    c. Least?
    d. What can teachers do to help them learn better?

4. Observe a teacher using some type of cooperative learning.
    a. How did the teacher prepare students for the activity?
    b. How were students divided into groups?
    c. How did the groups differ in terms of gender and ethnic background?
    d. What activities were students involved in within the groups?
    e. How did the teacher hold students accountable?
    f. How could the lesson have been improved?

5. Interview a teacher regarding the use and availability of computers.
    a. Does each classroom have some, or are they clustered in certain rooms?
    b. How many are there in the school?
    c. How modern and up to date are they?
    d. How modern and up to date are the software that go with them?
    e. How does the teacher use them instructionally?
    f. How does the teacher use them for lesson planning and record keeping?

6. Interview a teacher about inclusion.
    a. How many students with exceptionalities are included in the classroom?
    b. How has the teacher adapted instruction to meet the needs of these students?
    c. What assistance does the teacher have in working with these students?
    d. What suggestions does the teacher have to make the process more effective?

TOOLS FOR TEACHING

Print References

Banks, J. (2006). *An introduction to multicultural education* (4th ed.). Boston: Allyn & Bacon. A readable introduction to the field of multicultural education.

Brophy, J. (2004). *Motivating students to learn* (2nd ed.). Boston: McGraw-Hill. This text on motivation has several excellent chapters on motivating struggling students placed at risk.

Gollnick, D., & Chinn, P. (2006). *Multicultural education in a pluralistic society* (7th ed.). Upper Saddle River, NJ: Merrill/Prentice Hall. Describes how multicultural education fits into educating our pluralistic society.

Peregoy, S., & Boyle, O. (2005). *Reading, writing, and learning in ESL* (4th ed.). New York: Longman. Provides a comprehensive and readable account of how to instruct English-language learners in the classroom.

Sapon-Shevin, M. (2007). *Widening the circle: The power of inclusive classrooms.* Boston: Beacon Press. Describes the advantages of inclusive classrooms and how to make them happen.

Web Sites

http://www.tesol.edu Provides excellent information about different ways to help ELL learners succeed in the classroom.

http://www.uni.edu/coe/inclusion This site has good information about how to make inclusion happen in your classroom.

http://www.learningstyles.net Contains useful information about learning styles and the effects on classroom learning.

http://pzweb.harvard.edu/PIs/HG_MI_after_20_years.pdf An interesting look at the area of multiple intelligences and how our views of intelligence have changed over the years.

http://www.cec.sped.org This is the Web site for the Council for Exceptional Children and contains valuable information about working with students with exceptionalities.

UNIT FOUR

Standards and Assessing Instruction

Chapter 11 Assessing Learning in an Era of Standards
and Accountability

Assessing Learning in an Era of Standards and Accountability

INTRODUCTION

We are now at the final phase of the teaching cycle. Having considered both the planning and the implementation of lessons, we now turn our attention to assessment, which includes the techniques for determining whether students reach the goals we specified during the planning phase.

Because this book is not a text that focuses in the assessment of learning, we will not attempt to provide the coverage you would find in a book devoted solely to that topic. We will, however, examine the role of assessment and show how the processes of planning, implementing, and assessing student learning are interrelated. This role has become increasingly important in recent years as the implementation of standards and holding teachers and students accountable for meeting them becomes more prominent.

OBJECTIVES

After completing your study of Chapter 11, you should be able to do the following:

- Describe the characteristics of classroom assessment
- Explain the differences between formal and informal assessment
- Discuss the differences between effective and ineffective assessment items
- Prepare items to measure concepts and generalizations
- Explain the assignment of grades based on assessment data

APPLYING ASSESSMENTS IN THE CLASSROOM

Following is a case study in which three teachers employ differing assessments. As you read the case study, consider the following questions:

- What are the characteristics of each of the assessments?
- Explain the differences between the assessments?
- Are any of the assessments formal assessments?
- Are any of the assessments informal assessments?

Jim Gorman's class is passing their prealgebra homework in to him. They had exchanged papers, scored the homework, and discussed the problems causing the most difficulty.

"How many got all the problems right?" he asks the class.

"Good!" he smiles in response to their show of hands. "You get this stuff. Remember that we have a test on this chapter on Friday, but now we're going to move on to subtraction of integers."

Kelly Morris gives her chemistry class a one- or two-problem quiz every other day. She is scoring the students' answers to a problem in which the mass of an element in grams is converted to moles and number of atoms. "I need to do some more of these," she thinks. "They can convert moles to grams, but they can't go the other way."

Barbara Fisher's fourth graders are working on the rules for forming plural nouns. After putting several words on the board, Barbara circulates among the students, making periodic comments.

"Check this one again, Nancy," she says when she sees that Nancy had written "citys" on her paper. She continues this process for 10 minutes before she moves to another activity.

Later she comments at lunch, "My kids just can't seem to get the rules straight. They get so mixed up when they change the 'y' to 'i' and add 'es.' What do you do about it? If I spend much more time on it, we won't get all the objectives covered."

CLASSROOM ASSESSMENT

Classroom assessment includes all the processes involved in making decisions about students' learning progress (Nitko, 2004). It includes observations of students' written work, their answers to questions in class, and performance on teacher-made and standardized tests. It also includes performance assessments, such as watching first graders print or observing art students create a piece of pottery. In addition, it involves decisions such as reteaching a topic or assigning grades. Both Jim's conclusion, "You get this stuff," and Barbara's, "My kid's just can't seem to get the rules straight," are part of the assessment process, as is Kelly's decision to "do some more of these."

Assessment is an integral part of teaching and learning. Despite its importance and the amount of time it requires—experts estimate up to a third of teachers' professional time—teachers often feel ill prepared to deal with its demands (Stiggins, 2004, 2005).

Functions of Classroom Assessment

Increasing learning is the primary function of classroom assessment. For example, the students' performance on Kelly's quiz suggested that they did not fully convert the mass of an element to moles and numbers of atoms, so she decided to provide them with more practice. Without the information she gathered through her assessment (her short quizzes), making decisions that increase learning is impossible.

Research indicates that students learn more in classes where assessment is an integral part of instruction than in those where it is not, and brief assessments that provide frequent feedback about learning progress are more effective than long, infrequent ones, like once-a-term tests (McGlinchey & Hixson, 2004; Stiggins, 2005).

Research also indicates that a well-designed assessment system increases students' motivation to learn (Black, Harrison, Lee, Marshall, & William, 2004; Ross, Rolheiser, & Hogaboam-Gray, 2002). Think about your own experiences. Almost certainly, you study the hardest and learn the most when you are thoroughly assessed and given informative feedback.

Formal and Informal Assessment

Teachers gather information through both informal and formal assessments. **Informal assessment** is the process of gathering incidental information about learning progress and making decisions based on that information. For example, if a teacher sees a student "drifting off" and she decides to call on him to bring him back into the lesson, she is involved in informal assessment. In contrast, **formal assessment** is the process of systematically gathering information and making decisions about learning progress. Kelly, for example, was involved in formal assessment when she gave the students a quiz and decided to provide the students with more practice. Teachers use tests and quizzes in formal assessment, and teachers also use observable performances, such as a physical education teacher's observing the number of situps a student can do.

The Need for Formal Assessment.   Informal assessment is essential in helping teachers make the many decisions required in their work (Black et al., 2004). For example, it helps them decide who to call on, how long the student is given to answer, and how quickly to move through a lesson. Without it, making these decisions would be impossible (Rose, Williams, Gomez, & Gearon, 2002).

Informal assessments provide an incomplete picture of learning, however (Green & Mantz, 2002). For example, concluding that all students understand an idea on the basis of responses from only a few (who usually have their hands up) is a mistake that teachers often make. And they sometimes make decisions as important as assigning grades on the basis of informal assessment. Students who readily respond, have engaging personalities, and are physically attractive are often awarded higher grades than their less fortunate peers (Ritts, Patterson, & Tubbs, 1992). Systematically gathering information with formal assessments is important in preventing these potential biases. As we saw earlier, Kelly's quiz was a formal assessment. All students responded to the same items, so they gave her a comprehensive look at the students' understanding.

Formal assessment is particularly important in the lower elementary grades, where teachers often use performance measures, such as handwriting samples or students' verbally identifying written numerals. These assessments are often subjective, influenced by factors other than the students' understanding. The question "Could I document and defend this decision to a parent if necessary?" is a helpful guideline in this process.

Assessment Accuracy.   As with all assessments, the ones teachers make differ in accuracy. For instance, a teacher can obtain more precise assessments of Juan's knowledge of multiplication tables than of Juan's creative ability. A child's knowledge of the alphabet can be measured more precisely than a child's reading comprehension.

Additionally, assessment accuracy is determined by the instruments used to make the assessments. For instance, standardized reading tests, when administered and interpreted correctly, can give a more accurate assessment of a child's reading level than informal methods.

Teachers should continually try to increase the accuracy of assessments. The purpose of this chapter is to help you learn to measure student understanding as accurately as possible.

Accountability Issues in Assessment

Over the past several years, reformers have expressed concerns about American students' lack of knowledge and skills. For example, in a survey of 18- to 24-year-olds, 6 in 10 respondents could not find Iraq on a map of the Middle East, and about half could not locate New York state (Manzo, 2006). Other studies lead to doubts about our science, reading, writing, and math knowledge as well. For example, results from the National Assessment of Educational Progress indicate that only 38% of U.S. eighth graders can calculate a 15% tip on a meal, even when given five choices to select from (Stigler & Hiebert, 2000).

Social commentators have written much about these inadequacies, and educators have responded by promoting **standards-based education,** the process of focusing curricula and instruction on predetermined goals or standards and holding students and teachers accountable for meeting the standards. **Standards** specify what students at different ages and in particular content areas should know and be able to do, and **accountability** is the process of requiring students to demonstrate that they have met specified standards and making teachers responsible for students' performance.

No Child Left Behind.   The accountability movement received a big boost from the passage of the **No Child Left Behind Act** (NCLB) of 2001, which one expert calls "the most significant change in federal regulation of public schools in three decades" (Hardy, 2002, p. 201). Signed by President George W. Bush, NCLB was the reauthorization of the Elementary and Secondary Education Act, which began in 1965 and resulted in billions of dollars being spent on compensatory education programs for disadvantaged students. Assessment is at the heart of the act.

The NCLB calls for assessment and accountability at several levels. For example, states are required to create standards for what every child should know for all grades. States were to develop standards for math and reading immediately, and standards for science were due by the 2005–2006 school year. States must implement these standards and gather information about their attainment in order to receive continued federal funding. Individual schools are held accountable for ensuring that every child in that school is making satisfactory progress. Schools, districts, and states must keep records of performance to document achievement of different groups of students by race, ethnicity, gender, and English proficiency.

If a school fails to make adequate yearly progress with any of these student subgroups for 2 consecutive years, students may transfer to another school. If a school's performance is subpar for 3 years, students are entitled to outside tutoring at district expense. After 4 years, the school will be placed on probation and corrective measures taken. States, districts, individual schools, and teachers within those schools are feeling the pressures of this accountability, virtually all of which depends on standardized test results (Christie, 2003).

High-Stakes Tests.   **High-stakes tests** are standardized tests designed to measure the extent to which standards are being met (Linn & Miller, 2005; Popham, 2004). High-stakes testing, also called minimum competency testing, has three components: (a) an established standard for acceptable performance, (b) a requirement that all students of designated grades (such as 5th, 8th, and 10th) take the tests, and (c) the use of test results for decisions about promotion and graduation. When students cannot move to the next grade level or graduate from high school because they fail a test, for example, the "stakes" are very high, thus the term "high-stakes tests."

As you would expect, high-stakes testing is controversial. Advocates claim the process helps clarify the goals of school systems, sends clear messages to students about what they should be learning, and provides the public with hard evidence about school effectiveness (Hirsch, 2000). While conceding that teacher preparation, materials, and the tests themselves need to be improved, advocates also argue that the tests are the fairest and most effective means of achieving the aim of democratic schooling—a quality education for all students. Further, they assert, educational systems that establish standards and use tests that thoroughly measure the extent to which the standards are met greatly improve achievement for all students, including those from disadvantaged backgrounds (Bishop, 1995, 1998). Hirsch (2000) summarized the testing advocates' position: "They [standards and tests that measure achievement of the standards] are the most promising educational development in half a century" (p. 64).

Critics counter that teachers spend too much class time helping students practice for the tests, the tests do not reflect the curriculum being taught, and they do not accurately assess student learning (Amrein & Berliner, 2002; Behuniak, 2002; Berliner, 2005; Meier, 2002). They also contend that the cutoff scores are arbitrary and that the instruments are too crude to be used in making crucial decisions about students, teachers, and schools (Popham, 2004). In addition, the tests have had a disproportionately adverse impact on minority students, particularly those with limited proficiency in English (Hafner, 2001; Neill, 2003; Popham, 2003).

In spite of the criticisms, standards-based education and high-stakes testing are widespread. While you will not be involved in creating high-stakes tests, you will be required to design classroom assessments designed to meet specified standards, and this is the reason we include this section in the chapter.

EXERCISE 11.1

Read the scenario that follows and decide whether each numbered statement describes an informal assessment (ia) or a formal assessment (fa).

Karen Anthony wanted her kindergarten students to be prepared for written symbol recognition so that they could pick out the symbol when its sound was made. So she needed to determine if her kindergarten class needed more work in sound discrimination before they went into recognition of the written symbols. She decided to pronounce the words *bird, dog, ball, dad, man, none, nose*, and *milk* to the children individually and ask them to tell her which ones had the same first sound _____ (1). She then checked the students to see if they could match the sounds, and she found that 8 of her 20 students matched all four pairs of sounds correctly, while the other 12 incorrectly matched one or more of the pairs _____ (2).

She separated the children into a group of 12 and a group of 8, which she started on written letter recognition activities _____ (3). Then, in order to have smaller groups, Karen divided the group of 12 into those whose first names started with A through M and those whose names started with N through Z, which made six students per group. She decided to practice first-letter sounds with both of these groups by presenting pictures of objects and pronouncing the words.

While Karen worked with the first group of six, she saw Joey poke Mary and pull her hair _____ (4). She also noticed Joey glancing at her as he performed his little disruptions _____ (5). She recalled that he had been making himself conspicuous in other activities as well _____ (6). She then decided that she would not call more attention to Joey by reprimanding him _____ (7). She noticed that Mary seemed to be paying little attention to him _____ (8).

After Karen completed her weeklong activity with her two groups of six, she gave each child a set of 15 pictures and told them to put all the pictures that started with the sound of *b* in one pile, those with *d* in a second pile, those with *m* in a third, and those with *n* in a fourth _____ (9). Based on the results, Karen moved the top eight students into symbol recognition but held the bottom four students back for more work _____ (10).

PREPARING EFFECTIVE ASSESSMENT ITEMS

As we begin our discussion of preparing assessment items, we want to emphasize that the process is more complex than it appears on the surface. For example, a multiple-choice item actually measures at least three aspects of learning: (a) the learners' understanding of the content, (b) their ability to respond to multiple-choice items, and (c) reading ability. Each of these factors affects the accuracy of the assessment. Keep these factors in mind as you prepare items.

One way of dealing with the problem is to increase the frequency of your assessments and use a variety of formats. Increased frequency gives students practice with the particular format, such as multiple choice, and variety allows them to capitalize on their strengths; for example, students who are good writers can capitalize on essay items.

Paper-and-pencil tests are widely used not because they are more accurate than other forms but because they are more efficient. It is time consuming to discuss a topic with each student in a large class, but giving a single paper-and-pencil test can be accomplished quickly. We neither support nor oppose paper-and-pencil tests; rather, we describe ways of making written items as accurate as possible. A good discussion of different item formats can be found in Linn and Miller (2005). Let's turn now to a more specific discussion of assessment.

Assessing Fact Learning

As you saw in Chapter 4, facts are forms of information learned through drill, and assessment of their attainment would be classified in the cell where *factual knowledge* intersects with *remember* in the taxonomy developed by Anderson and Krathwohl (2001). For example, an appropriate item that could be used to measure whether learners know the American presidents during major events in history might be the following:

The president during the Civil War was

  a. Alexander Hamilton
  b. Robert E. Lee
  c. Abraham Lincoln
  d. William Jennings Bryan

The example is a recognition item, meaning that the learner merely had to "recognize" the correct choice. A question in the form of a production item for the same objective could be

Who was president during the Civil War?

In this case, the student must "produce" the answer. Obviously, production items are more demanding than recognition items, and teachers should keep this factor in mind when considering their goals and assessment items.

Assessing Understanding of Concepts

First, while concepts can be assessed at the factual *knowledge-remember* level, measuring them would be more commonly classified in the cell where *conceptual knowledge* intersects with *understand*. This is accomplished quite easily by asking students to identify unique examples of the concept. To refresh your understanding of the taxonomy table (Anderson & Krathwohl, 2001), you might want to refer back to Chapter 4. For example, suppose you want preschool students to understand the concept *between*. Their understanding could be measured using the item in Figure 11.1.

Now let's turn to a discussion of assessing concepts at different levels. Note in the following discussion that some of the objectives go beyond the understanding of a concept

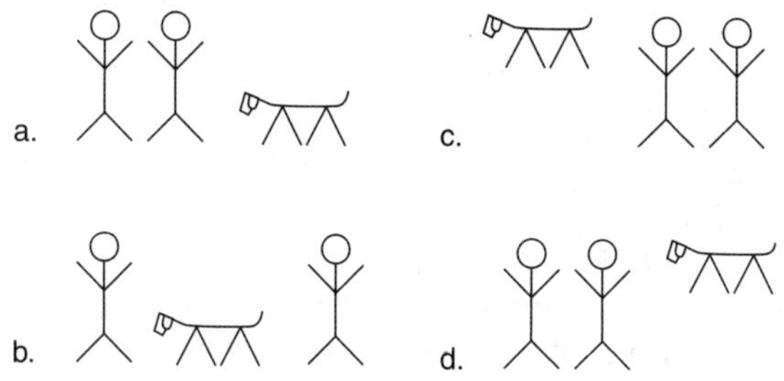

Figure 11.1   Recognition Test Item

Place an X on the picture where the dog is between the two boys.

per se and into the analysis of relationships. As we noted previously, understanding concepts themselves is primarily a *conceptual knowledge-understand* task.

Let's look at an example with the concept *noun*. Suppose your goal is for the students to "understand" nouns. What does this mean? Some possibilities are the following:

1. Write the definition of nouns
2. Identify the definition of nouns from a list of definitions
3. In a list of words, circle all those that are nouns
4. Write grammatically correct sentences using nouns
5. Underline all the nouns in a list of sentences
6. Describe the author's intent by interpreting the meaning of the nouns in the context of a written passage
7. Select the best interpretation of the meaning of nouns in context when given several interpretations

We see that deciding what "understanding" means is not simple. We listed seven possibilities, and there are undoubtedly more. The decision depends on the teacher's careful judgment.

Let's look now at possibilities and discuss them in the context of the material we have presented so far. First, each could become a formal assessment designed to provide data to help teachers assess their students' understanding of nouns. This is in contrast with informal assessments, such as observing the students at work or hearing a variety of responses from them.

Second, the possibilities represent different levels. Items 1 and 2 are in the *factual knowledge-remember* cell, items 3 and 5 are in the *conceptual knowledge-understand* cell, item 4 is in the *procedural knowledge-application* cell, and 6 and 7 are in the *procedural knowledge-analyze* cell. Our goal in discussing this information is for you to be aware of the advanced cells of the taxonomy table so that you can encourage your students to move beyond the *factual knowledge-remember* cell, where much of the instruction in schools exists.

Third, some of the possibilities require production, and others require only recognition. Items 1, 4, and 6 require production; the students were asked to produce, respectively, a definition, a sentence, and an analysis. Items 2, 3, 5, and 7 are recognition items; the students must recognize a definition, nouns in a list, nouns in a sentence, and a correct interpretation of noun's use.

Let's look now at recognition and production in a bit more detail. First, production items are generally more difficult than recognition items at the same taxonomic level. Items 1 and 2 are both *factual knowledge-remember* items, but recalling and stating the definition is more difficult than merely recognizing it. Another example of how recognition is simpler than production is found in our vocabulary. It is generally believed that our comprehension vocabulary is several times larger than our speaking vocabulary. In other words, we recognize the meaning of many more words than we use in conversation.

Second, recognition items are much easier for the teacher to score. A production item results in each student giving a slightly different response, leaving you in a position of having to decide whether the produced statement represents an adequate understanding of the concept. For example, compare item 6 to item 7. Item 6 puts much more demand on learners; they must interpret what is being asked, organize their thoughts, and put them down on paper. In item 7, they must merely select the choice they believe is best. In addition, in item 6, students will give a variety of responses since this is not a convergent question (question requiring a single answer), as in item 7. Therefore, the teacher needs to make more evaluation decisions with item 6 than with 7, where it would be much easier to be consistent in scoring.

One other factor to consider in deciding on the item format is the amount of work involved. Production items are easier to prepare, but recognition items are easier to score. The decision of which to use depends on your goals. If you want to have students learn to express themselves in writing, you may choose to use a production item. You must keep in mind, of course, that you would be measuring writing ability in addition to the understanding of the concept.

These factors are not mentioned to suggest that accurate assessment is impossible. On the contrary, measuring can be an enjoyable task because it gives you information about your students and your own teaching. Instead, these factors are a reminder of considerations you must make in measuring—again, all in an effort to increase sound decision making.

EXERCISE 11.2

Write a multiple-choice item to measure a kindergarten child's concept of mammal.

Assessing Understanding of Generalizations

Generalizations, as with concepts, can be measured at the knowledge and the comprehension levels. In addition, however, they can readily be measured at the *conceptual knowledge-apply* level and the *procedural knowledge-apply* levels.

Let's look now at the different levels. Measuring a generalization at the *factual knowledge-remember* level involves simply asking students to recall or identify one in a list.

Measuring generalizations at higher levels is quite another task. Let's look at the following goal:

Psychology students will understand the generalization that intermittent reinforcement produces persistent behavior and slow extinction.

Consider the following item:

Which of the following illustrates the generalization that intermittent reinforcement produces persistent behavior and slow extinction? Circle the letter of all choices that apply.

a. Mrs. Williams was trying to encourage Johnny's seat work. For a week, she gave him a reward every 5 minutes whenever he was working quietly at his desk.
b. Mr. Smith assigns homework nightly but checks it only periodically.
c. Johnny, a spirited third grader, acts up often. Generally his teacher is firm and strict. Sometimes, though, Johnny's behavior is so funny that she has to laugh.
d. When encountering a locked door, people generally wiggle it a few times and then leave or hunt for a key.
e. Mr. Jones put 50 cents into the washing machine at the Laundromat. It did not come on, so he tried another machine.
f. People who go to Las Vegas usually lose, but they win every once in a while.
g. Mr. Anderson caught a fish in a particular spot in the St. Johns River. Now he fishes in that spot whenever he can and does fairly well.

In this recognition item, the students have to identify cases where the generalization is illustrated; in other words, they are identifying examples of the generalization. In this regard, the assessment is similar to having the students identify examples of a concept, which is also a comprehension-level task.

Note the format of the item. The student, in responding, makes a decision about each choice individually. The item then essentially operates in a true-or-false format. The directions could just as easily have read as follows:

Mark as true the following cases that illustrate the generalization that intermittent reinforcement results in persistent behavior and slow extinction.

To make the item multiple choice, you would simply have to reduce the number of choices to four or five, with only one of them correct.

The following is an example of using the multiple-choice format to measure application-level understanding of the generalization that reinforcement is most effective following desired behavior:

People in an institution were being paid 50 cents a day for doing maintenance work around the grounds. After the work was done, the trustee who inspected the work would come and pay the workers. After a while, since the work was always satisfactory and the workers always got paid, the administrators decided that they would just pay all the inmates in the morning at roll call and save the management the problem of paying people when the trustee came around.
Which of the following best describes the consequence of the change in routine?

a. There would be no change, and the operation would proceed more smoothly.
b. The inmates would like it better because they knew they would get paid, and, consequently, they would work harder.

Effective teachers employ a wide range of alternative assessments.

    c. The inmates would not work as hard because they got paid whether they did the work or not.

    d. The inmates would not work as hard because they would be insulted by the small amount they were being paid.

Notice in this example that students were asked to predict the consequences of the generalization, which is an application-level task.

Note in each of the previous examples that measuring understanding of a generalization required a short vignette either in the stem of the item or in the distracters. When measuring generalizations, this will often be the case since a generalization is broader and more inclusive than a concept. With practice, you will learn how to write vignettes that can be used in questions to measure your students' understanding of generalizations.

Let's look now at an example that does not require a vignette. Suppose a teacher wants the students to understand the following:

When two vowels are together in a word, the first is long, and the second is silent.

An item to measure this generalization could be as follows:

[Teacher reads] Look at the list of words in front of you. I'm going to pronounce each word, and you mark the ones in which this rule is generalized: When two vowels are together in a word, the first is long and the second is silent.

    beat   boat

    meet   main

    beak

Notice in this item that both the words and their pronunciations were required because the rule linked the sound of the word to its spelling. Merely showing the students the words and asking them to state in which cases the rule applied would not be appropriate. In order to respond correctly, a student would have to know how the word was pronounced; that being the case, the example could not be unique, which would mean that the item was only at the knowledge level. This example is an excellent illustration of the teacher's need to think carefully about the assessment process.

EXERCISE 11.3

Develop a one-paragraph vignette and write a multiple-choice item to measure the following objective:

For students to understand the generalization that climate affects culture, so that when given a description of a culture, they will identify a statement that illustrates the generalization.

Assessing Inquiry Skills

Now we will briefly consider the assessment of inquiry skills. This represents a departure from the themes of the text up to this point because measuring inquiry learning amounts to measuring an intellectual skill. The skill involved is the ability to relate data to a hypothesis or the ability to decide which of two or more hypotheses is most supported in light of the data. As an example, consider the situation shown in Figure 11.2 involving the relationship of data to hypotheses:

Both cities are on the coast and exist at the mouths of rivers. However, Jonesburg is a large and busy transportation center, whereas Williamsborough is small and insignificant. The following were proposed hypotheses that explained the reason for this difference:

1. While both Williamsborough and Jonesburg are on the coast and are at the mouths of rivers, Williamsborough's harbor is smaller than Jonesburg's, and the winds and tricky local currents made entrance dangerous in the early years when sailing ships were used.

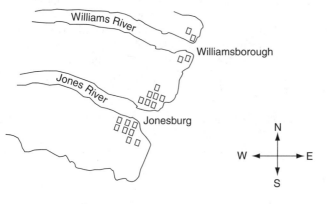

Figure 11.2 A Partial Map of a Coastline

2. The coastal range of mountains isolated Williamsborough but dwindled to foothills by the time they reached Jonesburg, which left it accessible to overland shipping.

The following data were gathered in reference to the hypotheses. Based on the data, decide which hypothesis is more logical and explain your choice briefly.

1. The current along the coast runs from north to south.
2. Jonesburg's harbor is larger than Williamsborough's.
3. About the same number of ships ran aground near Jonesburg as ran aground near Williamsborough in the sailing days.
4. Jonesburg and Williamsborough are more than 100 miles apart.
5. The mountains around Williamsborough are more rugged than the mountains around Jonesburg.
6. The local winds around Jonesburg are more variable than they are around Williamsborough.

Keep in mind here that you are measuring the student's ability to relate data to hypotheses, meaning that the particular content of the item is not important. An inquiry lesson could present a topic in science, while the item could involve social studies content. This is appropriate because you are measuring an intellectual skill on the part of the students rather than information about an area of content. This is often a unique experience for a student and initially can be difficult. However, once this ability is developed, the students have acquired a powerful thinking skill.

EXERCISE 11.4

Read the following example of an inquiry situation and then respond to the data that follow.

A study reported an investigation of longevity in various groups of people around the world. The investigators found two particular groups with a wide disparity in the average life expectancy between them. Group A (the long-lived group) had a much lower overall standard of living than Group B (the shorter-lived group). The average expectancies were Group A—85 years and Group B—70 years. The investigators proposed the following explanation for this startling phenomenon:
While the standard of living for Group A is lower, they live in a manner conducive to good health. They are basically agrarian people, leading active and hardworking lives tending livestock and farms. Hence, they stay slim and avoid becoming overweight. They live in the mountains away from the psychological stresses of urban living. Their intake of potentially harmful items such as alcohol, tobacco, and high-cholesterol foods is kept at a minimum. On the other hand, Group B was sampled from an urban environment where psychological stress causing blood pressure problems is high, the air is dirty from factories, and the people lead sedentary lives.

The following are data that were found relative to the two groups. In each case, decide if the data support the explanation (s) or do not (ns).

_____ 1. Group A people averaged about 5 feet 10 inches and about 190 pounds, while Group B people averaged about 6 feet 0 inches and approximately 180 pounds.

_____ 2. The average protein intake per capita per day was

Group A: All sources—60 g
            Animal sources—1 g

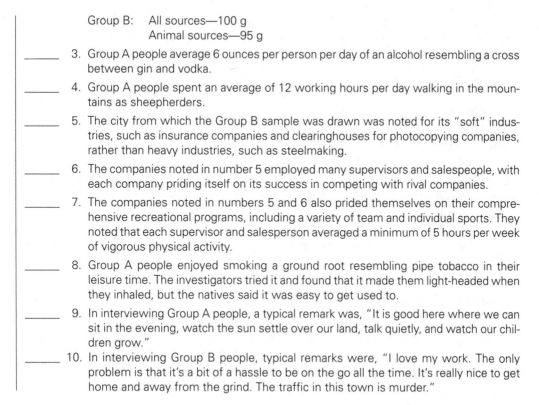

Group B: All sources—100 g
            Animal sources—95 g

_____ 3. Group A people average 6 ounces per person per day of an alcohol resembling a cross between gin and vodka.

_____ 4. Group A people spent an average of 12 working hours per day walking in the mountains as sheepherders.

_____ 5. The city from which the Group B sample was drawn was noted for its "soft" industries, such as insurance companies and clearinghouses for photocopying companies, rather than heavy industries, such as steelmaking.

_____ 6. The companies noted in number 5 employed many supervisors and salespeople, with each company priding itself on its success in competing with rival companies.

_____ 7. The companies noted in numbers 5 and 6 also prided themselves on their comprehensive recreational programs, including a variety of team and individual sports. They noted that each supervisor and salesperson averaged a minimum of 5 hours per week of vigorous physical activity.

_____ 8. Group A people enjoyed smoking a ground root resembling pipe tobacco in their leisure time. The investigators tried it and found that it made them light-headed when they inhaled, but the natives said it was easy to get used to.

_____ 9. In interviewing Group A people, a typical remark was, "It is good here where we can sit in the evening, watch the sun settle over our land, talk quietly, and watch our children grow."

_____ 10. In interviewing Group B people, typical remarks were, "I love my work. The only problem is that it's a bit of a hassle to be on the go all the time. It's really nice to get home and away from the grind. The traffic in this town is murder."

You have now seen what is perhaps a unique form of assessment for teachers and students—assessment of the inquiry process. Of course, the teacher could still measure the students' understanding of the content of a lesson in one of the conventional ways previously discussed. Our purpose here is to give you a brief introduction to the idea of measuring for inquiry skills. This introduction is sketchy because complete discussion of measuring for inquiry skills is beyond the scope of this text, but we hope that this initial exposure will help you get started toward developing an important thinking skill in your students.

ALTERNATIVE ASSESSMENT

While paper-and-pencil tests are widely used in education, they continue to be criticized. Some reasons include the following:

- Paper-and-pencil tests tend to focus on low levels of learning.
- Paper-and-pencil tests provide little insight into the way learners think.
- Paper-and-pencil tests do not measure learners' ability to apply their understanding to real-world problems (Shepard, 2001).

In response to these criticisms, **authentic assessments** are being emphasized. Often used interchangeably with performance assessments and alternative assessments, authentic assessments directly measure student performance through "real-life" tasks (Herman, Aschbacher, & Winters, 1992; Worthen, 1993). Some examples include the following:

- Explaining a real-world problem, such as why clothes tend to "stick" together when they come out of the dryer
- Writing a letter to a pen pal in another country
- Designing and conducting an experiment to measure different effects on the growth of plants
- Creating an original piece of sculpture

In addition to products, such as the written explanation for the clothes sticking together, the letter, the description of the experiment, or the sculpture, teachers want to examine learners' thinking when they use authentic assessments (Gronlund, 1993). For example, a portfolio of essays that illustrate improvement in writing or systematic observation of students as they work might be considered.

Let's look at two forms of authentic assessments: performance assessments and the use of portfolios.

Performance Assessment

A middle school science teacher notices that her students have difficulty designing and conducting simple science experiments, such as determining which brand of aspirin dissolves faster.

A health teacher reads in a professional journal that the biggest problem people have in applying first aid is not the mechanics per se but knowing what to do when. In an attempt to address this problem, the teacher has a periodic unannounced "catastrophe" day. Students entering the classroom encounter a catastrophe victim with an unspecified injury. Each time, they must first diagnose the problem and then apply first aid interventions. (Eggen & Kauchak, 2007)

These teachers are using **performance assessments** to gather information about students' thinking. Performance assessments measure skill and understanding by directly observing student performance in a natural setting.

Two common performance assessment methods are checklists and rating scales. **Checklists**—written descriptions of dimensions that must be present in an acceptable performance—extend systematic observation. When checklists are used, the students' behaviors are "checked off." For example, the science teacher wanting to assess learners' ability to design and conduct the experiment with plant growth might prepare a checklist such as the one that appears in Figure 11.3. (Notes could be added if desired, which would then combine elements of both checklists and systematic observations.)

Checklists are useful when the behaviors either exist or they do not, such as "Identifies variables that must be controlled." However, in cases such as "Writes a description of results," the results are not merely present or absent; some written descriptions will be better than others. This leads us to rating scales.

Rating scales are written descriptions of dimensions and scales of values on which each dimension is rated. They allow a more precise assessment of quality than is possible with checklists. A sample rating scale, based on the checklist in Figure 11.3, is illustrated in Figure 11.4.

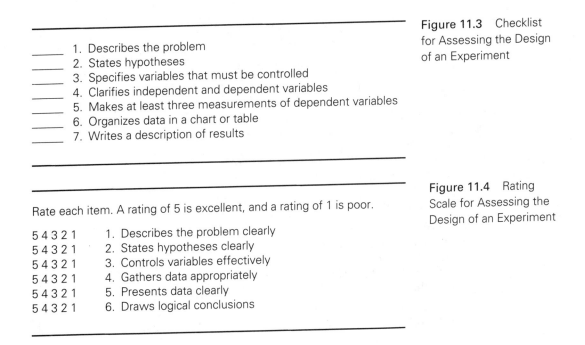

Figure 11.3 Checklist for Assessing the Design of an Experiment

_____ 1. Describes the problem
_____ 2. States hypotheses
_____ 3. Specifies variables that must be controlled
_____ 4. Clarifies independent and dependent variables
_____ 5. Makes at least three measurements of dependent variables
_____ 6. Organizes data in a chart or table
_____ 7. Writes a description of results

Figure 11.4 Rating Scale for Assessing the Design of an Experiment

Rate each item. A rating of 5 is excellent, and a rating of 1 is poor.

5 4 3 2 1   1. Describes the problem clearly
5 4 3 2 1   2. States hypotheses clearly
5 4 3 2 1   3. Controls variables effectively
5 4 3 2 1   4. Gathers data appropriately
5 4 3 2 1   5. Presents data clearly
5 4 3 2 1   6. Draws logical conclusions

Portfolio Assessment

Portfolios are collections of work that are reviewed against preset criteria (Stiggins, 2005). They are a second type of authentic assessment. Using them allows students to be involved in the processes of collecting and assessing their own work. Portfolios are collections of products, such as samples of student writing; they are not the assessment. The assessments are the teachers' and students' evaluation of the products.

Portfolios have two characteristics: (a) they include products of student work that have been gathered over a long period of time, and (b) students are involved in decisions about what materials will be included and how they will be evaluated.

Portfolios should reflect learning progress. For example, different essays indicate changes that occur during a grading period, semester, or entire course. These samples can then be used in parent–teacher conferences and as feedback for students themselves.

Using Rubrics with Alternative Assessments

A commonly used guideline that assists teachers in determining more accurate assessments and evaluations involves the construction of rubrics. **Rubrics** are guidelines for making scoring decisions, which are commonly presented as individual grade sheets that clearly provide expectations, guidance, and motivation for an assignment. They are presented in a clear, simple format using child-appropriate language. A rubric consists of a series of descriptors referring to a single criterion and arranged in a descending scale. Each descriptor specifies what is expected at that level and facilitates clarity of thought (Huffman, 1998). An example of a rubric is illustrated in Figure 11.5 (Fiderer, 1998).

Figure 11.5   Rubric for Assessing Story Predictions

Story Predictions

Assessing Written Predictions

- Select a story that has a character, problem, and solution
- Photocopy for each child a portion of the story—just enough to provide information about the character and the problem
- Photocopy the My Story Prediction planning form for each child
- Copy the Make a Prediction response for each child

Conduct the Assessment

- Allow at least 30 minutes for children to read the story beginning, complete the planning form, and write their predictions
- Distribute the My Story Prediction planning form and read the directions
- Distribute the Make a Prediction response form
- Encourage them to reread their story maps before they begin to write their ideas about how the story will end

My Story Prediction: Read the unfinished story. Think about how the story might end. Write about the story on the lines below.

1. Tell what the main character is like.

_____

_____

2. Tell what happened in the story so far.

_____

_____

Make a Prediction: Think about the character or characters and what happened in the story so far. Look at your story prediction form. Use what you know about the story to predict (guess) how it might end.

Write your ideas on the lines below.

I predict that . . . _____

_____

_____

_____

_____

Figure 11.5   (continued)

I made that prediction because. . . _____

_____

_____

_____

_____

Story Predictions Rubric

Score

Rating = 3

The response is complete. The prediction is logical and sequenced and indicates an excellent understanding of the character and story event.

Rating = 2

The response is partial. The prediction is reasonable and indicates a fairly good understanding of the story. The response is connected to a part of the story and does not take some events into account.

Rating = 1

The response is fragmentary. The prediction is barely connected to the story and may be illogical. It indicates minimal understanding of the story's events and characters.

Rating = 0

The response is illogical. The prediction indicates serious misunderstanding of the story.

The following is another example of a rubric used to assess the checklist in Figure 11.3:

Rating = 5
  The problem is stated clearly. Students appear to understand the topic and why the problem is important. It presents a framework for forming hypotheses.

Rating = 4
  Problem is quite clear. It is adequate, but more important problems could have been identified. An adequate basis for stating hypotheses is provided.

Rating = 3
  The statement of the problem is uncertain. The basis for hypothesizing solutions is not clear.

Rating = 2
  The statement is made, but it is not in the form of a problem. It is not clear from the statement whether learners understand the significance of the problem.

Rating = 1
  A problem is not stated.

A rubric for each of the other dimensions would also be prepared in a form similar to the preceding example. Using these descriptions, observers can achieve acceptable levels of reliability for both student performance and products.

The use of rubrics is essential in a standards-based system of performance assessment (Falk & Ort, 1998). Rubrics have the following advantages (Baker, 1997):

- Specifications provide a relatively efficient way to translate standards into assessments.
- General scoring rubrics reduce the load on teachers; in elementary classrooms (where teachers are responsible for all the content areas), they need to remember only one set of criteria (principles, prior knowledge, and so on) that can be applied to different topics.
- General scoring rubrics reduce the cost of scoring.
- Rubrics can be used for both summative (formal) assessments (used by districts and states) and formative assessments (used at the classroom level by teachers).

Although we have seen an increased use of rubrics, educators need to be aware of and avoid potential flaws, including the following (Popham, 1997):

- Rubrics are often linked to specific behaviors instead of overall skill mastery.
- Criteria are often so general that the rubric essentially becomes worthless.
- Many textbook-based rubrics are too long and too wordy.
- The rubric is often treated as the skill itself. Teachers must instruct toward the skill represented by the performance test, not toward the test.

Rubrics can help teachers in the assessment process, but, more important, they provide feedback about instruction. Well-designed rubrics provide teachers with invaluable information about the effectiveness of their instruction and the extent to which goals, learning activities, and assessments are aligned (Falk & Ort, 1998).

DIVERSITY IN THE CLASSROOM

Reducing Bias in the Classroom

When teachers assess their students, they gather data to make decisions about student progress and improve their instruction. Learner diversity, however, often complicates this process. For example, students from minority groups may lack experience with general testing procedures, different test formats, and test-taking strategies, and they may not understand the purpose of assessments. In addition, because most assessments are strongly language based, language may be another obstacle (Heubert & Hauser, 1999; Land, 1997). Teachers can respond to diversity by modifying their assessment procedures in at least three ways: (a) carefully wording items, (b) making provisions for nonnative English speakers, and (c) accommodating diversity in scoring.

Carefully Wording Items

Content bias is always a possibility when assessing students with diverse backgrounds (Hanson, Hayes, Schriver, Lemahien, & Brown, 1998). For example, learners from minority groups can have difficulties with items that contain information about things uncommon in their culture, such as transportation like cable cars, sports like American football, and musical instruments like the banjo (Cheng, 1987). In addition, holidays like Thanksgiving or U.S. historical figures like Abraham Lincoln, well known to most Americans, may be unfamiliar to these students. When these types of terms and events are included in assessment items, teachers are measuring both the intended topic and students' understanding of American vocabulary and culture. As a result, validity suffers.

There is no easy solution to this problem, but teacher awareness and sensitivity are starting points. In addition, encouraging students to ask questions and discussing tests thoroughly after they are given can help uncover unintended bias.

Making Provisions for Nonnative English Speakers

What would you do if your next exam in this class were presented in Russian? This prospect gives you some idea of the problems facing nonnative English-speaking students during tests. The most effective ways to help these students is to modify the test or the testing procedures. Some suggestions for doing so include the following:

- Provide extra time to take tests
- Allow students to use a glossary or dictionary
- Read directions aloud (in native language, if possible)
- Read the test aloud and clarify misunderstandings
- Simplify test language
- Provide visual supports

Of these suggestions, providing extra time for students to use a glossary or dictionary appear most promising (Abedi, 1999).

Accommodating Diversity in Scoring

Essay exams and alternative assessments can be effective for measuring students' ability to organize information, think analytically, and apply their understanding to real-world problems. However, they also place an extra burden on students who are wrestling with both content and language. What can teachers do? Valid assessment often requires the use of essays and alternative formats, and teachers cannot ignore students' grammatical errors. One solution is to evaluate essays and performance assessments with two grades: one for content and another for grammar, spelling, and punctuation (Hamp-Lyons, 1992; Scarcella, 1990). Breaking the score into two parts allows the teacher to discriminate between understanding of content and the ability to use language. These modifications are designed to ensure, as much as possible, that test scores reflect differences in achievement and not cultural bias related to background knowledge, vocabulary, or testing sophistication.

GRADES AND GRADING

Grades and grading are somewhat controversial, and their merits have been argued for decades. Some argue that they are inherently destructive, pitting students against each other (Kohn, 1996). Grades are unlikely to disappear, however, since both parents and students expect them. A variety of systems, such as "satisfactory," "satisfactory plus," and so on, have been implemented, but they are little more than substitute terms for the traditional letter grades.

We will not debate the effectiveness or appropriateness of grades in this text. They have always been a part of schooling, and they are likely to be a part in the future.

Norm-Referenced and Criterion-Referenced Grading Systems

When decisions are made about student progress and grades are assigned based on how they compare with other students, this is **norm-referenced grading**. Most standardized tests are norm referenced; the performance of learners in a class, school, or district on tests is compared with other students across the country.

Few classroom teachers use norm-referenced evaluations, however. They are more likely to use **criterion-referenced grading,** which assesses the extent to which learners have reached a preset standard.

A common form of criterion referencing uses a percentage system, and this is what you are most likely to encounter when you begin teaching. A sample percentage system could be the following:

93–100% A

85–92%   B

76–84%   C

67–75%   D

With this system, a teacher determines each student's average percentage at the end of a grading period, and this percentage determines the grade. A thorough discussion of the issues involved in grading can be found in Linn and Miller (2005).

Purposes of Assigning Grades

Grades serve two primary purposes: providing feedback and meeting school needs. Let's look at them.

Providing Feedback.   Most important, grades provide feedback for students and parents. In doing so, a grade becomes an indicator of achievement during a course of study over a specified period of time, most commonly 9 weeks. If feedback is to be useful, the students and their parents must be familiar with the grading system. The most common is the letter-grade system that uses A, B, C, D, and F grades, which essentially represent excellent, good, average, poor, and failing, respectively.

In some areas, you might encounter a pass/fail (P/F) or an honors/satisfactory/unsatisfactory system (H/S/U). Whatever the system being used, its purpose is to communicate the educational progress of the pupil.

Meeting School Needs.   Grades are also used to meet a range of institutional needs. For example, they are one of the factors used as a basis for grouping students, and they are used by school systems to promote students from one grade level to the next or to graduate students from different levels within the system. They are often used to identify honor students, and awards and scholarships are based on them. They may even determine whether a student is eligible to engage in extracurricular activities.

Finally, grades are a major factor for college admission and eligibility to participate in athletics. For example, the National Collegiate Athletic Association, in implementing a rule called Proposition 48, has stated that any high school graduate with less than an overall C average is ineligible to participate in intercollegiate athletics at an NCAA member university. (A minimum score of 700 on the SAT or 17 on the ACT is also part of Proposition 48.)

The original purpose of grades was to provide information about student progress and achievement. However, as educational institutions have grown, grades have become a critical factor to the success in the adult world of today's students. This is true not only in the professions but also in any area that requires the student to exhibit mastery of a skill.

Inappropriate Uses of Grades

As we said earlier, the primary purpose of grades is to indicate a level of achievement and communicate this achievement to students and their parents. However, grades are used in classrooms in many other ways. Sometimes, a higher, inappropriate grade is assigned to a student whose achievement has been low but whose effort has been high. In this way, the grade is designed as an incentive to keep trying regardless of the degree achievement. When this takes place, the grade becomes more important than the achievement, which is often undesirable. The problem is that a student might have solid grades but low scores on the standardized assessments, confusing and frustrating parents and aggravates administrators and school boards. If the function of a grade is to transmit information regarding student achievement, one must avoid communicating inaccurate information.

The teacher should also avoid using grades as a management axe. If a student achieves at the B level, it is illogical to report C achievement because of a lack of participation, poor attendance, or a management/discipline problem. Those situations should be handled in other ways, as discussed earlier in the text.

Affective areas should also be communicated in other ways. Grades should not be used to help students maintain a positive self-concept or help them move away from a negative one. Grades should not be given to reward the cooperative or to punish the uncooperative student.

The best way to support students is to review and upgrade the quality of instruction continually. This will allow increased numbers of students to achieve academically, which will then be reflected in higher grades.

FEEDBACK SYSTEMS

Feedback to Students

Students receive feedback from teachers in both verbal and written forms. Verbal feedback is common in question-and-answer sessions. One of the most common written forms is a grade on a formal assessment, such as a paper-and-pencil test. As we said earlier, students should understand that grades are designed to clearly communicate the level of achievement.

Teachers also write comments on papers. Again, the point is that all feedback regarding communication of achievement must be comprehensible.

Your grading policies and system should be simple and clear to the student. As we have emphasized throughout this book, students have a right to understand their learning situations, the objectives they are expected to meet, and at what level they must perform to succeed. Feedback regarding performance and achievement should be continuous, and students should know how they are performing at all times.

Feedback to Parents

The most common form of communicating grades to parents is the report card. The high school report card offers grades that should reflect academic achievement, whereas the elementary report card serves the same function in addition to providing information on satisfactory or unsatisfactory performance in nonacademic areas.

Parents should be familiar with as much performance information as the school can provide, most often presented in the form of grades. However, this information must be usable by clearly communicating levels of achievement. A letter grade of B in one class might not mean the same as a B in another class. As we said earlier, parents seeing satisfactory grades on report cards and low percentiles on standardized tests often do not understand how this could happen.

What teachers should remember is that the reason for a report card or any other communication device is to increase parents' awareness of their children's educational progress. The report card is only one way of achieving this goal.

Feedback should be constructive, supportive, and understandable.

Another method of communicating progress is a written report. Such reports should be clear and easy to read, and no reference to a grade should be made. In everyday language, teachers must communicate the general academic situation, being concerned with both what they are trying to say and how they are trying to say it.

The most effective way of communicating with parents is through a conference. Face-to-face verbal communication allows the parent to ask questions and the teacher to provide understandable information. As stated earlier, parents need to know what grades mean, and in a conference, the teacher can clearly discuss observable achievement as well as learning difficulties. The teacher should also realize that the parent conference is a two-way street and provides the opportunity to gain valuable information about the student and the student's home environment. Such information may become instrumental in helping the teacher promote further achievement.

TECHNOLOGY IN THE CLASSROOM

Improving Assessment

Frequent classroom assessment is an essential part of the teaching-learning process. Frequent assessment requires a great deal of teachers' time and effort, however. Technology can help.

Because they enable users to store, manipulate, and process large amounts of data quickly, computer technologies are especially valuable in classroom assessment. Computers can serve three important and time-saving assessment functions (Newby, Stepich, Lehman, & Russell, 2006; Roblyer, 2006). They include the following:

- Planning and constructing tests
- Analyzing test results
- Maintaining student records

Let's look at them.

Planning and Constructing Tests

Software test generators have at least three advantages over general word processing programs. First, they produce a standard layout; the teacher does not have to worry about spacing or format. Second, they automatically produce various forms of the test—helpful for makeup tests and preventing "wandering eyes." Third, they can be used with commercially prepared test banks, making it easier for teachers to combine the best of the commercially produced items with items they have constructed. These time- and effort-saving features can make classroom assessment more effective and efficient.

Many test creation programs are commercially available. The programs can be used to do the following:

- Develop a test file in a variety of formats. Within a file, items can be organized by topic, chapter, objective, or difficulty level.

- Select items from the created file bank either randomly, selectively, or by categories to generate multiple versions of a test.
- Modify items and integrate these into the total test.
- Produce student-ready copies and an answer key.

Analyzing Test Data

Technology can also assist in the process of scoring tests and reporting results, saving time for the teacher and providing students with more informative feedback. Software programs are available to machine score tests, and these programs can perform the following functions:

- Score objective tests and provide descriptive statistics such as test mean, median, mode, range, and standard deviation
- Generate a list of items showing difficulty level, the percentage of students who selected each response, the percentage of students who did not respond to an item, and the correlation of each item with the total test
- Sort student responses by score, grade/age, or gender (Merrill et al., 1992)

The time and energy saved provide teachers with opportunities to analyze and improve individual items as well as the entire test, thus improving student learning.

Maintaining Student Records

An effective assessment system frequently gathers information about student performance from a variety of sources. If this information is to be useful to the teacher, it must be stored in an easily accessible and usable form. Computers provide an efficient way to store, analyze, and report student assessments. One teacher commented,

> I keep my grades in an electronic gradebook. By entering my grades into an electronic gradebook as I grade papers, I always know how my students are progressing and exactly where my students stand in relation to each other. It does take a little time to enter the grades, but it makes my job easier during reporting periods. All I have to do is open my disk and record my students' grades on the grade sheet. (Morrison, Lowther, & DeMuelle, 1999, p. 355)

For teachers with some background in technology, general spreadsheet programs can be converted into individualized grade sheets (Forcier & Descy, 2005). Commercial software is also available, and most of the programs designed to analyze individual test score data also have the following capabilities:

- Begin a new class file for each class or subject. The files can be organized by name and/or student identification number.
- Average grades, create new grades or change old ones, and add extra credit.
- Compute descriptive statistics (such as the mean, median, mode, and standard deviation) for any test or set of scores.

- Weigh numerical or raw scores and translate into letter grades.
- Record the type of activity and the point value for each activity.
- Average grades on a quarterly, semester, and/or yearly basis.

In addition to saving teachers time and energy, these programs are accurate and imme-diate. If the entered data are correct, teachers can generate grades at the end of a grading period at the touch of a button. In addition, records are readily available at any time, pro-viding students with instant and accurate feedback (Roblyer, 2006). Some programs even have the capacity to print student reports in languages other than English (Forcier & Descy, 2005).

Technology and Portfolios

Technology can also be used to organize, store, and display student portfolios (Newby et al., 2006; Stiggins, 2005). Electronic portfolios address problems of space and accessi-bility and improve usability because they are stored in a computer. Teachers who have dealt with the logistical problems involved in multiple boxes of student portfolios attest to the advantages of electronic storage.

Technology is revolutionizing the teaching-learning process. Nowhere is this impact more important than in the assessment process, and technology's capacity to help assess-ment contribute more strongly to learning is continually increasing.

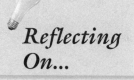

Reflecting On...

CLASSROOM ASSESSMENT
INTASC Principles 3, 8, and 10
Think about the discussion of assessing student learning in this chapter.

SUMMARY

Assessment is the process of gathering information about learning, and evaluation is the process of making decisions based on the assessments.

Assessments accuracy depends on well-designed items used to determine the extent to which students understand facts, concepts, and generalizations. They can usually be assessed with either recognition or supply-type items.

Alternative assessments, which include performance assessment and portfolios, provide options for teachers who are skeptical of the validity of traditional assessment. Scoring rubrics should be used when performance assessments are used.

Determining and communicating grades mark the last step of the three-phase model. When determining grades, teachers must first decide whether they are going to compare students to students or students to preset standards. Once this decision is made, the next step is to select an appropriate grading system that allows the teacher to assign letter grades objectively. It is important to note that a certain amount of subjectivity is always present no matter how objective the grading system.

Once letter grades have been assigned, the next step is to clearly and understandably communicate them to both students and parents. The critical point here is that the letter grade must accurately represent student performance. Once this step is accomplished, the use of the three-phase model is complete.

As a final point, it should be understood that using this model involves a never-ending process. Although the process of assigning and communicating grades completes the assessing phase, the teacher must now examine student achievement to plan, implement, and evaluate subsequent instruction. Therefore, using the three-phase model is a circular situation in which the teacher is engaged in an endless instructional series. Only through such a process can teachers hope to improve instruction on a continual basis and thereby promote student achievement and a success-oriented environment.

KEY CONCEPTS

Accountability   329

Authentic assessments   339

Checklists   340

Classroom assessment   327

Criterion-referenced grading   346

Formal assessment   328

High-stakes tests   330

Informal assessment   328

No Child Left Behind Act   329

Norm-referenced grading   346

Performance assessments   340

Portfolios   341

Rating scales   340

Rubrics   341

Standards-based education   329

PREPARING FOR YOUR LICENSURE EXAMINATION

Read the following case study and, using information from this chapter, answer the questions that follow.

Marianne Milligan, a communications teacher at Rio Grande High School, begins her class by distributing an example of a persuasive essay to each of her students and asks them to retrieve their worksheet with the "power questions." She then instructs the students to take out a piece of paper and place their name, the date, and the period in the upper right-hand corner. She told them to title the paper "Dissect an Essay."

"OK," Marianne begins, "we are now ready to start. Look at the essay on your desk. Every essay has a title. Whatever it is, write it on your sheet under 'Dissect an Essay.'"

"Is this a title page?" Jon inquires.

"You are not going to do a title page. You are just going to use this sheet to undertake the assignment," Marianne responds. "Now, what we are going to do is work on a five-paragraph essay that has a structure that shows that you know how to persuade somebody to believe what you think. We are going to start by dissecting the essay bit by bit. These essays you are dissecting are from another class and they dissected your essays earlier today to get even with you, so everybody is dissecting everybody."

Marianne then moves to the overhead projector, on which she places a sample essay. She asks the students to look at the first of the power questions on the handout. "We are looking for the theme, which should appear in the introductory paragraph. The theme of this essay [on the overhead] is, 'I think students with HIV should not, and the key here is not, be allowed to play basketball in school!' So, for the answer to number 1, you would write that down. That statement is the theme of the essay, the main idea. Next, it says, 'What is the first reason the author uses to develop the theme?' This usually comes in the first part of the second paragraph. It says here you can't play in the National Basketball Association, so why should you be allowed to play in high school? Is that correct?"

"Yes," Elizabeth says.

"OK," Marianne says, "so for number 2 you would write that the NBA doesn't allow athletes with HIV to play so why should schools? That is the reason this person is using to support the theme or main idea. The next question calls for citing an example. What does that mean . . . Robert?"

"It means note or list," he says.

"Or making us aware of an example," Maria adds.

"Great," Marianne says. "Now what is it in the essay on the overhead?"

"All I see is a description of how the NBA works," Mercedes says.

"That's fine because it supports the first reason." Using the overhead, Marianne continues to work through the structure, which calls for a second reason and an example to support the second reason and a third reason followed by a support example.

"Now," she continues, "our last power question asks us to identify a concluding sentence in the last paragraph. What is it in this essay . . . Toby?"

"It says, 'I don't think HIV victims should be allowed to play basketball.'"

"Good. We have dissected this essay; we've looked at the bone structure of it. We looked at the introduction, reason 1 and example, reason 2 and example, reason 3 and example, followed by the conclusion. Now, let's do it again with another essay on the overhead that takes the opposite position and says students who are HIV positive should, and the key word here is should, be allowed to play basketball."

Marianne then guides the students through the second persuasive essay and its structural components. She then instructs the students to repeat the process with the sample essay on their desk by writing the answers to the power questions on their sheets. Marianne and her bilingual aide spent the remainder of the class observing and facilitating the assignment.

1. How is an informal assessment being used in Ms. Milligan's lesson?
2. How would you assess the students' understanding of the concept persuasive essay?
3. What is an example of an alternative assessment that could be employed to determine student achievement?

4. Note in the last paragraph that Marianne had a bilingual aide. What kind of provision(s) would you make for nonnative English speakers?

VIDEO EXERCISE

Go to MyEducationLab and select the topic "Assessment" and watch the video "Portfolios." Respond to the questions that follow the video episode.

DEVELOPING YOUR PORTFOLIO

The purpose of this activity is to help you begin to design a grading system that you might use in your classes or classroom.

- Describe how much weight you will assign tests and quizzes in your system.
- Describe how you will handle homework in your system and how much weight you will assign to homework.
- Describe how you will help the students keep track of where they stand with respect to their grades in your system.

QUESTIONS FOR DISCUSSION

1. Does assessment enhance, detract from, or have no effect on the amount students learn? Provide evidence to support your position.

2. Does assessment enhance, detract from, or have no effect on learner motivation? Provide evidence to support your position.

3. To what extent should assessment be used for motivational purposes? Explain why you feel this way.

4. To what extent should you use assessment for grading and reporting compared with using assessment to enhance learning? Explain.

5. Traditional paper-and-pencil tests are commonly criticized as measuring low-level learning in students. Do you agree with this criticism? Explain.

6. Since traditional paper-and-pencil tests are so strongly criticized, do you believe that eventually they will no longer be used? Explain why or why not.

7. Imagine 5 years and then 10 years from now. Do you believe that authentic assessments will be more or less prominent than they are today? Why do you think so?

8. Why do you believe that traditional (A, B, C, and so on) grading has endured for so long? Will these traditional grades eventually disappear? Why or why not?

SUGGESTIONS FOR FIELD EXPERIENCE

1. Interview a teacher. Questions you might ask are the following:
   a. How important do you feel assessment is for promoting learning?
   b. How do you assess? Would you describe your assessment system? How do you include homework, projects, and tests and quizzes in your assessment system?
   c. Do you use authentic (or alternative or performance) assessments in your system? If so, how do you count them in your grading?
   d. How do you communicate assessment results to parents beyond sending home report cards and interim progress reports?
   e. Do you do any specific test preparation for your students before you give tests, such as the day before?
   f. Do you go over tests with your students after you give them? Why or why not?
   g. How often do you test?

2. Observe a teacher the day before a test is given. Does the teacher do anything to prepare the students for the test?

3. Observe a teacher the day a test is handed back to students. Does the teacher discuss the test with them? If so, describe specifically what the teacher does as part of the discussion.

4. Gather a sample of teachers' tests. As you study them, you might consider the following questions:
   a. At what level in the cognitive taxonomy are most of the items written? Are they primarily knowledge level, or do they measure higher-level thinking?
   b. What format is used for most of the items? Are they primarily objective, such as multiple choice, matching, or true or false, or do they use another format, such as fill in the blank or essay?
   c. Are most of the items clear (i.e., is it unlikely they would be misinterpreted)?

5. If the teacher uses portfolios of students' work, examine the contents of a portfolio. Describe the contents and be prepared to discuss them with your peers.

TOOLS FOR TEACHING

Print References

Emmer, E. T., Evertson, C. M, & Worsham, M. E. (2006). *Classroom management for middle and high school teachers* (7th ed.). Boston: Allyn & Bacon. A widely respected text that provides detailed suggestions for responding to classroom management problems in middle and high schools.

Evertson, C. M., Emmer, E. T., & Worsham, M. E. (2006). *Classroom management for elementary teachers* (7th ed.). Boston: Allyn & Bacon. A widely respected text that provides detailed suggestions for responding to classroom management problems in elementary schools.

Evertson, C. M., & Weinstein, C. S. (Eds.). (2006). *Handbook of classroom management research, practice, and contemporary issues.* Mahwah, NJ: Lawrence Erlbaum Associates. This handbook provides a comprehensive overview of research and effective practice in classroom management.

Good, T. L., & Brophy, J. E.. (2008). *Looking in classrooms* (10th ed.). Boston: Allyn & Bacon. This well-known and widely used text includes a chapter specifically devoted to effective responses to disruptive behavior.

Marzano, R. J., Marzano, J. S., & Pickering, D. J. (2003). *Classroom management that works: Research-based strategies for every teacher.* Alexandria, VA: Association for Supervision and Curriculum Development. This research-based resource provides specific strategies for responding to classroom management problems.

Web Sites

www.adprima.com/managemistakes.htm Identifies a series of common mistakes that new teachers make in responding to classroom management issues.

www.adprima.com/managing.htm Offers suggestions for responding to classroom management issues as well as other suggestions for creating an orderly classroom.

www.4faculty.org/includes/images/solutionstable.pdf Identifies a series of classroom management issues and suggests possible solutions to each.

www.kde.state.ky.us/KDE/Instructional+Resources/Career+and+Technical+Education/Classroom+Management.htm Offers one state's approach to offering suggestions to teachers about dealing with classroom management issues.

Glossary

Abstractions. Ideas used to describe, understand, and simplify the world.

Academic disciplines (as source of goals). The subject-matter knowledge considered to be useful to an educated person.

Accountability. The process of requiring students to demonstrate that they have met specific standards and making teachers responsible for student performance.

Active learning. Learning that gives students considerable input on the direction of learning.

Affective domain. The domain that focuses on attitudes, values, and feelings.

Assertive discipline. A management system in which the teachers establish their rights, rules, and procedures and are enforced with reinforcers and punishments.

Assessing. The process of gathering information about student performance and achievement.

Assistive technology. Adaptive technology tools that help students use computers and other types of technologies to learn content.

Attitudes. The ways in which teachers view their students emotionally, psychologically, and intellectually.

Authentic assessments. Direct measurements of student performance through real-life tasks.

Backward design. An approach to planning that first identifies desired learning objectives, then specifies ways to assess whether these objectives are met, and finally establishes learning experiences to reach the objectives.

Behavioral objectives. Learner outcomes that include a performance, condition, and criterion.

Caring. Teachers who genuinely care about their students.

Checklists. Written descriptions of dimensions that must be present in an acceptable performance.

Child (as source of goals). Objectives designed to meet the needs of individuals.

Clarity. Precise communication with respect to desired student behavior.

Classroom assessment. Processes involved in making decisions about students' learning progress.

Classroom climate. A learning environment that supports positive student emotional feelings.

Classroom discipline. Teacher responses to student misbehavior.

Classroom management. Strategies that create and maintain order in the classroom.

Closure. A teacher review that comes at the end of a lesson.

Cognition. The way students think and process information.

Cognitive domain. The domain that focuses on storing and processing information.

Concepts. A group of ideas or objects that share common characteristics.

Constructivism. An approach to learning that provides students with opportunities to construct useful understanding while engaged in purposeful learning activities.

Content outline. A blueprint for the lessons to be taught in a unit of instruction.

Convergent questions. Questions for which there is generally only one correct response.

Cooperative learning. A general term for a collection of teaching strategies designed to foster group cooperation and interaction among students. Common to all these strategies is students working together in small groups on common learning goals.

Criterion-referenced grading. Assessments based on students meeting a preset standard.

Critical thinking. Intellectual processes that promote student ability to process information through reasoning.

Culturally responsive teaching. Instruction that acknowledges and accommodates cultural diversity in classrooms.

Decision making. The process in which teachers make decisions with regard to the planning, implementing, and assessing of learning experiences.

Desist. Getting students to stop a behavior by addressing them directly.

Developing understanding (direct instruction). The segment of the direct instruction lesson in which the teacher explains new content, perhaps the most important phase of direct instruction.

Direct instruction. An instructional strategy designed to teach essential knowledge and skills that are needed for later learning; useful when skills can be broken down into specific steps and has been found to be particularly effective in working with low achievers and students with exceptionalities.

Discussions. Instructional strategies that use teacher–student and student–student interactions as the primary vehicle for higher-level learning goals.

Divergent questions. Questions for which there is a wide range of acceptable student responses.

English-language learners. Those students for whom English is not their first language.

English-language learning (EEL) Programs. Emersion programs with a heavy emphasis on content acquisition.

Evaluation statement. That part of a goal that contains a student performance, condition, and criterion.

Extrinsic. Tangible, external rewards for students.

Facts. Statements that are observable and typically singular in occurrence.

Feedback. Information about the accuracy and appropriateness of student responses

Firmness. Holding students accountable for their actions; communicating to students that teachers mean what they say.

Formal assessment. The process of systematically gathering information and making decisions about student learning progress.

Formative assessment. Gathering information about student learning progress during instruction to provide students with feedback and aid the teacher in diagnosing learner background knowledge and subsequent adjustments to instruction.

Generalizations. Statements that represent patterns that suggest a causal relationship.

Goal statement. That part of a goals objective that specifies who the learner is and what is to be achieved in general terms.

Goals objectives. Statements that include both general and specific learner outcomes.

Group investigation. A cooperative learning strategy that places students together in teams of three to six to investigate or solve some common problem.

Group work. An instructional strategy that uses students working together to supplement other strategies such as teacher-centered direct instruction or lecture-discussion.

Guided discovery. An instructional strategy designed to teach concepts and relationships among them; teachers present students with examples, guide them as they attempt to find patterns in the examples, and come to closure when students are able to describe the idea that the teacher is attempting to teach.

Guided practice (direct instruction). The phase of direct instruction that provides students with opportunities to try out the new skill or concept and for teachers to provide feedback about learning progress.

High expectations. Teachers' positive views of student work and achievement

High-level questions. Questions that require students to process information

High-stakes tests. Standardized tests designed to measure the extent to which standards are met.

"I" message. Ways to ensure that students understand rules and procedures.

Immersion language programs. Language acquisition programs that emphasize rapid transition to English, with little or no attempt to preserve the first language.

Implementation. The part of the Three-Phase Model of Teaching that includes the teacher's presentation of content, strategies, and materials designed to promote student learning.

Inclusion. A comprehensive approach to educating students with exceptionalities that advocates a total, systematic, and coordinated web of services.

Independent practice (direct instruction). The final phase of direct instruction designed to provide additional opportunities for students to practice the new content.

Indirect cues. Attending to student off-task behavior by not addressing them directly.

Individualized education plan. A comprehensive description of an individualized curriculum designed for each student.

Individuals with Disabilities Education Act. (P. L. 94–142.) Federal law that requires that children with disabilities be provided with a free and appropriate education.

Informal assessment. The process of gathering incidental information about student learning progress and making decisions based on that information.

Inquiry strategies. Instructional strategies that use the inquiry processes of answering questions and solving problems based on the logical examination of facts and observations to teach content and to help students think analytically.

Instructional objectives: *See* Behavioral objectives.

Intrinsic. The reward of the feeling of internal worth.

Introduction and review (direct instruction). The first part of a direct instruction lesson designed to attract students' attention, pull them into the lesson, and remind them of previously learned content.

Jigsaw. A cooperative learning strategy that places students in small groups to investigate a common topic.

Knowledge. The acquisition of intellectual, moral, and prepositional information and the ability to manifest or employ it.

Learner-centered instruction. Instruction in which teachers facilitate rather than direct student learning.

Learner diversity. The significant ways in which children differ.

Learning styles. Also called *cognitive styles*, students' preferred ways of learning, solving problems, or processing information.

Least restrictive environment. The concept that all children have the right to learn in an environment that fosters their academic and social growth to the maximum extent possible.

Lecture-discussion. An instructional strategy designed to teach organized bodies of information in an interactive manner; occurs in four phases: introduction and review, presenting information, comprehension monitoring, and integration.

Lesson assessment. The ways in which teachers evaluate student learning.

Lesson content. The major ideas a teacher plans to present.

Lesson focus. Ways to attract and maintain student attention.

Lesson goals. The general learner outcomes of a lesson.

Lesson materials. A wide range of resources used to facilitate student learning.

Lesson objectives. The intended specific learner outcomes of a lesson.

Lesson procedures. Strategies used to facilitate instruction.

Lesson rational. Reasons for presenting a lesson to the students.

Local goals. An outcomes considered important in a specific school district.

Long-range goals. Goals to be achieved over a long period of study.

Low-level questions. Questions that are generally of a recall nature.

Mainstreaming. The process of placing students with disabilities into "regular" classrooms.

Maintenance language programs. Language programs that place the greatest emphasis on using and sustaining the first language. Students receive some instruction in their native language and some in English, gradually increasing the English.

Metacognition. Students' awareness of the ways they learn most effectively and their ability to control these factors.

Modeling enthusiasm. Teachers communicating genuine interest in student work.

Motivation. The internal drive that increases a student's desire to learn and achieve.

Multicultural education. A comprehensive term for a variety of strategies that schools use to accommodate cultural differences and provide educational opportunities for all students.

Multiple intelligences. A view of intelligence that proposes that our intellect is composed of several different kinds or dimensions of intelligence.

National goals. A goals deemed important nationwide.

Negative questions. Teacher questions that shift students from correct to incorrect answers.

No Child Left Behind Act. Federal regulations that require states to create standards and assess those standards at several levels.

Norm-referenced grading. Decisions made about student progress and grades based on how students compare to each other.

Objective condition. What the student is given, or not given, at the time of assessment.

Objective criterion. Acceptable level for an objective at which students must perform.

Objective observed behavior. The performance component of a behavioral objective.

Open-ended questions. See divergent questions.

Organization. Being prepared to facilitate smooth and effective learning experiences.

Organized bodies of knowledge. Topics that connect facts, concepts and principles and make the relationships among them explicit.

Overlapping. The teacher's ability to do more than one thing at one time.

Pairs check. A group work strategy that involves student pairs working at their desks while focusing on problems with convergent answers.

Passive learning. Learning activities in which students are receivers of information.

Performance assessments. The measurement of student skill and understanding by directly observing student performance in a natural setting.

Planning. The component of the Three-Phase Model of Teaching in which the teacher establishes the unit of instruction and selects the objectives to be learned and the rationale for learning those objectives.

Portfolios. Collections of student work that are reviewed against preset criteria.

Positive questions. Questions that help students change a wrong provisional answer into the right final answer.

Praise. Ways in which teachers positively support student responses or behavior.

Probing. A questioning technique in which the teacher requires the student to provide additional information or a more in-depth response.

Problem-based instruction. A broad family of strategies designed to teach problem-solving and inquiry skills. Uses a problem as a focal point for student investigation and inquiry.

Problem solving. A problem-based teaching strategy in which teachers help students learn to solve problems through hands-on learning experiences.

Procedures. Established routines students follow on a daily basis.

Prompting. See positive questioning.

Psychomotor domain. The domain that focuses on physical activities and abilities.

Rating scales. Written descriptions of dimensions and scales of values on which each dimension is rated.

Redirection. A questioning technique in which the teacher poses the same question to a number of students.

Reflection. The process in which a teacher revisits instruction in terms of how it can be more effective.

Review. Teacher summaries of previous work and links to that which is to come.

Rubrics. Guidelines for making scoring decisions.

Rules. Established standards for student behavior.

Skills. A wide range of desired behaviors students exhibit in the classroom.

Society (as source of goals). Goals that are designed to help students meet the challenges of society effectively.

Standards. Attempts by states and national organizations to clearly specify what students need to learn and know.

Standards (as source of goals). Goals that are established for the curriculum of a given state.

Standards-based education. The process of focusing curricular instruction on predetermined goals and holding students and teachers accountable for meeting the standards

State goals. *See* Standards.

Student-centered instruction. *See* Active learning; Constructivism.

Student teams achievement division. A cooperative learning strategy in which high- and low-ability students are paired on evenly matched teams of four or five and team scores are based on the extent to which individuals improve their scores on skills tests. Students are rewarded for team performance, encouraging group cooperation.

Students placed at risk. Those students in danger of failing to complete their education with the skills necessary to survive in modern society.

Teacher-centered instruction. Instruction in which the teacher's role is to present the knowledge to be learned and to direct, in a rather explicit manner, the learning process of the students.

Think-pair-share. A group-work strategy in which the teacher asks a routine question, but instead of calling on one student, the teacher asks all students to think about the answer (the think part of the strategy) and discuss it with their partner (the pair-share aspect of the strategy).

Transition language programs. Language programs that maintain the first language until students acquire sufficient English.

Unit content outline. That part of a unit plan that outlines the lessons designed to facilitate the unit goal.

Unit goal. Part of the unit plan that set forth the learner outcomes in general terms.

Unit planning. The process in which teachers determine what is to be learned in general terms, why it is to be learned, and what lessons will facilitate the learner outcomes.

Unit rationale. The teacher's justification for including the unit outcomes in the curriculum.

Wait time. The time in which a teacher pauses after asking a question.

Withitness. Teachers being aware of what is going on in the classroom.

References

Abedi, J. (1999, Spring). CRESST report points to test accommodations for English language learning students. *The CRESST Line*, 6–7.

Abedi, J., Hofstetter, C., & Lord, C. (2004). Assessment accommodations for English language learners: Implications for policy-based empirical research. *Review of Educational Research, 74*(1), 1–28.

Adams State College Conceptual Framework (2002). Alamosa, CO: Adams State College.

Alberto, P., & Troutman, A. (1999). *Applied behavior analysis for teachers* (4th ed.). Upper Saddle River, NJ: Merrill/Prentice Hall.

Alexander, P., & Murphy, P. (1998). The research base for APA's learner-centered psychological principles. In N. Lambert & B. McCombs (Eds.), *How students learn: Reforming schools through learner-centered education* (pp. 25–60). Washington, DC: American Psychological Association.

Amrein, A., & Berliner, D. (2002). High-stakes testing, uncertainty, and student learning. *Education Policy Analysis Archives, 10*(18). Retrieved October 1, 2002, from http://epaa.asu.edu/epaa/v10n18/

Anderson, L., & Krathwohl, D. (Eds.). (2001). *A taxonomy for learning, teaching, and assessing: A revision of Bloom's taxonomy of educational objectives.* New York: Addison Wesley Longman.

Arends, R., Winitzky, N., & Tannenbaum, M. (2001). *Exploring teaching: An introduction to education* (2nd ed.). Boston: McGraw-Hill.

Armstrong, D. (2003). *Curriculum today.* Upper Saddle River, NJ: Merrill/Prentice Hall.

Armstrong, D., Henson, K., & Savage, T. (2005). *Teaching today: An introduction to education.* Upper Saddle River, NJ: Pearson Education.

Aronson, E., Wilson, T., & Akert, R. (2005). *Social psychology* (5th ed.). Upper Saddle River, NJ: Pearson.

Attewell, P. (2001). The first and second digital divides. *Sociology of Education, 74(3)*, 252–259.

Baker, E. (1997). Model-based performance assessment. *Theory Into Practice, 36*(4), 247–253.

Banks, J. (2006a). *An introduction to multicultural education* (4th ed.). Boston: Allyn & Bacon.

Banks, J. (2006b). *Cultural diversity and education* (6th ed.). Boston: Allyn & Bacon.

Barak, M., & Dori, Y. J. (2005). Enhancing undergraduate students' chemistry understanding through project-based learning in an IT environment. *Science Education, 89*, 117–139.

Barnoski, L. (2005). My purpose. *Education Week, 25*(13), 37.

Barr, R., & Parrett, W. (2001). *Hope fulfilled for at-risk and violent youth* (2nd ed.). Boston: Allyn & Bacon.

Behuniak, P. (2002). Consumer-referenced testing. *Phi Delta Kappan, 84*, 199–206.

Berk, L. (2006). *Child development* (7th ed.). Boston: Allyn & Bacon.

Berk, L. (2007). *Development through the lifespan* (4th ed.). Boston: Allyn & Bacon.

Berliner, D. (1994). Expertise: The wonder of exemplary performances. In J. Mangieri & C. Collins (Eds.), *Creating powerful thinking in teachers and students* (pp. 161–186). Ft. Worth, TX: Harcourt Brace.

Berliner, D. (2005). Our impoverished view of educational reform. *Teachers College Record,* August 2. ID Number: 12106. Retrieved January 12, 2006, from http://www.tcrecord.org

Beyer, B. (1988). Developing a scope and sequence for thinking skills instruction. *Educational Leadership, 45*(7), 26–30.

Biklen, S., & Pollard, D. (2001). Feminist perspectives on gender in classrooms. In V. Richardson (Ed.), *Handbook of research on learning* (4th ed., pp. 695–722). Washington, DC: American Educational Research Association.

Bishop, J. (1995). The power of external standards. *American Educator, 19,* 10–14, 17–18, 42–43.

Bishop, J. (1998). The effect of curriculum-based external exit systems on student achievement. *Journal of Economic Education, 29,* 171–182.

Black, P. (1998). Inside the black box: Raising standards through classroom assessment. *Phi Delta Kappan, 80*(2), 139.

Black, P., Harrison, C., Lee, C., Marshall, B., & William, D. (2004). Working inside the black box: Assessment for learning in the classroom. *Phi Delta Kappan, 86*(1), 9–21.

Bloom, B., & Bourdon, L. (1980). Types and frequencies of teachers' written instructional feedback. *Journal of Educational Research, 74,* 13–15.

Bloom, B., Englehart, M., Furst, E., Hill, W., & Krathwohl, D. (1956). *Taxonomy of educational objectives: The classification of educational goals: Handbook 1. The cognitive domain.* White Plains, NY: Longman.

Blumenfeld, P., Pintrich, P., & Hamilton, V. L. (1987). Teacher talk and students' reasoning about morals, conventions, and achievement. *Child Development, 58,* 1389–1401.

Bohn, C. M., Roehrig, A. D., & Pressley, M. (2004). The first days of school in the classrooms of two more effective and four less effective primary-grades teachers. *Elementary School Journal, 104,* 269–288.

Borg, W., & Ascione, F. (1982). Classroom management in elementary mainstreaming classrooms. *Journal of Educational Psychology, 74,* 85–95.

Borich, G. (1996). *Effective teaching methods* (3rd ed.). Englewood Cliffs, NJ: Prentice Hall.

Bracey, G. (2003). *On the death of childhood and the destruction of public schools.* Portsmouth, NH: Heinemann.

Bransford, J., Brown, A., & Cocking, R. (Eds.). (2000). *How people learn: Brain, mind, experience, and school.* Washington, DC: National Academy Press.

Brisk, M. E. (1998). *Bilingual education: From compensatory to quality schooling.* Mahwah, NJ: Erlbaum.

Brophy, J. (1981). On praising effectively. *Elementary School Journal, 81,* 269–278.

Brophy, J. (1996). *Teaching problem students.* New York: Guilford Press.

Brophy, J. (1999). Perspectives of classroom management. In J. Freiberg (Ed.), *Beyond behaviorism: Changing the classroom management paradigm* (pp. 43–56). Boston: Allyn & Bacon.

Brophy, J. (2004). *Motivating students to learn* (2nd ed.). Boston: McGraw-Hill.

Brophy, J., & McCaslin, M. (1992). Teachers' reports of how they perceive and cope with problem students. *Elementary School Journal, 93*(1), 3–68.

Brosvic, G. M., & Epstein, M. L. (2007). Enhancing learning in the introductory course. *The Psychological Record, 57,* 391–408.

Browne, M., & Keeley, S. (1990). *Asking the right questions: A guide to critical thinking* (3rd ed.). Englewood Cliffs, NJ: Prentice Hall.

Brualdi, A. (1998). Classroom questions. *ERIC Clearinghouse on assessment and evaluation.* College Park, MD: Catholic University of America.

Bruning, R., Schraw, G., Norby, M., & Ronning, R. (2004). *Cognitive psychology and instruction* (4th ed.). Upper Saddle River, NJ: Prentice Hall.

Burbules, N., & Bruce, B. (2001). Theory and research on teaching as dialogue. In V. Richardson (Ed.), *Handbook of research on teaching* (4th ed., pp. 1102–1121). Washington, DC: America Educational Research Association.

Burstyn, J., & Stevens, R. (1999, April). *Education in conflict resolution: Creating a whole school approach.* Paper presented at the annual meeting of the American Educational Research Association, Montreal, Quebec, Canada.

Cameron, C., & Lee, K. (1997). Bridging the gap between home and school with voice-mail technology. *Journal of Educational Research, 90*(2), 182–190.

Campbell, L., Campbell, B., & Dickinson, D. (2004). *Teaching and learning through multiple intelligences.* Boston: Pearson Education.

Canter, L. (1988). Let the educator beware: A response to Curwin and Mendler. *Educational Leadership, 46*(2), 71–73.

Canter, L., & Canter, M. (1992). *Assertive discipline.* Santa Monica, CA: Lee Canter & Associates.

Carbo, M. (1997). Reading styles times twenty. *Educational Leadership, 54(7),* 38–42.

Carnine, D., Silbert, J., Kame'enui, E., Tarver, S., & Jongjohann, K. (2006). *Teaching struggling and at-risk readers: A direct instruction approach.* Upper Saddle River, NJ: Prentice Hall.

Casserly, M. (2002). Can the Bush school plan work? How to keep 'No Child Left Behind' from dissolving into fine print. *Education Week, 22*(14), 39, 48.

Castle, K. (1993). Rule-creating in a constructivist classroom community. *Childhood Education, 70*(2), 77.

Cheng, L. R. (1987). *Assessing Asian language performance.* Rockville, MD: Aspen.

Christie, I. (2003). States ain't misbehavin' but the work is hard! *Phi Delta Kappan, 84,* 565–566.

Clark, R. C., & Mayer, R. E. (2003). *E-learning and the science of instruction: Proven guidelines for consumers and designers of multimedia learning.* San Francisco: Pfeiffer/Wiley.

Clifford, M. (1990). Students need challenge, not easy success. *Educational Leadership, 48*(1), 22–26.

Cognition and Technology Group at Vanderbilt. (1992). The Jasper Series as an example of anchored instruction: Theory, program description, and assessment data. *Educational Psychologist, 27,* 291–315.

Cognition and Technology Group at Vanderbilt. (1997). *The Jasper Project: Lessons in curriculum, instruction, assessment, and professional development.* Mahwah, NJ: Erlbaum.

Colorado Model Content Standards for Geography. (1995, June). Denver: Colorado Department of Education.

Cook, M. (1999). *Effective coaching.* New York: McGraw-Hill.

Cooper, H., Robinson, J., & Patall, E. (2006). Does homework improve academic achievement? A synthesis of research, 1987–2003. *Review of Educational Research, 76*(1), 1–62.

Cooper, J. (Ed.). (2003). *Classroom teaching skills* (7th ed.). Boston: Houghton Mifflin.

Corbett, D., & Wilson, B. (2002). What urban students say about good teaching. *Educational Leadership, 60*(1), 18–22.

Cornelius-White, J. (2007). Learner-centered teacher-student relationships are effective: A meta-analysis. *Review of Educational Research, 77*(1), 113–143.

Crocker, R., & Brooker, G. (1986). Classroom control and student outcomes in grades 2 and 5. *American Educational Research Journal, 23,* 1–11.

Cuban, L. (1993). *How teachers taught: Constancy and change in American classrooms: 1890–1980* (2nd ed.). New York: Teachers College Press.

Cuban, L. (2005). *Growing instructional technology in U.S. classrooms.* 2005 J. George Jones & Velma Rife Jones Lecture: University of Utah, Salt Lake City.

Darling-Hammond, L. (2001). Standard setting in teaching: Changes in licensing, certification, and assessment. In V. Richardson (Ed.), *Handbook of research on teaching* (4th ed., pp. 751–776). Washington, DC: America Educational Research Association.

Deering, P., & Meloth, M. (1990). *An analysis of the content and form of students' verbal interactions in cooperative groups.* Paper presented at the annual meeting of the American Educational Research Association, Boston.

Delgado-Gaitan, C. (1992). School matters in the Mexican American home: Socializing children to education. *American Educational Research Journal, 29*(3), 495–516.

Dempster, F. (1991). Synthesis of research on reviews and tests. *Educational Leadership, 48*(7), 71–76.

Denham, C., & Lieberman, A. (1980). *Time to learn.* Washington, DC: National Institute of Education.

Denig, S. J. (2003, April). *A proposed relationship between multiple intelligences and learning styles.* Paper presented at the annual meeting of the American Educational Research Association, Chicago.

Dewey, J. (1906). *Democracy and education.* New York: Macmillan.

Dewey, J. (1910). *How we think.* Boston: DC Health.

Dewey, J. (1923). *The school and society.* Chicago: University of Chicago Press.

Dewey, J. (1938). *Experience and education.* New York: Macmillan.

Ding, M., Li, X., Piccolo, D., & Kulm, G. (2007). Teacher interventions in cooperative-learning mathematics classes. *Journal of Educational Research, 100*(3), 162–176.

Doebler, L. (1998). Preservice teacher case study responses: A preliminary attempt to describe program impact. *Education, 119*(2), 349.

Doll, B., Zucher, S., & Brehm, K. (2004). *Resilient classrooms: Creating healthy environments for learning.* New York: Guilford Press.

Donovan, M. S., & Bransford, J. D. (2005). Introduction. In M. S. Donovan & J. D. Bransford (Eds.), *How students learn: History, mathematics, and science in the classroom* (pp. 1–26). Washington, DC: National Academies Press.

Doyle, W. (1986). Classroom organization and management. In M. Wittrock (Ed.), *Handbook of research on teaching* (3rd ed., pp. 392–425). New York: Macmillan.

Drajem, L. (2002, April). *Life stories: Successful white women teachers of ethnically and racially diverse students.* Paper presented at the annual meeting of the American Educational Research Association, New Orleans.

Dreikurs, R. (1968a). *The courage to be imperfect* [Speech]. Tempe, AZ: Arizona State University.

Dreikurs, R. (1968b). *Psychology in the classroom* (2nd ed.). New York: Harper & Row.

Dunn, R., & Dunn, K. (1993). *Teaching secondary students through their individual learning styles: Practical approaches for grades 7–12.* Boston: Allyn & Bacon.

Dunn, R., Dunn, K., & Price, G., (2000). *Learning style inventory.* Lawrence, KS: Price Systems.

Easton, L. (2002). Lessons from learners. *Educational Leadership, 60*(1), 64–68.

Eby, J., Herrell, A. (2005). *Teaching in the elementary school: A reflective action approach* (4th ed.). Upper Saddle River, NJ: Pearson/Prentice Hall.

Echevarria, J., & Graves, A. (2007). *Sheltered content instruction* (3rd ed.). Boston: Allyn & Bacon.

Eggen, P. (1998, April). *A comparison of inner-city middle school teachers' classroom practices and their expressed beliefs about learning and effective instruction.* Paper presented at the annual meeting of the American Educational Research Association, San Diego, CA.

Eggen, P., & Jacobsen, D. (2001). *Constructivism and the architecture of cognition: Implications for instruction.* Seattle, WA: American Education Research Association.

Eggen, P., & Kauchak, D. (1996). *Strategies for teachers: Teaching content and thinking skills* (3rd ed.). Needham Heights, MA: Allyn & Bacon.

Eggen, P., & Kauchak, D. (2007). *Educational psychology: Windows on classrooms* (7th ed.). Upper Saddle River, NJ: Pearson.

Ellis, S., Dowdy, B., Graham, P., & Jones, R. (1992, April). *Parental support of planning skills in the context of homework and family demands.* Paper presented at the annual meeting of the American Educational Research Association, San Francisco.

Ely, J. (1994). *Reflective planning, teaching & evaluation for the elementary school.* New York: Merrill.

Emmer, E. (1988). Praise and the instructional process. *Journal of Classroom Interaction, 23,* 32–39.

Emmer, E., & Gerwels, M. (2002). Cooperative learning in elementary classrooms: Teaching practices and lesson characteristics. *Elementary School Journal, 103*(1), 75–91.

Emmer, E., Evertson, C., & Worsham, M. (2006). *Classroom management for secondary teachers* (7th ed.). Boston: Allyn & Bacon.

Epstein. J., Sanders, M., Simon, B., Salinas, K., Jansorn, N., & van Voorhis, F. (2002). *School, family, and community partnerships: Your handbook for action.* Thousand Oaks, CA: Corwin Press.

Evans, C., Kirby, U., & Fabrigar, L. (2003). Approaches to learning, need for cognition, and strategic flexibility among university students. *The British Journal of Educational Psychology, 73,* 507–528.

Evertson, C. (1987). Managing classrooms: A framework for teachers. In D. Berliner & B. Rosenshine (Eds.), *Talks to teachers* (pp. 54–74). New York: Random House.

Evertson, C., Emmer, E., & Worsham, M. (2006). *Classroom management for elementary teachers* (7th ed.). Boston: Allyn & Bacon.

Fabiano, G. A., Pelham, W. E. Jr., & Gnagy, E. M. (2007). The single and combined effects of multiple intensities of behavior modification and methylphenidate for children with attention deficit hyperactivity disorder in a classroom setting. *The School Psychology Review, 36,* 195–216.

Falk, B., & Ort, S. (1998). Sitting down to score: Teacher learning through assessment. *Phi Delta Kappan, 80*(1), 59–64.

Farkas, R. (2003). Effects of traditional versus learning-styles instructional methods on middle school students. *Journal of Educational Research, 97*(1), 42–51.

Federal Interagency Forum on Child and Family Statistics. (2005). *Family structure and children's living arrangement.* Retrieved 4/23/06, from http://www.childstats.gov/americaschildren/pop6.asp

Fiderer, A. (1998). *35 rubrics and checklists to assess reading and writing.* New York: Scholastic Professional Books.

Finkelstein, E. (2005). Making PowerPoint quizzes. *Presentations, 19*(1), 18–20.

Forcier, R., & Descy, D. (2005). *The computer as an educational tool: Productivity and problem solving* (4th ed.). Upper Saddle River, NJ: Merrill/Prentice Hall.

Freiberg, H., & Driscoll, A. *Universal teaching Strategies* (3rd.). Boston: Allyn & Bacon.

Fullan, M., Hill, P., & Crevola, C. (2006). *Breakthrough.* Thousand Oaks, CA: Corwin.

Gardner, H. (2006). *Multiple intelligences: New horizons.* New York: Basic Books.

Gardner, H., & Moran, S. (2006). The science of multiple intelligences theory: A response to Lynn Waterhouse. *Educational Psychology, 41*(4), 227–232.

Gay, G. (2005). Politics of multicultural teacher education. *Journal of Teacher Education, 56*(3), 221–228.

Gee, J. P. (2005). *Learning by design: Games as learning machines.* Retrieved 4/23/06, from http://labweb.education.wisc.edu/room130/papers.htm

Gijbels, D., Dochy, F., Van den Bossche, P., Segers, M. (2005). Effects of problem-based learning: A meta-analysis from the angle of assessment. *Review of Educational Research, 75*(1), 27–61.

Ginsburg-Block, M., Rohrbeck, C., & Fantuzzo, J. (2006). A meta-analytic review of social, self-concept, and behavioral outcomes of peer-assisted learning. *Journal of Educational Psychology, 98*(4), 732–749.

Gollnick, D., & Chinn, P. (2006). *Multicultural education in a pluralistic society* (7th ed.). Upper Saddle River, NJ: Merrill/Prentice Hall.

Good, T., & Brophy, J. (2008). *Looking in classrooms* (10th ed.). New York: Longman.

Gopaul-McNicol, S., & Thomas-Presswood, T. (1998). *Working with linguistically and culturally different children: Innovative clinical and educational approaches.* Boston: Allyn & Bacon.

Gordon, T. (1974). *Teacher effectiveness training*. New York: Wyden.

Gordon, T. (1975). *T.E.T.: Teacher effectiveness training*. New York: Wyden.

Gorman, J., & Balter, L. (1997). Culturally sensitive parent education: A critical review of quantitative research. *Review of Educational Research, 67,* 339–369.

Green, S., & Mantz, M. (2002, April). *Classroom assessment practices: Examining impact on student learning.* Paper presented at the annual meeting of the American Educational Research Association, New Orleans.

Griffith, J. (2002). A multilevel analysis of the relation of school learning and social environments to minority achievement in public elementary schools. *The Elementary School Journal, 102,* 349–366.

Gronlund, N. (1993). *How to make achievement tests and assessments.* Needham Heights, MA: Allyn & Bacon.

Gronlund, N. (2000). *How to write and use instructional objectives* (6th ed.). New York: Macmillan.

Gronlund, N., & Linn, R. (2000). *Measurement and evaluation in teaching* (8th ed.). Upper Saddle River, NJ: Prentice Hall.

Guillaume, A. (2004). *K-12 classroom teaching: A primer for new professionals* (2nd ed.). Upper Saddle River, NJ: Pearson Education.

Hafner, A. (2001, April). *Evaluating the impact of test accommodations on test scores of LEP students and non-LEP students.* Paper presented at the annual meeting of the American Educational Research Association, Seattle.

Hamp-Lyons, L. (1992). Holistic writing assessment for L.E.P. students. In *Focus on evaluation and measurement* (Vol. 2, pp. 317–358). Washington, DC: U.S. Department of Education.

Hanson, M., Hayes, J., Schriver, K., LeMahieu, P., & Brown, P. (1998). *A plain language approach to the revision of test items.* Paper presented at the annual meeting of the American Educational Research Association, San Diego, CA.

Hardman, M., Drew, C., & Egan, W. (2008). *Human exceptionality* (9th ed.). Needham Heights, MA: Allyn & Bacon.

Hardy, L. (2002). A new federal role. *American School Board Journal, 189*(9), 20–24.

Harris, K., Graham, S., & Mason, L. (2006). Improving the writing, knowledge, and motivation of struggling young writers: Effects of self-regulated strategy development with and without peer support. *American Educational Research Journal, 43*(2), 295–340.

Harris, L., Kagay, M., & Ross, J. (1987). *The Metropolitan Life survey of the American teacher: Strengthening links between home and school.* New York: Louis Harris & Associates.

Harrow, A. (1972). *A taxonomy of the psychomotor domain: A guide for developing behavioral objectives.* New York: David McKay.

Harry, B. (1992). An ethnographic study of cross-cultural communication with Puerto Rican American families in the special education system. *American Educational Research Journal, 29*(3), 471–488.

Hatch, J. (2002). Accountability shovedown: Resisting the standards movement in early childhood education. *Phi Delta Kappan, 83*(6), 457–462.

Hattie, J., & Timperley, H. (2007). The power of feedback. *Review of Educational Research, 77*(1), 81–112.

Henniger, M. (2004). *The teaching experience: An introduction to reflective practice.* Upper Saddle River, NJ: Pearson Education.

Henniger, M. (2005). *Teaching young children: An introduction* (3rd ed.). Upper Saddle River, NJ: Pearson/Prentice Hall.

Herman, J., Aschbacher, P., & Winters, L. (1992). *A practical guide to alternative assessment.* Alexandria, VA: Association for Supervision and Curriculum Development.

Heubert, J., & Hauser, R. (Eds.). (1999). *High stakes testing for tracking, promotion, and graduation.* Washington, DC: National Academy Press.

Heward, W. (2006). *Exceptional children* (8th ed.). Upper Saddle River, NJ: Merrill/Prentice Hall.

Hill, D. (1990). Order in the classroom. *Teacher, 1,* 70–77.

Hirsch, E. (1987). *Cultural literacy: What every American needs to know.* Boston: Houghton-Mifflin.

Hirsch, E. (2000). The tests we need and why we don't quite have them. *Education Week, 19*(21), 40–41.

Hopkins, J. (2006). All students being equal. *Technology & Learning, 26*(10), 26–28.

Hudley, C. (1992, April). *The reduction of peer-directed aggression among highly aggressive African American boys.* Paper presented at the Annual Meeting of the American Educational Research Association, San Francisco.

Huffman, E. (1998). Authentic rubrics. *Art Education, 51*(1), 64–68.

Ilg, T., & Massucci, J. (2003). Comprehensive urban high schools: Are there better options for poor and minority children. *Education and Urban Society, 36*(1), 63–78.

Individuals with Disabilities Education Act (IDEA). Public Law 94–142. 20 U.S.C. §1400[c]. (1975).

Individuals with Disabilities Education Act Amendments, Pub. L. No. 105–17, 1 (1997).

Jacobsen, D. (2002b). *Philosophy in classroom teaching: Bridging the gap* (2nd ed.). Upper Saddle River, NJ: Pearson Education.

Jacobsen, D. (2003a). *Historical foundations of cognitive and social constructivism: A philosophical perspective.* Chicago: Midwest History of Education Society.

Jacobsen, D. (2003b). *Philosophy in classroom teaching: Bridging the gap* (2nd ed.). Upper Saddle River, NJ: Prentice Hall.

Jarolimek, J., Foster, C., & Kellough, R. (2005). *Teaching and learning in elementary school* (8th ed.). Upper Saddle River, NJ: Prentice-Hall.

Jennings, J. (2002). Knocking on your door. *American School Board Journal, 189*(9), 25–27.

Jewett, A., & Mullan, M. (1977). Movement process categories in physical education in teaching-learning. *Curriculum design: Purposes and procedures in physical education teaching-learning.* Washington, DC: American Alliance for Health, Physical Education, and Recreation.

Johnson, A. P. (2005). *A short guide to action research* (2nd ed.). Boston: Pearson.

Johnson, D., & Johnson, R. (2006). *Learning together and alone: Cooperation, competition, and individualization* (8th ed.). Needham Heights, MA: Allyn & Bacon.

Johnson, R. (1997). Questioning techniques to use in teaching. *The Journal of Physical Education, 68*(8), 45.

Jonassen, D., Howland, J., Moore, J., & Marra, R. (2003). *Learning to solve problems with technology.* Columbus, OH: Merrill.

Jordan, W. (2001, April). *At–risk students during the first year of high school: Navigating treacherous waters.* Paper presented at the annual meeting of the Educational Research Association, Seattle, WA.

K-12 Principles Guide to No Child Left Behind. (2004). Alexandria, VA: National Association of Elementary School Principals.

Kagan, J., Pearson, L., & Welch, L. (1966). Conceptual impulsivity and inductive reasoning. *Child Development, 37,* 123–130.

Kaplan, D., Liu, X., & Kaplan, H. (2001). Influence of parents' self-feelings and expectations on children's academic performance. *Journal of Educational Research, 94*(6), 360–365.

Karweit, N. (1989). Time and learning: A review. In R. Slavin (Ed.), *School and classroom organization.* Hillsdale, NJ: Erlbaum.

Katz, A. (1999, April). *Keepin' it real. Personalizing school experiences for diverse learners to create harmony instead of conflict.* Paper presented at the annual meeting of the American Educational Research Association, Montreal, Quebec, Canada.

Kauchak, D., & Eggen, P. (2003). *Learning and teaching: Research-based methods* (4th ed.). Needham Heights, MA: Allyn & Bacon.

Kauchak, D., & Eggen, P. (2007). *Learning and teaching: Research based methods* (5th ed.). Boston: Allyn and Bacon.

Keefe, J. (1982). Assessing student learning styles: An overview. In National Association of Secondary School Principals (Ed.), *Student learning styles and brain behavior* (pp. 18–21). Reston, VA: Editor.

Keefer, M., Zeitz, C., & Resnick, L. (2000). Judging the quality of peer-led student dialogues. *Cognition and Instruction, 18*(1), 53–81.

Kellog, J. (1988) Forces of change. *Phi Delta Kappan,* 70, 199–204.

Kellough, R. (2000). *Resource guide for teaching: K–12.* (3rd ed.). Upper Saddle River, NJ: Prentice Hall.

Kent, M., Pollard, K., Haaga, J., & Mather, M. (2001). *First Glimpse from the 2000 U. S. census.* Retrieved October 1, 2002, fromn http://www.prb.org/AmeriState Template.cfm

Kerman, S. (1979). Teacher expectations and student achievement. *Phi Delta Kappan,* 60, 716–718.

Kher-Durlabhji, N., Lacina-Gifford, L., Jackson, L., Guillory, R., & Yandell, S. (1997, March). *Preservice teachers' knowledge of effective classroom management strategies.* Paper presented at the annual meeting of the American Educational Research Association, Chicago.

Kirschner, P., Sweller, J., & Clark, R. (2006). Why minimal guidance during instruction does not work: An analysis of the failure of constructivist, discovery, problem-based, experiential, and inquiry-based teaching. *Educational Psychologist, 41*(2), 75–86.

Klein, P. (2003). Rethinking the multiplicity of cognitive resources and curricular representations: Alternatives to "learning styles" and "multiple intelligences." *Journal of Curriculum Studies, 35,* 45–81.

Kohn, A. (1996). *Beyond discipline: From compliance to community,* Alexandria, VA: Association for Supervision and Curriculum Development.

Kounin, J. (1970). *Discipline and group management in classrooms.* New York: Holt, Rinehart & Winston.

Krathwohl, D., Bloom, B., & Masia, B. (1964). *Taxonomy of educational objectives: The classification of educational goals: Handbook 2. Affective domain.* New York: McKay.

Kroesbergen, E. H., van Luit, E. H., & Maas, C. J. (2004). Effectiveness of explicit and constructivist mathematics instruction for low-achieving students in the Netherlands. *Elementary School Journal, 104(2),* 233–251.

Lafee, S. (2005). Another weighty burden. *School Administrator, 62*(9), 10–16.

Lam, D. (2004). Problem-based learning: An integration of theory and field. *Journal of Social Work Education, 40*(3), 371–389.

Land, R. (1997). Moving up to complex assessment systems: Proceedings from the 1996 CRESST Conference. *Evaluation Comment, 7*(1), 1–21.

Landau, B. (2004). *The art of classroom management: Building equitable learning communities* (2nd ed.). Upper Saddle River, NJ: Pearson Education.

Lee, J., Pulvino, C., & Perrone, P. (1998). *Restoring harmony: A guide for managing conflicts in schools.* Columbus, OH: Merrill.

Lepper, M., & Hodell, M. (1989). Intrinsic motivation in the classroom. In C. Ames & R. Ames (Eds.), *Research on motivation in education* (Vol. 3, pp. 73–105). San Diego, CA: Academic Press.

Lever-Duffy, J., McDonald, J., & Mizell, A. (2003). *Teaching and learning with technology.* Boston: Allyn & Bacon.

Li, Y., Anderson, R., Nguyen-Jahiel, K., Dong, T., Archodidou, A., Kim, I., Kuo, L., Clark, A., Wu, X., Jadallah, M., & Miller, B. (2007). Emergent leadership in children's discussion groups. *Cognition and Instruction, 25*(1), 75–111.

Limber, S., Flerx, V., Nation, M., & Melton, G. (1998). Bullying among school children in the United States. In M. Watts (Ed.), *Cross-cultural perspectives on youth and violence.* Stamford, CT: JAI Press.

Linn, R., & Gronlund, N. (2000). *Measurement and assessment in teaching* (8th ed.). Upper Saddle River, NJ: Merrill/Prentice Hall.

Linn, R., & Miller, M. (2005). *Measurement and assessment in teaching* (9th ed.). Upper Saddle River, NJ: Pearson.

López, G., & Scribner, J. (1999, April). *Discourses of involvement: A critical review of parent involvement research.* Paper presented at the annual meeting of the American Educational Research Association, Montreal, Quebec, Canada.

Maccoby, E. (1992). The role of parents in the socialization of children: An historical overview. *Developmental Psychology, 28,* 1006–1017.

Madrid, L., Canas, M., & Ortega-Medina, M. (2007). Effects of team competition versus team cooperation in classwide peer tutoring. *Journal of Educational Research, 100*(3), 155–161.

Mager, R. (1962). *Preparing instructional objectives.* Belmont, CA: Fearon.

Mager, R. (1997). *Preparing instructional objectives: A critical tool in the development of effective instruction* (3rd ed.). Atlanta, GA: The Center for Performance.

Manning, M., & Bucher, K. (2001). *Teaching in the middle school.* Upper Saddle River, NJ: Prentice Hall.

Manzo, K. (2006). Young adults don't think world knowledge is vital. *Education Week, 25*(36), 8.

Marquez, E., & Westbrook, P. (2007). *Teaching money applications to make mathematics meaningful: Grades 7–12.* Thousand Oaks, CA: Corwin Press.

Martinez, M. (2006). What is metacognition? Phi Delta Kappan, 87(9), 696–699.

Marzano, R. (2003). *What works in schools.* Alexandria, VA: Association for Supervision and Curriculum Development.

Marzano, R., & Kendall, J. (2003). *Designing standards-based districts, schools, and classrooms.* Alexandria, VA: Association for Supervision and Curriculum Development.

Marzano, R., Marzano, J., & Pickering, D. (2003). *Classroom management that works: Research-based strategies for every teacher.* Alexandria, VA: Association for Supervision and Curriculum Development.

Marzano, R., & Pickering, D. (2007). Errors and allegations: About research on homework. *Phi Delta Kappan, 88*(7), 507–513.

Mathis, W. (2003). No Child Left Behind Act: Costs and benefits. *Phi Delta Kappan, 84,* 679–686.

Mayer, R. (2001). *Multimedia learning.* New York: Cambridge University Press.

Mayer, R. (2002). *The promise of educational psychology: Volume II. Teaching for meaningful learning.* Upper Saddle River, NJ: Merrill/Prentice Hall.

Mayer, R. (2004). Should there be a three-strikes rule against pure discovery learning? *American Psychologist, 59,* 14–19.

Mayer, R. (2008). *Learning and instruction.* Upper Saddle River, NJ: Pearson.

McCarty, H., & Siccone, F. (2001). *Motivating your students.* Boston: Allyn and Bacon.

McCaslin, M., & Good, T. (1992). Compliant cognition: The misalliance of management and instructional goals in current school reform. *Educational Researcher, 21*(3), 4–17.

McCombs, B., & Miller, L. (2007). *Learner-centered classroom practices and assessment.* Thousand Oaks, CA: Corwin.

McGlinchey, M., & Hixson, M. (2004). Using curriculum-based measurement to predict performance on state assessments in reading. *School Psychology Review, 33*(2), 193–203.

McLaughlin, H. J. (1994). From negation to negotiation: Moving away from the management metaphor. *Action in Teacher Education, 16*(1), 75–84.

McMillan, J. (2004). *Classroom assessment: Principles and practice for effective instruction.* Boston: Pearson Education.

Mehrabian, A., & Ferris, S. (1967). Inference of attitude from nonverbal behavior in two channels. *Journal of Consulting Psychology, 31,* 248–252.

Meier, D. (2002). Standardization versus standards. *Phi Delta Kappan, 84,* 190–198.

Meltzer, L. (Ed.) (2007). *Executive function in education: From theory to practice.* New York: Guilford.

Merrill, P., Hammons, K., Tolman, M., Christensen, L., Vincent, B., & Reynolds, P. (1992). *Computers in education.* Needham Heights, MA: Allyn & Bacon.

Meter, P., & Stevens, R. (2000). The role of theory in the study of peer collaboration. *Journal of Experimental Education, 69*(1), 113–127.

Miller, D. (1998). *Enhancing adolescent competence.* Belmont, CA: Wadsworth.

Moles, O. (1992, April). *Parental contacts about classroom behavior problems.* Paper presented at the Annual Meeting of the American Educational Research Association, San Francisco.

Moore, K. (1992). *Classroom teaching skills* (2nd ed.). New York: McGraw-Hill.

Moran, S., Kornhaber, M., & Gardner, H. (2006). *Orchestrating multiple intelligences.* Educational Leadership, 64(1), 24–27.

Moreno, R. (2004). Decreasing cognitive load for novice students: Effects of explanatory versus corrective feedback in discovery-based multimedia. *Instructional Science, 32,* 99–113.

Moreno, R., & Duran, R. (2004). Do multiple representations need explanations: The role of verbal guidance and individual differences in multimedia mathematics learning. *Journal of Educational Psychology, 96,* 492–503.

Morgan, B. (1999). Passing the torch: Performance assessment benchmarks for preservice teachers and mentor teacher training. *Education, 119*(3), 374.

Muñoz, M., & Portes, P. (2002, April). *Voices from the field: The perceptions of teachers and principals on the class size reduction program in a large urban school district.* Paper presented at the annual meeting of the American Educational Research Association, New Orleans, LA.

Murphy, J. (2007). Hey, Ms. A! One student teacher's success story. *Kappa Delta Pi Record, 43,* 52–55.

Nakamura, R. (2000). *Healthy classroom management: Motivation, communication, and discipline.* Stamford, CT: Wadsworth.

National Association of Elementary School Principals. (2004). *K–12 Principals' guide to No Child Left Behind.* Alexandria, VA: Author.

National Council for Accreditation of Teacher Education (NCATE). (2008). Available at http://www.ncate.org/. Accessed 1/9/08.

National Council of Teachers of Mathematics. (1989). *Curriculum and evaluation standards for school mathematics.* Reston, VA: Author.

Neill, M. (2003). High stakes, high risk. *American School Board Journal, 190*(2), 18–21.

Nesbit, J., & Adesope, O. (2006). Learning with concept and knowledge maps: A meta-analysis. *Review of Educational Research, 76*(3), 413–448.

Newby, T., Stepich, D., Lehman, J., & Russell, J. (2006). *Instructional technology and teaching and learning* (3rd ed.). Upper Saddle River, NJ: Merrill/Prentice Hall.

Nitko, A. (2004). *Educational assessment of students* (4th ed.). Upper Saddle River, NJ: Pearson.

Noblit, G., Rogers, D., & McCadden, B. (1995). In the meantime: The possibilities of caring. *Phi Delta Kappan, 76,* 680–685.

Noddings, N. (1995). Teaching the themes of care. *Phi Delta Kappan, 76,* 675–679.

Noddings, N. (1999, April). *Competence and caring as central to teacher education.* Paper presented at the annual meeting of the American Educational Research Association, Montreal, Quebec, Canada.

Nucci, L. (1987). Synthesis of research on moral development. *Educational Leadership, 44*(5), 86–92.

Nye, B., Hedges, L., & Konstantopoulos, S. (2001). Are effects of small classes cumulative? Evidence from a Tennessee experiment. *Journal of Educational Research, 94,* 336–341.

OELA (Office of English Language Acquisition). (2004). *National clearinghouse for language acquisition and language instruction programs.* Retrieved 3/2/06, from www.NCLE.gwu.edu/languages

Ogbu, J. (1992). Understanding cultural diversity and learning. *Educational Researcher, 21*(8), 5–14.

Ogbu, J. (1999, April). *The significance of minority status.* Paper presented at the annual meeting of the American Educational Research Association, Montreal, Quebec, Canada.

Olson, L. (2004). States seek OK for revisions. *Education Week, 23*(34), 1, 31.

Ormrod, J. (2000). *Educational psychology.* Columbus, OH: Merrill/Prentice Hall.

Ornstein, A., & Behar-Ornstein, L. (1999). *Contemporary issues in curriculum* (2nd ed., pp. 31–32). Boston: Allyn & Bacon.

Parsons, R., & Brown, K. (2002). *Teacher as reflective practitioner and action researcher.* Belmont, CA: Wadsworth.

Parsons, R., Hinson, S., & Brown, D. (2001). *Educational psychology: A practitioner-research model of teaching.* Belmont, CA: Wadsworth/Thomson Learning.

Peregoy, S., & Boyle, O. (2005). *Reading, writing, and learning in ESL* (4th ed.). New York: Longman.

Pfiffer, L., Rosen, L., & O'Leary, S. (1985). The efficacy of an all-positive approach to classroom management. *Journal of Applied Behavior Analysis, 18,* 257–261.

Piaget, J. (1952). *Origins of intelligence in children.* New York: International Universities Press.

Piaget, J. (1959). *Language and thought of the child* (M. Grabain, Trans.). New York: Humanities Press.

Pianta, R., Belsky, J., Houts, R., & Morrison, F. (2007). Opportunities to learn in America's elementary classrooms. *Science, 315,* 1795–1796.

Pintrich, P., & Schunk, D. (2002). *Motivation in education: Theory, research, and applications* (2nd ed.). Upper Saddle River, NJ: Prentice Hall.

Popham, W. (1997). What's wrong—and what's right—with rubrics. *Educational Leadership, 55,* 72–75.

Popham, W. (2003). The seductive lure of data. *Educational Leadership, 60*(5), 48–51.

Popham, W. (2004). *American's failing schools: How parents and teachers can cope with No Child Left Behind.* New York: Routledge Falmer.

Popham, W. (2006). Diagnostic assessment: A measurement mirage? *Educational Leadership, 64,*(2), 90–91.

Popham, W. (2007). The lowdown on learning progressions. *Educational Leadership, 64*(7), 83–84.

Porche, M., & Ross, S. (1999, April). *Parent involvement in the early elementary grades: An analysis of mothers' practices and teachers' expectations.* Paper presented at the annual meeting of the American Educational Research Association, Montreal, Quebec, Canada.

Powell, S. (2005). *Introduction to middle school.* Upper Saddle River, NJ: Pearson/Prentice Hall.

Presidential Task Force on Psychology in Education. (1993). *Learner-centered psychological principles: Guidelines for school redesign and reform.* Washington, DC: American Psychological Association.

Pressley, M., Raphael, L., & Gallagher, J. G. (2004). Prodience-St. Mel School: How a school that works for African American students works. *Journal of Educational Psychology, 96*(2), 216–235.

Public Agenda. (2004). *Teaching interrupted*. Retrieved June 12, 2004, from http://www/.publicagenda.org

Purkey, S., & Smith, M. (1983). Effective schools: A review. *Elementary School Journal, 83,* 427–452.

Radd, T. (1998). Developing an inviting classroom climate through a comprehensive behavior-management plan. *Journal of Invitational Theory and Practice, 5,* 19–30.

Reed, R., & Johnson, T. (2000). *Philosophical documents in education* (2nd ed., p. 91). New York: Longman.

Reed, S. (2006). Cognitive architectures for multimedia learning. *Educational Psychologist, 41*(2), 87–98.

Reynolds, R., Sinatra, G., & Jetton, T. (1996). Views of knowledge acquisition and representation: A continuum from experience-centered to mind-centered. *Educational Psychologist, 31,* 93–194.

Ritts, V., Patterson, M., & Tubbs, M. (1992). Expectations, impressions, and judgments of physically attractive students: A review. *Review of Educational Research, 62,* 413–426.

Roblyer, M. (2006). *Integrating educational technology into teaching* (4th ed.). Upper Saddle River, NJ: Merrill/Prentice Hall.

Rodgers, C. (2002). Seeing student learning: Teacher change and the role of reflection. *Harvard Educational Review, 72,* 230–253.

Rodriguez, G. (1988). Teaching teachers to teach thinking. *Curriculum Review, 1,* 13–14.

Rose, K., Williams, K., Gomez, L., & Gearon, J. (2002, April). *Building a case for what our students know and can do: How trustworthy are our judgments?* Paper presented at the annual meeting of the American Educational Research Association, New Orleans.

Rose, L., & Gallup, A. (2007). The 39th annual Phi Delta Kappa/Gallup poll of the public's attitudes towards public schools. *Phi Delta Kappan, 89,* 33–51

Rosen, L., O'Leary, S., Joyce, S., Conway, G., & Pfiffer, L. (1984). The importance of prudent negative consequences for maintaining the appropriate behavior of hyperactive students. *Journal of Abnormal Child Psychology, 12,* 581–604.

Rosenshine, B. (1971). *Teaching behaviors and student achievement*. London: National Foundation for Educational Research.

Rosenshine, B. (1987). Explicit teaching. In D. Berliner & B. Rosenshine (Eds.), *Talks to teachers*. New York: Random House.

Rosenshine, B., & Furst, N. (1971). Research in teacher performance criteria. In B. O. Smith (Ed.), *Research in education* (pp. 37–66). Englewood Cliffs, NJ: Prentice Hall.

Ross, J., Rolheiser, C., & Hogaboam-Gray, A. (2002, April). *Influences on student cognitions about evaluation*. Paper presented at the annual meeting of the American Educational Research Association, New Orleans.

Rowe, M. (1974). Wait-time and rewards as instructional variables, their influence on language, logic, and fate control: Part One—Wait-time. *Journal of Research in Science Teaching, 11,* 81–94.

Rowe, M. (1986, January/February). Wait-time: Slowing down may be a way of speeding up. *Journal of Teacher Education,* 43–50.

Ryan, R., & Cooper, J. (2001). *Those who can, teach* (9th ed.). Boston: Houghton Mifflin.

Ryan, R., & Deci, E. (2000). Intrinsic and extrinsic motivations: Classic definitions and new directions. *Contemporary Educational Psychology, 25,* 54–67.

Sack-Min, J. (2007). The issues of IDEA. *American School Board Journal, 194*(3), 20–25.

Safer, N., & Fleischman, S. (2005). How student progress monitoring improves instruction. *Educational Leadership, 62*(5), 81–83.

Saltpeter, J. (2005). Telling tales with technology. *Technology & Learning, 25*(7), 18–24.

Sapon-Shevin, M. (2007). *Widening the circle: The power of inclusive classrooms*. Boston: Beacon Press.

Savage, T. (1991). *Discipline for self control*. Englewood Cliffs, NJ: Prentice Hall.

Scarcella, R. (1990). *Teaching language-minority students in the multicultural classroom.* Upper Saddle River, NJ: Prentice Hall.

Scheidecker, D., & Freeman, W. (1999). *Bringing out the best in students: How legendary teachers motivate kids.* Thousand Oaks, CA: Corwin Press.

Schibsted, E. (2006). Fighting for fitness. *Edutopia, 1*(9), 30–37.

Schwartz, W. (1998). Standards: Their impact on urban students "opportunity to learn" strategies). *Teacher Librarian, 26*(1), 28.

Serafini, F. (2002). Possibilities and challenges: The National Board for Professional Teaching Standards. *Journal of Teacher Education, 53,* 316–327.

Shepard, L. (2001). The role of classroom assessment in teaching and learning. In V. Richardson (Ed.), *Handbook of research on learning* (4th ed., pp. 1066–1101). Washington, DC: American Educational Research Association.

Shuell, T. (1996). Teaching and learning in a classroom context. In D. Berliner & R. Calfee (Eds.), *Handbook of educational psychology* (pp. 726-764). New York: Macmillan.

Sieber, R. (1981). Socialization implications of school discipline, or how first graders are taught to "listen." In R. Sieber & A. Gordon (Eds.), *Children and their organizations: Investigations in American culture* (pp. 18–43). Boston: G. K. Hall.

Silver-Pacuilla, H., & Fleischman, S. (2006). Technology to help struggling students. *Educational Leadership, 63*(5), 84–85.

Singh, N., Lancioni, G., Joy, S., Winton, A., Sabaawi, M., Wahler, R. & Singh, J. (2007). Adolescents with conduct disorder can be mindful of their aggressive behavior. *Journal of emotional and behavioral disorders,* 15, 56–63.

Slavin, R. (1995). *Cooperative learning: Theory, research, and practice* (2nd ed.). Needham Heights, MA: Allyn & Bacon.

Slavin, R., Karweit, N., & Madden, N. (Eds.). (1989). *Effective programs for students at risk.* Needham Heights, MA: Allyn & Bacon.

Sleeter, C., & Grant, C. (1987). An analysis of multicultural education in the United States. *Harvard Educational Review, 57*(4), 421–444.

Smith, A., & Bondy, E. (2007). "No! I Won't!" Understanding and responding to Defiance. *Childhood Education, 83,* 151–157.

Spring, J. (2006). *American education* (12th ed.). Boston: McGraw-Hill.

Stahl, S. A. (1999). Why innovations come and go (and mostly go): The case of whole language. *Educational Researcher, 28*(8), 13–22.

Stiggins, R. (2004). New assessment beliefs for a new school mission. *Phi Delta Kappan, 86*(1), 22–27.

Stiggins, R. (2005). *Student-centered classroom assessment* (4th ed.). Upper Saddle River, NJ: Merrill/Prentice Hall.

Stiggins, R. (2007). Assessment through the student's eyes. *Educational Leadership, 64*(8), 22–26.

Stigler, J., & Hiebert, J. (2000). *The teaching gap.* New York: Free Press.

Stipek, D. (2002). *Motivation to learn: Integrating theory and practice* (4th ed.). Boston: Allyn & Bacon.

Stipek, D. (2004). Head Start: Can't we have our cake and eat it too? *Education Week, 23*(34), 52, 43.

Sungur, S., & Tekkaya, C. (2006). Effects of problem-based learning and traditional instruction on self-regulated learning. *Journal of Educational Research, 99*(5), 307–318.

Swanson, C. (2006b). Tracking U.S. trends. *Education Week, Technology Counts, 2006, May,* 50–52.

Tan, I., Sharan, S., & Lee, C. (2007). Group investigation effects on achievement, motivation, and perceptions of students in Singapore. *Journal of Educational Research, 100*(3), 142–154.

Thompson, G. (2002). African-American teens discuss their elementary teachers. *Educational Horizons, 80*(3), 147–152.

Tomlinson, C. (2000). Reconcilable differences? Standards-based teaching and differentiation. *Educational Leadership, 58*(1), 6–11.

Trawick-Smith, J. (2000). *Early childhood development: A multicultural perspective* (2nd ed.). Upper Saddle River, NJ: Merrill/Prentice Hall.

Turnbull, A., Turnbull, R., Shank, M., Smith, S., &. Leal, D. (2007). *Exceptional lives: Special education in today's schools* (5th ed.). Upper Saddle River, NJ: Merrill/Prentice Hall.

Tyler, R. (1949). *Basic principles of curriculum and instruction.* Chicago: University of Chicago Press.

U.S. Bureau of Census. (2003). *Statistical abstract of the United States* (123rd ed.). Washington, DC: U.S. Government Printing Office.

U.S. Bureau of Census. (2005). *Income, poverty, and health insurance coverage in the United States, 2004.* Washington, DC: U.S. Government Printing Office.

U.S. Department of Education. (1994). *The national educational goals.* Washington, DC: Author.

U.S. Department of Education. (2000). *Digest of education statistics, 1999.* Washington, DC: National Center for Educational Statistics.

U.S. Department of Education. (2002). *Twenty-fourth annual report to Congress on the implementation of the Individuals with Disabilities Education Act.* Washington, DC: U.S. Government Printing Office.

U.S. Department of Education. (2005). *The condition of education in 2005 in brief.* Washington DC: National Center for Education Statistics.

Utah Department of Education.(2007). *State of Utah curriculum standards.* Available online at: http://www.usoe.k12.ut.us

Vaughn, S., Bos, C., Candace, S., & Schumm, J. (2006). *Teaching exceptional, diverse, and at-risk students in the general education classroom* (3rd ed.). Boston: Allyn & Bacon.

Viadero, D. (1999). Tennessee class-size study finds long-term benefits. *Education Week, 18*(34), 5.

Victor, E., & Kellough, R. (2004). *Science K-8: An integrated approach* (10th ed.). Upper Saddle River, NJ: Pearson.

Wang, M., Haertel, G., & Walberg, H. (1993). Toward a knowledge base for school learning. *Review of Educational Research, 63*(3), 249–294.

Wassermann, S. (1999). Shazam! You're a teacher facing the illusory quest for certainty in classroom practice. *Phi Delta Kappan, 80*(6), 464.

Webb, N., Farivar, S., & Mastergeorge, A. (2002). Productive helping in cooperative groups. *Theory into Practice, 41,* 13–20.

Weiner, L. (2002, April). *Why is classroom management so vexing to urban teachers? New Directions in theory and research about classroom management in urban schools.* Paper presented at the annual meeting of the American Educational Research Association, New Orleans.

Wentzel, K. (1991). Relations between social competence and academic achievement in early adolescence. *Child Development, 62,* 1066–1078.

Wentzel, K. (1997). Student motivation in middle school: The role of perceived pedagogical caring. *Journal of Educational Psychology, 89,* 411–419.

Wiggins, G., & McTighe, J. (2005). *Understanding by design* (2nd ed.). Upper Saddle River, NJ: Pearson Education.

Wiles, J. (1999). *Curriculum essentials.* Boston: Allyn & Bacon.

Wiley, D., & Harnischfeger, A. (1974). Explosion of a myth: Quantity of schooling and exposure to instruction, major education vehicles. *Education Researcher, 3,* 7–12.

Williams, S., Bareiss, R., & Reiser, B. (1996, April). *ASK Jasper: A multimedia publishing and performance support environment for design.* Paper presented at the annual meeting of the American Educational Research Association, New York.

Winitzky, N. (1994). Multicultural and mainstreamed classrooms. In R. Arends (Ed.), *Learning to teach* (3rd ed., pp. 132–170). New York: McGraw-Hill.

Wolfgang, C., & Glickman, C. (1986). *Solving discipline problems* (2nd ed.). Boston: Allyn & Bacon.

Wolfinger, D., & Stockard, J. (1997). *Elementary methods: An integrated curriculum.* White Plains, NY: Longman.

Worthen, B. (1993). Critical issues that will determine the future of alternative assessment. *Phi Delta Kappan, 74,* 444–454.

Zehr, M. (2002). Early bilingual programs found to boost test scores. *Education Week, 22*(1), 6.

Index